EGON RONAY'S

GOOD FOOD in PUBS & BARS 1990

D1343847

Establishment research is conducted by a team of full-time professional inspectors, who are trained to achieve common standards of judgement with as much objectivity as this field allows. Their professional identities are not disclosed until they seek information from the management after paying their bills. The Guide is independent in its editorial selection and does not accept advertising, payment or hospitality from establishments covered.

Egon Ronay's Guides,
City Wall House,
Basing View, Basingstoke,
Hampshire RG21 2AP

Design and illustrations *Indent Designers and Illustrators*
Marketing and sponsorship consultants *Spero Communications*

Cover design *Quadraphic*

Cartography by the *Automobile Association, Information Division*

The contents of this book are believed correct at the time of printing. Nevertheless, the publisher can accept no responsibility for errors or omissions or changes in the details given.

Distributed by the Publishing Division of The Automobile Association, Fanum House, Basingstoke, Hampshire RG21 2EA.

ISBN 0 7495 0012 3

Typeset in Great Britain by *Servis Filmsetting Limited*

Printed by *Butler & Tanner Ltd,
Frome, Somerset*

Contents

Contents

The Entries

How to Use This Guide

Good bar food

We include establishments where our team of professional inspectors found excellent-quality bar food. Such pubs are indicated by the word **FOOD** printed in the entry. Pub restaurants are also mentioned when we feel the standard is high, and their opening times are given in the entry.

Two typical dishes from the bar menu are listed, with prices valid at the time of our visit. Prices may, however, have risen a little since then.

We indicate when bar food is served and also any times when food is not available, but changes may occur after going to press.

Those establishments serving outstanding food are indicated by a star alongside the description and a photograph.

Those pubs which we have recommended for accommodation or atmosphere (see below) may also serve bar food, but if we do not consider it to be up to our standards then it is not mentioned in the entry.

Good accommodation at pubs

We also inspected the accommodation, and those pubs recommendable for an overnight stay are indicated by the letters **B&B** in the entry.

We list the number of bedrooms, and a symbol shows the minimum price (including VAT) for bed and a full cooked breakfast for two in a double room at the time of going to press:

£A over £50   **£B** £45–50   **£C** £35–44   **£D** under £35

Rooms have also been given a grading symbol – G1, G2 or G3 – according to the degree of comfort and facilities offered.

If residents can check in at any time, we print *all day*; if check-in is confined to certain hours, or if it is advisable to arrange a time when booking we print *by arrangement*.

Pubs with atmosphere

Pubs recommended as pleasant or interesting places for a drink rather than for their bar food or accommodation are indicated by the letter **A** in the entry.

Family pubs

Those pubs we suggest as suitable for families (denoted by ❧) are ones that have a specific room or indoor area without a bar where children are allowed whether eating or not. Many pubs welcome children if they are eating bar food and some pubs make a feature of outdoor play areas, but readers should note that these are *not* the qualifications on which we base our category. Restrictions on children staying overnight are mentioned in the entries, and pubs with the ⛌ symbol welcome children overnight unless otherwise stated.

Draught beers
We indicate whether an establishment is a free house or brewery-owned. After the 🍺 symbol we list the names of a number of beers and lagers available on draught. We print *No real ale* where applicable.

Opening times
Opening hours vary throughout the country. Some pubs have a six-day licence. Any regular weekday closure is given in the entry. As most pubs close at some time during Christmas and New Year, it is advisable to check during that period.

Order of listing
London entries appear first and are in alphabetical order by establishment name. Listings outside London are in alphabetical order by location within the regional divisions of England, Scotland, Wales, Channel Islands and Isle of Man.

Map references
Entries contain references to the main map section at the end of the book, or to the enlarged area maps.

London telephone numbers
From 6th May 1990, all 01 numbers will have a new code, either 071 or 081, depending on the area. In the entries, the relevant new code appears in brackets after 01 (which it will replace) and before the actual number.

Index
An index of establishments classified by county has been included for easy location of entries.

Symbols

FOOD	Recommended for bar food
B&B	Recommended for accommodation
A	Recommended for atmosphere
★	Outstanding bar food
Credit	Credit cards accepted
⛌	Children welcome
🍺	On draught
☺	Dairy Crest Cheese Symbol of Excellence (see p.54)
♈	Good wine by the glass
£A–D	Cost of B&B
G1–3	Grade of rooms

THE GENUINE TASTE OF IRELAND

FOUNDED IN 1792 AND SITUATED IN CORK, IRELAND, BEAMISH & CRAWFORD HAVE BEEN BREWING STOUTS FOR NEARLY 200 YEARS.

BEAMISH IS NOW AVAILABLE IN THE U.K. ON DRAUGHT AND IN CAN TO THE DISCERNING DRINKER.

FOR MORE INFORMATION ON HOW YOU CAN DISCOVER BEAMISH FOR YOURSELF PLEASE CONTACT THE BEAMISH SALES OFFICE ON...

01-543 3135

Publisher's Introduction

As the licensing trade is still in a state of flux, following the liberalisation of opening hours and with the prospect of further government intervention regarding ownership, it is more difficult than ever to predict future developments. Our standards nevertheless remain unchanged, and for this year's *Coca-Cola Guide to Good Food in Pubs and Bars* we devoted a full three months of our inspection period solely to finding new entries in all areas of the country. Although this inevitably produced a large number of non-recommendations, many 'little gems' of the pub world were unearthed.

Readers' recommendations

Some of these new recommendations were brought to our attention by readers on the Reader's Comments pages included towards the end of the book, of which we receive many hundreds each year. The majority do not lead to new entries in the Guide, however, so we thought it would be helpful to take a few pages to explain *exactly* what our criteria for including a pub are. This resulted in the feature entitled 'Our Kind of Pub', to be found on pages 47–52, which also includes a description of the 1989 Pub of the Year and the philosophy of its landlords.

Special investigation

Following the 'explosion' of cheap pub restaurants, as highlighted in our introduction to last year's Guide, we decided to conduct a special investigation into the major chains offering such a service. Our interesting conclusions can be found on pages 35–44. Most of these chain pubs are targeted towards the family market, which is an increasingly important area.

Family pubs

For the 1990 Guide, we have been stricter than ever before in awarding our 'children welcome' rocking-horse symbol, so that *every* pub which has the symbol provides a family area or children's room in which there is no bar. Other pubs without this symbol may also welcome children when eating or provide an outdoor play area; these facts are mentioned in the description if the pub does not get a symbol. We hope that this will make life much easier for parents when deciding on an appropriate pub for a family outing. More information on this topic can be found in the 'Coca-Cola Family Pub of the Year' section on pages 26–9.

Pub restaurants

In former years we have not mentioned individual pub restaurants in this Guide, but they are now becoming an increasing feature of the industry. Consequently, we felt that it was time to include a mention of a pub restaurant within the entries if the food is worthy of attention. Bar food is still our main priority, but almost without exception a good restaurant on the premises ensures a high standard of food in the bar, although the reverse is not always so true.

Grading of accommodation

Another change in the entries is the introduction of a grading system for the bedrooms in our accommodation pubs. Each has been given a grading from 1 to 3: Grade 3 indicates basic and practical accommodation; Grade 2 modest but with a reasonable degree of comfort; Grade 1 excellent degree of comfort, mainly en suite facilities and good extras. Together with the price band indication we hope that this will aid considerably in the process of choosing where to stay.

Constructive criticism

We have not been frightened to make the odd criticism where we feel it is justified, and intend this as a constructive aid to our landlords. After all, a certain standard of excellence has already been achieved for actual inclusion in the Guide, so small improvements can only better an already good service.

Finally, we hope that all the improvements we have made to the Guide for the 1990 edition and the continuing high standard of the pubs recommended will combine to make the book more useful and informative than ever before.

AN
EGON RONAY'S
GUIDE
ONLY INCLUDES
THE BEST.

LIGHT-DRY

CARTA BLANCA

RUM

Ron
BACARDI
Superior

BACARDI & CO., L
Nassau, Bahamas

Coca-Cola

NOTHING FEELS LIKE BACARDI® AND COKE®

Foreword

'You Can't Beat the Feeling' of top-quality bar food accompanied by the great taste of Coca-Cola, and now for the third consecutive year Coca-Cola is sponsoring *Egon Ronay's Guide to Good Food in Pubs and Bars*.

The Guide is firmly established as the leading authority on good food in pubs and bars and as always continues to strive to encourage high standards paying tribute to the British publicans who take pride in the food they serve.

As we move into the nineties the face of the British pub is changing from the traditional public drinking house to a social meeting place for all ages. Coca-Cola, the most popular soft drink for adults and children alike, is the refreshing complement to quality fare in pubs and bars.

Coca-Cola is pleased to continue its association with the search for excellence demonstrated in the Guide and to promote high standards in pub and bar catering.

'You Can't Beat the Feeling' of Coca-Cola with good-quality pub food.

Pub of the Year

The Pub of the Year award is a hand-painted and gilded octagonal decanter by Mason's Ironstone, engraved with the name of the winner, who will retain it. The runners-up will receive similar decanters. As in previous years, the main criteria for the award are a very high standard of bar food and a pleasant, congenial atmosphere.

WINNER

Silver Plough, Pitton

Skills in the kitchen lift the Silver Plough well out of the ordinary category, and make the converted farmhouse a haven for pub gourmets. In a lovely Wiltshire village, it is a perfect spot for enjoying excellent seafood, suckling pig or game from an extensive and mouthwatering menu, followed by home-made sweets or fine cheeses and accompanied by English country wines.

RUNNERS-UP

Three Acres Inn, Shelley

Bar food, restaurant and overnight accommodation are all of top quality here, high in the Pennines above Huddersfield. A copper-hooded fireplace and a grand piano are focal points in the bar, where first-class snacks are served at lunchtime: excellent soups, salads, sandwiches and a few hot dishes. More elaborate meals are provided in the restaurant, and the immaculate, pretty bedrooms are filled with plenty of extras.

Masons Arms, Cartmel Fell

Directions are definitely required in order to locate this picturesque pub in a fairytale setting, but when you finally arrive it is well worth all the trouble. Noted for its vast selection of bottled beers from all over the world, the Masons Arms also offers excellent bar food ranging from chicken burritos, cider-braised pork chops and fennel crumble to rum and raisin cheesecake.

Outstanding Bar Food

The following list highlights a very select number of pubs where our inspectors judge the food to be of particularly high quality. The gazetteer entries for these establishments carry a star symbol.

England

Brightling, East Sussex: *Fullers Arms*
Brimfield, Shropshire: *Roebuck*
Burton, Wiltshire: *Plume of Feathers*
Cartmel Fell, Cumbria: *Masons Arms*
Haslemere, Surrey: *Crowns*
Ivy Hatch, Kent: *The Plough*
Kingsclere, Hampshire: *Swan*
Kingsteignton, Devon: *Old Rydon Inn*
Monksilver, Somerset: *Notley Arms*
Newton, Cambridgeshire: *Queens Head*
Pitton, Wiltshire: *Silver Plough*
Ramsbury, Wiltshire: *Bell*
Shelley, West Yorkshire: *Three Acres Inn*
Stow Bardolph, Norfolk: *Hare Arms*
Stuckton, Hampshire: *Three Lions*
Warenford, Northumberland: *Warenford Lodge*
West Ilsley, Berkshire: *Harrow*
Winchester, Hampshire: *Wykeham Arms*
Yattendon, Berkshire: *Royal Oak*

Scotland

Kilberry, Strathclyde: *Kilberry Inn*

Wales

Llyswen, Powys: *Griffin Inn*

AN EXCITING NEW WORLD
OF COCKTAIL SNACKS

Wine Pub of the Year

Egon Ronay's Guides and the Wine Development Board have continued for a second year their joint initiative aimed at improving the quality of wine served in the British Pub. Those pubs which our inspectors consider offer a good glass of wine over the bar have been awarded, in recognition, a special 'good wine' symbol in the 1990 Egon Ronay's Coca-Cola Pub Guide.

In awarding this symbol, here are a few pointers of style and content that we look for in a 'good wine' pub:

Quality
Wines of good quality from reliable shippers and growers.

Choice
Good span of four wines of different styles – for example Muscadet, Soave, Beaujolais, Côtes du Rhone.

Service
Wines served at the correct temperature (whites chilled but not iced, reds at room temperature) in practical glasses of proper shape. Ravenhead 'Winemaster' and Durand 'Elegance' are two inexpensive, readily available types which will stand up to glass-washing machines.

Proper measure
The voluntary code of practice for sales of still wines by the glass recommends that the quantity of wine given for the price should be clearly indicated. This means using marked glasses (e.g. 125 ml and 175 ml), preferably with a good 'head' above the marker in order to appreciate the aromas of the wine.

Wine by the bottle
Sale of bottles of wine over the bar to be encouraged. The choice should be selective and interesting, rather than overwhelming. New World wines from Australia, California, Chile and New Zealand are nowadays a common feature on good pub wine lists. Long lists of famous Châteaux from 'off' years do not impress.

We have also made awards this year to a number of regional 'Best Wine' pubs. Although regional winners have been required to offer a good choice of wines, they have not necessarily been expected to carry an extensive range to qualify. It is quality, discerning selection and service of the wines that count.

From these winners Britain's Best Wine Pub of the Year, the overall winner, has been selected.

BEST WINE PUB 1990

Inn at Whitewell, Whitewell, Lancashire
Good well-kept wines by the glass; positive 'house' claret and a changing vintage selection which includes Côtes du Rhone Cuvée Personelle (Pascal) '83 and Pinot d'Alsace (Albrecht) '86. About 100 wines by the bottle; try the excellent Rhine Riesling (Mitchelton) from Australia for under £5. Our North of England regional winner.

The other regional winners are:

London
White Horse on Parsons Green, SW6
An impeccable selection from around the world at keen prices. Rhine Riesling from South Australia, excellent Gewürztraminer from Alsace, fine reds from Penedès. Wines by the glass are served in prime condition.

South of England
Dundas Arms, Kintbury, Berkshire
Good wines by the glass include a delicious Dulong vin de table from Bordeaux. The list of wines by the bottle is magnificent and also competitively priced. The selection of burgundies is perhaps the finest in the country.

South-West of England
New Inn, Cerne Abbas, Dorset
Excellent selection of up to a dozen wines by the glass, changed on a weekly basis. Wide-ranging choice of wines by the bottle includes Oakwood Chardonnay from Australia. Service and presentation of wines are exemplary.

East of England
Crossways Inn, Scole, Norfolk
Highly drinkable Côtes du Rhone and Muscadet by the glass. Exceptional list of fine wines by the bottle includes mature clarets from the sixties, '76 great burgundies and Château d'Yquem '57. Not surprisingly the landlord used to work in the wine trade.

Heart of England
Pheasant, Keyston, Huntingdonshire
The approach to wine is intelligent, selective, highly imaginative and keenly priced. Five delicious whites and five serious reds are served in prime condition from the Canadian Wine Machine: Santa Rita Chilian Chardonnay '87 (£2.30), Merlot del Piave '86 (£1.90). Excellent wines by the bottle include an aromatic Morey St Denis (Dujac) '84, a snip at £14.75.

Scotland

Champany Inn Chop & Ale House, Linlithgow, Lothian

The wine selection here provides a model for other publicans and innkeepers. In no way has Clive Davidson tried to ape the great cellar in his grand restaurant next door. The pub list is admirable for its tight selection and friendly prices. Around eight own label imports available by the glass (try the Pinotage) and fifteen good wines by the bottle with a 1983 Cahors for just £9.

Wales

Crown at Whitebrook, Gwent

Wines by the glass are sound fruity vins de table from Georges Duboeuf and a delicious Liebfraumilch (yes Liebfraumilch) from Kleebach. Every bottle on the list is worth drinking: champagne from Joseph Perrier, Riojas from Faustino and a 1980 Beaune Grèves from Chanson are typical of the careful selection.

Outstanding Wine Pubs

London
White Horse on Parsons Green, SW6

England
Appleby, Cumbria – *Royal Oak Inn*
Beauworth, Hampshire – *Milbury's*
Biddenden, Kent – *Three Chimneys*
Brightwell Baldwin, Oxfordshire – *Lord Nelson*
Cerne Abbas, Dorset – *New Inn*
Chilgrove, West Sussex – *White Horse Inn*
Clare, Suffolk – *Bell Hotel*
Doddiscombsleigh, Devon – *Nobody Inn*
Dorchester-on-Thames, Oxfordshire – *George Hotel*
Falmouth, Cornwall – *The Pandora Inn*
Fotheringhay, Northamptonshire – *Falcon*
Huntingdon, Cambridgeshire – *Old Bridge Hotel*
Keyston, Huntingdonshire – *Pheasant*
Kintbury, Berkshire – *Dundas Arms*
Lancing, West Sussex – *Sussex Pad Hotel*
Mayfield, East Sussex – *Rose & Crown*
Moulton, North Yorkshire – *Black Bull Inn*
Oakwoodhill, Surrey – *Punchbowl Inn*
Port Gaverne, Cornwall – *Port Gaverne Hotel*
Saffron Walden, Essex – *Eight Bells*
Saffron Walden, Essex – *Saffron Hotel*
Scole, Norfolk – *Crossways Inn*
Shelley, West Yorkshire – *Three Acres Inn*
Shipston-on-Stour, Warwickshire – *White Bear*
Shipton-under-Wychwood, Oxfordshire – *Lamb Inn*
Southwold, Suffolk – *The Crown*
Staple Fitzpaine, Somerset – *Greyhound Inn*
Whitewell, Lancashire – *Inn at Whitewell*
Winchester, Hampshire – *Wykeham Arms*
Yattendon, Berkshire – *Royal Oak*

Scotland
Canonbie, Dumfries & Galloway – *Riverside Inn*
Invermoriston, Highland – *Glenmoriston Arms*
Linlithgow, Lothian – *Champany Inn Chop & Ale House*

Wales
Babell, Clwyd – *Black Lion Inn*
Chepstow, Gwent – *Castle View Hotel*
Crickhowell, Powys – *Nantyffin Cider Mill Inn*
Whitebrook, Gwent – *The Crown at Whitebrook*

Coca-Cola Family Pub of the Year

Once again this year our judges began looking for the Coca-Cola Family Pub of the Year, and as the top choice for soft drinks refreshment in family pubs Coca-Cola provides an ideal association for this annual search for excellence. Selecting the finalists was no easy task, because with British pubs fast becoming social meeting places for all ages the positive factors contributing to the 'complete family pub' are more in evidence than ever. Pubs are now catering for members of the family from nine to ninety offering a range of facilities to provide maximum family enjoyment.

Many landlords and their staff now welcome parents accompanied by their children and set aside separate play areas where children can occupy themselves safely without disturbing other pub users.

The long licensing hours have enabled more families to take the opportunity of dining out together in comfort. Standards of pub food are improving rapidly and many pubs now cater specifically for family tastes with careful thought behind the choice of food and drink on offer. Coca-Cola is the first choice for soft drink refreshment for all the family and is the ideal accompaniment to good food in pubs.

This year our selected finalists offered that unique combination of factors which we consider contribute to the making of the 'complete family pub' and provide an ideal leisure environment for all the family. The winner is announced below, and will receive a hand-painted Chinacraft plaque.

Pubs, children and the law

Generally speaking, the law in this country prohibits children under 14 from being in a bar on licensed premises, unless the bar is set apart for table meals and is not used for the sale of alcohol except for consumption by persons having table meals there and as an ancillary to the meal, or they are there solely for the purpose of passing to or from some place on the premises, such as a specially designated children's room, which is not a bar.

Our list starting on page 62 includes only those pubs which provide a family area or separate children's room *without* a bar. These pubs have all been awarded the rocking-horse symbol. Other pubs provide outdoor play areas and children's portions or menus, and such items are mentioned in the entry. This should make life easier for parents trying to choose an appropriate pub for a family outing.

WINNER

Wight Mouse Inn, Chale, Isle of Wight

Part of the Clarendon Hotel, all ages of children are positively encouraged here, in the midst of a popular holiday area. Much thought has gone into providing facilities for youngsters, and extra time and care is also taken by John and Jean Bradshaw and their staff in keeping them amused. There are play areas both inside and out, the latter with swings, seesaw and slide in the terraced garden from which you can see the Needles on a clear day. One of the two downstairs children's rooms features stained-glass skylights depicting white mice stealing scraps. Children's portions and their own menu are also on offer, featuring Jean's home-made pizzas and burgers.

27

RUNNER-UP

Fox, Ansty, Dorset

Deep in rural Dorset, reached only by country lane, the Fox has recently been extended with the younger element very much in mind. A new bar area has been opened up for family eating, just off which there is a children's room complete with giant ludo board, fish ride and TV with cartoon videos. Food is still mainly carvery-style, and either small portions or something from their 'Freddie the Fox Cub' menu will keep the children happy. If not, a fun pack with crayons and a colouring pack should do the trick! Outside there is a garden with Wendy house, two slides and a swimming pool. On the accommodation side, there are five family rooms in the old main building.

28

RUNNER-UP

Royal Oak, Over Stratton, Somerset

A splendid thatched pub where children are excellently catered for. In the garden (with barbecue) is a play area with sandpit, slides, swings, trampoline and even a junior assault course! Families can use the dining room at one end of the building to enjoy some substantial meals from the main menu (small portions available) or items from the children's menu, which offers the usual (sausage, fish or scampi and chips) and the unusual (King Charles' Booty Box – a picnic box filled with a selection of tasty morsels). Parents can savour mushroom soup, curried fish cocktail, beef in stout, salmon pie, lamb in filo, vegetarian dishes, salads, steaks and so on, all accompanied by a very good wine list.

A taste of the Caribbean

The story of BACARDI rum started more than a century and a quarter ago in the warmth of the Caribbean, on the island of Cuba.

Soon its light, dry taste found favour with American visitors to the island and in 1898 a US Army lieutenant celebrating Cuba's independence from Spain tried mixing Bacardi rum with the latest soft drink from America, Coca-Cola. Today BACARDI and Coke or the 'Cuba Libre' is still the world's favourite way of enjoying BACARDI rum.

The original BACARDI rum Distillery in 1862.

And not just with Coke...

The ideal base for many refreshing drinks, BACARDI rum is now increasingly drunk with orange juice, tonic or lemonade, while many enjoy it straight with a little ice or mixed as the famous Daiquiri — an icy blend of BACARDI rum and lime juice.

To recreate the original taste of a BACARDI daiquiri add 1½ measures of BACARDI rum to 1 measure of lemon or lime juice. Add 2 or 3 teaspoonsful of sugar, according to taste and stir well. Serve with plenty of ice.

For those who prefer a richer, mellower flavour there's Bacardi Gold rum too — especially good with orange juice.

With friends or on its own, BACARDI rum feels good. Sociable, friendly and warm. Nothing feels like BACARDI rum!

Free drinks guide

Now you can enjoy many more famous BACARDI rum drinks with the full colour BACARDI rum Drinks Guide. There are almost 100 recipes ranging from Daiquiris through to punches and hot drinks. For your *free* copy, write to Good Food in Pubs & Bars, Bacardi rum Drinks Guide Offer, Dept PA, c/o Transom House, Victoria Street, Bristol BS1 6AH (don't forget to include your own address and postcode).

Enjoy the recipes — Nothing feels like BACARDI rum!

diet Coke

Just for the taste of it.

One Calorie. Sugar Free.

Enjoy
diet
Coca-Cola
REGD. TRADE MARK

Pub Chain Restaurants

Designed to appeal to a broad cross-section of the public, many 'pub chains' offer special prices (and menus) to attract, for instance, the elderly to a mid-week lunch or parents of young families to an early-evening meal. Most outlets have children's rooms within, and/or extensive play areas outside, as well as their trendy (though junky) kids' menus. Many also offer extended opening, and almost universally are open all day on Sundays.

The product

The chain pubs to which we refer contain many of those less endearing features which we tend to find unacceptable in pubs we research for this Guide: loud intrusive taped music, multifarious gaming machines, lack of choice in the variety of real beers and wines offered; and also, in too many cases, offhand impersonal service.

The type of houses we have reviewed can be divided roughly into two sectors: the carvery operations of Barnaby's, Roast Inn and Toby Carving Rooms, and the steak house chains as run by Berni, Beefeater, Harvester and Toby Grills.

The most significant aspect of their *menus* in either case is that they are standard throughout each chain, even to the extent that in one chain (Beefeater) their latest speciality dishes are now trademarked to discourage imitation. Herein lies the advantage for the public, who can choose between chains secure in the knowledge of what will be on offer; the comparative disadvantage lies in the uniformity of each product, with little opportunity for individuality in menu dishes which are 'designed' and imposed on their outlets from a central head office.

The selection of wines is generally limited and of indifferent quality; the range of 23 at Toby Grills quite easily offers the best choice and value. Berni, however, should be recognised for their larger (200ml) glass offered to diners at a more reasonable price.

The food

For the reasons outlined above, our inspectors can only have expected to find the food similar in pubs operated by the individual chains. It was rather a surprise, however, to find individual dishes *identical* the length and breadth of the country. Nowhere is this more clearly illustrated than in the salad bars operated by both Berni Inns and Barnaby's, where concoctions such as tuna and pasta salad, or cream cheese and pineapple with sultanas, came in for criticism at *every* outlet visited. The worst case, however, involved Barnaby's 'mini Scotch eggs', which have clearly been conceived without consultation with the poultry population, and contain a quite disgusting filling of dried egg.

We have also been universal in our condemnation of the carveries' hot food. The very nature of their operation causes the roast meats to stand, often for hours, under halogen lamps which cannot fail further to cook and dry out the exposed surfaces of the roasts. Equally, the effect on vegetables of standing for long periods in a bain-marie can only be an extension of the cooking time, either by steaming or immersion, to the ruination of their texture, flavour and nutritional content. Worse still was the number of times when up to three roast meats were served up with a single gravy, usually a thickened brown liquid whose effect was totally to mask the inherent flavours of the individual meats.

The findings

The best food we found was generally the plainest. You can get a good steak at any of the steak houses, but from the alternatives tried and tested throughout the Berni, Beefeater, Harvester and Toby Grills branches we have been largely discouraged from recommending diners to be too adventurous.

There is, also a lack of finesse in the cooking – chips, or baked potato, and peas are the most common vegetables. We *never* had a grilled tomato, and in the majority of cases mushrooms were tinned or boiled rather than fresh, then grilled or fried. There was a variation in presentation and service which suggests (as one might expect) that the larger outlets generally benefit from better-trained management and staff. At the bottom end of the scale we found poor food and badly trained staff which were indicative of incompetent management, in most cases conspicuous by its absence.

In the opinion of one of our inspectors these pubs 'succeed in providing *cheapness* rather than value for money, and the public has come to accept all that this implies: convenience foods, plastic products (butter portions, UHT creams, etc) as the necessary trappings of what they actually came out for – roast and four veg or steak and chips'.

The chain pubs are *faring* well enough; but in terms of food quality, service to their public and value for money they are *performing* badly.

Hotels

Berni/Chef & Brewer, Toby and Beefeater also offer a hotel service, which our inspectors sampled as well. Their impressions can be summed up as follows: 'poor management and shoddily kept facilities are the general hallmarks of this rapidly expanding breed of journeyman hostelries; they have neither the personal touch of our recommended pubs nor the class of our hotels'. A lack of public rooms and room service, coupled with fairly high prices, exacerbate the problems.

Barnaby's

Barnaby's got the wooden spoon in our survey, for the following reasons. There is a large selection at the 'starter table', but you only get a small plate; so, for the set price per *visit*, you are limited to what you can get on it. Salads are standard throughout the country, so unlikely to be fresh, and all are mayonnaise-based. Other choices include mini Scotch eggs (from mini hens?), spicy chicken wings (mostly skin and bone, tough and rubbery) and 'cold water prawns' which were just that – full of cold water! There is also a cauldron of soup of the day, one of which (leek and potato) was freshly made, hearty and palatable. Shredded seafood sticks had no taste ('like eating wet string') and cocktail sausages were 'wizened and skinless'.

The carvery was consistently condemned by our inspectors. Turkey was 'overcooked to the extent that the chef was having the greatest difficulty carving it', and the beef, pork and ham were also very dry, sitting as they do under strong heat lamps for long periods. Only one (unpleasant) gravy was provided for all the meats, the Yorkshire pudding was 'very heavy and cake-like' and the vegetables were 'boiled to a pulp'. Other main-course choices were steak and mushroom pie or salmon and haddock bake.

The sweet selection was unimaginative, with apple pie (microwaved with the custard over it, and difficult to tell which was the cardboard-like pastry and which the 'papier mâché' apple), treacle sponge (commercial-mix sponge, but plenty of treacle) and various ice-cream based desserts.

Self-service is the main order of the day, but the waitresses were generally quite friendly; one glass of wine was totally forgotten, however, and there was a general lack of management supervision.

Barnaby's also came bottom of our poll for both pleasantness of surroundings and facilities for children, being rather stark and 'plastic' places with standard green decor.

Best: Northampton 50%

37

Beefeater

Owned by Whitbread, Beefeater came out second in our overall survey (just!) but third for food service alone. Menus differ slightly from winter to summer. As with Berni, their steaks are of decent quality and usually cooked as ordered, but other aspects let the side down.

Starters include 'seven-spice prawns' (a trademarked 'Cajun' recipe, according to the menu), a dish which consists of poor-quality chewy prawns in a hotly spiced unappetising bread-crumb, with a lemon wedge garnish. Salmon mousse was creamy enough, but lacked colour, texture and flavour; chicken and sweetcorn soup was also flavourless; 'country-style pâté' had a minced texture and an unsubtle taste.

Cooking of the steaks varied from branch to branch, but the meat was usually good; accompaniments, however, were disappointing. Vegetables consist of the ubiquitous peas, jacket potatoes or chips, with new potatoes in the summer; all as usual overcooked and on the cool side. Salad costs extra, but is a better bet. Other main courses range from steak with a turkey kebab, in which the steak was reasonable but the pieces of turkey dry and chewy; chicken Oscar was awful – 'the chicken breast was burnt underneath so the black bits went everywhere and the main constituent of the broccoli, prawn and smoked salmon accompaniment was

water'. Vegetable lasagne caters for vegetarians, and fish dishes are available as well.

Treacle pudding was poor sponge with jelly-like golden syrup and lumpy custard; summer pudding consisted of 'thick gelatinous sponge and sharp evil-tasting fruit'; 'seven-fruit tarte' in one case appeared to have only six fruits, and had either a tough pastry base or a soggy one depending on the amount of syrup it was sitting in.

Service was variable from poor to efficient, even if (in the opinion of one our inspectors) the staff do look a little silly in their uniforms. One bill was made out wrongly, and courses were often hurriedly brought. In one instance, however, staff were well-trained and extremely friendly.

Value for money was quite highly rated, and they cater fairly well for children.

Best: Doncaster 63%

Berni

'We're famous for our steaks' claim Berni, and with some justification, as the steaks themselves turned out to be of good-quality meat and usually capably cooked to order: a good, dependable option. The standard menu announces that no item contains any artificial colours, flavours or sweeteners, which is a welcome move. Other aspects of the food operation, however, were not so good.

Starters include bland mass-produced soup of the day, the ever-present prawn cocktail, and chicken tikka (fatty chicken pieces in 'greasy yellow paste'). The salmon or asparagus and smoked ham mousse were quite acceptable, in some cases, but not in others.

Main courses, apart from steaks, are fish, poultry, pork, gammon or a vegetarian option ('approved by the Vegetarian Society'), none of which were of particularly high quality. If you sensibly opt for the steak, have it plain; the speciality sauces were generally quite poor. Chasseur sauce was far too tomatoey, and béarnaise too oily (on one occasion); but these and the cooking of the steaks themselves did vary from branch to branch. Plain steaks come with ungrilled tomatoes and mushrooms, a major gripe among our inspectors. Vegetables consist of chips or jacket potatoes, peas or beans, again quite variable in quality, and

there is a salad bar offering a very familiar choice of mainly sauce-based salads, which range from 'excellent' to having 'seen better days'.

Sweets were disappointing. 'Strawberry Imagination' consisted of strawberries with strawberry-flavoured yogurt ice-cream, which was refreshing enough but scarcely lived up to its title. Mango melba was very sickly, as was the topping on a raspberry torte, and the fudge cake tasted mass-produced. One welcome touch was the provision of fresh fruit on one visit.

Service gained the highest mark in our survey: staff were friendly and helpful on the whole.

The standard decor is pleasant enough, and there are both children's and braille menus, but there could have been more parking spaces provided.

Best: Stratford-upon-Avon 65%

Harvester

One of our worst experiences in the whole survey occurred at a Harvester (a chain owned by Trusthouse Forte) – despite prominent advertising of lunch service from 12 to 2.30pm, our inspector was refused admittance for lunch at 1.50pm. He was eventually given what they had left: two hot sausages and a roll (no butter). We decided that, appalling though this was, it was unfair actually to include the resulting marks in the survey; but be warned!

Winter and summer menus are available. Starters include savoury mushrooms, which were deemed 'a better effort than most'; country pâté was 'a sort of soggy red mince that tasted rather like corned beef'; salmon mousse was 'a mite powdery', but quite pleasant. A plus here was the fact that real butter was served with rolls or toast.

Steaks, although still acceptable, were considered the least good offered by the steak house chains; our inspectors thought the meat was of slightly inferior quality. Sauces again are best avoided, and the vegetables and salad cart also disappointing, with a very poor choice. Other main courses include various unimaginative chicken dishes and plaice or scampi. 'Lemon chicken and butterfly shrimps' was spoiled by deep-fried 'shrimps' which were all crisp coating and fresh air, and devoid of much real flavour. The chicken breast was much better.

Sweets are simple ice-cream based or frozen. 'Lemon surprise' was a lemon-flavoured mousse on a sponge with cream, and was considered quite good; chocolate fudge cake was rather dried out; toffee and apple pudding was 'microwaved to ruination with a rubbery ball of apple sponge dowsed in a sticky coating of toffee custard strangely reminiscent of glue!'.

Service varied wildly from 'the friendliest and most efficient' in the survey to 'just one waitress struggling to cope'. In one branch, a waiter insisted on trying to sell our inspector a sweet even after he had declined four times!

Other aspects were not particularly inspiring either, although amenities and cleanliness did gain the highest mark.

Best: Peterborough 63%

41

Roast Inn

The menu here is split between kitchen-cooked items and a carvery, but our inspectors did not think much of either! Starters include baked mushrooms, which looked unappetising, had very little taste, and were garnished with greasy, misshapen croutons. Deep-fried prawns were slightly better, but disappointingly served with just tartare sauce from a jar. Soup was either French onion or vegetable, neither very appealing.

The carvery itself was very poor in all the branches we visited. Some counters had no heat lamps, and so all the meats looked cold. Beef and pork were dry, stringy and flavourless, and both meats shared the same gravy with the turkey. There was so much fat on the beef in one instance that our inspector's dog consumed more of it than he did. Yorkshire pudding was universally hard, leathery and cold, and the vegetables were overdone, watery and tasteless. Roast potatoes were also cold, and very hard. Kitchen-cooked items include steak and kidney pudding, which was again hard and rubbery, and accompanied by the same poor vegetables. Plus points were the salads – the counter was well stocked, and the salads themselves were reasonably fresh and pleasant – and the selection of wines by the glass, which included Muscadet, Frascati and a wine of the week.

Puddings varied. One syllabub was 'the best part of the meal', but treacle tart was overdone to the point that the treacle had caramelised and the pastry was rock hard. Steamed sponge pudding could not be served without the custard (a real giveaway), which itself was thick and unappetising. Pina colada ice-cream 'totally missed out on flavour'.

Service was only average, varying from branch to branch. Customers serve themselves to most things, but even simple tasks like bringing bread rolls seemed to cause problems for the staff, and one bill was wrong. In one case, though, the waitress showed a caring attitude – she replaced an obviously cold Yorkshire pudding with a hot one (but equally leathery!).

Unfortunately there was nothing outstanding about Roast Inns to counteract the poor quality of the food. All other aspects were just average.

Best: Bournemouth 57%

Toby

Grills

Toby Grills easily came out top of our list for quality of food and value for money. The menu is noticeably more extensive and the cooking and service quite decent; there is also more choice for children, and a better wine list, than offered by its competitors.

Starters ranged from mushroom coriander (good fresh-tasting mushrooms in a quite passable white wine sauce) to seafood provençale (although the prawns were too small and chewy, the sauce 'came close to an acceptable effort'). Steaks are of good quality and flavour, and this time the speciality sauces are worth trying. Baked potatoes are excellent, but let down by the greasy onion rings, and the stir-fry vegetables at least represented an attempt to be different even if they were frozen. Other main courses include barbecued chicken, which was moist and tasty with a spicy but less than imaginative sauce, and the salad (freshly prepared) had a rather sharp vinaigrette.

Desserts are very convenience-based, but the apple pie and custard were at least hot. Service was pretty good, compared to what our inspectors had become used to, and management were actually in evidence.

Carving rooms

This was voted the best of the carveries, although it was still pretty poor. They use the same starters as the Grills, but with more variable results: seafood provençale which was reasonable in the Grills was a poor relation here; the mushroom coriander this time had a sauce which was 'thick like porridge'.

The roast meats were dry and fairly tasteless and served up with the same gravy for all. Pork was fatty and the crackling was nowhere near crisp enough. Vegetables were of the usual overdone variety and Yorkshire pudding was tough and leathery. At one branch, the sour smell as the lids were removed almost caused our inspector to keel over!

At some branches they offer alternatives to the carvery, but the cooking is a let-down. Sirloin steak was 'nearly 30% fat and sinew', and again served with raw tomato and an awful chasseur sauce.

Sweets were rated higher than at most of the other chains, but as with the Grills were obviously convenience products. Service was reasonable and friendly, but not outstanding.

Best Grill: Worcester 70%
Best Carving Room: Saltash and Banbury 54% each

Our Ratings

Our inspectors awarded marks firstly for the standard of food, wine and table service (see Table 1), and then for other aspects of the operation (see Table 2).

Table 1:

Food, Wine and Table Service

	Marks out of	Toby Grills	Berni	Beefeater	Toby Carveries	Harvester	Roast Inn	Barnabys
Starters	20	11	9	9	9	9	8	6
Main Courses	40	26	21	20	15	17	12	12
Desserts	20	12	8	8	10	8	6	6
Wine	10	7	5	6	6	6	6	6
Service	10	8	7	6	6	6	5	5
Total	%	64	50	49	46	46	37	35

Table 2:

Overall Service

	Marks out of	Toby Grills	Beefeater	Berni	Toby Carveries	Harvester	Roast Inn	Barnabys
Food (see Table 1)	100	64	49	50	46	46	37	35
Amenities & Cleanliness	20	12	11	12	13	12	12	11
Children's Facilities	20	14	13	12	12	9	12	9
Layout & Surroundings	10	7	7	8	7	7	7	5
Value for Money	20	15	13	11	11	11	11	10
Parking	10	10	9	7	9	9	9	9
Toilets	20	12	9	9	10	10	10	5
Total	%	67	55.5	54.5	54	52	49	42

As good as gold

Your best bet for a fuller flavour

Our Kind of Pub

Every year we receive hundreds of letters from hopeful readers recommending their particular favourite pub for the Guide, and no doubt the majority are disappointed to find when the new Guide is published that it has been omitted once more. This is very probably because what *we* look for in a good pub is not always what is provided by the 'friendly local' where many regulars often meet in an almost club-like atmosphere. Have you ever walked into a pub full of people and immediately felt totally isolated? This can happen when most of the clientele already know each other, and you may have unwittingly sat in old Joe's favourite chair by the fire. Fine if you are a member of the 'club', but not so pleasant if you are a stranger.

On their travels, our inspectors are invariably 'strangers', and gauge a pub on how well they are received and looked after as such. There is no point in recommending an otherwise lovely old inn somewhere in the wilds, if visitors to the area are not going to feel welcome once inside. So this is our first priority: a warm welcome and a relaxed, friendly atmosphere.

Some pubs are recommended solely because they have fascinating historical connections, command a beautiful setting or have some other significant point of interest. These are our 'atmosphere' pubs: places we could not bear to leave out even though we do not particularly rate the standard of food or accommodation.

Inside the Silver Plough at Pitton in Wiltshire, one of our starred pubs.

Then there are the ones in which the food is not only a bonus but on occasion a positive highlight. Fresh ingredients are essential, whatever the ambitions of the menu, and we often find that simple food done well can be better than attempts at more elaborate dishes. Little touches can reveal the general quality. Are the milk, butter and cream real and nicely served, or do they come out of tubs, packets or spray cans? Are you given a bowl of sugar, or packets? Are the vegetables fresh and crisp, and more than just chips and peas? Are the sweets home-made, or of the standard shop-bought variety? Even if you are not a food expert, these aspects can be readily assessed. If the menu is not printed but handwritten daily, this suggests that fresh seasonal ingredients are used.

We like the pub itself to be spotlessly clean from the bars to the toilets, and free of game machines, juke boxes and background music. Bedrooms, too, should be clean and comfortable, not necessarily large or with televisions, but just homely, warm and relaxing.

One of our major problems is the rapidity with which pubs can change hands. It is very disappointing when a pub recommended in our current Guide is sold to a new landlord whose standards are not as high as those of the previous one. This proves that in many cases we are recommending not the pub itself but the efforts of its landlord. Where landlords excel in all aspects of running their pub, we award the rare accolade of a 'star'. Having achieved this, they are then also in the running for the Pub of the Year Award, which if won can bring in a great deal of extra business. The 1989 Pub of the Year was the Griffin Inn in Llyswen, a village in Powys, Wales, and it is well worth a visit, at any time of year.

Griffin Inn, Llyswen

After a lovely drive through the Welsh countryside, whatever the weather, your first glimpse of the Griffin with its spring flowers or summer windowboxes, as you drive or walk through the village, is delightful, and first impressions for once are entirely accurate. Inside, Richard and Di Stockton treat you as guests in their own home from the moment you enter the uncluttered, peaceful bar area. Armchairs, plush carpets, solid furniture, a log fire in winter, beams and exposed stonework, fresh flowers, two dogs and a cat (all pristine, including the animals) create an immediately comforting environment in which the hum of the locals' conversation is the only background noise. Colourful characters in the bar include the village poacher, who always makes a strong impression on visitors staying at the Griffin for their fishing (they have a full-time ghillie) or shooting weekends.

The food is worth a long journey to sample, all cooked by Eileen Havard (who originally worked at the pub as a washer-up), and the menus, handwritten by Richard, change daily, making excellent use of seasonal game and fish. Salmon and trout are caught locally in the Wye, and sea fish is supplied from Cornwall. You could choose anything from sandwiches cut to order, one dish from the bar menu or a full à la carte meal in the

The Griffin Inn in the spring.

separate dining room, and the Stocktons would not flinch. One Christmas they threw a lunch party for a number of their regular customers, who enjoyed it so much that they now repeat the experience once a month! The wine list consists of around 40 wines from France, Italy, Spain, Germany and California.

Richard Stockton, whose background lies in the engineering and haulage industry, and his wife Di took over the pub in March 1984, after three years of living 'the good life' in Worcestershire where they kept chickens and ducks, and started baking and selling from their cottage door. This operation snowballed and gave them the idea of running their own business, possibly bed and breakfast in a large country house. When the Griffin Inn was offered to them, they snapped it up, having stayed there themselves before and knowing its strategic position and vast potential. Since then they have gradually improved and refurbished throughout, and have further plans to increase their accommodation capacity. At present there are six bedrooms (two single) in the rear extension, all named after fishing flies (Yellow Torrish, Silver Wilkinson, Jack Scott, Green Highlander, Mar Lodge and Durham Ranger) and again festooned with the flower arrangements done by Mrs Stockton senior.

Expansion at all costs is not the Stockton's main aim, however; they are keen above all to retain the 'local' tag and not to drive away the village clientele. The pub has a table quoits team which plays the other pubs in the area, match nights always being quite an event. Their only problems are lack of lounge space for residents at present (there being just a small area on the landing), the perennial difficulty with getting staff to serve and clean (they do most of the cleaning themselves) and the old story of only making a small profit on their £300,000 turnover. 'Enough for a holiday', said Richard, but the Griffin Inn is so much a part of their life that they never really enjoy being away. Perhaps that is the secret of how to win an award like Pub of the Year: total devotion to the job, a businesslike attitude, and a constant attention to detail. A highly personable character helps, too!

The Griffin's dining room laid out for the regulars' monthly party.

A publican's lot

It came over forcefully from talking to the Stocktons how single-minded and uncompromising they have been to achieve standards which they themselves consider acceptable to the type of customer they are trying to attract – and yet how careful they have been to retain the local character of the Griffin as a pub. This has taken the form of personal supervision of every aspect of the operation: careful stage-by-stage improvements to bars and bedrooms, and meticulous attention to menus, beer cellar and wine lists. They pay attention equally to their oft-returning residents' comforts and the sometimes demanding regulars' enjoyment of *their* local.

All this has its price, in sixteen-hour working days, and takes its toll; their weekly retreat to a cottage 'hidden in the hills' and snatched four-day trips to France test their powers of recuperation to the limit. The pub is not simply their living, it is their life, and a contribution to its success of near to 100 working hours per week (each) cannot be otherwise. Here we are, showering our 'Publicans of the Year' with high praise, and yet their story is increasingly familiar amongst other licencees we talk to. One freeholder who recently sold his business of some twelve years calculates that he saw his 'status' on his own payroll slide gradually from the top of the pay scale to 'somewhere in the bottom half' over the last six years. Another couple of our acquaintance recently purchased the freehold of their pub, having calculated their earnings in their first years as tenants of the brewery to be below 50p per hour!

Part of the comfortable bar area at the Griffin Inn.

Our inspectors' most common complaint over recent months has been that pubs with truly good food are becoming increasingly hard to find. Our editors' disquiet lies in the near 10% of entries annually which are lost to the Guide through the natural wastage of proprietors retiring or simply selling up and moving on.

We are told, for instance, that around half of all first-time buyers leave the industry within five years amid rising disillusion at the rigours of the trade, and current estimates put the annual turnover of free houses as high as 20% annually. This is occurring at a time when the extension of opening hours and greater freedom from brewery ties is being hailed as a golden opportunity for expansion in the free trade sector. The next five years could yet show the opposite to be true.

The root cause may well lie simply in the burgeoning costs of freehold property, which amongst Britain's 34,000 'Free Houses' tends to mirror house prices, and has seen an increase in property values of 30% per annum since 1980. Whereas ten years ago a rule of thumb was considered to be that '£1 of investment will buy £1 of turnover', as we approach 1990 60 pence per pound invested is as much as a prospective purchaser may expect in potential gross turnover. To date, as individual investment has increased, so has the involvement of the 'Big Six' brewers whose offer of 'soft loans' in exchange for the exclusive supply of their products has underpriced many an over-capitalised publican. The consequences of

51

government intervention to discontinue this practice will take some time to assess, but the outlook for totally 'free' pubs (and for potential private investors in them) is not rosy.

Amongst the small band of current independent publicans, such as the Stocktons, however, there appears to be a rising tide of contributory adverse factors. As competition increases from the brewery-owned and managed houses with their seemingly limitless source of development capital (not to mention the plethora of convenience-minded chicken, burger and pizza houses) virtually no suburban, village or country pub will survive unless it is capable of providing a food service. The sensible considerations of the 'Don't drink and drive' campaign have only served to emphasise this fact.

Demands, therefore, for a good quality of food and service are greater than ever before. Yet the dual factors of low pay and unsocial hours increase the difficulty of hiring competent staff, and the onus falls very heavily on the beleaguered licensee.

Whereas ten years ago there maybe was room for the gifted and often charismatic amateur to struggle by, such 'creative' entrepreneurs have all too often proved to be catastrophically unmercenary, and frequently chaotically unbusinesslike. An inevitable consequence is that food quality cedes to profitability as a desirable goal in the publican's ongoing struggle against shrinking profit margins, and this loss of flair and ingenuity (in food terms) signals the onset of mediocrity.

The advent of the microwave, and supplier-produced 'speciality' menu items then spells the inevitable 'convenient' way out; no further investment is required in capable trained cooks (who are at a premium anyway), nor time-consuming preparation techniques, nor even expensive traditional cooking equipment.

Thus is born a new generation of 'pub grub' which proliferates on the blackboards of our pubs and inns, and is easily identified as such by our eagle-eyed inspectors; to the point that in many cases individual frozen food suppliers can be identified by their proprietory brands of specialities.

Nor, finally, is the general public fooled (despite the feeling amongst a very few of our readers that their local's microwave excels over all others!) but they have become conditioned, almost, to accept the lowest common denominator of quality and price . . . for convenience's sake.

Our Publicans of the Year, past and present, our starred pubs and our nominees for future such awards look ever in danger of becoming the 'dodos' of Britain's vaunted pub heritage, and they are fighting for survival against what appear at times to be overwhelming odds.

We salute them!

Coca-Cola
Coca-Cola
Coke
You Can't Beat The Feeling!
Enjoy
Coca-Cola
REGISTERED TRADE MARK
Enjoy
Coke

The Dairy Crest Symbol of Excellence

Wherever you see this sign, you will be entering an establishment where the quality and presentation of cheeses is excellent.

The Dairy Crest Symbol of Excellence is only awarded by the Egon Ronay's Guides' team of inspectors where they find a high standard of cheese available – whether presented on a cheeseboard or included in a meal or snack.

Now in its third year, the Award is an on-going sign of commitment from Britain's leading cheese manufacturer, Dairy Crest Foods, to the improvement of cheese quality, variety and presentation.

The Symbol is recognised nationally by caterers who strive to reach its high standards, and by the ever more discerning public who are seeking nothing but the best when eating in hotels, restaurants, pubs and cafes.

So, wherever you see the Egon Ronay's Guide Dairy Crest Symbol of Excellence, you will enjoy guaranteed quality of:

TASTE – through expert selection, handling and storage

VARIETY – through imaginative use of traditional, new and local cheeses

PRESENTATION – through the use of colour, texture and shape to give a mouth-watering display

INFORMATION – through the caterer's knowledge and understanding

Where you find English cheeses at their best, you will be sure to find Dairy Crest's own excellent cheeses, such as the famous Lymeswold range, the reduced-fat Tendale range and the full selection of England and Welsh traditional cheeses and prize-winning Cheddars and Stilton.

DAIRY CREST

Outstanding Cheeseboards

London
Alma SW18
Lamb & Flag WC2

England
Bainbridge, North Yorkshire: *Rose & Crown Hotel*
Bedford, Bedfordshire: *Park*
Bridport, Dorset: *George Hotel*
Brightwell Baldwin, Oxfordshire: *Lord Nelson*
Broom, Bedfordshire: *Cock*
Chinnor, Oxfordshire: *Sir Charles Napier*
Doddiscombsleigh, Devon: *Nobody Inn*
Levington, Suffolk: *Ship*
Pitton, Wiltshire: *Silver Plough*
Staple Fitzpaine, Somerset: *Greyhound Inn*
Stilton, Cambridgeshire: *Bell*
Trent, Dorset: *Rose & Crown*
Yattendon, Berkshire: *Royal Oak*

Wales
Llandissilio, Dyfed: *Bush Inn*
Llyswen, Powys: *Griffin Inn*

John Selden
1854–1654

'Tis not the eating, nor 'tis not the drinking that is to
be blamed, but the excess.
Table Talk

Leon de Fos

For the man who would eat like a glutton,
A good stomach is worth more than mutton,
For what use is the best
If you cannot digest,
And your teeth are exceedingly rotten.
'Gastronomia'

William Shakespeare
1564–1616

Will the cold brook, candied with ice, caudle thy
morning taste, to cure thy o'-er-night's surfeit.
Timon of Athens

Mauduit

Intoxication . . . embraces five stages: jocose,
bellicose, lachrymose, comatose, and morotose.
The Vicomte in the Kitchen (1933)

Anonymous

The glances over cocktails
That seemed to be so sweet
Don't seem quite so amorous
Over the Shredded Wheat.
'Wine, Women and Wedding'

Just Desserts

Thankfully, the days when a pub lunch consisted of a slice of not-quite-fresh bread with a mean portion of rubbery cheese and a dollop of pickle are over. Countrywide, pubs now offer traditional fare or appetisingly different hot dishes. Generous portions, realistic prices and evening menus means that dining à la public house can be a pleasing experience.

Still something of a surprise feature are desserts, particularly when the choice extends beyond fruit pie, gâteau or cheesecake. So we thought you might like to sample some of the splendid sweet options available – a devilishly rich chocolate mousse, an imaginative cream ice or a light and fruity roulade.

Not necessarily for every day, these sweets are the ideal occasional indulgence. We might feel guilty about eating sugar, but for good health our bodies need a regular supply of proteins, carbohydrates, fats, fibre, minerals and vitamins. Sugar is one type of carbohydrate that is easily digested and constitutes a valuable source of energy; so when eaten as part of a sensibly balanced diet it deserves to be enjoyed! Remember that one level teaspoon containing 4 grams provides just 16 calories.

Next time you want to bring a meal to a spectacular end, forget your elaborate cookbooks and try one of these specialities from the best of British pubs.

58

Chocolate Ring with Vanilla Custard
Rupert Willcocks, Silver Plough, Pitton

This rich chocolate mousse is flavoured with brandy and toasted chopped almonds and served with a light, vanilla-flavoured custard.

Serves 12–16

450 g/1 lb best plain dessert
   chocolate
225 g/8 oz unsalted butter
4 eggs, separated
100 g/4 oz caster
   sugar
100 g/4 oz blanched
   almonds, chopped
   and toasted
30 ml/2 tbsp brandy

Vanilla custard
6 egg yolks
65 g/2½ oz caster sugar
2 vanilla pods
550 ml/18 fl oz milk

Lightly oil a 1.4-litre/2½-pint capacity ring mould (20–23 cm/8–9 inches in diameter, depending on depth). Melt the chocolate and butter together in a bowl over a pan of hot water. Do not allow the water to boil.

Beat the egg yolks with the sugar until pale and very creamy. Off the heat, add the almonds to the chocolate mixture and stir in the brandy. Fold in the creamed yolks, then whisk the egg whites until stiff and fold them in also. Do not allow the chocolate mixture to cool before folding in the remaining ingredients or it will become too stiff. Turn the mixture into the prepared ring mould and chill for a few hours, until firmly set.

To make the vanilla custard, beat the yolks and sugar together until pale and creamy. Bring the milk to the boil with the vanilla pods, then set it aside to cool for 30 seconds. Strain the hot milk on to the egg mixture, stirring, and set the bowl over a pan of hot water. Do not allow the water to boil or the custard may overheat and curdle. Cook, stirring continuously, until the custard is thick enough to coat the back of the spoon. Cover the surface of the custard with damp greaseproof paper or cling film to prevent a skin forming, and leave to cool. Chill until required.

Turn the chocolate ring out onto a 30-cm/12-inch tray or platter and surround it with some vanilla custard. Decorate with grated chocolate, almonds and a dusting of cocoa over the custard. Serve the remaining custard separately.

Glayva Cream Ice
Kathy Leadbeater, Kilberry Inn, Kilberry

An unusual iced dessert, this recipe uses concentrated frozen orange juice as a base, then enriches the mixture with whipped cream. Decorate individual portions with slices of fresh orange if you like.

Serves 6–8

1 × 178 ml/6½ fl oz can frozen
*   orange juice*
175 g/6 oz caster sugar
75 g/3 oz golden syrup

grated rind and juice of 1 lemon
600 ml/1 pint whipping cream
30 ml/2 tbsp Glayva (Drambuie
*   may be used instead)*

Turn the undiluted, frozen juice into a bowl. Add the sugar, syrup, lemon rind and juice, then whisk the mixture with an electric beater until smooth. Make sure that the ice particles are broken down to give a smooth result.

Gently stir in the cream and Glayva until all the ingredients are thoroughly combined. When the cream is smooth, and no streaks of orange remain, pour it into a deep, rigid freezer container. Leave a little headspace as the cream will expand slightly on freezing, then freeze until firm.

Transfer the cream to the refrigerator 25 minutes before it is to be served, then scoop it into individual dishes.

Variation
Follow the above recipe, making up a half-quantity. Make up a second batch, again using half-quantities, substituting frozen grapefruit juice for the orange and Cointreau for the Glayva. Freeze the creams in separate containers, then serve scoops of both cream ices together in individual dishes.

Pineapple Roulade
Eileen Havard, Griffin Inn, Llyswen

A light sponge roulade filled with slightly sweetened whipped cream and tangy pineapple. Instead of using canned fruit, you can substitute fresh pineapple when it is relatively inexpensive.

4 eggs, separated
150 g/ 5 oz caster sugar
50 g/2 oz plain flour
grated rind of 1 orange or lemon
30 ml/2 tbsp orange or lemon juice
pinch of salt

Filling
300 ml/ ½ pint double cream
icing sugar to taste
30 ml/2 tbsp Kirsch
1 × 227 g/8 oz can pineapple pieces
    or chunks, well drained and
    halved if large

Line and grease a 23 × 33 cm/9 × 13 inch Swiss roll tin. Set the oven at 180°C/350°F/Gas 4.

Beat the egg yolks with 100 g/4 oz of the sugar until thick and creamy. Fold in the flour, then fold in the fruit rind and juice. Whisk the egg whites with the salt until they stand in stiff peaks. Add the remaining caster sugar and continue to whisk until the whites are glossy and stiff. Fold the whites into the yolks, then pour the mixture into the prepared tin and spread it evenly and lightly. Bake for about 15 minutes, until risen, golden and firm. Leave to cool for 5 minutes, then cover with a damp cloth and leave to cool completely.

For the filling, whip the cream with a little icing sugar to taste and the Kirsch. Turn the roulade out on to sugared greaseproof paper and spread the cream over it. Top with the pineapple, then use the greaseproof paper as a guide to roll up the roulade. Dust with icing sugar and serve cut into slices.

Note
The roulade can be decorated with piped whipped cream and pineapple or quartered slices of orange or lemon if liked.

Pubs for Families

London
Bulls Head W4
Dickens Inn E1
George Inn SE1

England
Alrewas, Staffordshire: *George & Dragon*
Ansty, Dorset: *Fox*
Appleby, Cumbria: *Royal Oak Inn*
Armathwaite, Cumbria: *Dukes Head Hotel*
Ashwell, Hertfordshire: *Three Tuns Hotel*
Askham, Cumbria: *Queens Head Inn*
Askrigg, North Yorkshire: *Kings Arms Hotel*
Aston Cantlow, Warwickshire: *Kings Head*
Bantham, Devon: *Sloop Inn*
Beetham, Cumbria: *Wheatsheaf Hotel*
Belford, Northumberland: *Blue Bell Hotel*
Bewdley, Hereford & Worcester: *Black Boy Hotel*
Bibury, Gloucestershire: *Catherine Wheel*
Bretforton, Hereford & Worcester: *Fleece*
Bridport, Dorset: *George Hotel*
Broad Chalke, Wiltshire: *Queens Head*
Broom, Bedfordshire: *Cock*
Burwash, East Sussex: *Bell Inn*
Casterton, Cumbria: *Pheasant Inn*
Castleton, Derbyshire: *Castle Hotel*
Cauldon, Staffordshire: *Yewtree*
Caxton, Cambridgeshire: *Caxton Gibbet Inn*
Cerne Abbas, Dorset: *New Inn*
Chale, Isle of Wight: *Clarendon Hotel*
Chale, Isle of Wight: *White Mouse Inn*
Chapel Amble, Cornwall: *Maltster's Arms*
Chedworth, Gloucestershire: *Seven Tuns*
Chenies, Hertfordshire: *Bedford Arms Thistle Hotel*
Chester, Cheshire: *Ye Olde Kings Head*
Chorleywood, Hertfordshire: *Sportsman Hotel*
Churchstow, Devon: *Church House Inn*
Clanfield, Oxfordshire: *Clanfield Tavern*
Clavering, Essex: *Cricketers*
Clifton Hampden, Oxfordshire: *Barley Mow*
Cotherstone, Co. Durham: *Fox & Hounds*
Croscombe, Somerset: *Bull Terrier*
Crowell, Oxfordshire: *Catherine Wheel*
Dedham, Essex: *Marlborough Head*
Dowlish Wake, Somerset: *New Inn*
Dragon Green, West Sussex: *George & Dragon*
Dunwich, Suffolk: *Ship Inn*
Eastling, Kent: *Carpenters Arms*
Ewen, Gloucestershire: *Duck Inn*
Falmouth, Cornwall: *Pandora Inn*
Faringdon, Oxfordshire: *Bell Hotel*
Fonthill Bishop, Wiltshire: *Kings Head*
Ford, Wiltshire: *White Hart at Ford*
Fordwich, Kent: *Fordwich Arms*
Fossebridge, Gloucestershire: *Fossebridge Inn*
Fovant, Wiltshire: *Cross Keys Hotel*
Freeland, Oxfordshire: *Shepherds Hall Inn*

Gibraltar, Buckinghamshire: *Bottle & Glass*

Goldsborough, North Yorkshire: *Bay Horse Inn*

Gretton, Gloucestershire: *Royal Oak*

Guisborough, Cleveland: *Moorcock Hotel*

Hatherleigh, Devon: *George Hotel*

Hawkshead, Cumbria: *Drunken Duck Inn*

Hawkshead, Cumbria: *Queen's Head*

Haytor Vale, Devon: *Rock Inn*

Helmsley, North Yorkshire: *Feathers Hotel*

Heydon, Cambridgeshire: *King William IV*

Holywell, Cambridgeshire: *Ye Olde Ferryboat Inn*

Horns Cross, Devon: *Hoops Inn*

Horton, Dorset: *Horton Inn*

Hubberholme, North Yorkshire: *George Inn*

Kingscote, Gloucestershire: *Hunters Hall Inn*

Kingston, East Sussex: *Juggs*

Kirk Langley, Derbyshire: *Meynell Arms Hotel*

Knapp, Somerset: *Rising Sun*

Lancaster, Lancashire: *Farmers Arms Hotel*

Linwood, Hampshire: *High Corner Inn*

Little Milton, Oxfordshire: *Lamb Inn*

Little Washbourne, Gloucestershire: *Hobnails Inn*

Loweswater, Cumbria: *Kirkstile Inn*

Lyddington, Leicestershire: *Marquess of Exeter*

Lydford, Devon: *Castle Inn*

Lyndhurst, Hampshire: *Waterloo Arms*

Marhamchurch, Cornwall: *Bullers Arms*

Market Drayton, Shropshire: *Corbett Arms Hotel*

Marshside, Kent: *Gate Inn*

Melmerby, Cumbria: *Shepherds Inn*

Metal Bridge, Cumbria: *Metal Bridge Inn*

Metherell, Cornwall: *Carpenters Arms*

Minster Lovell, Oxfordshire: *Old Swan Hotel*

Monksilver, Somerset: *Notley Arms*

Montacute, Somerset: *Kings Arms Inn*

Moretonhampstead, Devon: *White Hart Hotel*

Needingworth, Cambridgeshire: *Pike & Eel Hotel*

North Petherton, Somerset: *Walnut Tree Inn*

North Wootton, Somerset: *Crossways Inn*

Nunney, Somerset: *George Inn*

Oakwoodhill, Surrey: *Punchbowl Inn*

Ockley, Surrey: *King's Arms*

Old Dalby, Leicestershire: *Crown Inn*

Ollerton, Cheshire: *Dun Cow*

Oswaldkirk, North Yorkshire: *Malt Shovel Inn*

Over Stratton, Somerset: *Royal Oak*

Pendoggett, Cornwall: *Cornish Arms*

Pensax, Hereford & Worcester: *Bell Inn*

Perranuthnoe, Cornwall: *Victoria Inn*

Peter Tavy, Devon: *Peter Tavy Inn*

Petworth, West Sussex: *Angel*

Pewsham, Wiltshire: *Lysley Arms*

Porlock Weir, Somerset: *Anchor Hotel & Ship Inn*

Port Gaverne, Cornwall: *Port Gaverne Hotel*

Ramsbury, Wiltshire: *Bell*

Ringmore, Devon: *Journeys End Inn*

Ripley, Surrey: *Seven Stars*

Ripon, North Yorkshire: *Unicorn Hotel*

Rosedale Abbey, North Yorkshire: *Milburn Arms Hotel*

Saffron Walden, Essex: *Eight Bells*

Salisbury, Wiltshire: *Coach & Horses*

Scole, Norfolk: *Crossways Inn*

Seahouses, Northumberland: *Olde Ship Hotel*

Semley, Wiltshire: *Benett Arms*

Shave Cross, Dorset: *Shave Cross Inn*

Shiplake, Oxfordshire: *Baskerville Arms*

Shipston-on-Stour, Warwickshire: *White Bear Hotel*

Snettisham, Norfolk: *Rose & Crown Inn*

Sonning-on-Thames, Berkshire: *Bull Inn*

South Harting, West Sussex: *White Hart*

South Zeal, Devon: *Oxenham Arms*

Sproughton, Suffolk: *The Beagle*

St Margarets at Cliffe, Kent: *Cliffe Tavern*

St Mawes, Cornwall: *Rising Sun Inn*

Stanford Dingley, Berkshire: *Bull Inn*

Stanford St John, Oxfordshire: *Star Inn*

Stockbridge, Hampshire: *Grosvenor Hotel*

Stopham Bridge, West Sussex: *White Hart*

Stow Bardolph, Norfolk: *Hare Arms*

Summerhouse, Co. Durham: *Raby Hunt Inn*

Sutton, South Yorkshire: *Anne Arms*

Symonds Yat West, Hereford & Worcester: *Old Court Hotel*

Talkin Village, Cumbria: *Hare & Hounds Inn*

Tarrant Monkton, Dorset:

Langton Arms

Testcombe, Hampshire: *Mayfly*

Thornham, Norfolk: *Lifeboat Inn*

Trebarwith, Cornwall: *Mill House Inn*

Trent, Dorset: *Rose & Crown*

Upton Grey, Hampshire: *Hoddington Arms*

Wasdale Head, Cumbria: *Wasdale Head Inn*

West Ilsley, Berkshire: *Harrow*

West Pennard, Somerset: *Red Lion*

West Wycombe, Buckinghamshire: *George & Dragon*

Whatcote, Warwickshire: *Royal Oak*

Whitewell, Lancashire: *Inn at Whitewell*

Willerby, Humberside: *Cedars at Grange Park Hotel*

Winfrith Newburgh, Dorset: *Red Lion*

Winterton-on-sea, Norfolk: *Fisherman's Return*

Withington, Gloucestershire: *Mill Inn*

Wolverton Common, Hampshire: *Hare & Hounds*

Wooler, Northumberland: *Tankerville Arms*

Woolverton, Somerset: *Red Lion*

Wye, Kent: *New Flying Horse Inn*

Wykeham, North Yorkshire: *Downe Arms*

Yattendon, Berkshire: *Royal Oak*

Scotland

Ardentinny, Strathclyde: *Ardentinny Hotel*

Brae, Shetland: *Busta House Hotel*

Busby, Strathclyde: *Busby Hotel*

Clachan-Seil, Strathclyde: *Tigh-an-Truish*

Edinburgh, Lothian: *Rutland Hotel*

Kilberry, Strathclyde: *Kilberry Inn*

Kippen, Central: *Cross Keys Inn*

Lewiston, Highland: *Lewiston*

Arms Hotel
Loch Eck, Strathclyde: *Coylet Inn*
New Abbey, Dumfries &
   Galloway: *Criffel Inn*

Wales
Cenarth, Dyfed: *White Hart*
Crickhowell, Powys: *Bear Hotel*
East Aberthaw, South Glamorgan:
   Blue Anchor
Felindre Farchog, Dyfed:
   Salutation Inn
Llandovery, Dyfed: *Kings Head
   Inn*
Raglan, Gwent: *Beaufort Arms
   Hotel*

Waterside Pubs

London

Anchor SW1
Angel SE16
Bulls Head W4
Dickens E1
Dove W6
Grapes E14
Mayflower SE16
Old Ship W6
Prospect of Whitby E1
Ship SW18
Trafalgar Tavern SE10

England

Baginton, Warwickshire: *Old Mill Inn*
Bedford, Bedfordshire: *Embankment Hotel*
Beer, Devon: *Anchor Inn*
Bidford on Avon, Warwickshire: *White Lion Hotel*
Brendon, Devon: *Stag Hunters Hotel*
Bucklers Hard, Hampshire: *Master Builders House Hotel*
Burnham-on-Crouch, Essex: *Ye Olde White Harte Hotel*
Burton upon Trent, Staffordshire: *Riverside Inn*
Carey, Hereford & Worcester: *Cottage of Content*
Clifton Hampden, Oxfordshire: *Barley Mow*
Cockwood, Devon: *Anchor Inn*
Darmouth, Devon: *Royal Castle Hotel*
Eastergate, West Sussex: *Wilkes Head*
Falmouth, Cornwall: *Pandora Inn*
Fen Drayton, Cambridgeshire: *Three Tuns*
Ford, Wiltshire: *White Hart at Ford*
Fordwich, Kent: *Fordwich Arms*
Fossebridge, Gloucestershire: *Fossebridge Inn*
Helford, Cornwall: *Shipwrights Arms*
Himley, West Midlands: *Crooked House*
Holywell, Cambridgeshire: *Ye Olde Ferryboat Inn*
Hubberholme, North Yorkshire: *George Inn*
Hungerford, Berkshire: *John O'Gaunt Inn*
Huntingdon, Cambridgeshire: *Old Bridge Hotel*
Kintbury, Berkshire: *Dundas Arms*
Knightwick, Hereford & Worcester: *Talbot Hotel*
Lancaster, Lancashire: *Farmers Arms Hotel*
Lincoln, Lincolnshire: *Woodcocks*
Lynmouth, Devon: *Rising Sun Inn*
Marshside, Kent: *Gate Inn*
Metal Bridge, Cumbria: *Metal Bridge Inn*
Minster Lovell, Oxfordshire: *Old Swan Hotel*
Monksilver, Somerset: *Notley Arms*
North Cerney, Gloucestershire: *Bathurst Arms*
North Dalton, Humberside: *Star Inn*
Ovington, Hampshire: *Bush Inn*
Port Gaverne, Cornwall: *Port Gaverne Hotel*
Ruckhall, Hereford & Worcester: *Ancient Camp Inn*
Seahouses, Northumberland: *Olde Ship Hotel*
Seaview, Isle of Wight: *Seaview Hotel*
Sennen Cove, Cornwall: *Old Success Inn*
Shepperton, Middlesex: *Warren Lodge*
Southpool, Devon: *Millbrook Inn*

St Mawes, Cornwall: *Rising Sun Inn*

Stopham Bridge, West Sussex: *White Hart*

Testcombe, Hampshire: *Mayfly*

Umberleigh, Devon: *Rising Sun*

Wasdale Head, Cumbria: *Wasdale Head Inn*

Wath in Nidderdale, North Yorkshire: *Sportsmans Arms*

Whitewell, Lancashire: *Inn at Whitewell*

Whitney-on-Wye, Hereford & Worcester: *Rhydspence Inn*

Winkton, Dorset: *Fishermans Haunt Hotel*

Withington, Gloucestershire: *Mill Inn*

Yarmouth, Isle of Wight: *Bugle Hotel*

Scotland

Ardentinny, Strathclyde: *Ardentinny Hotel*

Brae, Shetland: *Busta House Hotel*

Busby, Strathclyde: *Busby Hotel*

Canonbie, Dumfries & Galloway: *Riverside Inn*

Clachan-Seil, Strathclyde: *Tigh-an-Truish*

Killin, Central: *Clachaig Hotel*

Kirkwall, Orkney: *Kirkwall Hotel*

Loch Eck, Strathclyde: *Coylet Inn*

Maidens, Strathclyde: *Bruce Hotel*

Spean Bridge, Highland: *Letterfinlay Lodge Hotel*

Tarbert, Strathclyde: *West Loch Hotel*

Tayvallich, Strathclyde: *Tayvallich Inn*

Wales

Abergavenny, Gwent: *Llanwenarth Arms*

Chepstow, Gwent: *Castle View Inn*

Felindre Farchog, Dyfed: *Salutation Inn*

Penmaenpool, Gwynedd: *George III Hotel*

Channel Islands

Pleinmont, Guernsey: *Imperial Hotel*

St Aubin's Harbour, Jersey: *Old Court House Inn*

Isle of Man

Peel, Isle of Man: *Creek Inn*

London Pubs by Area

Bayswater & Notting Hill
Slug & Lettuce, W2
Swan Tavern, W2
Victoria, W2
Windsor Castle, W8

Bloomsbury & Holborn
Lamb, WC1
Museum Tavern, WC1
Princess Louise, WC1
Ye Olde Mitre Tavern, EC1

Chelsea
Admiral Codrington, SW3

City
Black Friar, EC4
Cock Tavern, EC1
Fox & Anchor, EC1
Hand & Shears, EC1
The Old Dr Butler's Head, EC2
Ye Old Watling, EC4

Covent Garden
Lamb & Flag, WC2
Nell of Old Drury, WC2
Salisbury, WC2

East London
Dickens Inn, E1
Grapes, E14
Prospect of Whitby, E1

Fleet Street
Old Bell Tavern, EC4
Seven Stars, WC2
Ye Olde Cheshire Cheese, EC4

Knightsbridge
Grenadier, SW1
Paxton's Head, SW1

Mayfair
Shepherd's Tavern, W1

North & North-West London
Albion, N1
Eagle, N1
Flask, N6
Jack Straw's Castle, NW3
Slug & Lettuce, N1
Spaniards Inn, NW3

St James's
Two Chairmen, SW1

Soho & Trafalgar Square
Sherlock Holmes, WC2

South-East London
Anchor, SW1
Angel, SE16
George Inn, SE1
Mayflower, SE16
Trafalgar Tavern, SE10

South-West London
Ship, SW14
Ship Inn, SW18
Sun Inn, SW13
White Horse on Parsons Green, SW6

Victoria & Westminster
Albert, SW1
Cask & Glass SW1
Two Chairmen, SW1

West London
Bull's Head, W4
Dove, W6
Old Ship, W6

Admiral Codrington

17 Mossop Street SW3 2LY   `FOOD`
Map 14 B5
01(071)-589 4603
Parking *difficult*

Bar food *12–4 & 6.30–10.30, Sun 12–3*
No bar food *Sun eve*

Landlord *Mel Barnett*
Brewery *Charrington*
🍺 *Bass; Charrington IPA; Worthington Best Bitter; Carling Black Label; Tennent's Extra; Lamot Pils.* 🍷 ☺

A delightful pub with gaslights casting a mellow glow on well-seasoned wood and Victorian prints on the walls. At the rear is a conservatory with a grapevine and cast-iron garden furniture. There is also a bar with Liberty-print cloths on the tables where customers may dine on home-made pies, salads and fish dishes. Desserts include apple pie and cakes.
Typical dishes Steak & kidney pie £3.95 Treacle tart £1.50

Credit Access, Amex, Diners, Visa

Albert

52 Victoria Street SW1H 0EU   `A`
Map 14 C4
01(071)-222 5577
Parking *difficult*

Landlords *Roger & Gill Wood*
Owner *Chef & Brewer*
🍺 *Webster Yorkshire Bitter; Ruddles County, Best Bitter; Guinness; Foster's; Carlsberg.* 🍷

On a corner site in a street dominated by modern office blocks, this solid, red-brick Victorian pub provides a contrasting setting for a drink. Inside, despite modernisation, the spacious, open-plan bar area retains many features of a bygone age including engraved glass windows and panels, carved woodwork and a lofty ceiling. Note, too, the set of old prints depicting the evils of alcohol, and the traditional solid wood bar.

Credit Access, Amex, Diners, Visa

Albion

10 Thornhill Road N1 1HW   `FOOD`
Map 13 D1
01(071)-607 7450
Parking *difficult*

Bar food *12–2.30 & 7.30–9.30*
No bar food *Sun*

Landlords *Michael & Shirley Parish*
Owner *Chef & Brewer*
🍺 *Ruddles Best Bitter, County; Webster Yorkshire Bitter; Holsten; Budweiser; Foster's.* ☺

A pub of some character in a quiet Islington street. The front bar, full of china and brass ornaments, has a Victorian feel, and there is another, more rustic bar, a comfortable lounge and a pretty garden. Bar food is simple, homely and very good on a menu that rings the changes daily between dishes like hot salt beef, braised beef with vegetables and Friday's fresh fish. Sandwiches are available at lunchtime.
Typical dishes Steak & kidney pudding £4 Shepherd's pie £3.25

Credit Access, Amex, Diners, Visa

NEW ENTRY   Alma

499 Old York Road   `FOOD`
SW18 1FT
Map 12 B6
01(081)-870 2537
Parking *limited*

Bar food *12–11 pm, Sun 12–2.30 & 7–10*

Landlord *Charles Gotto*
Brewery *Young*
🍺 *Young Bitter, Special; Beamish Stout; Guinness; Young London Lager; Tuborg Pilsner.* 🍷 ☺

Red check-clothed tables surround a central display of fine cheeses, salamis and seafood in the back room of this Victorian pub, creating a decidedly continental air amid the traditional surroundings. Snacks such as croque-monsieur continue the mood, while more substantial dishes include chicken fricassée, grilled lemon sole and beef with mushrooms in red wine. Book for late (3pm-ish) Sunday roast lunch.
Typical dishes Taramasalata £2.25 Lamb cutlets with mustard sauce £4.75

Credit Access, Amex, Visa

Anchor

Bankside, 34 Park Street   A
SE1 9DN
Map 12 D4
01(071)-407 1577
Parking limited

Landlord Jon Davidson
Free house
🍺 Courage Best Bitter, Directors;
Guinness; Kronenbourg 1664; Hofmeister.

Standing between the two Southwark bridges is a historic pub with a waterside patio for fine weather drinking. The original Anchor was burnt down ten years after the Great Fire, but the present Georgian building retains plenty of atmosphere with its fine panelling, beams and four small and simple bars. Neighbouring buildings in the 17th century included the Globe theatre and the notorious Clink prison, and it was in a private room within the tavern that Dr Johnson wrote his celebrated dictionary.

Credit Access, Amex, Diners, Visa

Angel

101 Bermondsey Wall   A
East SE16 4NB
Map 12 D4
01(071)-237 3608
Parking ample

Landlord Peter Sutch
Owner Pierhouse Inns
🍺 Courage Best Bitter, Directors; John Smith's Yorkshire Bitter; Guinness; Kronenbourg 1664; Foster's.

A 15th-century riverside pub, the Angel offers views down to the Pool of London in one direction and, to the other, a classic perspective of Tower Bridge. The original landlords were the monks of Bermondsey Priory, but by the 18th century it had become a haunt for smugglers and famous Londoners like Samuel Pepys. Outside there is a balcony over the river and it was from here that Pepys bought cherries for his wife as recounted in his diary.

Credit Access, Amex, Diners, Visa

Black Friar

174 Queen Victoria Street   A
EC4 4BY
Map 13 D3
01(071)-236 5650
Parking difficult

Closed Sat, Sun & Bank Hols

Landlords Mr & Mrs D. McKinstry
Free house
🍺 Adnams Bitter; Bass; Tetley Bitter; Boddingtons Bitter; Castlemaine XXXX; Tennent's Extra.

So named for occupying the site of a 13th-century friary, the Black Friar is a Victorian wedge-shaped pub next to a railway viaduct. It is distinctive both inside and out. The exterior 19th-century walls sport carved friars in various stages of intoxication, from just tipsy to plain drunk. Inside a positive efflorescence of art nouveau in marble, stained glass and copper bas-reliefs has the religious itinerants playing medieval instruments. There is also a grotto with a vaulted mosaic ceiling. Extraordinary.

Bull's Head

15 Strand-on-the Green   A
W4 3PQ
Map 12 A5
01(081)-994 1204
Parking limited

Landlords Mr & Mrs R.D. Smart
Owner Chef & Brewer
🍺 Webster Yorkshire Bitter; Ruddles County, Best Bitter; Carlsberg; Budweiser; Foster's.

White-painted with black shutters, this pub overlooks the Thames from the pretty Strand-on-the-Green. As headquarters for Cromwell, it is likely that councils of war were held here. Today the spacious bar promotes a more peaceful mood. Fine river views can be enjoyed from window seats and there are cosy corners for quieter drinks. A sheltered beer garden adjoins the games room bar and on sunny days the terrace is popular. Children welcome lunchtimes only.

Credit Access, Visa

Cask & Glass

39 Palace Street SW1E 5HN FOOD
Map 14 C4
01(071)-834 7630
Parking *difficult*

Bar food *12–2.45 (eves & Sun lunch by request)*
Closed *3 days Xmas*

Landlords *R. & M. Beatty*
Owner *Chef & Brewer*
🍺 *Watney Special; Webster Yorkshire Bitter; Carlsberg.*

With its hanging baskets, window boxes and white patio furniture, this pretty little pub is a riot of colour in summer. The low-ceilinged, comfortable bar provides a cosy setting for enjoying a filled sandwich on good brown bread (made in advance for lunchtime trade, to order in the evening). They range from various cold meats and cheese and chutney, to salad, or hot sausage.
Typical dishes Cream cheese with chives sandwich £1.20 Egg salad sandwich £1.20

Cock Tavern

Poultry Avenue, Central Markets EC1A 9LH FOOD
Map 13 D3
01(071)-248 2918
Parking *limited*

Bar food *5.30–10.30 am & 11.30–3*
Closed *eves, Sat, Sun & Bank Hols*

Landlord *Mike Callaghan*
Free house
🍺 *Courage Best Bitter; John Smith's Yorkshire Bitter; Hofmeister.* 🍷 ⊖

Tucked away in a cellar close to the heart of Smithfields, excellent food draws meat porters and businessmen alike to this comfortable tavern. Breakfast (starting at 5.30 am!) is whatever takes your fancy – T-bone steaks, toast, kippers or hash browns. Meat, not surprisingly, features strongly on the menu as grills, steaks, roasts and the ever-popular hot salt beef sandwich.
Typical dishes Breakfast £3.85 Roast loin of pork £3

Credit Access, Amex, Visa

Dickens Inn

St Katharine's Way E1 9LB A
Map 12 C4
01(071)-488 1226
Parking *ample*

Landlord *Mr Bingham*
Brewery *Courage* ⌇
🍺 *Dickens Special; Courage Best, Directors; Guinness; Kronenbourg 1664; Hofmeister.*

Standing right in the cobbled heart of St Katharine's Dock redevelopment area, this 18th-century former brewery warehouse escaped demolition in the seventies to be reconstructed in the style of a galleried inn. The heavy beamed, low-ceilinged bars with their old wooden settles and polished brass display much of the original timber and ironwork and make an atmospheric setting for enjoying real ale and spirits drawn from the wood.

Credit Access, Amex, Diners, Visa

Dove

19 Upper Mall W6 9TA A
Map 12 A5
01(081)-748 5405
Parking *difficult*

Landlord *Brian Lovrey*
Brewery *Fuller Smith & Turner*
🍺 *Fullers ESB, London Pride; Guinness; Fullers K2 Lager; Tennent's Lager; Heineken.*

Although it is in a quiet backwater, the Dove has nevertheless made its mark in the arts – it featured in A.P. Herbert's *The Water Gypsies* as The Pigeons, and James Thomson composed *Rule Britannia* here. Its history is uncertain but food and drink have been served on the premises since Charles II and Nell Gwynne drank here together. Nowadays it has a simple, rustic feel inside and the terrace is a fine spot for al fresco drinking above the Thames.

Eagle Tavern

2 Shepherdess Walk N1 7LB A
Map 11 D3
01(071)-253 4715
Parking *limited*

Closed *Sat, Sun & Bank Hols*

Landlords *Leonard & Jean Deadfield*
Brewery *Charrington*
🍷 *Charrington IPA; Bass; Fullers ESB;*
Carling Black Label; Tennent's Extra.

Immortalised in the old nursery rhyme 'Pop Goes the Weasel', this is the Eagle where the money went after its customers had pawned their possessions – or popped the weasel. The Royal Grecian Theatre once stood next door, and amongst the many famous performers who appeared on stage there was the much-loved vaudeville star Marie Lloyd. Today, posters and a model of the theatre serve as reminders in the convivial bar. Garden.

Credit Access, Amex, Diners, Visa

Flask

77 Highgate West Hill A
N6 6BU
Map 11 C2
01(081)-340 7260
Parking *ample*

Landlords *Margaret & Peter Mather*
Brewery *Taylor Walker*
🍷 *Taylor Walker Bitter; Ind Coope Burton Ale; Guinness; Skol; Castlemaine XXXX.*

Dating back to 1663, this characterful pub takes its name from the flasks which were obtained from the premises filled with chalybeate spa water from Hampstead Wells. The two original low-beamed and panelled bars (the Committee Room and Snug Bar) have been joined by a larger third formed by knocking through to the adjoining cottage. A former visitor to the pub was William Hogarth, who used to paint here. In summer, drinks can be enjoyed outside on the pleasant patio.

Credit Access, Amex, Visa

Fox & Anchor

115 Charterhouse St FOOD
EC1M 6AA
Map 13 D2
01(071)-253 4838
Parking *limited*

Bar food *7.30–10.30 am & 12–2.30*
No bar food *eves*
Closed *Sat, Sun, 1 wk Aug & 1 wk Xmas*
Landlord *Seamus O'Connell*
Brewery *Taylor Walker*
🍷 *Taylor Walker Bitter; Ind Coope Burton Ale; Tetley Bitter; Castlemaine XXXX.* 🍷 ⊖

From 7.30 in the morning till 10.30 this traditional Victorian pub, complete with red flock wallpaper and a stuffed fox, serves beefy breakfasts to workers from nearby Smithfield market. Appropriately the forte at lunchtime is quality meat. Chump chops, steaks and sausages are grilled to order. Alternatives include prawn, chicken or ham salads, home-made soups and sandwiches.
Typical dishes Smoked haddock £8 Fillet steak £9

Credit Access, Visa

George Inn

77 Borough High Street, A
Southwark SE1 1NH
Map 12 D4
01(071)-407 2056
Parking *difficult*

Landlord *John Hall*
Brewery *Whitbread* ☎
🍷 *Flowers Original; Boddingtons Bitter; Greene King Abbot Ale; Brakspear Bitter; Stella Artois.*

London's last surviving galleried inn originally occupied three sides of a courtyard where Shakespeare's plays were performed by actors from the nearby Globe Theatre. Rebuilt in 1677 after the Great Fire of Southwark, the inn lost two sides through demolition in the 19th century and later suffered damage in the blitz. However, the old beamed bar where Dickens reputedly made notes for *Little Dorrit* survives, and upstairs a once-secret passage leads to charming half-timbered dining rooms.

Credit Access, Amex, Diners, Visa

Grapes

76 Narrow Street,   FOOD
Limehouse E14 8BP
Map 12 D4
01(071)-987 4396
Parking *difficult*

Bar food *12–2.30 & 6–9*
No bar food *Mon eve & all Sun*
Closed *Bank Hols & 1 wk Xmas*

Landlord *Frank Johnson*
Brewery *Taylor Walker*
🍺 *Taylor Walker Bitter; Ind Coope Burton Ale; Friary Meux Bitter; Löwenbräu.*

A 16th-century pub right in the heart of London's docklands, with an enclosed riverside terrace. Downstairs is a split-level bar in a long, narrow room, and upstairs is a tiny restaurant specialising in fish simply and traditionally cooked. The range includes Dover sole, turbot, halibut, plaice and trout, with a couple of meat dishes. In the bar, sandwiches, fish and chips and fish pies are on offer.
Typical dishes Whole fried plaice £3.10 Prawn curry £2.95

Credit Access

Grenadier

18 Wilton Row SW1X 7NR   A
Map 14 B4
01(071)-235 3074
Parking *difficult*

Landlord *Mr Dodgson*
Owner *Chef & Brewer*
🍺 *Ruddles County, Best Bitter; Webster Yorkshire Bitter; Guinness; Holsten; Carlsberg.*

A pub that takes some finding – tucked away down a quaint cobbled mews and hidden behind a facade of vines, it is only noticeable from the red sentry box in front. Built in 1802, it was originally the officers' mess and was patronised by the Duke of Wellington; military prints and weapons adorn the cramped front bar to remind you of its origins. It is apparently haunted by the ghost of a guardsman flogged to death for cheating at cards!

Credit Access, Amex, Diners, Visa

Hand & Shears

1 Middle Street, Cloth Fair   A
EC1A 7JA
Map 13 D2
01(071)-600 0257
Parking *difficult*

Closed *Sat & Sun*

Landlord *Chris Ife*
Brewery *Courage*
🍺 *Courage Directors, Best Bitter; Guinness; Foster's; Kronenbourg 1664; Hofmeister.*

The present building dates only from 1839, but the original 12th-century pub attracted tailors from the Cloth Fair – hence the name and the pub sign, which depicts the emblem of the guild of Merchant Tailors. A more gruesome historical note is that prisoners from Newgate were sentenced in an upstairs room and were allowed a final drink before proceeding to the hangman's noose. Today's patrons are mainly staff from nearby Barts and tourists on the heritage trail.

Jack Straw's Castle

North End Way NW3 7ES   A
Map 11 B2
01(071)-435 8885
Parking *limited*

Landlord *Mr Guarino*
Brewery *Charrington*
🍺 *Charrington IPA; Worthington Best Bitter; Guinness; Tennent's Extra, Pils; Carling Black Label.*

Named after Wat Tyler's second-in-command, during the Peasants' Revolt of 1381, whose hut or 'castle' once stood here, this striking weatherboarded pub perched high on Hampstead Heath later gained notoriety as the haunt of Dick Turpin. The custom of Victorian artists and writers – including Dickens, who rented a suite of rooms – helped restore its reputation, and although the original tavern was badly damaged in the 1940 blitz, it was faithfully rebuilt in the sixties. Garden.

Lamb

94 Lamb's Conduit Street A

WC1N 3LZ
Map 13 D2
01(071)-405 0713
Parking *difficult*

Landlords *Mr & Mrs Whyte*
Brewery *Young*
🍺 *Young Bitter, Special, Winter Warmer;*
Beamish Stout; John Young Premium
Lager; Tuborg.

The fine cut-glass snob screen would have
hidden Charles Dickens' face from the hoi
polloi when he drank here in its days as a
cider house, his own house being just
around the corner. Dark polished wood, the
low pillared ceilings and original sepia
photographs of Victorian and Edwardian
music-hall stars retain the period feel. The
facade's dark green tiles reflect the
bright window-boxed daffodils enticing
springtime pavement drinkers. Patio at
rear.

Credit Access, Amex, Diners, Visa

Lamb & Flag

33 Rose Street WC2E 9EB FOOD

Map 13 C3
01(071)-836 4108
Parking *difficult*

Bar food *12–9.30, Sun 12–2.30 & 7–10*

Landlord *Adrian Zimmerman*
Brewery *Courage*
🍺 *Courage Best Bitter, Directors; John*
Smith's Yorkshire Bitter; Kronenbourg
1664; Hofmeister; Foster's. ✆

Behind the Georgian frontage is the only
surviving example in the West End of a
17th-century timber-framed building. The
major attraction now is the excellent range
of cheeses – Somerset Brie, Sage Derby,
Blue Cheshire and Blue Shropshire are just
a few – and pâtés served with hot or French
bread. Other items on the menu range from
pies and quiches to curries and chilli con
carne.
Typical dishes Lasagne £2.95 Italian
meatballs £2.95

Mayflower

117 Rotherhithe Street A

SE16 4NF
Map 12 D4
01(071)-237 4088
Parking *difficult*

Landlords *Richard Crofton & Richard*
Emslie
Owner Vintage Inns
🍺 *Charrington IPA; Bass; Guinness;*
Carling Black Label; Tennent's Extra.

The captain of the Mayflower received his
orders to transport the Pilgrim Fathers to
the New World while drinking at the
Mayflower. From the renovated jetty,
today's customers can view the spot where
that famous ship was moored prior to her
historic voyage in 1620. The links with
America survive through the pub's unique
distinction of being licensed to sell both
British and American stamps. Note the
heavy steel floodgates once necessary for
the jetty doors. Upkeep could be better.

Credit Access, Amex, Diners, Visa

Museum Tavern

49 Great Russell Street A

WC1B 3BA
Map 13 C3
01(071)-242 8987
Parking *difficult*

Landlords *Michael & Judith Clarke*
Free house
🍺 *Greene King IPA, Abbot Ale; Brakspear*
Special; Everards Tiger; Guinness;
Hurlimann.

Karl Marx, Dylan Thomas and assorted
members of the Bloomsbury set all in their
time sought refreshment here, as the
Tavern is conveniently sited opposite the
British Museum and its celebrated Reading
Room. Handsome mounted gas lighters
brighten the exterior, while inside the
spacious open-plan bar all is splendidly
Victorian, from the ornate carved mahogany and etched mirrors to stained and
frosted glass and gilded columns.

Credit Access, Amex, Diners, Visa

Nell of Old Drury

29 Catherine Street   A
WC2B 5JS
Map 13 D3
01(071)-836 5328
Parking *difficult*

Closed *Bank Hol lunches & all Sun*

Landlords *Mr & Mrs M. Dunphy*
Brewery *Courage*
🍺 *Courage Directors Bitter, Best Bitter;
John Smith's Yorkshire Bitter; Guinness;
Kronenbourg; Foster's.*

Named after Nell Gwynne, good friend of
Charles II and one-time seller of fruit to the
patrons of the Theatre Royal opposite, this
charming little bow-fronted pub is the
oldest in Covent Garden. Today's theatre-
goers can admire the old playbills which
adorn the walls of the simply appointed bar
– where the Theatre Royal's intermission
bell can clearly be heard! Sadly, the tunnel
from the cellars to the theatre can no longer
be used by patrons.

Old Bell Tavern

95 Fleet Street EC4Y 1DH   A
Map 13 D3
01(071)-583 0070
Parking *difficult*

Closed *Sat, Sun & Bank Hols*

Landlady *Mrs N.P. Healy*
Free house
🍺 *Boddingtons Bitter; Tetley Bitter; Young
Bitter; Marston Pedigree; Castlemaine
XXXX.*

Built just before the Great Fire, the Old Bell
Tavern has seen many patrons come and
go. The earliest ones were the builders of
Christopher Wren's nearby St Bride's
church, who used it as a handy lodging
house, and it is reasonable to suppose that
Wren himself might have dropped in for the
odd pint when he came to check up on
progress. Until recently a favourite haunt of
hacks and printers, it is now mainly filled
with City types.

The Old Dr Butler's Head

Mason's Avenue,   A
Coleman Street EC2V 5BT
Map 12 D4
01(071)-606 3504
Parking *difficult*

Closed *Sat & Sun*

Landlord *Nigel Field*
Free house
🍺 *Tolly Cobbold Original; Marston
Pedigree; guest beer; Kronenbourg 1664;
Foster's.* 🍺

The eponymous William Butler was a
distinguished chemist in the reign of James
I who appeared to cure his monarch of
sciatica with a draught of his own ale, and
was consequently granted the honorary
title of Doctor. Standing next to the site of
the original Mason's Hall, the pub was
rebuilt in 1667 after the Great Fire and is
full of atmosphere with its blackened
beams, wood panelling and sawdust-
strewn floors.

Credit Access, Amex, Diners, Visa

Old Ship

25 Upper Mall W6 9TD   A
Map 12 A5
01(081)-748 3970
Parking *difficult*

Landlady *Mrs M. McCormack*
Brewery *Watney Combe Reid*
🍺 *Ruddles County, Best Bitter; Webster
Yorkshire Bitter; Guinness; Budweiser;
Foster's.*

The pretty terrace of this fine old Thames
pub, festooned as it is with flowers and
shrubs, makes a delightful vantage point
from which to watch the boat race. Inside
the beamed bars there is almost more
boating paraphernalia than the eye can take
in – rowing sculls and ships' wheels hang
from the ceiling, anchors, baskets, lanterns,
oars and old shipping prints adorn the
walls. Good-quality red upholstery and
gleaming brasses give a clean, well-cared-
for look.

Paxton's Head

153 Knightsbridge   A
SW1X 7PA
Map 14 B4
01(071)-589 6627
Parking *difficult*

Landlord *Robert Cook*
Brewery *Taylor Walker*
🍺 *Ind Coope Burton Ale; John Bull Bitter; Tetley Bitter; Skol; Castlemaine XXXX.*

A very attractively designed pub which provides a welcome haven from the roar and bustle of Knightsbridge. Named after Joseph Paxton, MP for Coventry and builder of the fountain and conservatory at Chatsworth and of Crystal Palace, it has a traditional Victorian feel inside, although the interior in fact dates from the early 1970s. A huge wood-panelled circular bar, panelled walls and marble-topped tables make for pleasing surroundings in which to enjoy a drink.

Credit Access, Amex, Visa

NEW ENTRY   *Phoenix & Firkin*

5 Windsor Walk, Denmark   FOOD
Hill SE5 8BB
Map 12 D6
01(071)-701 8282
Parking *limited*

Bar food *11–3 & 5.30–11 (Sat from 6), Sun 12–2 & 7–10.30*

Landlord *Mr S.A. Smith*
Free house
🍺 *Phoenix Bitter, Dogbolter; Beamish Stout; Carlsberg; Holsten.*

Part of the Denmark Hill Station building, and a fine example of restoration done with taste and practicality. The railway theme (day-trip posters, brightly painted signal boards) works well on the two levels, and the customers are relaxed, informal and mainly young. Good simple fare ranges from giant wholemeal baps and a selection of quiches to cold pies and some hot choices in winter.

Typical dishes Giant filled bap £1.20
Quiche with four salads £2.10

Princess Louise

208 High Holborn   A
WC1V 7BW
Map 13 C3
01(071)-405 8816
Parking *difficult*

Landlord *Ian Phillips*
Free house
🍺 *Vaux Samson, Wards Sheffield Best Bitter; Greene King Abbot Ale; Guinness; Tuborg Pilsner; Stella Artois.* 🍷

Built in 1872, a busy, characterful pub which was given a complete facelift some 20 years later, and its late-Victorian features remain virtually unchanged to this day. A popular drinking pub for its selection of real ales, the ground-floor bar is invariably packed at lunchtime with local office workers. Note the contrast of bare-wood floors with splendid etched mirrors, ornate moulded ceilings and fin-de-siècle glazed tiles. The plusher upstairs bar provides a quieter haven.

Prospect of Whitby

57 Wapping Wall E1 9SP   A
Map 12 D4
01(071)-481 1095/1317
Parking *difficult*

Landlord *Philip Howells*
Owner *Grand Met*
🍺 *Ruddles County, Best Bitter; Webster Yorkshire Bitter; Carlsberg; Holsten Export; Foster's.* 🍷

Known as the Devil's Tavern during the Bloody Assizes, when Judge Jeffreys came here to watch felons being hanged following his judgments, this characterful, timber-framed Thames-side pub was renamed in 1790 after a collier moored nearby. Samuel Pepys was a regular patron when Secretary to the Admiralty, while Turner and Whistler both painted river scenes from here. Open fires warm the wooden-floored bar and there is a small riverside patio for summer sipping.

Credit Access, Amex, Diners, Visa

Salisbury

90 St Martin's Lane   `A`
WC2N 4AP
Map 13 C3
01(071)-836 5863
Parking *difficult*

Landlords *Kevin & Patricia Lee*
Owner *Clifton Inns*
🍺 *Ind Coope Burton Ale; Tetley Bitter;
John Bull Bitter; Taylor Walker Bitter;
Löwenbräu; Castlemaine XXXX.*

Originally the Salisbury Stores, then turned into an ornate late-Victorian pub upon being leased from the 3rd Earl of Salisbury in 1892, this busy hostelry enjoys a favoured setting in the heart of theatreland. It is popular with those meeting before curtain-up and those relaxing after work, and the lavishly authentic bars (faithfully restored in 1963) provide the perfect atmosphere with their moulded ceilings, etched glass screens and carved gilded statuettes.

Credit Access, Amex

Seven Stars

53 Carey Street WC2 2JB   `A`
Map 13 D3
01(071)-242 8521
Parking *difficult*

Closed *Sat, Sun & Bank Hols*

Landlord *John Crawley*
Brewery *Courage*
🍺 *Courage Best Bitter, Directors;
Guinness; Foster's; Kronenbourg.*

Rub shoulders with members of the Bench and Bar at this tiny, ever-busy pub positioned between Lincoln's Inn Fields and the Law Courts. Rear entrance to the latter august establishment is nearby, giving rise to the old expression for bankruptcy, 'to be in Carey Street'. Caricatures of many distinguished legal gentlemen by the celebrated cartoonist Spy decorate one end of the wooden-floored bar and there is an interesting 17th-century fire mark on the exterior wall.

Shepherd's Tavern

50 Hertford Street W1   `A`
Map 14 B4
01(071)-499 3017
Parking *limited*

Landlords *David Morton & Sue Ames*
Owner *Chef & Brewer*
🍺 *Ruddles County; Watney Special;
Webster Yorkshire Bitter; Carlsberg;
Foster's; Holsten Export.*

Telephone calls are made from a converted sedan chair that once belonged to the Duke of Cumberland, younger son of George II and vanquisher of Bonnie Prince Charlie at Culloden in 1746, at this fine 300-year-old tavern in Shepherd Market. A favourite with airforce fighter and bomber crews during World War 2, it is now the haunt of local business people and office workers.

Credit Access, Amex, Diners, Visa

Sherlock Holmes

10 Northumberland Street   `A`
WC2N 5DA
Map 14 C4
01(071)-930 2644
Parking *difficult*

Landlords *Eddie & Joan Hardcastle*
Brewery *Whitbread*
🍺 *Boddingtons Bitter; Flowers Original;
Greene King Abbot Ale; Stella Artois;
Heineken.* 🍷

A pub which is known worldwide to devotees of the great detective, and which started life as the Northumberland Arms in the days when Sir Arthur Conan-Doyle drank here. Immortalised in *The Hound of the Baskervilles*, it is today a veritable shrine of Holmes memorabilia and early forensic instruments. Upstairs is Conan-Doyle's study, while behind the bar long-serving landlords Eddie and Joan Hardcastle are now celebrities in their own right.

Credit Access, Amex, Diners, Visa

Ship

Jews Row, Waterside,   FOOD
Wandsworth SW18 1TB
Map 12 B6
01(081)-870 9667
Parking *limited*

Bar food *12–10, Sun 12–2.30 & 7–9.30*

Landlord *Mr C.C. Gotto*
Brewery *Young*
Young Bitter, Special; Guinness; Young Premium Lager.

A conservatory-style bar and large patio make the most of the Thames-side setting here at a characterful pub tucked under Wandsworth Bridge. Spicy meatballs, pork and mushroom pie and beef and potato curry typify the lunchtime choice here, while the evening brings elegant 'nibbles' such as various dips, assorted salamis and eggs Benedict or Florentine. Summer barbecues are an added attraction.
Typical dishes Chicken fricassee £3.25 Lentil soup £1.20

Credit Access, Amex, Diners, Visa

Ship

10 Thames Bank,   A
Riverside SW14 7QS
Map 12 A6
01(081)-876 1439
Parking *ample*

Owner *Chef & Brewer*
Watney Combes Bitter; Ruddles County, Best Bitter; Guinness; Holsten Export; Foster's.

Certainly the perfect vantage point on Boat Race day, an excellent view of the winning post is gained from the pub's riverside terrace. Inside, the rowing theme is continued, with paddles and sculls hanging from the lofty ceiling, and mementoes of past Oxford–Cambridge battles mingling with old Thames maps and nautical prints. The bar, although dating back to Elizabethan times, has a relaxed, spacious and Victorian feel, with raised areas housing window benches.

Credit Access, Amex, Diners, Visa

Slug & Lettuce

47 Hereford Road W2 5AH   FOOD
Map 12 B4
01(071)-229 1503
Parking *difficult*

Bar food *11.30–2.30 & 5.30–9.30 (Sun from 7)*

Landlady *Rebecca Bennett*
Brewery *Watney Combe Reid*
Ruddles Best Bitter; Webster Yorkshire Bitter; Holsten; Budweiser; Foster's.

Polished woodwork and numerous cosy corners add to the warm and friendly atmosphere at this lively pub with a predominantly youthful clientele. Consult the blackboard for the day's imaginative selection of enjoyable dishes – perhaps baked garlic mushrooms with crispy bacon, tagliatelle napoletana, cheesy spinach and egg bake or sautéed chicken livers served atop a muffin.
Typical dishes Tagliatelle £3.25 Salmon fishcakes £4.50

Credit Access

Slug & Lettuce

1 Islington Green N1   FOOD
Map 13 D1
01(071)-226 3864
Parking *difficult*

Bar food *12–2.45 & 6–9.30, Sat 12–8.30, Sun 12–2.30 & 7–9.30*

Landlords *Hugh Corbett & David Salisbury*
Brewery *Watney Combe Reid*
Ruddles County, Best Bitter; Webster Yorkshire Bitter; Guinness; Carlsberg; Holsten.

Popular with a young and arty crowd (the Screen on the Green is opposite), this attractive, bustling pub does a tasty line in savoury snacks prepared in the skillet. Appetising alternatives from the blackboard menu might include ham and lentil soup followed by chicken with mango and a sweet like baked bananas in rum. Waitress service Sunday brunch in the upstairs lounge.
Typical dishes Chicken and avocado £5.50 Steak sandwich £3.25

Spaniards Inn

Spaniards Road NW3 7SS   `A`
Map 11 B2
01(081)-455 3276
Parking *ample*

Landlord *David Roper*
Brewery *Charrington* ☙
● *Charrington IPA; Bass; Young Bitter;*
Highgate Mild; Carling Black Label.

Once the home of the Spanish Ambassador to James I, this atmospheric whitewashed pub was later patronised by Dick Turpin, who favoured an upstairs window seat from which to select his next victim from among the passing carriages. The Gordon rioters also paused for refreshment, while happier associations link the pretty garden complete with aviary to Keats (it inspired his *Ode to a Nightingale*) and Dickens, who based the tea party scene in *Pickwick Papers* here.

Credit Access, Visa

NEW ENTRY   ## Sun Inn

7 Church Road, Barnes   `A`
SW13 9HE
Map 12 A5
01(081)-876 5256
Parking *ample*

Landlords *Len & Jan Harris*
Brewery *Taylor Walker*
● *Ind Coope Burton Ale; Tetley Bitter;*
Taylor Walker Bitter; Skol; Castlemaine
XXXX.

The pub dates from the 18th century, but the bowling green at the rear has a much longer history – according to legend, Drake and Walsingham taught Elizabeth I to play bowls there. Inside, a maze of small rooms with wooden tables, bare floorboards, prints of old London and old wooden wall cabinets displaying clay pipes, pots and mugs give a truly old world atmosphere. There is a particularly fine Victorian fireplace with cubbyholes containing antique knick-knacks.

Swan Tavern

66 Bayswater Road W2 3PH   `FOOD`
Map 13 A3
01(071)-262 5204
Parking *limited*

Bar food *11 am–10 pm (Sun till 9.30)*

Landlord *Tim Headey*
Brewery *Watney Combe Reid*
● *Tetley Bitter; Younger's IPA; Taylor*
Walker Bitter; Holsten; Foster's;
Carlsberg. ⊖

A traditional white-painted pub which does a roaring trade refreshing tourists from nearby hotels and those who have worked up a thirst tramping Hyde Park across the road. Imaginative, well-prepared food is available all day and you can take your choice from the display cabinet or from the blackboard menu, which offer fare such as roast of the day, boeuf bourguignon, curries and pasta.
Typical dishes Roast beef & Yorkshire pudding £5.20 Shepherd's pie £3.20

Credit Access, Amex, Diners, Visa

Trafalgar Tavern

Park Row, Greenwich   `A`
SE10 9NL
Map 10 D3
01(081)-858 2437
Parking *ample*

Landlord *Roger Wormull*
Owner *Chef & Brewer*
● *Ruddles County, Best Bitter; Webster*
Yorkshire Bitter; Holsten Export; Foster's;
Carlsberg.

The Thames laps against the walls of this substantial pub, which dates from 1837. On the first floor there is a fine period ballroom and a bar arranged as the forecastle of a sailing ship. The main bar downstairs has a nautical flavour, with oil paintings of an admiral (not Nelson!) and an old sailing ship. Old fireplaces, jugs and bottles add to the atmosphere and there are splendid river views through a large bow window.

Credit Access, Amex, Diners, Visa

Two Chairmen

39 Dartmouth Street   A
SW1H 9BP
Map 14 C4
01(071)-222 8694
Parking *difficult*

Closed *Sat eve, all Sun & Bank Hols*

Landlady *Penny Allcorn*
Owner *Chef & Brewer*
🍺 *King & Barnes Sussex Bitter; Webster Yorkshire Bitter; Ruddles County, Best Bitter; Watney Special; Foster's.*

The two sedan chairmen in question are depicted on the sign hanging outside this historic tavern, formerly an 18th-century coffee house, and once inside it is easy to imagine the pub as it must have looked two hundred or so years ago. The mural depicting just such a scene, the open fire and panelling further enhance the atmosphere. Tables with parasols are put outside on the pavement during the summer months.

Credit Access, Amex, Diners, Visa

Two Chairmen

Warwick House Street, off   A
Cockspur Street SW1Y 5AT
Map 14 C4
01(071)-930 1166
Parking *difficult*

Closed *Sun eve*

Landlord *James O'Hare*
Brewery *Courage*
🍺 *Courage Best Bitter, Directors; Guinness; Miller Lite; Foster's.*

Built in 1683 and reconstructed some 200 years later in Queen Victoria's reign, this popular little drinking pub tucked away down an alley near Trafalgar Square is named after the sedan chairmen who plied their energetic trade in the City during the 17th and 18th centuries. The intimate bar is very atmospheric and most appealing, its panelled walls being lined with fascinating prints of London life. Well-kept beers and real ales.

Victoria

10a Strathearn Place   A
W2 2NH
Map 13 A3
01(071)-262 5696
Parking *limited*

Landlords *Mr & Mrs Byrne*
Brewery *Charrington*
🍺 *Charrington IPA; Bass; Stones Bitter; Guinness; Carling Black Label; Tennent's Extra.* 🍷

Those with a taste for Victorian memorabilia will love the Victoria, where the good queen apparently dropped in for a snifter after opening Paddington Station. Inside the long bar there are cabinets with commemorative plates, mugs and jugs and each one of the many prints and paintings depicts her or events during her reign. A splendid bar counter, beautifully etched mirrors, fine mahogany panelling and an ornate plaster ceiling complete the picture of a period long gone.

Credit Access, Visa

White Horse on Parsons Green

1 Parsons Green SW6 4UL   FOOD
Map 12 B5
01(071)-736 2115
Parking *limited*

Bar food *12–3 (Sat & Sun from 11) & 7.30–10*
Closed *1 wk Xmas*

Landlady *Sally Cruickshank*
Brewery *Bass*
🍺 *Bass; Charrington IPA; Adnams Bitter; Highgate Mild; Carling Black Label.* 🍷 🌐

You will find some of the best pub food in town at the White Horse, a fine corner pub dating back to the 19th century. Inside, it has an airy, spacious feel, with high ceilings, fans and hanging baskets, and there is also a shady roadside patio overhung with trees. The well-presented home-made fare on offer includes imaginative salads, excellent cold meats, cheeses, jacket potatoes and a selection of hot daily specials.
Typical dishes Courgette and tomato pie £2.80 Lasagne £3.70

Windsor Castle

114 Campden Hill Road [A]
W8 7AR
Map 12 B4
01(071)-727 8491
Parking *limited*

Landlord *Mr A.J. Owen*
Brewery *Charrington*
🍺 *Charrington IPA; Bass; Guinness;
Carling Black Label; Tennent's Extra;
Lamot Pils.*

The exterior of the Windsor Castle does not promise much, but inside it is a real old-fashioned pub which has not been tampered with at all. The series of little dark-panelled, uncarpeted rooms have built-in elm benches, smoky yellow ceilings, large copper pots and hunting prints. There is even a small open fire. For summer drinking, the garden and terrace are shaded by plane, lime and cherry trees and equipped with sturdy teak seats.

Credit Access, Visa

Ye Olde Cheshire Cheese

145 Fleet Street EC4A 2BU [A]
Map 13 D3
01(071)-353 6170
Parking *difficult*

Closed *Sun eve*

Landlord *Gordon Garritty*
Free house
🍺 *Samuel Smith's Old Brewery Bitter,
Museum Ale, Pils.*

Journalists, lawyers and tourists crowd the tiny bars and narrow courtyard of a bustling pub tucked away off Fleet Street. A victim of the Great Fire, it was rebuilt in 1667 and only the ancient vaulted cellars remain of the original tavern. Dr Johnson lived nearby and regularly drank here; today's customers can admire his portrait while relishing the period charms of sawdust-strewn floors, high beams, fine panelling and an open fire in winter.

Credit Access, Amex, Diners, Visa

Ye Olde Mitre Tavern

1 Ely Court, Ely Place, [A]
Holborn EC1N 6SJ
Map 13 D3
01(071)-405 4751
Parking *difficult*

Closed *Sat, Sun & Bank Hols*

Landlord *Mr D. O'Sullivan*
Brewery *Taylor Walker*
🍺 *Ind Coope Burton Ale; Friary Meux
Bitter; Tetley Bitter; Löwenbräu;
Castlemaine XXXX; Skol.*

An earlier inn of the same name was built in 1546 on the site of the palace of the Bishops of Ely, and until fairly recently the area was ecclesiastically part of Cambridgeshire. The present 18th-century pub is a cosy spot with dark panelling and rustic tables. Also within is the stump of a cherry tree that marked the limit of the Bishop's land. There are some seats outside between the pub and St Ethelreda's Church.

Ye Olde Watling

29 Watling Street EC4N 9BR [A]
Map 12 D4
01(071)-248 6252
Parking *difficult*

Closed *Sat, Sun & Bank Hols*

Landlord *Mr G. Thornton*
Brewery *Charrington*
🍺 *Bass; Charrington IPA; Young Bitter;
Carling Black Label; Tennent's Extra.*

The pub was built in 1604 to house the workers on St Paul's, and stands on London's oldest street overlooking the great cathedral from its doorway. Today, the beamed and panelled ground-floor bar with its leaded windows, red velvet curtains and bright copper jugs is a favourite rendezvous for after-office drinks. The upstairs bar, Wren's Room, has a chintzy Victorian charm, while at the rear lies a small games room offering darts and pool.

Credit Access, Amex, Diners, Visa

ALDBOURNE   NEW ENTRY   *Crown at Aldbourne*

Nr Marlborough SN8 2DU   `B&B`
Area Map 4 D5 *Wiltshire*
Marlborough (0672) 40214
Parking *ample*

Landlords *Rod & Chris Chorlton*
Brewery *Usher*
🍺 *Usher Best Bitter; Ruddles County;
Webster Yorkshire Bitter; Guinness;
Holsten.*

Accommodation *3 bedrooms* **£D G2**
Check-in by arrangement

Overlooking the duck pond, the Crown is a
spick-and span 18th-century inn with very
friendly staff. Beams and brasses give a
traditional feel to the bar, and the courtyard
is a pleasant spot for summer sipping. Two
of the neat bedrooms have shower rooms
and toilets, the third just a toilet. The best
room boasts a stylish four-poster. No radios
or telephones, but they will provide a TV on
request. Outdoor play area for children,
who are welcome overnight.

Credit Amex, Visa

ALDERMINSTER   *Bell*

Shipston Road, Nr   `FOOD`
Stratford-upon-Avon
CV37 8NX
Map 10 A1 *Warwickshire*
Alderminster (078 987) 414
Parking *ample*

Bar food *12–2.30 & 7–10*
Closed *Mon eve*

Landlords *Keith & Vanessa Brewer*
Free house
🍺 *Flowers IPA, Original; Whitbread Best
Bitter, Poacher Bitter; Stella Artois.* 🍷 ⊖

Once a coaching inn, the Bell now serves
imaginative and well-prepared food to a
more discerning clientele. The pub's character has been carefully maintained – white
walls hung with prints, oak beams with
wicker baskets and bric-a-brac, stripped
pine tables and old settles. The blackboard
menu may include haddock in Stilton sauce
or lamb and aubergine koresh with ginger
and apricot pudding to finish.
Typical dishes Shrimp phoebe £3.50
Calf's liver a la crème £7.50

Credit Access, Visa

ALFRISTON   *George Inn*

High Street, Nr Polegate   `B&B`
BN26 5SY
Area Map 6 F5 *East Sussex*
Alfriston (0323) 870319
Parking *difficult*

Landlord *Mr M. Gregory*
Free house
🍺 *Ruddles Best Bitter, County; Webster
Yorkshire Bitter; Guinness; Holsten;
Carlsberg Hof.*

Accommodation *8 bedrooms* **£A G2**
Check-in all day

Tourists love this friendly, well-run little
place, so overnight guests are advised to
book well ahead. It is a flint and timbered
building dating back some 300 years and
stands in a picture-postcard smugglers'
village. Blackened beams abound, and the
bar is characterised by a handsome inglenook. The best bedroom boasts a very
splendid four-poster and some carefully
preserved original plaster; some of the
others are more ordinary. Six have neat
little bathrooms en suite. *No dogs.*

Credit Access, Amex, Diners, Visa

ALREWAS   *George & Dragon*

Main Street, Nr Burton   `B&B`
upon Trent DE13 7AE
Map 7 B1 *Staffordshire*
Burton upon Trent (0283) 790202
Parking *ample*

Landlords *Ray & Mary Stanbrook*
Brewery *Marston* ⌁
🍺 *Marston Pedigree, Albion Bitter;
Guinness; Marston Pilsner; Stella Artois.*

Accommodation *16 bedrooms* **£C G1**
Check-in all day

Overnight guests at this friendly inn set in a
picturesque village just off the A38 stay in
the adjoining Claymar Hotel. All the bright,
compact bedrooms have good private facilities and offer everything from TVs, direct-
dial telephones, radio-alarms and tea-
makers to trouser presses and hairdryers.
There is a choice of convivial bars, as well
as a patio and children's play area – making
it a popular summer stop for family
refreshments.

Credit Access, Visa

ANSTY   NEW ENTRY   *Fox*

Nr Dorchester DT2 7PN
Area Map 7 C4 *Dorset*
Milton Abbas (0258)
880328
Parking *ample*

FOOD
B&B

Bar food *11.45–2.30 & 6.45–10,
Sun 12–2.15 & 7–9.30* ⊃

Landlords *Gary & Kathryn Witheyman*
Free house
🍺 *Wadworth 6X; Hall & Woodhouse
Badger Best; Tetley Bitter; guest beer;
Guinness; Carlsberg Hof.* ⬤

Deep in Hardy country, down narrow
country lanes, the Fox pops up in an
imposing fashion. A large brick and flint,
steep gabled building, its character has
recently been diminished by a large open-
plan extension. Yet the Platter Bar remains
unchanged where a vast collection of plates
festoon the walls, likewise the famous Toby
Bar displaying over 800 toby jugs. The
extension makes the pub available to families, with its children's room. Three types of
eating are available: fixed-price cold meats,
quiches and cheeses with an extensive
choice of good help-yourself salads; a
barbecue serving steaks, gammon, chops
and ribs; and elsewhere there are jacket
potatoes with up to fourteen different
fillings. Children have their own menu.
Garden.

Typical dishes Lamb and pork kebabs
£4.75 Stuffed rainbow trout £5

Accommodation *14 bedrooms* £C **G1/2**
Check-in all day

Of fourteen en suite bedrooms, those in the
new extension offer better standards, being
light and airy with matching floral fabrics
and good compact en suite bathrooms. All,
however, are clean and comfortable.

Credit Access, Amex, Visa

APPLEBY   *Royal Oak Inn*

Bongate CA16 6UN
Map 3 C2 *Cumbria*
Appleby (0930) 51463
Parking *ample*

FOOD
B&B

Bar food *12–2 & 6.30–9 (Sun from 7)* ⊃

Landlords *Colin & Hilary Cheyne*
Free house
🍺 *McEwan's 70/-, Export; Yates
Westmoreland Bitter; Murphy Stout;
McEwan's Lager.* ⬤ ⊝

Dating back as far as 1100 in parts, this
ancient black and white coaching inn just
outside town looks most attractive with its
leaded dormer windows and hanging
baskets. Inside, there are a cosy snug and a
comfortable panelled lounge bar which
leads to the dining room (candlelit by
night). The lengthy menu, available in both
bar and restaurant, ranges from apple and
Stilton pancakes, garlic mushrooms and
potted shrimps among starters to such
appetising main courses as Cheddar
chicken, local lamb cutlets, shark steak and
cheesy crumble-topped vegetable casserole.
Sandwiches, salads and ploughman's are
also offered, and there is a selection of
desserts, gâteaux, ice creams or cheeses to
finish the meal.

Typical dishes Leek and tomato croustade £2.95 Seafood mornay £4.35

Accommodation *7 bedrooms* £C **G2**
Check-in all day

Homely little beamed bedrooms, with
uneven floors and an attractive co-ordinated decor, all have TVs and tea-makers;
four offer en suite facilities. The peaceful
residents' lounge looks out towards
Appleby Castle.

Credit Access, Amex, Diners, Visa

APPLETREEWICK   *Craven Arms*

Burnsall, Nr Skipton   A
BD23 6DA
Area Map 2 D4 *North Yorks*
Burnsall (075 672) 270
Parking *ample*

Landlord *Jim Nicholson*
Free house
☛ *Tetley Bitter; Younger's Scotch; Theakston Best Bitter, XB, Old Peculier; Carlsberg Hof.*

Jim Nicholson is the friendly new host at a sturdy, stone-built pub dating back to 1625. Standing amid the rolling hills of this splendid national park, it is a great favourite with walkers and ramblers. Join them beside the huge cast-iron range in the homely main bar, where a collection of African guns and bright copper kettles decorate the heavily beamed ceiling. There is also a cosy little snug, a garden and patio.

ARMATHWAITE   *Duke's Head Hotel*

Front Street, Nr Carlisle   B&B
CA4 9PB
Map 3 B1 *Cumbria*
Armathwaite (069 92) 226
Parking *ample*

Landlord *Peter Lynch*
Brewery *Whitbread*
☛ *Whitbread Castle Eden, Trophy; Heineken.*

Accommodation *6 bedrooms* £D G2
Check-in all day

A modest but welcoming pebbledash pub offering simple overnight accommodation in six pleasant bedrooms. Traditional furnishings and candlewick bedspreads strike a homely note and two rooms have en suite facilities; the rest share two public bathrooms. Downstairs, the main bar is a warm and cosy spot with its open fire, wheelback chairs and collection of pewter beer mugs; the public bar offers darts and pool. Garden. Children welcome overnight.

ASHWELL   *Bushel & Strike Inn*

Mill Street, Nr Baldock   FOOD
SG7 5LY
Map 10 D1 *Hertfordshire*
Ashwell (046 274) 2394
Parking *ample*

Bar food *12–2 & 7–10*

Landlords *Sandy & Tony Lynch*
Brewery *Wells*
☛ *Wells Eagle Bitter; Bombardier, Silver Special; Guinness; Red Stripe; Talisman.* ▮ ☺

One of those pubs where food is a prime concern, making its village location and white-painted brick exterior a mere visual preamble to the extensive and cosmopolitan menu. There is fish pie, Cajun chicken, whitebait, pâté en croûte, jugged hare and rainbow trout. An inviting cold buffet on a pine table and dresser brings up the rear with various meats and fresh salads. Lovely trifle. Separate restaurant. Garden.
Typical dishes Spring rolls £2 Venison pie £4.25

Credit Access, Amex, Diners, Visa

ASHWELL   *Three Tuns Hotel*

High Street, Nr Baldock   B&B
SG7 5NL
Map 10 D1 *Hertfordshire*
Ashwell (046 274) 2387
Parking *ample*

Landlady *Elizabeth Harris*
Brewery *Greene King* ☙
☛ *Greene King Abbot Ale, IPA, XX, Mild; Guinness; Kronenbourg.*

Accommodation *10 bedrooms* £D G2
Check-in by arrangement

Dating back to 1806, this welcoming inn stands in the heart of a pretty little village some four miles from the end of the A1(M). Neatly kept bedrooms, including four in a nearby Victorian house with their own shower cubicles, are attractively decorated and furnished in solid, traditional style. All offer TVs, tea-makers and radio-alarms and there are three gleaming public bathrooms. Enjoy a pint in the inviting bars or large garden.

Credit Access, Amex, Diners, Visa

ASKHAM   *Queen's Head Inn*

Nr Penrith CA10 2PF   `B&B`
Area Map 1 E1 *Cumbria*
Hackthorpe (093 12) 225
Parking *ample*

Landlord *Graham Ferguson*
Brewery *Vaux* ☙
☞ *Vaux Samson; Wards Sheffield Best Bitter; Lorimer's Best Scotch; Labatt's.*

Accommodation *6 bedrooms* **£C G2**
Check-in all day

You can enjoy the model railway in the grounds of this fine 17th-century coaching inn, or just relax with a drink in the mellow lounge bar or atmospheric beamed public bar with its brassware and oak furniture. Books, pot-pourri and ornaments lend a homely air to the charming bedrooms, which share two thickly carpeted bathrooms. Residents also have the use of a comfortably furnished TV lounge. Patio. *No dogs.*

ASKRIGG   *King's Arms Hotel*

Market Place,   `B&B`
Wensleydale DL8 3HQ
Area Map 2 C2 *North Yorks*
Wensleydale (0969) 50258
Parking *ample*

Landlords *Mr & Mrs R. Hopwood*
Free house ☙
☞ *Younger's No 3, Scotch; Newcastle Exhibition; McEwan 80/-, Tartan Bitter.*

Accommodation *10 bedrooms* **£D G1**
Check-in all day

If you are a James Herriot fan, you will be fascinated to drink in the splendid main bar here, which is the setting for the pub in 'All Creatures Great and Small'. Local photos, hunting prints and tack create a striking impression, and some of the bedrooms sport heavy antique beds or half-testers. All rooms are spacious with en suite facilities and tea-makers, and each is individually decorated and furnished to give plenty of character. Improvements are continually being made.

Credit Access, Amex, Diners, Visa

ASTON CANTLOW   *King's Head*

Bearley Road, Nr Stratford-   `A`
upon-Avon B95 6HY
Map 10 A1 *Warwickshire*
Great Alne (078 981) 242
Parking *ample*

Landlords *Mr & Mrs Saunders*
Brewery *Whitbread Flowers* ☙
☞ *Flowers IPA, Original, Best Bitter; Stella Artois; Heineken.*

It would be showing less than commercial acumen for a pub in the Stratford region not to claim some acquaintance with its most famous son. The boast here is that this is where Shakespeare's parents held their wedding breakfast. Validity matters little for the King's Head is nevertheless a fine place for a pint. Half-timbered outside and flagstone-floored inside, with old wooden settle seating, a snug, an open fireplace and fresh sprays of flowers brightening the dimness. Garden.

ASWARBY   *Tally Ho*

Nr Sleaford NG34 8SA   `B&B`
Map 8 D1 *Lincolnshire*
Culver Thorpe (052 95) 205
Parking *ample*

Landlords *Rachel & Christopher Davis*
Free house
☞ *Bateman Best Bitter; Adnams Bitter; Greene King Abbot Ale; Stella Artois; Ayingerbräu.*

Accommodation *6 bedrooms* **£D G2**
Check-in all day

Just south of Sleaford before the turning off the A15 to Aswarby stands a mellow inn dating back some 200 years. The pleasant bar boasts a great deal of exposed stone and brickwork, and country prints adorn the walls. An adjacent stable block houses well-kept bedrooms, four of which have neat modern bathrooms, the others little shower rooms. Decor is restful, heating is effective and there is ample writing and hanging space. Garden. Children welcome overnight.

BAGINTON NEW ENTRY *Old Mill Inn*

Mill Hill, Nr Coventry `B&B`
CV8 2BS
Map 7 B2 *West Midlands*
Coventry (0203) 303588
Parking *ample*

Landlord *Bill Johnson*
Owner *Chef & Brewer*
🍺 *Webster Yorkshire Bitter; Ruddles Best, County; Guinness; Carlsberg; Foster's.*

Accommodation *20 bedrooms* **£A G1**
Check-in all day

A super place to stay, handy for the A45 and A46 yet tucked away peacefully in pine-studded grounds running down to the river Sowe. Public areas still retain many features of the 19th-century working mill, and outside a riverside patio is linked by bridge to the garden. A well designed modern block houses the bedrooms, where you will find pine furniture and Laura Ashley designs, remote-control TVs, direct-dial phones and en suite bathrooms. Children welcome overnight. *No dogs.*

Credit Access, Amex, Diners, Visa

BAINBRIDGE *Rose & Crown Hotel*

Nr Leyburn DL8 3EE `B&B`
Area Map 2 C2 *North Yorks*
Wensleydale (0969) 50225
Parking *ample*

Landlady *Penny Thorpe*
Free house
🍺 *Younger's Scotch; John Smith's Bitter; Theakston Best Bitter; Guinness; Beck's Bier; Carlsberg Pilsner.* 🍺

Accommodation *13 bedrooms* **£C G2**
Check-in all day

One of the finest of the handsome old buildings that skirt the village green, this is a splendid 15th-century coaching inn. The famous Bainbridge horn, traditionally blown to guide lost travellers, stands in the entrance hall, beyond which are a mellow bar, a cosy little snug and a very comfortable residents' lounge complete with log stove. Bedrooms, all prettily decorated and clean as a whistle, are provided with TVs, tea-makers and books. Children welcome overnight.

Credit Access, Visa

BAMFORD *Rising Sun Hotel*

Castleton Road S30 2AL `B&B`
Map 4 D4 *Derbyshire*
Hope Valley (0433) 51323
Parking *ample*

Landlords *Michael & Anne Humphries*
Free house
🍺 *Mansfield Bitter, Light, Lager; Foster's.* No real ale.

Accommodation *13 bedrooms* **£C G2**
Check-in all day

A fairly average black-and-white roadside pub, but a useful overnight stop for anyone travelling the busy A625 Castleton-Hathersage High Peak route. Bedrooms are pretty plain and functional in looks, but all have private bath or shower rooms, colour TVs, direct-dial telephones, hair-dryers and tea-makers. Front rooms can be noisy, so go for a rear one looking towards the High Peaks across gardens complete with dovecote, peacock and brown goat. Children welcome overnight.

Credit Access, Amex, Visa

BANTHAM *Sloop Inn*

Nr Kingsbridge TQ7 3AJ `B&B`
Map 9 B3 *Devon*
Kingsbridge (0548) 560489
Parking *limited*

Landlord *Neil Girling*
Free house 🛏
🍺 *Usher Best Bitter; Bass; Flowers IPA; Worthington Best Bitter; Carlsberg; Stella Artois.*

Accommodation *5 bedrooms* **£D G2**
Check-in by arrangement

Flagstone floors once trod by smuggler and 16th-century landlord John Widdon now bear the nautical paraphernalia of a bygone era. A ship's cabin bar adds to the fantasy of the bar games at this sturdy pub which stands just 300 yards from the sea. Pretty quilts complement the generous-sized bedrooms with their modern style of furniture. Four have en suite facilities, and the fifth uses the corridor bathroom. Children's room. Patio. Accommodation closed December to January.

BARTLOW   *Three Hills*

Nr Linton CB1 6PW   `FOOD`
Map 10 D1 *Cambridgeshire*
Cambridge (0223) 891259
Parking *ample*

Bar food *12–2.45 & 7–9.30 (Sun till 9)*

Landlords *Sue & Steve Dixon*
Brewery *Greene King*
🍺 *Greene King IPA, Abbot Ale;*
Kronenbourg 1664. 🍷 ⊖

The Dixons have created a welcoming atmosphere at the Three Hills, where the cosy bar features fresh flowers, polished brasses and an inglenook fireplace. The printed menu is augmented by daily specials such as soup, pâté, quiche and apple pie. From the main menu, vegetarians are offered four choices and there are simple meat dishes, pizzas and snacks. Sunny Sundays see barbecues in the garden.
Typical dishes Plaice stuffed with prawns £7.95 Fruit pavlova £2.20

BASSENTHWAITE LAKE   *Pheasant Inn*

Nr Cockermouth CA13 9YE   `FOOD`
Area Map 1 C1 *Cumbria*   `B&B`
Bassenthwaite Lake
(059 681) 234
Parking *ample*

Bar food *12–1.45 (Sun till 1.30)*
No bar food *eves*

Landlord *Mr W.E. Barrington-Wilson*
Free house
🍺 *Theakston Best Bitter; Younger's*
Scotch; Bass; Guinness; Carlsberg Hof.

Originating from a 400-year-old farm, the Pheasant is long and low with a rustic porch, whitewashed walls and a mossy slate roof, all set in lovely gardens that lead to beech woods. The residents' rooms are blissfully peaceful with parquet floors, oriental rugs, walls hung with sporting prints and shotguns and a log fire burning in a copper-hooded fireplace. A bar menu runs the gamut of cold light snacks from smoked mackerel fillet to quail eggs with hazelnut mayonnaise. Garden.

Typical dishes Potted Silloth shrimps £2.95 Smoked Herdwick lamb with melon £3.10

Accommodation *20 bedrooms* **£A G1**
Check-in by arrangement

The bedrooms help make this an outstanding pub to stay in. All are delightfully different, some with modern fitted units, others with antiques. One has a half-tester bed, another is all old pine. Most enjoy fine views. Fabrics are tasteful and well-coordinated without a too-formal 'designed' look. Bathrooms are tiled and bright and mostly new. Children welcome overnight. *No dogs.*

Prices given are as at the time of our research and thus may change.

BATHAMPTON   *George Inn*

Mill Lane, Nr Bath BA2 6TR   `FOOD`
Map 10 A3 *Avon*
Bath (0225) 25079
Parking *ample*

Bar food *12–2 & 6–9.45 (Sun 7–9.30)* 🛏

Landlord *Walter John Hall*
Brewery *Courage*
🍺 *Courage Best Bitter, Directors; John*
Smith's Yorkshire Bitter; Guinness;
Foster's. ⊖

The last official duel in England was fought at this delightful creeper-clad 15th-century pub by the Kennet and Avon canal. Today, enjoyable snacks are cheerfully served in the numerous cosy beamed lounge areas, with choices like leek and potato soup, prawn and salmon pancake, spit-roast chicken and delicious apple and walnut sponge. Children's play area and garden.
Typical dishes Beef in Stilton and red wine sauce £5.90 Queen of puddings £1.65

BEAUWORTH   *Milbury's*

Nr Cheriton SO24 0PB   A
Map 7 C4 *Hampshire*
Bramdean (096 279) 248
Parking *ample*

Landlords *Len & Jan Larden*
Free house
🍺 *Gales HSB; Flowers Original; Wadworth 6X; Hermitage Bitter; Guinness; Stella Artois.*

First the Hare and Hounds, then the Fox and Hounds, the 17th-century inn has been restored to something like its original order, with flagstones, beams and an old brick fireplace. Its most unusual feature is a massive treadwheel, some 250 years old, which was used to draw water from a 300ft well, the latter now covered by glass. Historical notes to the inn say that it was once renowned for smugglers and 'strange goings-on'.

Credit Access, Diners, Visa

BECKLEY   *Abingdon Arms*

Nr Oxford OX3 9UU   FOOD
Area Map 4 F2 *Oxfordshire*
Stanton St John (086 735) 311
Parking *ample*

Bar food *12.15–2.15 & 7.15–9.45*
No bar food *Sun eve*

Landlords *Brian & Mary Greatbatch*
Free house
🍺 *Wadworth 6X; John Bull Bitter; Guinness; Löwenbräu; Castlemaine XXXX.* 🍷 😊

Mary Greatbatch just has to be a fine cook with a name like that, and her short, seasonally changing menus are full of interest at this pleasant country pub. Tempting cold dishes might include smoked trout with beetroot and horse-radish sauce or Parma ham and peaches, while equally delicious hot options embrace flavoursome bouillabaisse, poached salmon and sliced smoked chicken. Good choice of sweets and cheeses. Garden.
Typical dishes Rare roast beef £3.95 Chicken curry £4.25

BEDFORD   *Embankment Hotel*

The Embankment MK40 3PD   B&B
Map 10 C1 *Bedfordshire*
Bedford (0234) 261332
Parking *ample*

Landlord *John Bradnam*
Owner *Toby Restaurants*
🍺 *Charrington IPA; Worthington Best Bitter; Toby Bitter; Carling Black Label; Tennent's Pilsner, Extra.*

Accommodation *20 bedrooms* £C G1
Check-in all day

A large town-centre hotel which overlooks the river Ouse, and provides excellent overnight accommodation. An informal sitting area at reception is attractive and comfortable, and the Raj bar is well designed and full of character with its artefacts and prints. Twenty spacious upstairs bedrooms feature radios, TVs, trouser presses and tea-makers. All rooms are en suite with shower facilities. Accommodation closed 3 days Christmas. *No dogs.*

Credit Access, Amex, Diners, Visa

BEDFORD   *Park*

98 Kimbolton Road   FOOD
MK40 2PF
Map 10 C1 *Bedfordshire*
Bedford (0234) 54093
Parking *limited*

Bar food *12–2*
No bar food *eves & all Sun*

Landlords *Bob & Janet Broomhall*
Brewery *Charles Wells*
🍺 *Wells Bombardier, Eagle Bitter, Talisman; Red Stripe; Kellerbräu.* 😊

Over 20 English cheeses are temptingly displayed every lunchtime (except Sundays) at this substantial mock-Tudor pub north of the town centre. Enjoy your selection as part of a ploughman's, or choose something hot like home-made soup served with good wholemeal bread, chilli or cottage pie. The handsome beamed bar and airy conservatory with patio doors opening on to the garden are pleasant places to eat.
Typical dishes Scotch broth £1.25 Pork and cheese platter £2.95

Credit Access, Amex, Diners, Visa

BEER — *Anchor Inn*

Fore Street EX12 3ET — B&B
Map 9 C2 *Devon*
Seaton (0297) 20386
Parking *limited*

Landlord *David Boalch*
Free house
🍺 *Flowers IPA; Courage Best Bitter; Hall & Woodhouse Badger Best; Stella Artois; Foster's; Heineken.* 🍷

Accommodation *9 bedrooms* **£C G2**
Check-in by arrangement

Most of the bedrooms enjoy fine sea views at this sturdy pub in a little fishing village. Neat and bright, all have modern fitted furniture, matching floral fabrics and wallpapers, plus TVs and tea-makers. Four offer en suite facilities, while remaining rooms share two public bathrooms. The spacious bars are comfortable and well lit and there is a homely reception lounge with TV for residents' use. Accommodation closed one week Christmas. Children welcome overnight. *No dogs.*

Credit Access, Visa

BEETHAM — *Wheatsheaf Hotel*

Nr Milnthorpe LA7 7AL — B&B
Area Map 1 E5 *Cumbria*
Milnthorpe (044 82) 2123
Parking *ample*

Landlady *Mrs F. Miller*
Free house ☙
🍺 *Thwaites Bitter; Stones Bitter; Younger's Scotch; Guinness; Carlsberg.* 🍷

Accommodation *7 bedrooms* **£D G2**
Check-in all day

The Miller family have been dispensing good old-fashioned hospitality for over 27 years at their fine old coaching inn just off the A6. Black and white gables and leaded windows distinguish the facade; inside, the three beamed bars are full of character and there is a comfortable upstairs TV lounge for residents' use. Attractively appointed bedrooms with TVs and tea-makers all have private bathrooms (two are not en suite).

BELFORD — *Blue Bell Hotel*

Market Place NE70 7NE — B&B
Map 2 D5 *Northumberland*
Belford (066 83) 543
Parking *ample*

Landlords *Carl & Jean Shirley*
Free house ☙
🍺 *Newcastle Exhibition; McEwan's Scotch; Drybrough Heavy; Theakston Best Bitter; Carlsberg Pilsner.*

Accommodation *15 bedrooms* **£A G1**
Check-in all day

Lots of changes at the Shirleys' fine old creeper-clad inn, but none, happily, that alter its delightful, traditional character. A new public bar will leave the charming cocktail bar for residents and diners, and the lounge will be even more comfortable with its new carpets and matching upholstery. Bedrooms are pretty and homely, with period-style furnishings, a couple of armchairs and ornaments galore, plus TVs, direct-dial telephones and neat bathrooms. Two new annexe rooms.

Credit Access, Amex, Diners, Visa

BENENDEN — *King William IV*

The Street TN17 4DJ — FOOD
Area Map 5 B4 *Kent*
Benenden (0580) 240636
Parking *ample*

Bar food *12–2 & 7.30–9.30*
No bar food *Mon eve & all Sun*

Landlords *Nigel & Hilary Douglas*
Brewery *Shepherd Neame*
🍺 *Shepherd Neame Master Brew, Hurlimann Sternbräu; Guinness; Steinbock Lager.* 🍷

Fresh flowers on plain wooden tables, a log fire in the inglenook and exposed beams add to the homely, well-lived-in air inside a traditional tile-hung pub. Simple, satisfying snacks – home-made soup, toasted sandwiches, sausages and mash, chilli con carne and fish pie served with delicious red cabbage – go down well with the largely local clientele. Strangers could be made more welcome.
Typical dishes Ham and leek mornay £2.50 Arabian spiced kebabs £4.25

BERKELEY ROAD   *Prince of Wales Hotel*

Nr Berkeley GL13 9HD   B&B
Map 6 E4 *Gloucestershire*
Dursley (0453) 810474
Parking *ample*

Landlord *Mr P.K. Downe*
Free house
🍺 *Wadworth 6X; Marston Pedigree; Tetley Bitter; Guinness; Löwenbräu.*

Accommodation *8 bedrooms* £B G2
Check-in all day

New owners have given this well-run, freshly painted inn alongside the A38 a thorough facelift. Popular with business travellers for its proximity to junctions 13 and 14 of the M5, decent overnight accommodation is provided by neat uniformly decorated bedrooms, now all with en suite facilities as well as TVs, telephones, tea-makers and hairdryers. Best of the bedrooms is large and cheerful and boasts a half-tester. Garden and play area. Children welcome overnight.

Credit Access, Amex, Visa

BEWDLEY   *Black Boy Hotel*

Kidderminster Road   FOOD
DY12 1AG   B&B
Map 7 A2 *Hereford & Worcs*
Bewdley (0299) 402119
Parking *ample*

Bar food *11.30–2*
No bar food *eves & all Sun* 🌣

Landlord *Mr A.R. Wilson*
Free house
🍺 *Mitchells & Butlers Brew XI, Springfield Bitter; Tennent's Pilsner; Carling Black Label.* No real ale.

Accommodation *28 bedrooms* £D G3
Check-in all day

A solidly built 17th-century inn with two pleasantly traditional beamed bars, one devoted to displays of regimental insignia of the British Army. Lunchtime bar snacks chosen from a small menu with daily-changing additions are carefully and enjoyably prepared by their chef of 35 years together with the landlord's daughter. As well as standard favourites like plain and toasted sandwiches, ploughman's, steaks and omelettes, there are also delicious specials such as flavourful carrot and coriander soup followed by baked ham with parsley sauce, and lovely treacle or Bakewell tart for afters.

Typical dishes Cottage pie £1.95 Garlic mushroom omelette £2.95

Best bedrooms are those with private facilities in the Georgian annexe: bright and light, they have a comfortable, homely feel. Rooms in the oldest part of the inn are looking very shabby and would benefit from refurbishment. Residents have the use of three lounge areas, including a delightfully chintzy Georgian room with cream-painted panelling.

Credit Access, Amex, Visa

BIBURY   *Catherine Wheel*

GL7 6DJ   FOOD
Area Map 4 C2 *Gloucs*   B&B
Bibury (028 574) 250
Parking *ample*

Bar food *12–2 & 7–10* 🌣

Landlord *Bill May*
Brewery *Courage*
🍺 *Courage Best Bitter, Directors; John Smith's Yorkshire Bitter; Guinness; Hofmeister; Foster's.* ⊜

Attentive service here goes beyond pulling pints to the brim and wiping the tables. The landlord, when not out shooting pheasants to supplement the menu, selects from his collection classical music appropriate to the mood. The pub chips in its pennyworth of character with low beamed ceilings, dark wood seats and tables, a restrained use of brass and copper implements and a log fire. A good chicken and ham soup comes with warm granary bread and ratatouille gratinée comes packed with vegetables, the sauce lightly herbed and pleasantly thick.

There is a regular menu and daily blackboard listing a dozen specials such as sherried kidneys and pheasant casserole. Traditional Sunday lunch.

Typical dishes Escalope of pork with wine and mushroom sauce £4.50 Mushrooms in garlic sauce £4

Accommodation *2 bedrooms* **£D G3**
Check-in by arrangement

Two pretty, homely bedrooms have pretty floral fabrics, dried flowers, ornaments and TVs, and share a large, clean carpeted bathroom with separate shower cubicle. Garden. Accommodation closed three days Christmas.

BIDDENDEN   *Three Chimneys*

TN27 8LW   `FOOD`
Area Map 5 B4 *Kent*
Biddenden (0580) 291472
Parking *ample*

Bar food *11.30–2 & 6.30–10, Sun 12–2 & 7.15–10* ☙

Landlords *Mr & Mrs C. F. Sayers*
Free house
🍺 *Adnams Bitter; Hook Norton Old Hookey; Goacher Maidstone Ale; Marston Pedigree; Guinness; Stella Artois.* ▮ ☺

A gem of a country pub, formed from a pair of ancient timbered cottages and named after the three lanes (*trois chemins*) on which it stands. An extensive choice of home-made snacks is offered in the Garden Room and tiny beamed bars, ranging from venison pâté, devilled crab soup and excellent ploughman's to duck and pheasant casserole, seafood pie and lemon and ginger pudding. Garden.
Typical dishes Veal and pork terrine £2.40 Mexican pork £4.75

BIDFORD-ON-AVON   *White Lion Hotel*

High Street B50 4BQ   `B&B`
Map 10 A1 *Warwickshire*
Stratford (0789) 773309
Parking *ample*

Landlords *Mr & Mrs Lilley*
Free house
🍺 *Younger's IPA, Scotch; Bass Special; Beck's Bier; Tennent's Export; Carlsberg Export.*

Accommodation *10 bedrooms* **£A G1**
Check-in all day

Enjoying a pretty setting beside an old stone bridge on the banks of the Avon, this attractively refurbished hotel offers most appealing overnight accommodation. The ten well-kept bedrooms all have good dark wood furnishings (including one four-poster) and a nicely co-ordinated decor, plus neat modern bathrooms, TVs and tea-makers. Downstairs, the smart bar blends contemporary bamboo-style chairs with original beams. Children welcome overnight.

Credit Access, Amex, Diners, Visa

BINFIELD   *Stag & Hounds*

Forest Road RG12 5HA   `A`
Map 10 C3 *Berkshire*
Bracknell (0344) 483553
Parking *ample*

Landlord *Mr B. Howard*
Brewery *Courage* ☙
🍺 *Courage Directors, Best Bitter; John Smith's Bitter; Kronenbourg 1664; Foster's.* ▮

Built as a royal hunting lodge in the heart of Windsor Great Forest over 600 years ago, the Stag & Hounds oozes old-world atmosphere. Blackened beams, low ceilings and open fires characterise the five cosy little bars with their darkwood settles and sturdy wooden tables, while gleaming horse brasses and a collection of thimbles decorate the pleasant lounge bar. In the garden remains the stump of the ancient elm that marked the centre of the forest.

Credit Access

BIRCHOVER   *Druid Inn*

Nr Matlock DE4 2BL   `FOOD`
Map 6 F1 *Derbyshire*
Winster (062 988) 302
Parking *ample*

Bar food *12–2.15 & 7–10.15*

Landlord *Brian Bunce*
Free house
*🍷Marston Pedigree; Mansfield Bitter;
Guinness; Carlsberg.* ▮ ☺

The Druid nestles right under the Row Tor
rocks above Darley Dale in renowned
walking country. There is ample space for
eating in its cosy bars and two-storey
dining area. Blackboard menus offer an
extensive choice, from Stilton and walnut
pâté and hot garlic prawns among starters
to steak and oyster pie, fresh salmon and
red kidney bean bake. Sweets are limited,
but supplemented by locally made ice
creams and English cheeses.
Typical dishes Haddock and prawn tagliatelle £5.70 Vegetable curry £4.20

BIRMINGHAM   NEW ENTRY   *Barton Arms*

144 High Street, Aston   `FOOD`
B6 4UP
Map 7 B1 *West Midlands*
021-359 0853
Parking *limited*

Bar food *12–2 (Sun till 3)*

Landlord *Stephen Lefevre*
Brewery *Mitchells & Butlers*
*🍷M&B Brew XI, Mild; Guinness;
Tennent's Export.* ☺

Two miles north of the city centre at a
crossroads on the A34 stands an Edwardian landmark, unmissable among Aston's
anonymous modern blocks. The convivial
bars are roomy and extravagant, with
stained and etched glass, brightly decorated tiles, carved wood and many little
corners. Bar food centres round a cold
buffet, but there are also hot things like
steak and kidney pie, lasagne or seafood
platter.
Typical dishes Cornish pasty £1.70
Roast lamb chop £2.50

BISHOP WILTON   *Fleece Inn*

Nr York YO4 1RU   `B&B`
Area Map 3 C5 *Humberside*
Bishop Wilton (075 96) 251
Parking *ample*

Landlord *Leslie Wells*
Free house
*🍷John Smith's Yorkshire Bitter; Tetley
Bitter; Guinness; Beamish Stout; Skol.*

Accommodation *6 bedrooms* £D G2
Check-in all day

The Fleece has a superb village setting
looking over the green, where a small
bridge traverses a stream, to the Norman
spire of the parish church and beyond to the
North Wolds escarpment. Within, it is
villagey too, a central bar dividing lounge
and public areas, with a breakfast room to
the rear. Accommodation comprises three
bedrooms sharing a bathroom and lounge
above the pub, and three new ones, self-
contained and en suite, in a pantiled block.
Children welcome overnight.

Credit Access, Amex, Diners, Visa

BLAKESLEY   *Bartholomew Arms*

Nr Towcester NN12 8RE   `B&B`
Map 10 B1 *Northamptonshire*
Blakesley (0327) 860292
Parking *ample*

Landlords *Mr & Mrs C.A. Hackett*
Free house
*🍷Marston Pedigree; Younger's Scotch,
Tartan Bitter; Guinness; Beck's Bier.*

Accommodation *5 bedrooms* £D G2
Check-in all day

The Hacketts are delightful hosts and their
pub oozes originality and charm. A model
of the Cutty Sark, bequeathed by a local, is
part of the public bar's model ship collection. The lounge bar's themes are guns and
cricket, and an old bathchair sits on the
landing. Homely bedrooms complete with
ornaments, magazines, TVs and hand-
basins are well maintained with modern
units. One has en suite facilities, the others
share a simple, carpeted bathroom. Children welcome overnight.

BLEDINGTON   *King's Head Inn*

Nr Kingham OX7 6HD   `B&B`
Area Map 4 D1 *Oxfordshire*
Kingham (060 871) 365
Parking *ample*

Landlords *Michael & Annette Royce*
Free house
🍺 *Wadworth 6X; Hook Norton Best Bitter;*
Tetley Bitter; Guinness; Löwenbräu.

Accommodation *7 bedrooms* **£C G1**
Check-in all day

A complete picture of rural idyll, next to the village green with its stream and ducks, the King's Head is also splendid inside. The low-ceilinged bar has fine old beams, a recessed inglenook, rough stone walls and flagstone floors. Four new bedrooms have recently been added to the three existing ones, and all are white-painted with co-ordinated floral fabrics and antique pine furniture. En suite facilities, TVs and direct-dial telephones are standard. Children welcome overnight. *No dogs.*

BLICKLING   *Buckinghamshire Arms Hotel*

Nr Aylsham NR11 6NF   `B&B`
Map 8 F1 *Norfolk*
Aylsham (0263) 732133
Parking *ample*

Landlord *Nigel Elliott*
Free house
🍺 *Adnams Bitter; Greene King IPA, Abbot*
Ale; Löwenbräu; Hansa.

Accommodation *3 bedrooms* **£B G2**
Check-in all day

A splendid 17th-century inn standing deferentially at the gates of the even more splendid 1619 Blickling Hall, built on the site of the Boleyn family house. Two of three bedrooms have dramatic night views of the floodlit hall. The rooms themselves have four-poster-bed character and share a tidy bathroom and its old-fashioned tub. The bars, too, have an ambience mindful of the pub's history with open fires and old pine. Garden and play area. Children welcome overnight.

Credit Access, Visa

BLOCKLEY   NEW ENTRY   *Crown Inn*

High Street GL56 9EX   `FOOD` `B&B`
Map 10 A1 *Gloucestershire*
Blockley (0386) 700245
Parking *ample*

Restaurant *12–2 (Sun till 2.30) & 7–10*

Landlord *J.H. Champion & Sons*
Free house
🍺 *Butcome Bitter; Wadworth 6X; Greene*
King Abbot Ale; Guinness; Marston
Pedigree; Carlsberg. 🍷 ☻

Accommodation *15 bedrooms* **£A G1**
Check-in all day

Head straight for the restaurant in the converted coach house here, where the food from the set menus is far better than that on offer in the bar. Starters such as terrine of cheese, king prawns or beef and carrot soup followed by poached salmon, breast of chicken with curry and peach sauce, tender breast of duck with mango sauce or fillet of pork moutarde are sympathetically cooked from good fresh ingredients and served with crisp vegetables. Sweets might be cheesecake or fruit pie in season.
Set lunch £11.95 Set dinner £15.95 (no à la carte)

The main pub building has been well restored by the Champion family, and the quaintly rural bar is very popular with the locals. For residents there is a 'dry' lounge on the first floor. All the bedrooms are light, bright and fresh, having been carefully converted and improved. Cotswold stone and beams feature in many, as do hairdryers, beverage facilities and direct-dial telephones. All have small en suite bath or shower rooms. Children welcome overnight.

Credit Access, Amex, Diners, Visa

BODLE ST GREEN   NEW ENTRY   *White Horse Inn*

Herstmonceux BN27 4RE   `FOOD`
Map 8 E4 *East Sussex*
Herstmonceux (0323) 833243
Parking *ample*

Bar food *12–2.30 & 7–10.30*
(Fri & Sat till 11)
Closed *Mon*

Landlords *Ray & Dianne Tiney*
Free house
🍺 *Harveys Best Bitter; M&B Mild;*
Worthington Best Bitter; Toby Bitter;
Carling Black Label; Tennent's Extra.

Standing at a junction in a small country
lane, the White Horse Inn is a bright,
cheerful pub run by a particularly charming and convivial couple. Wholesome
home-cooked bar food is a big attraction,
typified by smooth, tasty pâté, deep-fried
Camembert and pasta with smoked haddock, prawns and mushrooms. Sunday
additionally features a three-course roast
beef lunch.
Typical dishes Deep-fried pâté-stuffed
mushrooms £1.85 Chicken curry and rice
£2.95

BOLTER END   *Peacock*

Lane End, Nr High   `FOOD`
Wycombe HP14 3LU
Map 10 C2 *Buckinghamshire*
High Wycombe (0494) 881417
Parking *ample*

Bar food *12–2 & 7–10*
No bar food *Sun eve*

Landlords *Peter & Janet Hodges*
Brewery *ABC*
🍺 *ABC Best Bitter; Bass; Guinness;*
Murphy Stout; Löwenbräu.

A pleasing country pub situated on the
B482 between Lane End and Stokenchurch.
Beams, nooks and crannies give character
to the traditional bars where you can find a
good range of enjoyable dishes. Pies,
salads, vegetarian dishes and baked
potatoes are always on offer and the daily
specials include cod and prawn mornay and
marinated grilled breast of chicken; finish
with treacle and walnut tart. Garden.
Typical dishes Steak & kidney pie £3.50
Satay £5

Credit Access, Amex, Visa

BOOT   *Woolpack Inn*

Eskdale, Holmbrook   `B&B`
CA19 1TH
Area Map 1 C3 *Cumbria*
Eskdale (094 03) 230
Parking *ample*

Landlords *Fred & Ann Fox & Bernard &*
Elaine Dickinson
Free house ☻
🍺 *Younger's Scotch, IPA; Theakston Best*
Bitter; Guinness; Carlsberg Hof; Harp.

Accommodation *7 bedrooms* £D G3
Check-in all day

Standing at the head of Eskdale Valley, this
17th-century inn is a welcome sight for fell
walkers who have just tackled Hardknott
pass. Join them in the convivial public bar,
or retreat to the pleasant, stone-walled
lounge bar. Bright, traditional bedrooms
thoughtfully provide tea-makers, electric
blankets and cosy candlewick bedspreads.
Four have their own shower cabinets and
all share one neat public bathroom. There is
a chintzy lounge for residents' use. *No dogs.*

Credit Access, Visa

BOURTON-ON-THE-HILL   *Horse & Groom Inn*

Nr Moreton-in-Marsh   `B&B`
GL56 9AQ
Map 10 A1 *Gloucestershire*
Blockley (0386) 700413
Parking *ample*

Landlords *Mr & Mrs J. L. Aizpuru*
Free house
🍺 *Bass; Worthington Best Bitter;*
Guinness; Carling Black Label.

Accommodation *3 bedrooms* £D G3
Check-in all day

Standing on the hill at the top end of the
village is a solid inn from which there are
fine views over the Cotswold countryside.
The rustic stone-walled bars are hung with
equestrian prints, reflecting the Basque
landlords' love of English racing, an enthusiasm shared by many of their customers.
Upstairs, three neat bedrooms with primarily modern decor all have shower cubicles
and washbasins, and share a bathroom.
Accommodation closed Christmas week.
No children under ten overnight. No dogs.

BOWLAND BRIDGE   Hare & Hounds

Grange-over-Sands   `B&B`
LA11 6NN
Map 3 B2 *Cumbria*
Crosthwaite (044 88) 333
Parking *ample*

Landlords *Peter & Barbara Thompson*
Free house
🍺 *Greenall Whitley Local Bitter, Original;*
Guinness; Labatt's.

Accommodation *16 bedrooms* **£C G2**
Check-in all day

One of the Lakeland's busiest pubs where people flock to sit in the garden, or at roadside tables under parasols. Eight of the bedrooms are recent additions; these have oak beams and Stag furniture, and six command views across the fells. All rooms are bright and airy; most have private facilities, but share a bathroom. All are good-sized, cheerful and well-kept with fitted furniture, TVs and beverage facilities. Children welcome overnight.

---

*Changes in data sometimes occur
in establishments
after the Guide goes to press.*

*Prices should be taken as indications
rather than firm quotes.*

BOX   NEW ENTRY   *Baylys*

High Street SN14 9NH   `FOOD`
Map 10 A3 *Wiltshire*   `B&B`
Box (0225) 743622
Parking *ample*

Bar food *12–2.30 & 7–10.30*
No bar food *Mon lunch*

Landlords *Jan & George Gynn*
Free house
🍺 *Wadworth 6X; Wiltshire Stonehenge
Best Bitter; Guinness; Stella Artois.* ⊖

Alongside the A4 Bath to Chippenham road is a solid-looking stone inn which used to be known as the Bear. Dating from the 1600s, the pub is now named after the original landlord, Jacob Bayly, whose will can be seen hanging in the bar. The vicar of the 11th-century church next door was barred from Baylys in 1656 by Oliver Cromwell. Bar food is now of interest, starting with beef broth or thick onion soup, going on to lemon sole, steaks, pies, roast beef, curry, liver and bacon, beef stew and dumplings or oriental seafood omelette, and finishing with apple crumble or vicar's tart.

Typical dishes Fish crock £3.95 Wiltshire whitepot £1.50

Accommodation *6 bedrooms* **£D G1**
Check-in all day

Six bedrooms are roomy and well fitted, with pink walls and floral fabrics blending with smart modern furniture. Four have excellent en suite facilities with high-class shower units, and the other two rooms share a public bathroom. Children welcome overnight. *No dogs.*

We publish annually so make sure you use the current edition.

BOXFORD NEW ENTRY *Bell*

Lambourn Road,
Nr Newbury RS16 8DD
Map 10 B3 *Berkshire*
Boxford (048 838) 253
Parking *ample*

`FOOD` `B&B`

Bar food *12–2 (Sun till 2.30) & 7–10*

Landlords *Paul & Helen Lavis*
Free house
🍺 *Courage Best Bitter, Directors; Arkell Kingsdown Ale, 3B; Morland Bitter; Guinness.* 🍷 ⊖

Accommodation *3 bedrooms* £B G2
Check-in by arrangement

A mood of cheery relaxation prevails here, and the wide selection of good food keeps the smiles on the customers' faces. It is a mock-Tudor pub at a country crossroads not far from Newbury, and its bar and restaurant menus cater for anyone from nibblers to the really ravenous. Ideal for the lighter appetite is the selection of tapas, including typically prawns in garlic, smoked octopus, deep-fried cockles, Spanish omelette and meat balls. Thick vegetable soup, herby chicken liver pâté and rump steak with an interesting Galliano-flavoured hot barbecue sauce were all very much to our taste, and everything gets even better with something from the rather good little wine list. Children's menu.

Typical dishes Singapore chicken £3.25 Port & Stilton pâté £2.95

The three decent-sized bedrooms are fresh and bright, with pretty floral duvets, modern furniture, TVs and radio-alarms. All have small but adequate shower/wc en suite. Building of a further eight rooms in a converted barn is under way. Children welcome overnight.

Credit Access, Amex, Diners, Visa

BRAINTREE *White Hart Hotel*

Bocking End CM7 6AB
Map 8 E2 *Essex*
Braintree (0376) 21401
Parking *ample*

`B&B`

Landlord *Ian Child*
Owner *Lansbury Hotels*
🍺 *Wethered Bitter; Greene King IPA, Abbot Ale; Whitbread Best Bitter; Heineken, Stella Artois.*

Accommodation *34 bedrooms* £A G1
Check-in all day

Standing right in the town centre, this former coaching inn offers today's traveller every modern comfort in an atmosphere of old-world charm. The traditional beamed bars have a friendly 'local' appeal, and there is a cosy residents' lounge upstairs. Bedrooms in the main house and more spacious extension have hairdryers, trouser presses, tea-makers and radio-alarms, while private bathrooms pamper with heated towel rails and full carpeting. Children welcome overnight. *No dogs.*

Credit Access, Amex, Diners, Visa

BRAMDEAN NEW ENTRY *Fox Inn*

Alresford SO24 0LP
Map 7 C4 *Hampshire*
Bramdean (0962 79) 363
Parking *ample*

`FOOD`

Bar food *12–2 & 7–9.30*

Landlords *Jane & Ian Inder*
Brewery *Marston*
🍺 *Marston Pedigree, Best Bitter, Border Ale; Guinness; Stella Artois; Heineken.* 🍷 ⊖

An attractive old white-painted pub set back off the A272. Soup, sandwiches, salads, steak pie and cauliflower cheese provide the main lunchtime choice in the tidy lounge bar. More formal evening fare ranges from succulent stuffed mushrooms with garlic mayonnaise to lamb noisettes, seasonal game and breast of chicken with sliced almonds and a lemony cream sauce. Traditional Sunday lunch.

Typical dishes Smoked salmon pâté £2.75 Halibut mornay £9.50

Credit Visa

BRANSCOMBE
Masons Arms

Nr Seaton EX12 3DJ
Map 9 C2 *Devon*
`FOOD`
`B&B`
Branscombe (029 780) 300
Parking *ample*

Bar food *12–1.45 & 7–9.30*

Landlady *Mrs Janet Inglis*
Free house
◆ *Bass; Hall & Woodhouse Badger Best, Tanglefoot; Guinness; Tennent's Pilsner; Hofbräu.* ⊖

Tucked into a hillside, with a pretty front terrace and colourful gardens, a delightful 14th-century, creeper-clad inn stands in the heart of an unspoilt Devon village. Inside, an enormous open fire not only warms the beamed and flagstoned main bar but also cooks the spit roasts offered on Thursday lunchtimes throughout winter. Alternatives range from ploughman's with locally baked crusty bread, sandwiches and salads to hot dishes like grilled lamb cutlets with garlic, chicken kebabs, omelettes and fresh local fish. Simple sweets include crème caramel and fruit pie with clotted cream. The choice of bar food is more limited at night, when the emphasis moves to the restaurant – also the venue for Sunday lunch.

Typical dishes Venison and mushroom pie £3.80 Crab gratinée £3.60

Accommodation *20 bedrooms* £B G2
Check-in all day

Exposed beams add to the charms of attractive bedrooms in the inn and nearby ancient cottages. All but two have en suite facilities, while TVs, telephones and tea-makers are standard throughout. The inviting residents' lounge commands lovely rural views. Children welcome overnight.

Credit Access, Amex, Visa

BRATTON
Duke

Nr Westbury BA13 4RW
`B&B`
Map 10 A3 *Wiltshire*
Bratton (0380) 830242
Parking *ample*

Landlords *Mick & Justine Considine*
Brewery *Usher*
◆ *Usher Best Bitter; Webster Yorkshire Bitter; Ruddles Best Bitter; Holsten; Carlsberg; Foster's.*

Accommodation *4 bedrooms* £D G3
Check-in all day

An unremarkable pub in an equally unremarkable village, the Duke nevertheless offers more than acceptable overnight accommodation. For preference choose one of the bedrooms at the back which overlook the peaceful little garden, but all the rooms are warm, comfortable and homely with good facilities. They share two bathrooms. Downstairs there is one main bar with black gloss-painted beams and frosted glass windows. Children welcome overnight. *No dogs.*

Credit Access, Amex, Visa

BRENDON
Stag Hunters Hotel

Nr Lynton EX35 1PS
`B&B`
Map 9 C1 *Devon*
Brendon (059 87) 222
Parking *ample*

Landlords *John & Margaret Parffrey*
Free house
◆ *Tetley Bitter; John Bull Bitter; Golden Hill Exmoor Ale; Guinness; Castlemaine XXXX.*

Accommodation *20 bedrooms* £C G3
Check-in all day

With a slightly disappointing exterior, the Stag Hunters stands nevertheless in a wonderful position by the East Lyn river, and makes a good base for guests wishing to explore Exmoor and the Doone Valley. Neat bedrooms in the main house and stone-built annexe all have tea-makers and half now offer carpeted bathrooms. Residents have the use of two lounges and there is a spacious public bar and cosy beamed lounge bar. Children welcome overnight. Accommodation closed January to end-March.

Credit Access, Amex, Diners, Visa

BRERETON GREEN   **Bears Head Hotel**

Nr Sandbach CW11 9RS   `B&B`
Map 3 C4 *Cheshire*
Holmes Chapel (0477) 35251
Parking *ample*

Landlord *Mr Tarquini*
Free house
🍺 *Bass; Burtonwood Best Bitter;
Worthington 'E'; Guinness; Carlsberg;
Carling Black Label.*

Accommodation *25 bedrooms* **£B G2**
Check-in all day

Run by the same family since 1936, this
timbered 17th-century pub stands less than
two miles from the M6. Pot plants and coal
fires in the characterful little beamed bars
are typically thoughtful touches, while
good-sized bedrooms (six in an adjacent
cottage, the remainder in a recent annexe)
reflect the same high standard of care. All
have modern furniture, telephones, TVs,
radios and tea-makers, together with
private facilities. Patio. Children welcome
overnight. *No dogs.*

Credit Access, Amex, Diners, Visa

BRETFORTON   NEW ENTRY   *Fleece*

The Cross, Nr Evesham   `A`
WR11 5JE
Map 10 A1 *Hereford & Worcs*
Evesham (0386) 831173
Parking *ample*

Landlords *Ian & Nora Davis*
Free house 🛏
🍺 *Ruddles Best Bitter; Hook Norton Best
Bitter; Mitchells & Butlers Brew XI; Uley
Old Spot, Pigs Ear; Tennent's Pilsner.*

The Saxon name of 'Brotforton' meant 'the
ford with planks', and the earliest docu-
mented deed from the village dates from the
year 714. The Fleece was originally a
mediaeval farmhouse and became an inn in
1848, when the beer was brewed in the back
kitchen. Since 1977 the pub has been owned
by the National Trust. There are three main
rooms – the Brewhouse, with its brewing
artefacts, the Dugout (originally the pantry)
and the Pewter Room, housing a world-
famous pewter collection. Garden.

BRIDGNORTH   **Falcon Hotel**

St John Street, Lowtown   `B&B`
WV15 6AS
Map 7 A1 *Shropshire*
Bridgnorth (074 62) 3134
Parking *ample*

Landlord *Mr P. Van Deventer*
Free house
🍺 *Courage Directors; John Smith's Bitter;
Talisman; Hofmeister; Foster's.*

Accommodation *15 bedrooms* **£C G2**
Check-in all day

The young landlord is improving the
standard of accommodation at his white-
painted 16th-century inn. Redecoration has
brightened the 15 small rooms, most of
which now offer en suite facilities. All have
matching duvet covers and curtains, plus
practical modern furnishings, TVs and
direct-dial telephones. Shabby public areas
would benefit from similar attention,
including the bar with its assorted bric-a-
brac and period pieces. Children welcome
overnight.

Credit Access, Amex, Diners, Visa

BRIDPORT   **Bull Hotel**

34 East Street DT6 3LF   `B&B`
Area Map 7 A5 *Dorset*
Bridport (0308) 22878
Parking *ample*

Landlords *Pursey family*
Free house ·
🍺 *Hall & Woodhouse Tanglefoot; Badger
Best; Bass; Palmer BB; Guinness;
Carlsberg Hof.*

Accommodation *22 bedrooms* **£C G2**
Check-in all day

New owners are extending and refurbish-
ing this white-painted 16th-century coaching inn standing in the historic town centre.
A pleasant reception area has been created
and both bar and first-floor lounge were
being smartly redecorated as we called.
Fabrics and wallcoverings in attractive soft
shades and cream-coloured units have
brightened bedrooms, largest of which are
at the front. Additional bathrooms will
increase the proportion of rooms en suite.
Children welcome overnight.

Credit Access, Amex, Diners, Visa

BRIDPORT   *George Hotel*

4 South Street DT6 3NQ
Area Map 7 A5 *Dorset*
Bridport (0308) 23187
Parking *limited*

FOOD
B&B

Bar food *12–3 & 7–9.30*
No bar food *Sun lunch & Bank Hols* ⊃

Landlord *John Mander*
Brewery *Palmer*
🍺 *Palmer IPA, Bridport Bitter, Tally Ho;
Guinness; Eldridge Pope Faust Pilsner;
Shilthorn Export.* ❸

A delightfully eccentric pub with a real character for a landlord in the shape of John Mander lies behind the formal facade of this Georgian listed building. Highlight of the extensive bar menu is the fresh fish bought daily straight from Bridport's quay, with choices like grilled whole plaice or lemon sole. Appetising alternatives range from sautéed kidneys, curry and grilled entrecôte steak to lighter bites such as garlic mushrooms on toast, hot sausage with French bread, ploughman's and cold meat salads. Finish with a pleasant sweet like chocolate mousse or bread and butter pudding – or opt for the fine English cheeseboard. Customers can eat in the dining room (where children are welcome) or lively bar with its loud jazz and jeans-clad staff.

Typical dishes Pigeon pie £2.50 Cauliflower cheese £1.95

Accommodation *4 bedrooms* **£D G3**
Check-in all day

Upstairs, four modest but cheerful little bedrooms share a public bathroom and all have washbasins and colour TVs. Accommodation closed Bank Holiday weekends.

BRIGHTLING   *Fullers Arms*

★   ★

**Oxley Green, Nr
Robertsbridge** TN32 5HD
Area Map 5 A5 *East Sussex*
Brightling (042 482) 212
Parking *ample*

FOOD

Bar food *12–2.30 & 7–10.30*
Closed *Mon except Bank Hols*

Landlords *Roger Berman & Shirl Telfer*
Free house
🍺 *Harvey Best Bitter; guest beers;
Theakston Old Peculier; Heineken; Stella
Artois.* 🍷 ❸

Cooking standards continue to improve here, and the menu remains unchanged since Roger Berman and Shirl Telfer took over. Their attitude is one of professionalism as well as unerring friendliness, and their remotely situated open-plan modern pub with its fresh flowers, bench seating and even kitchen chairs is consequently a wonderful place in which to eat. Enormous blackboards cover the walls – one listing savouries, one desserts and the other the daily specials. Savouries feature excellent pies (chicken and mushroom or sweetcorn, and prawn and halibut), gammon and onion pudding, cheesy leek and potato bake and lovingly prepared prawn pancakes. Vegetarians can choose from cashew and aubergine bake, mixed curried vegetables and cauliflower crumble. An impressive list of wines by the glass to accompany the meal is a bonus. Fine desserts include bread and butter pudding, jam sponge, banana and walnut or apricot and almond puddings.

Typical dishes Steak and kidney pudding £3.50 Cauliflower Stilton 95p Blackcurrant & apple crumble £3.50 Vegetarian spotted dick £1.50

BRIGHTON   *The Greys*

105 Southover Street, off FOOD
Lewes Road BN2 2 UA
Area Map 6 D4 *East Sussex*
Brighton (0273) 680734
Parking *ample*

Bar food *12.15–2*
No bar food *eves & all Sun*

Landlords *Mike Lance & Jackie Fitzgerald*
Brewery *Whitbread*
🍺 *Flowers Original; Fremlins Bitter;*
Marston Pedigree; Guinness; Stella Artois;
Heineken. ⊝

Jackie Fitzgerald's splendid cooking draws
the lunchtime crowds to this lively, popular
little pub run in friendly, extrovert style by
Mike Lance. Try vegetarian filo pastry
filled with feta cheese and spinach, a fresh
local fish special, tastily sauced pasta or a
hearty meat dish like pork in cider with
Dijon mustard. Sweets might include syllabub or apple and Calvados pancakes.
Booking is advisable.
Typical dishes Mediterranean fish stew
£3.50 Lamb brochette with wild rice £4.15

BRIGHTWELL BALDWIN   *Lord Nelson*

Nr Watlington OX9 5NP FOOD
Map 10 B2 *Oxfordshire*
Watlington (049 161) 2497
Parking *ample*

Bar food *12–2 & 6.30–10*
Closed *Mon (except Bank Hols)*

Landlords *Barry Allen &*
David & Muriel Gomm
Free house
🍺 *Brakspear Bitter; Webster*
Yorkshire Bitter; Carlsberg
Pilsner. ⊝

Standing opposite the village church, this
pretty, stone-built pub offers good food in a
cosy, welcoming setting. Traditional bar
snacks include salads, steak, chilli and
breaded scampi, or choose something more
elaborate from the restaurant menu:
perhaps garlic mushrooms or seafood pancake followed by veal cordon bleu or
chicken breast in prawn and asparagus
sauce. Sunday roast lunch available.
Typical dishes Prawn risotto £5.95 Fillet
of lemon sole £5.75

Credit Amex, Visa

BRIMFIELD   NEW ENTRY   *Roebuck*

Nr Ludlow SY8 4NE FOOD
Map 6 E3 *Shropshire* B&B
Brimfield (058 472) 230
Parking *ample*

Bar food *12–2 & 6.30–10*
No bar food *Sun eve & all Mon*

Landlords *John & Carole Evans*
Free house
🍺 *Ansells Bitter, Mild; Guinness; Skol,*
Löwenbräu.

Accommodation *3 bedrooms* **£A G1**
Check-in all day

Parts of this village pub just off the A456
date from the 15th century and the bars
retain much of their old-world character.
The food is the star attraction here, with
both bar and restaurant meals benefiting
from Carole Evans' first-class cooking. Bar
snacks are simpler – carrot and celery soup,
pigeon in red wine, nut and vegetable roll –
while the restaurant menu (also available in
the bar) is typified by spinach soufflé, rack
of lamb, roast Cornish lobster and lovely
sweets like chocolate marquise or home-
made ice cream in a brandy-snap basket.

Typical dishes Steak & kidney pie £4.70
Pigeon in red wine £4.90 Soup of the day
£1.50 Cheese & pickle lunch £2.70

The three new bedrooms are individually
decorated with fine fabrics, and the limed
oak furniture looks very handsome. Direct-
dial phones, remote-control TVs, and tea-
makers with Royal Worcester china. Two
of the bathrooms are shower/wc only.
Accommodation closed two weeks Feb. *No
children under 8 overnight. No dogs.*

Credit Access, Visa

BROAD CHALKE   *Queens Head*

Nr Salisbury SP5 5EN   `B&B`
Area Map 7 E3 *Wiltshire*
Salisbury (0722) 780344
Parking *ample*

Landlords *Bernard & Pamela Lott*
Free house ☞
🍺 *Wadworth 6X; Ringwood Best Bitter;
Ruddles Best Bitter; Guinness; Carlsberg;
Foster's.*

Accommodation *4 bedrooms* **£C G1**
Check-in all day

Once the village bakehouse, the Queens
Head has cleverly switched its monopoly
from cakes to ale having outlasted the three
other inns in the parish. The main Village
Bar has stone walls, a beamed ceiling and
an inglenook. There is a sheltered courtyard for outdoor drinking, across which
lies the new accommodation block housing
four light and airy bedrooms with floral
fabrics, some period furniture, remote-
control TVs and direct-dial telephones. *No
children under ten overnight. No dogs.*

Credit Visa

BROCKTON   *Feathers Inn*

Nr Much Wenlock TF13 6JK   `A`
Map 6 E2 *Shropshire*
Brockton (074 636) 202
Parking *ample*

Landlords *John & Maxine Littleton*
Free house
🍺 *Bass; Wood's Parish Bitter; Mitchells &
Butlers Springfield Bitter, Mild; Guinness;
Carling Black Label.*

Originally two Elizabethan cottages, themselves built with timbers salvaged from a
sailing ship (rope burns are evident on one
of the beams), the Feathers is oozing with
character. Outside a small stream runs by.
The inn brewed its own ale until the start of
this century and the well which supplied
the brewing water is still in daily use.
Inside, the huge bellows, rescued from the
local smithy, now serves as a table top. A
mellow and warm establishment. Patio.

BROME   *Oaksmere*

Nr Eye IP23 8AJ   `FOOD`
Map 8 F2 *Suffolk*
Eye (0379) 870326
Parking *ample*

Bar food *12–2 & 7–10*

Landlord *Michael Spratt*
Free house
🍺 *Adnams Bitter; Courage Directors, Best
Bitter; Guinness; Foster's.* ⊖

Imaginative snacks are justifiably popular
at this 16th-century country hotel surrounded by 20 acres of gardens and parkland. In the pubby beamed Tudor Bar, tuck
into carrot and coriander soup or fettucine
with cream and parmesan followed by a
daily special such as excellent stir-fried beef
with noodles or Cromer crab salad. Equally
appealing sweets include treacle tart and
plum crumble. Garden.
Typical dishes Scallop-stuffed chicken
£4.25 Turkey Madras £3.85

Credit Access, Amex, Diners, Visa

BROMHAM   *Greyhound*

Nr Chippenham SN15 2HA   `FOOD`
Map 10 A3 *Wiltshire*
Bromham (0380) 850241
Parking *ample*

Bar food *11–2 (Sun from 12) & 7–10.30
(Sun & in winter till 10)*

Landlords *George & Morag Todd*
Free house
🍺 *Wadworth 6X, IPA; Carling Black Label;
Stella Artois.* ⊖

Jovial proprietors George and Mo Todd
have built up a loyal following here, both
for their decorative techniques – walls and
ceilings festooned with bric-a-brac – or
their oddball menus, either standard or
daily. Hors d'oeuvre called 'Beginnings'
range from soup to clam fries, 'Middlings'
from swordfish steak to turkey mirin (fillets
fried in butter with a garlic, sherry, soy and
sugar sauce) and there are other fine
Malaysian dishes too. Garden.
Typical dishes Pork devils £4.50 Sambal
udang £5.10

BROMYARD   NEW ENTRY   *Falcon Hotel*

Broad Street HR7 4BT   `B&B`
Map 6 E3 *Hereford & Worcs*
Bromyard (0885) 483034
Parking *ample*

Landlord *E.J. Townley-Berry*
Free house
🍺 *Flowers Original; Whitbread Best Bitter;*
Heineken.

Accommodation *14 bedrooms* £B G1
Check-in all day

Once an important coaching stop, this splendid black-and-white inn dating from 1535 has been lovingly restored throughout. Many fine features abound, notably the lovely carved panelling in both the entrance foyer and restaurant, and the original Jacobean staircase. Particularly striking is the Judge's Bar, once the town's magistrates' courtroom. Charming little bedrooms have good-quality furnishings, coordinated fabrics and carpeted en suite bath/shower rooms. Children welcome overnight.

Credit Access, Visa

BROOM   *Broom Tavern*

High Street, Nr Alcester   `FOOD`
B50 4HL
Map 10 A1 *Warwickshire*
Stratford-upon-Avon (0789) 773656
Parking *ample*

Bar food *12–2 & 7–9.45*

Landlords *Gienek & Liz Zdanko*
Brewery *Whitbread*
🍺 *Flowers Original, Best Bitter, IPA;*
Whitbread Best Mild; Heineken; Stella
Artois. ⊖

Bar meals are a big draw in the friendly atmosphere of the village pub in Broom. The regular menu offers a wide and varied selection of dishes from starters like crispy mushrooms and French onion soup to main courses of grilled trout, beef goulash or chicken in prawn sauce. Specials might be duck pâté, rack of lamb, Cumberland pie, beef Wellington, or chicken marsala tandoori. Children's menu.
Typical dishes Steak and kidney pie £3.95 Lasagne verdi £4.15

Credit Visa

BROOM   *Cock*

23 High Street SG18 9NA   `FOOD`
Map 10 C1 *Bedfordshire*
Biggleswade (0767) 314411
Parking *ample*

Bar food *12–2 & 6.30–10, Sun 12–1.30*
& 7.30–9.30 🍴

Landlords *Brenda & Martin Murphy*
Brewery *Greene King*
🍺 *Greene King IPA, Abbot Ale; Harp.* ⊖

Part of a little row of ancient cottages, this unspoilt Victorian alehouse has several intimate, quarry-tiled rooms where amiable landlord Martin Murphy dispenses beer direct from the barrel. A fine selection of English cheeses, served with huge chunks of crusty bread, is the favourite accompaniment, and there are also succulent cold meats to enjoy with salad. Hot choices include home-made shepherd's pie, available every lunchtime except Sunday.
Typical dishes Game soup 65p Stilton platter £2.50

BUCKLER'S HARD   *Master Builder's House Hotel*

Beaulieu, Brockenhurst   `B&B`
SO42 7XB
Map 7 B4 *Hampshire*
Buckler's Hard (059 063) 253
Parking *ample*

Landlord *Richard Dawes*
Brewery *Allied Lyons*
🍺 *Ind Coope Burton Ale; Hall's Harvest*
Bitter; Tetley Bitter; Castlemaine XXXX;
Skol.

Accommodation *23 bedrooms* £A G1
Check-in all day

On the banks of the Beaulieu River in the heart of the Beaulieu Manor Estate, this former house of master shipbuilder Henry Adams is undergoing considerable modernisation and refurbishment. All bedrooms now offer en suite facilities, as well as trouser presses and hairdryers, and five in the original 18th-century house enjoy fine river views; remaining annexe rooms are bright, modern and compact. We hope that further changes and additions will not alter the character. Children welcome overnight.

Credit Access, Amex, Diners, Visa

BURCOT   *Chequers*

Nr Abingdon OX14 3DP   `FOOD`
Map 10 B2 *Oxfordshire*
Clifton Hampden (086 730) 7771
Parking *ample*

Bar food *12–2 (Sun till 1.45) & 6–9
(Sat till 9.30)*
No bar food *Sun eve*

Landlords *Michael & Mary Weeks*
Brewery *Usher*
🍺 *Usher Best Bitter; Ruddles County;
Webster Yorkshire Bitter; Guinness;
Holsten Export; Carlsberg.* 🍷 ☻

A charming 16th-century black and white
timbered, thatched pub on the A415, complete with grand piano. In the beamed and
quarry-tiled bars blackboards list the
extensive choice, from soup, salads and
ploughman's to flavoursome cassoulet,
fisherman's pie, beef and basil lasagne or
pork in ginger and pineapple. Mary's
disaster cake makes a rich chocolate finale,
or you can choose a refreshing sorbet.

Typical dishes Bacon & potato bake
£3.95 Sirloin steak £7.25
Credit Access, Visa

BURFORD   *Bull Hotel*

High Street OX8 4RH   `B&B`
Area Map 4 D2 *Oxfordshire*
Burford (099 382) 2220
Parking *limited*

Landlady *Mrs C. Cathcart*
Free house
🍺 *Wadworth 6X, IPA, Farmer's Glory;
John Smith's Yorkshire Bitter; Heineken;
Löwenbräu.*

Accommodation *14 bedrooms* £B G2
Check-in all day

Reputed to be the oldest hotel in Burford,
the Bull is situated on the town's main
thoroughfare. Downstairs is taken up with
two bars on different levels, and on the first
floor is the reception area which also serves
as a lounge. Two rooms have four-posters,
and all the furniture is modern and free-
standing. All rooms have TVs and beverage facilities, and ten have en suite bath or
shower rooms. The others share two neat
public bathrooms. Children welcome
overnight.

Credit Access, Amex, Diners, Visa

BURFORD   *Inn For All Seasons*

The Barringtons OX8 4TN   `B&B`
Area Map 4 D2 *Oxfordshire*
Windrush (045 14) 324
Parking *ample*

Landlords *John & Jill Sharp*
Free house
🍺 *Hall & Woodhouse Badger Best;
Wadworth 6X; Guinness; Carlsberg
Pilsner; Beck's Bier.*

Accommodation *10 bedrooms* £A G2
Check-in all day

If you are thinking of touring the Cotswolds, here is the ideal base, a solid stone
inn beside the A40 about 3 miles west of
Burford. It has been sympathetically preserved to retain its original 17th-century
charm, and delightfully furnished from the
bar and the residents' lounge to the neat
bedrooms. Front-facing rooms are double-
glazed, and all have TVs, tea-makers,
trouser presses and simple en suite bathrooms. *No children under ten overnight.
No dogs.*

Credit Access, Amex, Visa

BURFORD   NEW ENTRY   *Mermaid Inn*

High Street OX8 4QF   `FOOD`
Area Map 4 D2 *Oxfordshire*
Burford (099 382) 2193
Parking *ample*

Bar food *12–10.30 pm, Sun 12–2 & 7–10*

Landlords *Lynda & John Titcombe*
Brewery *Courage*
🍺 *Courage Directors, Best Bitter; Simonds
Bitter; Guinness; Foster's.* ☻

Behind the small frontage, flagstones,
beams, panelling and exposed stonework
make this a typical Cotswold pub. A large
menu of home-cooked dishes, available in
the bar or first-floor restaurant, include
light meals (pizza, ploughman's, seafood
casserole, tagliatelle) and main-course
dishes such as herby grilled plaice, poussin
chasseur and steaks.
Typical dishes Grilled lamb's kidneys
with granary toast £3.75 Stir-fried lamb
£7.95

Credit Visa

BURNHAM-ON-CROUCH   *Ye Olde White Harte Hotel*

The Quay CMO 8AS   `B&B`
Map 8 E3 *Essex*
Maldon (0621) 782106
Parking *limited*

Landlords *Lewis family*
Free house
🍺 *Tolly Cobbold Bitter, Mild; Adnams Bitter; McEwan's Export; Guinness; Carling Black Label.*

Accommodation *11 bedrooms* **£C G1**
Check-in all day

An old seaside inn where on sunny days you can take your drink to a terrace built out over the water. The two quaint wood-panelled bars, with their polished oak furniture and nautical flavour, have plenty of character; there is also a small, traditional residents' lounge. The bedrooms have been recently refurbished, with smart modern decor and simple furniture; five have windowseats overlooking the estuary. Some bathrooms have shower and bath. Children welcome overnight.

BURPHAM   NEW ENTRY   *George & Dragon Inn*

Nr Arundel BN18 9RR   `FOOD`
Area Map 6 B4 *West Sussex*
Arundel (0903) 883131
Parking *ample*

Bar food *12–2 & 7–10*
No bar food *Sun eve*

Landlords *Ian & Janet Wilson*
Free house
🍺 *Courage Directors; Ruddles County; Harvey Best Bitter; Guinness; Kronenbourg 1664; Red Stripe.* 🍷 ☕

An attractive, well-kept pub in a pretty Sussex Downs village. Cooking is sound and reliable, and among the regular favourites are deep-fried mushrooms with lemon mayonnaise, chicken breast with garlic, home-made meat pies, steaks and a variety of fresh salads. Sandwiches and ploughman's platters provide nourishing quick snacks, and there is always a vegetarian dish of the day, as well as daily specials.
Typical dishes Liver & bacon £3.75 Steak & kidney pie £4.65

Credit Access, Amex, Visa

BURTON   *Plume of Feathers*

Nr Chippenham SN14 7LP   `FOOD`
Map 10 A3 *Wiltshire*   `B&B`
Badminton (045 421) 251
Parking *ample*

Bar food *12–2 & 7–9.30 (Sun till 9)*

Landlords *June & Peter Bolin*
Free house
🍺 *Usher Best Bitter; Marston Pedigree; Guinness; Carlsberg Pilsner; Foster's.* 🍷

Accommodation *2 bedrooms* **£D G2**
Check-in all day

This 400-year-old West Country pub may be traditional but it certainly isn't typical. To stop off for only a pint of beer and a ham roll would be sacrilege. The menu commands reverential attention. By no means exceptional is Burgundy lamb en croûte, three grilled cutlets individually wrapped in puff pastry and cooked pink to perfection, the wine sauce with a hint of redcurrant, the broccoli and cauliflower crisp and fresh. The more adventurous customer might launch into Australian owner Peter Bolin's 'Orientalities' – Indian lamb or Burmese pork curries. On winter Sundays there is Ristaffel, a buffet of 20 or so Far Eastern dishes. Puddings are more English and excellent.

Typical dishes Pork schnitzel Amsterdam £3.95 Sinhalese chicken curry £3.80 Ristaffel £4.95 Blackberry and apple pancakes £1.50

Accommodation consists of two neat and clean twin rooms with duvets, matching curtains, radio-alarms, tea-makers and humble en suite facilities. Garden. *No children overnight.*

Credit Access, Visa

BURTON-UPON-TRENT   Riverside Inn

Riverside Drive, Branston `B&B`
DE14 3EP
Map 7 B1 *Staffordshire*
Burton-upon-Trent (0283) 511234
Parking *ample*

Landlord *Bruce Elliott-Bateman*
Brewery *Burton Inns Ltd*
🍺 *Bass Special; Marston Pedigree,*
Premium, Pilsner Lager; Tennent's Extra.

Accommodation *21 bedrooms* **£B G1**
Check-in all day

Front gardens extending down to the river
Trent and a large terrace make this welcoming old inn not far from the A38 a particularly popular spot in summer. Inside, the
comfortably traditional bar with bow
windows overlooking the river is an equally
appealing setting for a drink. A separate
wing houses the compact bedrooms, all of
which have fitted units and modern en suite
bathrooms. TVs, tea-makers, telephones
and radio-alarms are standard throughout.
Children welcome overnight. *No dogs.*

Credit Access, Amex, Visa

BURWASH   Bell Inn

High Street TN19 7EH   `B&B`
Area Map 5 A5 *East Sussex*
Burwash (0435) 882304
Parking *ample*

Landlords *Dee Mizel & A. Howard*
Brewery *Beard* 🐌
🍺 *Harvey Best Bitter; Fremlins Bitter;*
guest beer; Guinness; Stella Artois;
Carlsberg Hof.

Accommodation *5 bedrooms* **£D G3**
Check-in by arrangement

The inn dates from 1609 and a couple of the
bedrooms adduce half-timbering and sloping floors as evidence of its antiquity. Old-
fashioned furniture is used in the rooms,
which all have washbasins and share a
neat, functional bathroom. Appointments
are minimal, with no telephones or TVs.
Heavy carved wooden pews set off rich red
walls in the bar, where a log fire, beams and
yellowing plasterwork all add to the atmosphere. Friendly, well-run and clean.

Credit Access, Visa

---

*Any person using our name to obtain
free hospitality is a fraud.*

*Proprietors, please inform Egon Ronay's Guides
and the police.*

CALLINGTON   Coachmakers Arms

Newport Square PL17 7AS   `B&B`
Map 9 B2 *Cornwall*
Liskeard (0579) 82567
Parking *limited*

Landlords *Jon & Sandy Dale*
Free house
🍺 *Bass; Worthington Best Bitter;*
Charrington IPA; John Bull Bitter;
Guinness; Tennent's Pilsner.

Accommodation *4 bedrooms* **£C G2**
Check-in all day

You will find this bright 300-year-old inn
close to the centre of town alongside the
A388. Wooden settles and exposed beams
characterise the bar areas, and the bedrooms are furnished in neat, modern style.
Prints hang on the plain painted walls and
all rooms have duvets, TVs and tea-makers.
The largest room has its own patio, and
there is double glazing throughout. Private
facilities are standard, three with showers
and one with a bath. Children welcome
overnight.

Credit Access, Visa

CAMBRIDGE NEW ENTRY *Free Press*

7 Prospect Row CB1 1OU `FOOD`
Map 10 D1 *Cambridgeshire*
Cambridge (0223) 68337
Parking *difficult*

Bar food *12–2 & 7–9*

Landlords *Chris & Debbie Lloyd*
Brewery *Greene King*
🍺 *Greene King IPA, Abbot Ale; Guinness;
Harp; Kronenbourg.* 🍷 ☻

A small, highly atmospheric pub in a picturesque street near the city centre. Rowing photographs deck the bars, where out ahead among the snacks are delicious cold pies with fillings such as game, ham with mustard, or duck, walnut and orange. They also do good home-made soups and a few hot dishes, but most customers are happy to row in with those pies.
Typical dishes Turkey & cranberry pie with salad £3.70 Bacon with peach curry sauce £3

CANTERBURY *Falstaff Hotel*

St Dunstan's Street CT2 8AF `B&B`
Area Map 5 D2 *Kent*
Canterbury (0227) 462138
Parking *ample*

Landlord *Mr M.E. Nation*
Owner *Lansbury Hotels*
🍺 *Flowers Original; Fremlins Bitter;
Guinness; Stella Artois; Heineken.* 🍷

Accommodation *25 bedrooms* **£A G1**
Check-in all day

Dating back to 1403 in parts, this attractive tile-hung pub with its own flagstoned courtyard stands by the city's old West Gate. Inside, ancient beams and brickwork blend happily with modern furnishings in public areas like the snug lounge and softly lit bar. Cosy, oak-furnished bedrooms (including some with four-posters) offer TVs, telephones, hairdryers and trouser presses; all but one has a bath or shower en suite. Children welcome overnight. *No dogs.*

Credit Access, Amex, Diners, Visa

CAREY *Cottage of Content*

Hereford HR2 6NG `B&B`
Map 7 A2 *Hereford & Worcs*
Carey (043 270) 242
Parking *ample*

Landlord *Mike Wainford*
Free house
🍺 *Hook Norton Best Bitter, Old Hookey;
Worthington Best Bitter; Marston
Pedigree; Carlsberg Hof; Tennent's Pilsner.*

Accommodation *3 bedrooms* **£D G3**
Check-in by arrangement

Enjoying a tranquil rural setting beside a hump-backed bridge over a tributary of the river Wye is a delightful 500-year-old pub which is indeed aptly named. Staff are friendly and welcoming in the tiny beamed bars, where open fires and ancient settles add to the old-world charm. Upstairs, thick walls, beams and sloping floors are complemented by sturdy oak furnishings in the three cottage bedrooms. All have simple carpeted bathrooms, tea-makers and TVs. Children welcome overnight.

Credit Visa

CARTHORPE *Fox & Hounds*

Nr Bedale DL8 2LG `FOOD`
Area Map 2 F2 *North Yorks*
Thirsk (0845) 567433
Parking *ample*

Bar food *12–2 & 7–10 (Sun till 9.30)*
Closed *Mon*

Landlords *Bernadette & Howard
Fitzgerald*
Free house
🍺 *Cameron Traditional Bitter, Strongarm;
Younger's Scotch; Guinness; Hansa,
Export.* ☻

Part of this pub was once the village blacksmith's, serving the A1, and it still makes an ideal stop – nowadays, though, for its excellent food. All dishes are thoughtfully prepared by Howard Fitzgerald and his daughter. Start with broccoli and apple soup with toasted almonds or game terrine, and follow this with a packed seafood pancake, pork fillet with apple stuffing or chicken breast stuffed with Coverdale cheese.
Typical dishes Smoked salmon pâté £2.95 Lemon sole fillet £5.95

CARTMEL FELL **Masons Arms**

Head for Cartmel Fell and get directions, for it would be a great shame not to find this lovely, remote whitewashed pub set in the most glorious countryside. The views are marvellous, and in the beamy bars some 150 different beers provide ample elbow exercise. The blackboard menu is not quite so long but still offers a very wide variety: houmus with pitta bread and salad, chicken burritos, French-style fish soup and cider-braised pork chops are just a few examples of the excellent fare, all home-made from good fresh ingredients. Vegetarian dishes, marked up in a different colour, could include courgette and tagliatelle bake, fennel crumble and mushroom moussaka. Sandwiches and ploughman's platters make quick snacks and among the puddings are oat and apple crumble, rum and raisin cheesecake and lemon meringue pie.

Strawberry Bank, Nr Grange-over-Sands
FOOD
LA11 6NW
Area Map 1 E4 *Cumbria*
Crosthwaite (044 88) 486
Parking *ample*

Bar food *12–2 & 6–8.45 (Sun from 7)* ☺

Landlady *Mrs Helen Stevenson*
Free house
🍺 *Younger's No 3; Thwaites Bitter; guest beer; Murphy Stout; Furstenberg.* ☺

Typical dishes Spare ribs £3.60 Pork chops in cider £4.25 Blue cheese & cauliflower lasagne £3.60 Steak pie £4.40

Prices given are as at the time of our research and thus may change.

CASTERTON **Pheasant Inn**

Nr Kirkby Lonsdale
B&B
LA6 2RX
Area Map 1 F5 *Cumbria*
Kirkby Lonsdale (0468) 71230
Parking *ample*

Landlord *Mr D. Hesmondhalgh*
Free house ☺
🍺 *Tetley Bitter; Younger's Scotch; Löwenbräu; Castlemaine XXXX.* 🍷

Accommodation *10 bedrooms* £B G1
Check-in all day

Fronted by a little patio pleasant for summer drinks, this neat pebbledash pub in the centre of the village provides comfortable overnight accommodation. Antique furnishings (including one four-poster) grace a number of the bedrooms, while the remainder have white fitted units. TVs and tea-makers are standard, and all offer smart modern bathrooms. There is a comfortable residents' lounge and a mock-beamed bar with copper-topped tables and red plush seating.

Credit Access, Visa

We welcome bona fide recommendations or complaints on the tear-out pages at the back of the book for readers' comments.

They are followed up by our professional team, but do complain to the management on the spot.

CASTLE COMBE
Castle Hotel

Nr Chippenham SN14 7HN
Area Map 4 A5 *Wiltshire*
Castle Combe (0249)
782461
Parking *limited*

Bar food *12–2.15 & 7–9.45*

Landlords *Mr & Mrs S. J. Baker-Joy*
Free house
🍺 *Wadworth 6X, Old Timer; Charrington IPA; Eldridge Pope Royal Oak; Tennent's Extra; Kronenbourg 1664.* ⊖

In a picturesque, unspoilt Wiltshire village centre, with architectural heavyweights like the 14th-century cross and the church muscling for attention, the Castle Hotel nevertheless holds its own. Both pre-prandial drinks and meals can be had in the brick-lined cellars. The food is good when chef Ivan Reid is there, but only average when he isn't. Beyond the starters – Stilton and avocado soup, smoked haunch of venison with apricot chutney or cured salmon with salad – main dishes might be John Dory in lemon sauce or grilled red mullet. More common fare is offered in steak and kidney pie or black pudding.

Typical dishes Poached sole with crab sauce £4.45 Chicken breast with watercress sauce £6.10

Accommodation *11 bedrooms* **£A G1**
Check-in all day

Eleven bedrooms are neat, clean and all en suite. Creaking, sloping floors and corridors add atmosphere as do some decent-quality pieces of period furniture. Front bedrooms are biggest but attic rooms compete with 15th-century beams. Rather pricey. Children welcome overnight.

Credit Access, Amex, Visa

CASTLETON
Castle Hotel

Castle Street S30 2WG
Map 4 D4 *Derbyshire*
Hope Valley (0433) 20578
Parking *ample*

Landlord *Jose Luis Rodriguez*
Brewery *Bass North* ⧖
🍺 *Stones Bitter; Carling Black Label; Tennent's Pilsner.*

Accommodation *10 bedrooms* **£B G1**
Check-in all day

Accommodation is a strong point at this pleasant old inn dating back to the 17th century in parts. Comfortable bedrooms in the main house and stable block annexe are all prettily decorated, with solid darkwood furnishings, including three four-posters, and smartly tiled en suite facilities (two have whirlpool baths). Despite modernisation, the bars still offer plenty of old-world atmosphere – notably the Castle Bar with its flagstoned floors and low-beamed ceiling. Garden with play area.

Credit Access, Amex, Diners, Visa

CASTLETON
Ye Olde Nag's Head

Cross Street S30 2WH
Map 4 D4 *Derbyshire*
Hope Valley (0433) 20248
Parking *ample*

Bar food *12–2.30 & 7–10.30*

Landlords *Mr & Mrs G. Walker*
Free house
🍺 *Stones Bitter; Bass, Mild; Guinness; Carling Black Label.* 🍷 ⊖

Built of severe grey Derbyshire stone this 17th-century coaching house stands in the tiny Castleton village at the head of Hope Valley, under the hilltop site of historic Peveril Castle. In the warm, welcoming bar the emphasis on food is really lunchtime only, and an elegant two-tiered restaurant does the main evening business. Lunchtime brings a daily roast, traditional steak and kidney pie and fish dishes fried, grilled or poached. Soup and half a sandwich is a novel idea for a quick but satisfying snack.

Typical dishes Soup and sandwich platter £1.60 Poached cod £3.95

Accommodation *8 bedrooms* **£B G1**
Check-in all day

Accommodation comprises eight elegantly appointed and beautifully kept rooms in period style, three with four-posters and all with a good array of accessories, including direct-dial telephones, TVs, trouser presses and hairdryers. Top-of-the-range rooms boast spa baths, while some others have shower/wc only. On the first floor there is a bright and restful residents' lounge done out in a mixture of bamboo-style and chintz. Children welcome overnight. *No dogs.*

Credit Access, Amex, Diners, Visa

CASTLETON   *Moorlands Hotel*

Nr Whitby YO21 2DB   B&B
Area Map 3 C1 *North Yorks*
Castleton (0287) 60206
Parking *ample*

Landlords *Mr & Mrs Taylor &*
Mr & Mrs Forth
Free house
🍺 *John Smith's Magnet; Tetley Bitter;*
Guinness; Foster's. 🍺

Accommodation *10 bedrooms* **£C G2**
Check-in all day

With Baysdale Beck just east and Esk Dale minutes west Castleton can claim a rugged Moors pedigree, and the Moorlands has bedrooms views to prove it. It is a small, family-run hotel at the head of the village with a homely lounge, small TV room and a bar. Upstairs, modest but comfortable accommodation is simply decorated with pretty floral fabrics. Six bedrooms have their own rather compact shower rooms, while four others share two well-kept bathrooms. Children welcome overnight. *No dogs.*

---

*Our inspectors never book in the name of
Egon Ronay's Guides.*

*They disclose their identity only if they are
considering an establishment for inclusion
in the next edition of the Guide.*

CAULDON   NEW ENTRY   *Yew Tree*

Cauldon Lane ST10 3EJ   A
MAP 7 B1 *Staffordshire*
Waterhouses (0538) 308348
Parking *ample*

Landlord *Alan East*
Free house 🍺
🍺 *Bass; Mitchells & Butlers Mild; Burton*
Bridge Bitter.

Landlord Alan East's vast collection of antiques and bric-a-brac fills this celebrated pub nestling in the shadow of a yew tree near the A523. Persian rugs line the quarry-tiled floors, there are cast-iron copper-topped tables, a working pianola and giant Victorian music boxes which still operate for 2p. In summer, a restored 1928 charabanc plies a regular Sunday trade between the pub and nearby bus and rail stations. Garden and children's play area.

CAVENDISH   *Bull*

High Street CO10 8AX
Map 8 E2 *Suffolk*
FOOD
B&B
Glemsford (0787) 280245
Parking *ample*

Bar food *12–1.45 & 6–8.30*
No bar food *Sun–Wed*

Landlords *Lorna & Mike Sansome*
Brewery *Adnams*
🍺 *Adnams Old (Oct–Apr), Bitter; Carling Black Label.* 🍷 ⊖

Accommodation *3 bedrooms* **£D G3**
Check-in by arrangement

A homely, 500-year-old village pub run with great style by Lorna and Mike Sansome. Exposed wall timbers, beams, heavy settles and dogs lolling on the floor create a cosy, mellowed atmosphere in which to tuck into the simple food and quaff the carefully kept beer. The menu is very small, offering traditional English home cooking at its best, plus the usual sandwiches and ploughman's. The excellent puddings include the likes of apple crumble, bread and butter pudding and trifle.

Typical dishes Steak & kidney pie £3
Lasagne £2.80

Upstairs there are three decent-sized, cottagy bedrooms which share one neat bathroom and one shower room between them. With their characterful beams they need only their simple whitewood furniture and white walls to make them light, homely and charming. Morning tea is brought up to the rooms and residents can watch TV in the pleasing ground floor lounge. Garden and patio. Children welcome overnight.

We publish annually so make sure you use the current edition.

CAXTON   NEW ENTRY   *Caxton Gibbet Inn*

Nr Cambridge CB3 8PE
B&B
Map 10 D1 *Cambridgeshire*
Caxton (095 44) 8855
Parking *ample*

Landlady *Iris Stewart*
Free house ⌂
🍺 *Adnams Bitter; Webster Yorkshire Bitter; Flowers Original; Guinness; Carlsberg Pilsner; Hof.*
Accommodation *4 bedrooms* **£C G1**
Check-in all day

The old gibbet, or gallows, stands a few yards from the newly built roadside inn, and provides a chill reminder of less civilised times. The inn, though, is warm and welcoming, and for overnight guests there are four handsome, comfortable bedrooms, two with balconies, one with a fourposter. Two have en suite bathrooms, the others shower cubicles. Remote-control TVs and hairdryers are provided, and double glazing cuts out noise from the busy A14 and A45.

Credit Access, Diners, Visa

CERNE ABBAS   *New Inn*

14 Long Street DT2 7JF
B&B
Area Map 7 B5 *Dorset*
Cerne Abbas (030 03) 274
Parking *ample*

Landlord *Paul David Edmunds*
Brewery *Eldridge Pope* ⌂
🍺 *Eldridge Pope Dorchester Bitter, Royal Oak, Dorset Original IPA; Guinness; Faust Pilsner; Labatt's.* 🍷

Accommodation *5 bedrooms* **£D G3**
Check-in by arrangement

'New' refers to 16th-century modernisations to an 11th-century structure – a redbrick arch and steep slate roof – so no nasty architectural shocks here. Quite the opposite. With keen conservationist landlord Paul Edmunds already unearthing an inglenook and a priest's hole, his pub is moving back in time if anything. Five goodsized but modest bedrooms with beamed ceilings and uneven floors (TVs seem incongruous here) share two bathrooms. *No children under seven overnight. No dogs.*

Credit Access, Visa

CHADDLEWORTH   *Ibex*

RG16 0ER   **FOOD**
Area Map 4 E5 *Berkshire*
Chaddleworth (048 82) 311
Parking *ample*

Bar food *12–2 & 7–9.30*
No bar food *Sun eve*

Landlord *Colin Brown*
Brewery *Courage*
🍷 *Courage Best Bitter, Directors, Simonds;
Guinness; Foster's; Hofmeister.* ⧙ ⊖

Landlord Colin Brown was a professional jockey and that, coupled with the pub's proximity to racing stables, ensures plenty of horsy talk in the bar – not to mention a television for watching the racing. Restaurant and bar offer the same menu of straightforward fare such as soup, pâté and prawn cocktail for starters, gammon, steak and scampi for a main course and sturdy English puddings to finish. Garden, patio.
Typical dishes Steak & kidney pie £4.15
Lemon sole £6.95

Credit Visa

CHALE   *Clarendon Hotel*

PO38 2HA   **B&B**
Map 7 C4 *Isle of Wight*
Isle of Wight (0983) 730431
Parking *ample*

Landlords *John & Jean Bradshaw*
Free house ⛄
🍷 *Burt's VPA; Strong Country Bitter;
Gales HSB; Marston Pedigree; Murphy
Stout; Heineken.*

Accommodation *13 bedrooms* **£C G2**
Check-in all day

Named after a sailing ship wrecked at nearby Blackgang Chine in 1836, the Clarendon (a 17th-century coaching inn) is a restful and homely place for the whole family to stay. Individually decorated bedrooms with attractive floral fabrics and period furnishings all offer TVs, tea-makers and toiletries, while over half have bunk beds and/or cots. Both the residents' bar and sun lounge enjoy lovely views towards Freshwater Bay and the Needles.

CHALE   NEW ENTRY   *Wight Mouse Inn*

PO38 2HA   **FOOD**
Map 7 C4 *Isle of Wight*
Isle of Wight (0983) 730431
Parking *ample*

Bar food *12–10 pm (Sun 12–2.30 &
7–9.30)* ⛄

Landlords *John & Jean Bradshaw*
Free house
🍷 *Burt's VPA; Strong Country Bitter;
Gales HSB; Marston Pedigree; Murphy
Stout; Heineken.* ⊖

Adjoining the Clarendon Hotel is an atmospheric pub run in friendly, welcoming fashion by John ('Brad') and Jean Bradshaw. Children are positively encouraged here, with a choice of two family rooms, plenty of outdoor seating and a play area in the terraced garden. Jean's home-made pizzas and burgers will keep them further content, while mum and dad tuck into delicious fresh seafood, generously garnished steaks, salads and sandwiches.
Typical dishes Wiener schnitzel £3.75
Gravadlax £4.50

CHAPEL AMBLE   NEW ENTRY   *Maltster's Arms*

Nr Wadebridge PL27 6EU   **FOOD**
Map 9 B2 *Cornwall*
Wadebridge (020 881) 2473
Parking *limited*

Bar food *12–2 & 6–10 (Sun from 7)*

Landlords *Vivienne & Jeffrey Pollard*
Free house
🍷 *St Austell Tinners Ale, Hicks Special;
Courage Directors; Guinness; Stella Artois;
Carlsberg.* ⧙ ⊖

The Pollards are rapidly acquiring a reputation for excellent food at their unpretentious old Cornish pub in a hamlet north of Wadebridge. Follow duck's eggs on spinach or scallop chowder with chicken breast in a saffron and lemon sauce, garlic-baked monkfish or pork Marsala. Filled baguettes, ploughman's and a traditional roast available at lunchtimes; good sweets and cheeses to finish. Patio.
Typical dishes Tortellini with ricotta and parma ham £3.80 Toad-in-the-hole £2.65

Credit Access, Visa

CHARLTON NEW ENTRY *Horse & Groom*

Nr Malmesbury SN16 9DL `FOOD`
Area Map 4 B4 *Wiltshire*
Malmesbury (0666) 823904
Parking *ample*

Bar food *12–2 & 7.30–9.45 (Fri till 10)*
Closed *Sun eve & all Mon*

Landlord *Richard Hay*
Free house
🍺 *Mole's Cask Bitter; Wadworth 6X; Archers Village Bitter; Guinness; Tuborg Gold.* 🍷 ⊖

Picture the archetypal Cotswold stone pub and you might well be looking at the Horse and Groom, a really happy village pub where everyone seems to care. Sitting at antique furniture and warmed by log fires, visitors can tuck into excellent bar dishes like farmhouse pâté, grilled trout, burgundy beef kebabs and treacle tart. There is a similar evening restaurant menu. **Typical dishes** Cream of mushroom soup £1.35 Chargrilled chicken with lemon and thyme sauce £6.15

Credit Access, Visa

CHATTON NEW ENTRY *Percy Arms*

Nr Alnwick NE66 5PS `B&B`
Map 2 D5 *Northumberland*
Alnwick (066 85) 244
Parking *ample*

Landlords *Ken & Pam Topham*
Free house
🍺 *Newcastle Exhibition, 80/-; Younger's Scotch; Guinness; Carlsberg Hof.*

Accommodation *5 bedrooms* £D G3
Check-in all day

An angler's paradise – fishing with ghillie service on the Rivers Till and Tweed is on offer at this quiet, family-run pub, which dates from 1780. Modernisation has taken place inside, but the L-shaped bar area does not lack atmosphere. A wide Georgian staircase leads to the bedrooms, all of which have washbasins and share two public bathrooms (there are plans to make two of the rooms en suite). There is an indoor play area for children. *No dogs.*

CHEDWORTH *Seven Tuns*

Nr Cheltenham GL54 4AE `A`
Area Map 4 B2 *Gloucs*
Fossebridge (028 572) 242
Parking *ample*

Closed *Mon lunch in winter*

Landlords *Mr & Mrs B. Eacott*
Brewery *Courage* ⋈
🍺 *Courage Directors, Best Bitter; Beamish Stout; Hofmeister; Foster's.*

A delightful old village pub set among winding country lanes, its history as an alehouse dating back to 1610. The cottagy lounge bar with its high-backed wooden settles, log fire and hunting prints retains much period charm, and there is a simpler public bar (and family room) with a small games room attached. Across the road is the pretty walled beer garden – complete with miniature waterfall and old water wheel created from the village pond.

CHELSWORTH *Peacock Inn*

Nr Hadleigh IP7 7HU `B&B`
Map 8 E2 *Suffolk*
Bildeston (0449) 740758
Parking *ample*

Landlords *Tony Marsh & Lorna Bulgin*
Free house
🍺 *Greene King IPA, Abbot Ale; Mauldon's Bitter; Adnams Bitter; Guinness; Carlsberg.* 🍷

Accommodation *5 bedrooms* £C G2
Check-in all day

If it weren't for the hanging sign and legend over the door, the Peacock could pass for a pretty village cottage and abutting sweet-shop. Not that goings-on inside this oak-timbered, inglenooked inn are any less salubrious. Throughout everything is immaculate. Pictures adorn the walls, from country views to aeroplanes and drawings of Marilyn Monroe. Friday nights are jazz nights. Spotless cottage bedrooms have washbasins and TVs and share a beamed bathroom. Garden. *No children overnight. No dogs.*

CHENIES — Bedford Arms Thistle Hotel

Nr Rickmansworth WB3 6EQ FOOD
Map 10 C2 *Buckinghamshire* B&B
Chorleywood (092 78) 3301
Parking *ample*

Bar food *12–2.30* & *7–10* 😠

Landlord *Raymond Slade*
Owner *Thistle Hotels*
🍺 *Younger's No. 3, Scotch, IPA;*
McEwan's Export; Beck's Bier.

A pleasant old red-brick pub with seating at the front and a large garden sporting umbrella-topped picnic tables and an ornamental pool. Eat here or in the smartly rustic bars, choosing from an extensive snack menu that lists over 30 different varieties of sandwich (try ham with Gruyère, onion and French mustard or hot salt beef on rye with dill pickle and potato salad) as well as enjoyable daily specialities like tender, flavoursome braised oxtail, moules marinière and boiled brisket of beef with dumplings and pease pudding. Salads, jacket potatoes and traditional favourites such as chilli and cottage pie are also available, plus simple sweets.

Typical dishes Grilled kippers £3.20 Mortadella sandwich £1.90

Accommodation *10 bedrooms* £A G1
Check-in by arrangement

Comfortable, spacious bedrooms have been freshly decorated with Regency striped wallpapers, heavy curtains and new carpets running through to splendidly fitted en suite bathrooms. An exemplary range of accessories includes bathrobes, hairdryers, trouser presses, fresh fruit and even in-house movies. There is a cosy little lounge with comfortable winged armchairs.

Credit Access, Amex, Diners, Visa

CHESTER — Ye Olde King's Head

48 Lower Bridge Street B&B
CH1 1RS
Map 3 B4 *Cheshire*
Chester (0244) 324855
Parking *ample*

Landlord *Mr R. M. Defreitas*
Brewery *Greenall's* 😠
🍺 *Greenall's Original Bitter; Davenports Bitter; Guinness; Grünhalle; Labatt's.*

Accommodation *8 bedrooms* £B G1
Check-in all day

A typical example of one of the old black-and-white timbered buildings, with overhanging upper floors, for which Chester is famous. The pub was built by at least 1520 as a private home, and the splendid bedrooms combine the modern comforts of TVs, direct-dial telephones and tea-makers with a wealth of old beams and timbers. Pretty wallpapers and solid furnishings add to the appeal, and all have smartly tiled private facilities. *No dogs.*

Credit Access, Amex, Diners, Visa

CHICHESTER — Nags

3 St Pancras PO19 1FJ B&B
Area Map 6 A4 *West Sussex*
Chichester (0243) 785823
Parking *limited*

Landlord *John Speleers*
Brewery *Whitbread*
🍺 *Strong Country Bitter; Flowers Original; Whitbread Best Bitter; Heineken; Stella Artois.*

Accommodation *11 bedrooms* £C G3
Check-in by arrangement

Accommodation here is neat and fairly modest, arranged on two floors off wide, light corridors furnished with some sturdy stripped-pine chests. One bedroom has a full en suite bathroom, three others have showers and toilets, two have showers only and the rest share roomy public facilities. The lively bar has a stock of sporting reference books, which could come in handy for settling bar wagers. Garden and patio. Accommodation closed two weeks Christmas. *No dogs.*

Credit Access, Amex, Diners, Visa

CHIDDINGFOLD   Crown Inn

The Green GU8 4TX   `B&B`
Area Map 6 B2 *Surrey*
Wormley (042 879) 2255
Parking *ample*

Landlord *Mr Riley*
Owner *Harmony Leisure*
🍺 *Courage Best Bitter; Flowers Best Bitter; Whitbread Pompey Royal; Heineken; Stella Artois.*

Accommodation *8 bedrooms* **£A G1**
Check-in all day

The Crown stands on the village green opposite the church, and is a medieval timber-framed inn built as a guest house for pilgrims and Cistercian monks in 1258. Several bars retain this character, and the bedrooms divide equally between the old (exposed timbers, sloping floors, four-posters) and the modern (floral patterns and wooden units). All have smart en suite bathrooms, TVs; direct-dial phones, tea-makers, hairdryers and trouser presses. Children welcome overnight.

Credit Access, Amex, Diners, Visa

CHIDDINGFOLD   Swan

Petworth Road GU8 4TY   `FOOD`
Area Map 6 F4 *Surrey*
Wormley (042 879) 2073
Parking *ample*

Bar food *12–2.30 & 6.30–10.30, Sun 7–9.30*

Landlords *Jackie & Neil Bradford*
Brewery *Friary Meux*
🍺 *Friary Meux Bitter; King & Barnes Sussex Bitter; Tetley Bitter; Gales HSB; Skol; Castlemaine XXXX.* 🍷

Neil Bradford continues to cook good food in this pretty tile-hung pub. There is a little beamed restaurant but dishes from its menu can be eaten in the bar. The bar offers soup, pâté, omelettes and sandwiches. The restaurant menu includes whitebait and home-cured smoked sirloin and fish dishes. The choice widens with a daily changing blackboard menu. Traditional Sunday roast.
Typical dishes Steak & kidney pie £3.40
Lasagne £3.10

CHIDDINGLY   NEW ENTRY   Six Bells

BN8 6HE   `A`
Map 8 E4 *East Sussex*
Uckfield (0825) 872227
Parking *ample*

Landlord *Paul Newman*
Free house
🍺 *Courage Best Bitter, Directors; Harvey Best Bitter; Guinness.*

Behind the unassuming facade of this red-brick village pub lies a warm and welcoming establishment with a very individual character. Part of the well-worn and elaborately carved counter in the beamed main bar once did service as a makeshift bridge, while a second, smaller bar boasts a huge inglenook and an old pianola in working condition. Note, too, the collection of advertising signs that start on the outside garden wall and end in the gents' loo! Patio.

CHIEVELEY   Blue Boar Inn

North Heath, Newbury   `B&B`
RG16 8UA
Area Map 4 F5 *Berkshire*
Newbury (0635) 248236
Parking *ample*

Landlord *Mr N.J. Morton*
Free house
🍺 *Arkell BBB; Morland Best Bitter; Wadworth 6X; Guinness; Kronenbourg 1664; Carlsberg.*

Accommodation *16 bedrooms* **£A G1**
Check-in all day

Overlooking the Berkshire Downs, the Blue Boar is an attractive 16th-century thatched inn beside the B4494 with a homely, welcoming feel in its low-beamed main bar. Purpose-built bedrooms surrounding a central courtyard can be reached by a separate entrance and include both antique-furnished four-poster and half-tester rooms as well as compact singles. All offer carpeted bathrooms, TVs, tea-makers, direct-dial telephones and radio-alarms. Garden. *No children under six overnight. No dogs.*

Credit Access, Amex, Diners, Visa

CHILGROVE   *White Horse Inn*

Nr Chichester PO18 9HX   `FOOD`
Area Map 6 A4 *West Sussex*
East Marsden (024 359) 219
Parking *ample*

Bar food *12–2 (Sun till 3)*
No bar food *eves*
Closed *Mon, 3 wks Feb & 1 wk Oct*

Landlords *Barry & Dorothea Phillips*
Free house
🍺 *Antelope Ale; Webster Yorkshire Bitter; Courage Directors; Ind Coope Bitter; Guinness; Carlsberg.* 🍷

In a lovely position beneath the Sussex Downs, this attractive old inn offers a delightful setting for the short but appealing lunchtime menu. Choose from pâté, smoked salmon sandwiches, dressed crab salad, hearty braised oxtail and wood pigeon in red wine, followed by hazelnut meringue gâteau. There is also a restaurant (lunchtime and evening) and some splendid wines – many by the glass. Sandwiches only at night in the bar. Garden and patio.
Typical dishes Coq au vin £4.95 Grilled plaice £4.95

CHILHAM   *Woolpack*

High Street CT4 8DL   `FOOD`
Area Map 5 D2 *Kent*   `B&B`
Canterbury (0227) 730208
Parking *ample*

Bar food *12–2 & 7–9.30 (Sat till 10, Sun till 9)*

Landlord *John Durcan*
Brewery *Shepherd Neame*
🍺 *Shepherd Neame Master Brew Bitter; Hurlimann Sternbrau; Guinness; Shepherd Neame Steinbock Lager.* ⊖

Accommodation *17 bedrooms* **£B G2**
Check-in all day

It is not immediately apparent from the smart cream-painted exterior that the Woolpack dates from the reign of Henry VI, but when you step through the door you will instantly be transported back 400 years by the beams and old brick fireplace. Food is served both in the bar and in the Carvery, where steaks and cooked meats are offered in the evenings and a traditional roast at Sunday lunchtime. The bar menu includes beefburgers, ploughman's and salads, as well as blackboard specials such as yellow split pea and ham soup, beef stew or lasagne. Cheesecake or apple pie for afters. Children's menu and outdoor play area.

Typical dishes Cottage pie £2.50 Prawns in granary roll £2.95

Some of the seventeen bedrooms are in the main building, some in converted outbuildings and three in a stable block across the road, and all are pleasantly furnished and decorated. One has a four-poster, and fourteen have functional private bath or shower rooms. Children welcome overnight.

Credit Access, Amex, Diners, Visa

CHILLINGTON   *Chillington Inn*

Nr Kingsbridge TQ7 2JS   `B&B`
Map 9 C3 *Devon*
Kingsbridge (0548) 580244
Parking *difficult*

Landlords *Mr & Mrs D.R. Mooney*
Free house
🍺 *Palmer Bitter; Usher Best Bitter; Worthington Best Bitter; Guinness; Stella Artois; Carlsberg.*

Accommodation *3 bedrooms* **£D G2**
Check-in all day

Delightful overnight accommodation is offered at the Mooneys' friendly 17th-century village inn. Prettily decorated and charmingly furnished using modern and antique pieces, the three centrally heated bedrooms all provide TVs and tea-makers. Both main-house rooms have well-fitted bathrooms (not en suite), while the huge courtyard bedroom has its own private facilities. Enjoy a drink in the cosy bars with their open fires and carved wooden settles. Children welcome overnight.

Credit Access, Amex, Visa

CHINNOR   NEW ENTRY   *Sir Charles Napier*

Spriggs Holly OX9 4BX   FOOD
Map 10 C2 *Oxfordshire*
Radnage (024 026) 3011
Parking *ample*

Bar food *12.30–2*
No bar food *eves & Sun lunch*
Pub closed *Sun eve & all Mon*

Landlords *Griffiths family*
Free house
🍺 *Wadworth IPA.* 🍷 😊

Food plays an important part at this pleasant country inn with a delightful restaurant, where evenings (7.30–10) and Sunday lunchtimes (12.30–3) bring choices such as warm pigeon salad or herby baked mullet followed by, say, venison with juniper berries or poached salmon. Lovely puds and an excellent English cheeseboard. Lighter weekday bar lunches might include spinach and nutmeg soup.
Typical dishes Pasta with basil £6.50 Baked cod £6.50

Credit Amex, Diners

CHIPPING NORTON   *Crown & Cushion*

High Street OX7 5AD   B&B
Area Map 4 D1 *Oxfordshire*
Chipping Norton (0608) 2533
Parking *ample*

Landlord *Jim Fraser*
Free house
🍺 *Wadworth 6X, IPA; Donnington Best Bitter; Guinness; Kronenbourg 1664; Kestrel.*

Accommodation *29 bedrooms* **£A G1**
Check-in all day

The bar of this former coaching inn is full of character, with uneven flagstones, a huge inglenook and an abundance of blackened beams. Residents can join the locals here, or repair to their own quiet lounge. Bedrooms, decorated in restful cream, are well equipped (neat bathrooms, TVs, dial-out phones, tea-makers) and most are double-glazed. Eleven new bedrooms are larger and more luxurious, and several have four-posters. Children welcome overnight.

Credit Access, Amex, Diners, Visa

CHISLEHAMPTON   *Coach & Horses*

Nr Oxford OX9 7UX   B&B
Map 10 B2 *Oxfordshire*
Oxford (0865) 890 255
Parking *ample*

Landlords *Mr & Mrs McPhillips*
Free house
🍺 *Courage Directors, Best Bitter; Flowers Best Bitter; Morland Bitter; Carlsberg; Carling Black Label.*

Accommodation *9 bedrooms* **£C G1**
Check-in all day

Though pretty much modernised over the years, the Coach and Horses still keeps some traces of its 16th-century beginnings. The bedrooms, however, are just a few years old and form two sides of a courtyard at the back of the main building. Neatly furnished and smartly kept, they offer good, practical accommodation, with TVs and direct-dial phones in all rooms. Shower rooms are the norm, but a couple have bathtubs. The inn stands on the B480 south of Oxford. Children welcome overnight.

Credit Access, Amex, Diners, Visa

CHOLSEY   NEW ENTRY   *Morning Star*

Nr Wallingford OX10 9QL   FOOD
Map 10 B3 *Oxfordshire*
Wallingford (0491) 651413
Parking *ample*

Bar food *12–2 & 6–10, Sun 7–9.30*

Landlords *Bob & Sandra Price*
Brewery *Morlands*
🍺 *Morland Best Bitter, Old Ale, Mild; Guinness; Heineken; Stella Artois.* 😊

An old Great Western engine lends its name to a sturdy red-brick pub just off the A329, and the railway theme is continued in the pictures on the walls of the bar. A printed menu includes smoked haddock in cream and cheese sauce, lasagne, steaks, salads and filled baked potatoes, and the black-board specials might be pea and ham soup, king prawns Chinese-style, grilled herring or home-made beefburgers.
Typical dishes Rabbit stew £3.95 Cheese, onion & potato pie £1.95

Credit Access, Visa

CHORLEYWOOD   *Sportsman Hotel*

Station Approach WD3 5NB   `B&B`
Map 10 C2 *Hertfordshire*
Chorleywood (092 78) 5155
Parking *ample*

Landlord *Seamus Morgan*
Owners *Toby Hotels* ☙
☙ *Bass; Charrington IPA; Worthington Best Bitter; Carling Black Label; Tennent's Extra.*

Accommodation *18 bedrooms* **£A G1**
Check-in by arrangement

The Sportsman was built on a hillside across the road from the railway station, and dates from the late 19th century. Inside, 18 comfortable bedrooms with darkwood furniture and brass light fittings all have fully-tiled bath/shower rooms and are provided with trouser presses, TVs, tea-makers and direct-dial telephones. The Garden Bar with its plant-filled conservatory overlooking the garden and children's play area makes a bright and inviting spot for a drink.

Credit Access, Amex, Diners, Visa

CHRISTOW   *Artichoke Inn*

Village Road, Nr   `FOOD`
Moretonhampstead EX6 7NF   `B&B`
Map 9 C2 *Devon*
Christow (0647) 52387
Parking *ample*

Bar food *11.30–1.30 (Sun from 12) & 7–8.45*
No bar food *Sun & Mon eves (except for residents)*

Landlords *Mike & Sue Fox*
Brewery *Heavitree* ☙
☙ *Flowers Original, IPA; Whitbread Best Bitter; guest beer; Guinness; Heineken.* ℮

Accommodation *2 bedrooms* **£D G3**
Check-in by arrangement

Very much the village local, the Artichoke is a white-painted, thatched pub with an unpretentious appeal. At one end of the bar there is a formally laid dining area, where regular favourites on a pleasing menu include fresh trout and plaice. The fish comes regularly from Seaton, and lobsters are available with notice. The simplest snack is a jumbo sausage served in a baguette with onions, while steaks and a splendidly fiery chicken curry provide more substantial meaty dishes. Vegetarians are well looked after, and there is a small selection of home-prepared sweets; cream-filled nut meringues are very good. Book for traditional Sunday lunch.

Typical dishes Seafood mornay £3.50 Pork masala £5.95

The two bedrooms are modest but perfectly acceptable, and one has beds for a family of up to five (minimum two nights for this arrangement). Fluffy duvets with floral patterns match the curtains, and the addition of an en suite shower in the end room means that both rooms now offer private facilities. Accommodation closed 3 days Christmas. Garden. *No dogs.*

CHURCH ENSTONE   *Crown Inn*

OX7 4NN   `B&B`
Area Map 4 E1 *Oxfordshire*
Enstone (060 872) 262
Parking *ample*

Landlords *P.E. Gannon & J. Rowe*
Free house
☙ *Hook Norton Best Bitter; Flowers Best Bitter; Guinness; Stella Artois; Heineken.* ♟

Accommodation *3 bedrooms* **£C G2**
Check-in by arrangement

Accommodation is a strong point at the Crown, a Cotswold stone inn standing in a quiet village a couple of miles from the A34 Stratford–Oxford road. Bedrooms – all kept in apple-pie order – have pretty fabrics and furnishings, very comfortable beds, private bathrooms, TVs and tea-makers. The handsome flagstoned bar, usually full of lively local chat, serves well-kept real ale and decent wines. *No children overnight.*

CHURCHSTOW   *Church House Inn*

Nr Kingsbridge TQ7 3QW   FOOD
Map 9 C3 *Devon*
Kingsbridge (0548) 2237
Parking *ample*

Bar food *12–1.30 & 7–9* 🍴

Landlord *Mr H. Nicholson*
Free house
🍺 *Usher Best Bitter; Webster Yorkshire Bitter; Bass; Worthington Best Bitter; Guinness; Carlsberg.* 🍷

Once a rest home for Benedictine monks, a 13th-century inn separated from the local church by the A379. The 'Friar's Carvery' is unimpressive, but the daily specials are worth sampling. These range from potato and leek soup, whitebait and egg mayonnaise to braised beef and dumplings, mixed grill, rump steak, fish pie and sweet and sour pork. Blackberry and apple pie, bread and butter pudding or ice cream for afters.
Typical dishes Grilled trout £3.75 Devilled chicken £2.85

CLANFIELD   *Clanfield Tavern*

Nr Witney OX8 2RG   B&B
Area Map 4 D3 *Oxfordshire*
Clanfield (036 781) 223
Parking *ample*

Landlords *Keith & Ann Gill*
Free house 🍴
🍺 *Hook Norton Best Bitter; Morland Bitter; Morrells Bitter; Murphy Stout; Carlsberg.*

Accommodation *8 bedrooms* **£D G2**
Check-in all day

A colourful garden fronts this charming 17th-century village pub of Cotswold stone, whose interior has all the charms of uneven flagstoned floors, low-beamed ceilings and a large open fireplace. Three rooms are attractively furnished with a mixture of traditional and modern pieces, and these share a public bathroom. Five new bedrooms are planned for 1990, all en suite with TVs. One is to be suitable for disabled guests.
Credit Visa

CLARE   *Bell Hotel*

Market Hill CO10 8NN   B&B
Map 8 E2 *Suffolk*
Clare (0787) 277741
Parking *ample*

Landlords *Brian & Gloria Miles*
Free house
🍺 *Nethergate Bitter, Old Growler; Tetley Yorkshire Bitter; Löwenbräu; Stella Artois; Castlemaine XXXX.* 🍷

Accommodation *21 bedrooms* **£A G1**
Check-in all day

Stylish overnight accommodation is provided at this half-timbered 16th-century inn right in the town centre. Traditional furnishings (including four four-posters) and a striking decor characterise the courtyard bedrooms, which all offer smart modern bathrooms and hairdryers. Two of the cottage main-house rooms have en suite facilities; the rest share two public bathrooms. Guests can soak up the atmosphere in the convivial beamed bars with their open fires and splendid carved furnishings.
Credit Access, Amex, Diners, Visa

CLAVERING   NEW ENTRY   *Cricketers*

Nr Saffron Walden   FOOD
CB11 4QT
Map 10 D1 *Essex*
Clavering (0799) 550442
Parking *ample*

Bar food *12–2 & 7–10*
(Fri & Sat till 10.30)
No bar food *Mon* 🍴

Landlords *Mr & Mrs T.K. and S. Oliver*
Free house
🍺 *Flowers Original; Wethered Bitter; Guinness; Stella Artois; Heineken.* 🍴

Well-prepared snacks are served in traditional surroundings by particularly cheerful staff. A cricketing theme runs through the bar menu, with openers (homemade soup and pâté), middle order steaks, chicken tikka and Botham burgers, late cut sandwiches, full toss salads and second innings sweets. From the nets come plaice, trout and scampi, while towards the nursery end children's dishes are served.
Typical dishes Stuffed mushrooms £2.50 Veal escalope £5.50

Credit Access, Visa

CLAYGATE NEW ENTRY *Swan*

2 Hare Lane, Nr Esher `FOOD`
KT10 9BT
Map 10 C3 *Surrey*
Esher (0372) 62582
Parking *ample*

Bar food *12–2.30 & 6.30–9.30*

Landlords *Derek Swift & Sara Harris*
Owner *Chef & Brewer*
🍺 *Ruddles Best Bitter, County; Webster Yorkshire Bitter; Guinness; Holsten Export; Foster's.* 🍷 ⊖

In summer the pub becomes the 'pavilion' for the local cricket team, as its verandah handily overlooks the village green. Inside the atmosphere is distinctly Edwardian with books and prints. The food is appetising and filling without any pretentions – home-made steak and mushroom pie, fish pie and liver and bacon are some of the hot choices, and sandwiches, quiches, cheese and salads are also on display.
Typical dishes Lasagne £2.80 Lamb stew £2.80

Credit Access, Amex, Diners, Visa

CLEARWELL *Wyndham Arms*

Nr Coleford GL16 8JT `B&B`
Map 7 A3 *Gloucestershire*
Dean (0594) 33666
Parking *ample*

Landlords *John & Rosemary Stanford*
Free house
🍺 *Flowers Best Bitter, IPA; Bass; Carlsberg.*

Accommodation *16 bedrooms* £C G1
Check-in all day

A recently built annexe containing ten delightful bedrooms has added to the attractions of this splendid village inn dating from 1340. Airy and spacious, with a pale blue and cream decor, the new rooms are extremely stylish and, like their more traditional main-house counterparts, all have fresh flowers, tea-makers, radio-alarms and TVs, plus carpeted private bathrooms. Friendly staff and high standards of housekeeping. Children welcome overnight.

Credit Access, Amex, Visa

CLIFTON HAMPDEN *Barley Mow*

Nr Abingdon OX14 3EH `B&B`
Area Map 4 F3 *Oxfordshire*
Clifton Hampden (086 730) 7847
Parking *ample*

Landlady *Margaret Welch*
Owner *Westward Hosts* ⟴
🍺 *Webster Yorkshire Bitter; Usher Best Bitter; Ruddles County; Foster's; Carlsberg.*

Accommodation *4 bedrooms* £B G1
Check-in all day

Jerome K. Jerome mentioned the 14th-century Thames-side Barley Mow in his novel *Three Men in a Boat.* Low beams, oak panelling and button-back settees contribute to exceptional comfort. Bedrooms are pretty, though smallish, with Laura Ashley furnishings. One has en suite facilities; the others share two smart bathrooms. All have toilets, TVs and telephones. Garden. Accommodation closed Christmas week. *No children overnight. No dogs.*

Credit Access, Amex, Diners, Visa

COCKLEFORD *Green Dragon Inn*

Nr Cowley GL53 9NW `FOOD`
Area Map 4 B2 *Gloucs*
Coberley (024 287) 271
Parking *ample*

Bar food *11.30–2 & 6.30–10, Sun 12–2 & 7–10*

Landlords *Sue & Barry Hinton*
Free house
🍺 *Hook Norton Best Bitter; Wadworth 6X; Butcombe Bitter; Flowers Original; Bass; Stella Artois.* ⊖

An imaginative, weekly-changing menu attracts a loyal clientele to a friendly country inn in a converted 17th-century cider mill, reached by taking the Elkstone turning off the A435. Well-kept real ales complement such delights as pork in Stilton and cider, burgundy beef and West African ground nut stew, as well as plainer offerings: steaks, ploughman's, good soups and cold meats with granary bread. Excellent desserts include pear frangipane. Patio.
Typical dishes Steak and mushroom pudding £4.25 Three bean casserole £3.25

COCKWOOD   *Anchor Inn*

Starcross, Nr Exeter   FOOD
EX6 8RA
Map 9 C2 *Devon*
Starcross (0626) 890203
Parking *limited*

Bar food *12–2 (Sun till 2.30) & 6.30–10
(Sat & Sun from 7)*

Landlord *Mr J.D. Endacott*
Brewery *Heavitree*
🍺 *Eldridge Pope Royal Oak; Flowers
Original; Bass; Murphy Stout; guest beer;
Heineken.* 🍷 ⊖

Local seafood is the big attraction at this
atmospheric village inn by a peaceful
harbour off the Exe estuary. Tuck into
brandy-enriched crab soup followed by,
say, grilled plaice, baby clams, moules
marinière or prawn and lettuce salad. There
are a few meat dishes, too, plus simple
sweets like fruit crumble and trifle. Traditional Sunday lunch in winter. Patio and
terrace.
Typical dishes Seafood salad £10.95
Steak and kidney pie £3.60

Credit Access, Visa

COCKWOOD   *Ship Inn*

Nr Exeter EX6 8PA   FOOD
Map 9 C2 *Devon*
Starcross (0626) 890373
Parking *ample*

Bar food *12–2 & 7–10, Sun 12–1.45 &
7–9.30*

Landlady *Shirley Hoyle*
Brewery *Courage*
🍺 *Courage Directors, Best Bitter; John
Smith's Bitter; Guinness; Hofmeister;
Kronenbourg.* ⊖

A traditional food pub in a pleasant har-
bourside setting. Beyond the little bar and
lounge are seats for about 30, with waitress
service and a menu that is drawn almost
exclusively from the sea. Launch into crab
or lobster bisque, and follow up with
monkfish kebab, Cornish cod or a chunky
seafood pancake. 'Snack of fruits de mer' is
an open sandwich topped with crabmeat,
prawns and mussels. Garden.
Typical dishes Cockwood bouillabaisse
£6.50 Monkfish kebab £4.25

Credit Access, Amex

COLESBOURNE   *Colesbourne Inn*

Nr Cheltenham GL53 9NP   FOOD
Area Map 4 B2 *Gloucs*   B&B
Coberley (024 287) 376
Parking *ample*

Bar food *12–2 & 6.30–10, Sun 12–2.30
& 7–10, afternoon tea 3–5*

Landlords *Eric & Mary Bird*
Brewery *Wadworth*
🍺 *Wadworth 6X, Old Timer, Farmer's
Glory, IPA; Stella Artois; Heineken.*

The sturdy, listed Colesbourne Inn was
built some 200 years ago to serve the A435,
then the new main road from Cheltenham to
Cirencester. Open fires and ornaments add
a homely touch in the panelled bars, where
stalwarts like ploughman's, filled jacket
potatoes, steaks and savoury pies (try
salmon and broccoli) are served, together
with more elaborate blackboard specials
such as beef in red wine or skewered pork
with barbecue sauce. Apple pie and fruit
crumbles round off the meal nicely, and a
traditional roast lunch is available on
Sundays.

Typical dishes Steak and kidney pie with
ale £4.25 Smoked salmon with walnut
bread £4.95

Accommodation *10 bedrooms* **£C G1**
Check-in all day

A converted stable block houses the ten
decent-sized bedrooms, each individually
furnished with a mixture of antique and
period pieces. Trouser presses and hairdryers, tea-makers, TVs and direct-dial
telephones are standard, and all offer smart
modern bath or shower rooms. Children
welcome overnight.

COLESHILL — Swan Hotel

High Street B46 3BL `B&B`
Map 7 B1 *Warwickshire*
Coleshill (0675) 64107
Parking *ample*

Landlords *Mr S. A. Narey & Miss
V. B. Wright*
Brewery *Ansells*
🍺 *Tetley Bitter, Mild; Ansells Bitter;
Guinness; Skol.*

Accommodation *32 bedrooms* **£B G1**
Check-in all day

A listed building dating from the 17th century, the Swan is more of a hotel than a pub, although it does have a couple of bars. Bedrooms are uniform in size and decor, with modern fitted units and the odd sign of wear and tear. Trouser presses, hairdryers, TVs and direct-dial telephones head a useful list of accessories, and all rooms have either their own bath (8) or their own shower (24). Children welcome overnight.

Credit Access, Amex, Diners, Visa

---

*We welcome bona fide recommendations
or complaints on the tear-out pages at the back
of the book for readers' comments.*

*They are followed up by our professional team,
but do complain to the management on the spot.*

COLLYWESTON — Cavalier Inn

Nr Stamford DE9 3PQ `B&B`
Map 7 C1 *Northamptonshire*
Duddington (078 083) 288
Parking *ample*

Landlords *Noel & Andrew Haigh*
Free house
🍺 *Greene King IPA; Ruddles Best Bitter,
County; guest beer; Guinness; Foster's.* 🍷

Accommodation *5 bedrooms* **£C G2**
Check-in all day

Previously the Slaters Arms, the pub here changed its name when the slate mine closed and the workforce moved away. The inn itself is a terrace of small 19th-century cottages. Yet a glass window let into the bar floor reveals a much earlier stone spiral stairway to a tiny cellar. Refurbishment making five en suite bedrooms more spacious with sofas and armchairs should now be complete. Accommodation closed ten days over Christmas. Children welcome overnight. *No dogs.*

Credit Access, Diners, Visa

CONGLETON — Lion & Swan Hotel

Swan Bank CW12 1JR `B&B`
Map 3 C4 *Cheshire*
Congleton (0260) 273115
Parking *ample*

Landlord *Philip Greatwich*
Brewery *Burtonwood*
🍺 *Burtonwood Bitter, Dark Mild;
Guinness; Skol; Castlemaine XXXX;
Löwenbräu.*

Accommodation *21 bedrooms* **£B G2**
Check-in all day

Doric columns and stone lions flank the doorway of an imposing timbered coaching inn in the town centre. Inside, the cosy beamed bars are well kept and comfortable, with fresh flowers decorating the split-level lounge bar and heavily carved wooden settles adding character to the cocktail bar. Neat bedrooms in the original building and new wing have good modern furnishings plus TVs, tea-makers and direct-dial telephones. All but two have tiled private facilities. Children welcome overnight.

Credit Access, Amex, Diners, Visa

CONISTON   *Yewdale Hotel*

Yewdale Road LA21 8DU   `B&B`
Area Map 1 D4 *Cumbria*
Coniston (053 94) 41280
Parking *ample*

Landlords *Ken & Barbara Barrow*
Free house
🍺 *Hartley Bitter; Castle Eden Ale; Whitbread Trophy Bitter; Guinness; Heineken.*

Accommodation *11 bedrooms* **£C G2**
Check-in all day

Occupying a prime, village-centre site, this solidly built hotel is a pleasant place to visit and stay. Sit indoors in the pretty bar with its tall brass lamps and open fire or, on fine days, outside in the small paved area. Attractive bedrooms are furnished in pinks or greens and front rooms have splendid views of the fells; all have tea and coffee facilities, easy chairs and local information folders. Children welcome overnight.

Credit Access, Visa

CORSHAM   *Methuen Arms Hotel*

2 High Street SN13 0HB   `B&B`
Map 10 A3 *Wiltshire*
Corsham (0249) 714867
Parking *ample*

Landlords *Mike, Morwenna & Mark Long*
Brewery *Gibbs Mew*
🍺 *Gibbs Mew Wiltshire, Salisbury Best, Bishop's Tipple; Bass; Kronenbourg 1664; Harp.*

Accommodation *25 bedrooms* **£B G1**
Check-in all day

A 500-year history lies behind the Georgian facade of this fine old family-run inn, seen to most dramatic effect in the heavily beamed and stone-walled Long Bar. Modernised bedrooms in the main house sport pretty floral papers and fitted furniture; there is also more luxurious accommodation in the converted coach house. TVs, telephones and tea-makers are standard, and all but one room has en suite facilities. Delightful walled garden with play area. Children welcome overnight. *No dogs.*

Credit Access, Visa

CORTON   *Dove at Corton*

Nr Warminster BA12 0SZ   `FOOD`
Area Map 7 D1 *Wiltshire*
Warminster (0985) 50378
Parking *limited*

Bar food *12–2 & 7–9.30*
Closed *Sun eve, Mon (except Bank Hols), 2 wks mid-Jan & 1 wk Oct*

Landlords *Michael & Jane Rowse*
Brewery *Usher*
🍺 *Usher Best Bitter; Webster Yorkshire Bitter; Carlsberg.* 🍷 ☺

Michael and Jane Rowse are charming hosts at their immaculately kept Victorian pub, where attendant cooing doves add to its rustic charms. Light dishes include gazpacho and smoked pork loin with Charnwood smoked Cheddar, while a more substantial daily special might be savoury beef and vegetables in rich gravy. Irresistible sweets like 'silent ecstasy', a hot chocolate pudding with vanilla ice-cream.
Typical dishes Salmon mayonnaise £5.50 Pork and apricot curry £3.50

Credit Access, Visa

COTHERSTONE   NEW ENTRY   *Fox & Hounds*

Nr Barnard Castle DL12 9PF   `FOOD`
Map 3 C2 *Co. Durham*
Teesdale (0833) 50241
Parking *ample*

Bar food *12–1.45 & 7–9.15 (Sat 6.30–9.30)*

Landlords *Patrick & Jenny Crawley*
Free house ☺
🍺 *John Smith's Bitter, Magnet Ale.*

A coal fire glows in the bar, the seats are comfortably cushioned and healthy plants deck the window sills. Here, and in the adjoining restaurant, a reasonably imaginative menu covers fresh fish from Hartlepool, chicken tarragon, lamb and game. A rich, meaty broth is served with garlic and herb bread, and sweets include a wonderful chocolate crunch pie. Oily chips let the side down on our last visit.
Typical dishes Game casserole £4.95 Prawn pancakes £6.25

Credit Access, Visa

COUSLEY WOOD   *Old Vine*

Nr Wadhurst TN5 6ER   `FOOD`
Area Map 5 A4 *East Sussex*
Wadhurst (089 288) 2271
Parking *ample*

Bar food *11.30–2.30 & 6–11,*
Sun 12–2.30 & 7–10.30
No bar food *Sun eve (winter)*

Landlords *Tony & Jenny Peel*
Brewery *Whitbread*
🍷 *Flowers Original; Fremlins Bitter;*
Guinness; Heineken. ⊖

Food takes a top billing in a popular,
centuries-old pub. The bars owe their cosy,
traditional feel to benches, farmhouse
chairs, brasses and old prints. Blackboards
display a varied if mainly predictable
choice of soups, garlic mushrooms, chicken
curry, fried plaice and the like – all decently
cooked and served in energy-giving portions. Finish with mince pies or chocolate
cheesecake.
Typical dishes Moules marinière £2.25
Peppered chicken breast in cream £3.95

Credit Access, Diners, Visa

COXWOLD   *Fauconberg Arms*

YO6 4AD   `FOOD`
Area Map 3 B3 *North Yorks*   `B&B`
Coxwold (034 76) 214
Parking *ample*

Bar food *12–1.30*
No bar food *Sun & eves* ⛨

Landlords *Dick & Tricia Goodall*
Free house
🍷 *Younger's Scotch Bitter; Theakston*
Best; Tetley Bitter; Guinness; Carlsberg
Hof. 🍷

Dick Goodall, a former Lancashire baker
and confectioner, and his wife Tricia have
spent the last 24 years running their
charming stone pub in a pretty North
Yorkshire village. The bar is bright and
sparkling clean, with stone walls and
shining bric-a-brac. In the restaurant (12–
1.30 & 7–9), which is as traditional and
stolid in both decor and food as it was 20
years ago, the best choices are the fine
smoked salmon, rack of lamb and roast
duckling. To accompany the meal there is a
decent wine list. Puddings are conventional, but the Wensleydale cheese is a good
alternative. Bar snacks encompass home-
made soup, excellent sandwiches and a hot
dish of the day.

Typical dishes Crab sandwich £1.75
Fauconberg special sandwich £1.30

Accommodation *4 bedrooms* **£C G2**
Check-in all day

Solid comfort and a cottage feel characterise the four pristine bedrooms, whose
extras include generous-sized table lamps,
boxes of tissues and magazines. They share
a well-kept carpeted public bathroom, and
one bedroom has its own shower. *No dogs.*

Changes in data sometimes occur
in establishments
after the Guide goes to press.

Prices should be taken as indications
rather than firm quotes.

CRANBORNE   Fleur-de-Lys

5 Wimborne Street
BH21 5PP
Area Map 7 E4 *Dorset*
Cranborne (072 54) 282
Parking *ample*

FOOD
B&B

Bar food *12–2 & 7–10*

Landlords *Charles & Anne Hancock*
Brewery *Hall & Woodhouse*
🍺 *Hall & Woodhouse Badger Best,
Tanglefoot, Malthouse; Worthington Dark;
Guinness; Hofbräu Export.* ⊝

The cheery bar with its inglenook fireplace,
exposed beams and decorative corn dollies
makes an appealing setting for the fairly
predictable but enjoyable pub food offered
at the Hancocks' popular village pub. Daily
blackboard specials such as chicken à la
king, venison and ham pie and a vegetarian
dish supplement the printed menu of soup,
salads, ploughman's, sandwiches, fish
dishes and steaks. Choose the brown bread
rolls with your meal, as these are home-
baked. The best aspect here is the sweet
course – Pavlovas are a speciality (the
chocolate one is to be recommended), and
there are fruit pies and cheesecakes made
on the premises as well.

Typical dishes Steak pie £3.55 Raspberry pavlova £1.40

Accommodation *7 bedrooms* **£D G2**
Check-in all day

Original beams are a feature of some of the
well-kept, simply furnished bedrooms, all
but one of which offer en suite facilities
(mostly good modern shower cabinets).
Attractive duvet covers and dried flower
arrangements add a homely touch, and
TVs are standard throughout. Garden.
Accommodation closed one week Christmas. Children welcome overnight.

Credit Access, Amex, Diners, Visa

CRAWLEY   Fox & Hounds

Nr Winchester SO21 2PR
Map 7 B4 *Hampshire*
Sparsholt (096 272) 285
Parking *limited*

FOOD
B&B

Bar food *12–2 & 7–9.30*

Landlords *Mr & Mrs Sanz-Diez*
Free house
🍺 *Gales HSB; Wadworth 6X; Guinness;
Stella Artois; Carlsberg.*

A splendid red-brick pub built, like the rest
of the attractive village, at the turn of the
century and converted to look much older
than it is with a fine timbered facade and
bow windows. Simple, honest home-made
fare is the order of the day in the cosy little
main bar, with choices ranging from cauliflower soup or pâté accompanied by freshly
prepared garlic bread to chicken Provence
served with sauté potatoes and a good
salad, stuffed plaice, seafood pancakes,
cheese and lentil loaf and ploughman's.
Treacle tart or fruit pie to finish.

Typical dishes Chilled gazpacho soup
£1.50 Chicken Provence £5.50

Accommodation *3 bedrooms* **£C G2**
Check-in all day

The pristine accommodation comprises one
large en suite double and two twin rooms
which share a bathroom. Attractively
decorated in shades of peach and apricot,
with matching bedspreads and towels, all
three are simply furnished in light wood.
Garden. Children welcome overnight. *No
dogs.*

Credit Access, Visa

CRAZIES HILL   *Horns*

Nr Wargrave RG10 8LY   `FOOD`
Map 10 C3 *Berkshire*
Wargrave (073 522) 3226
Parking *ample*

Bar food *12–2 & 7–9*
No bar food *Sun & Mon eve*

Landlords *Mr & Mrs A. Wheeler*
Brewery *Brakspear*
🍺*Brakspear PA, Special; Stella Artois.* 🍷 ☻

Far-eastern dishes make a refreshing change on the blackboard menu at the Horns, a black and white timbered country pub. Mrs Wheeler's nasi goreng (Malaysian fried rice with ham and chicken) is a popular choice and there are also spicy sausages and curries with beef and lamb. More conventional offerings like lasagne and vegetarian broccoli and aubergine au gratin ring the changes. Garden.
Typical dishes Thai fried rice £2.35 Walnut, almond and cauliflower cheese £1.95

CROSCOMBE   *Bull Terrier*

Nr Wells BA5 3QJ   `B&B`
Area Map 7 B1 *Somerset*
Shepton Mallet (0749) 3658
Parking *limited*

Closed *Mon lunch (Nov–Mar)*

Landlords *Stan & Pam Lea*
Free house ☻
🍺*Butcombe Bitter; Greene King Abbot Ale; Guinness; Faust Pilsener.* 🍷

Accommodation *3 bedrooms* £D G2
Check-in all day

Renamed the Bull Terrier in 1976, this characterful 500-year-old inn has since become a popular meeting place for owners and breeders of the dog in question. Its flagstoned bars abound in rustic charm, while the bedrooms (a double with private facilities and two singles sharing a public bathroom) are equally inviting with their pretty, co-ordinating fabrics and good free-standing furniture. Garden. Accommodation closed one week Christmas. *No children or dogs overnight.*

CROWELL   NEW ENTRY   *Catherine Wheel*

Nr Chinnor OX9 4RR   `FOOD`
Map 10 C2 *Oxfordshire*
Kingston Blount (0844) 51431
Parking *ample*

Bar food *12–2 (Sat & Sun till 2.30) & 7–9*
No bar food *Sun & Mon eves* ☻

Landlords *Stuart & Lorraine Mackay*
Brewery *Aylesbury*
🍺*ABC Bitter; Bass; Guinness; Murphy Stout; Skol; Löwenbräu.* ☻

Good eating in a quaint old pub with an attractive country atmosphere. Cooking has always been a hobby of Lorraine's, and she has turned her hand confidently to catering for the public. Crispy fried mushrooms or tuna pâté will provide a tasty snack or starter, with chicken Dijon, vegetable pie or pork kebabs for a main course. Swordfish has penetrated many recent menus, and Lorraine's comes grilled, with a shrimp sauce.
Typical dishes Jambalaya £2.95 Butterfly prawns £2.25

CROYDE   *Thatched Barn Inn*

Hobbs Hill, Nr Braunton   `B&B`
EX33 1LZ
Map 9 B1 *Devon*
Croyde (0271) 890349
Parking *ample*

Landlords *Terry Pickersgill & Eddy Barough*
Free house ☻
🍺*Courage Best Bitter, Directors; Guinness; Foster's; Kronenbourg 1664.*

Accommodation *8 bedrooms* £C G2
Check-in all day

Former uses of this attractive building dating from between the 14th and 15th centuries include a storage area used by local monks, a tea room and a restaurant. It was converted to a pub in 1978. The five bedrooms in the main building and three across the road are plain and practical. Sloping ceilings and exposed beams add charm, as they also do in the bar areas. Duvets are standard, and six rooms have TVs. Children welcome overnight.

Credit Access, Visa

CROYDON — Windsor Castle

415 Brighton Road CR2 6EJ `B&B`
Map 10 D3 *Surrey*
01-680 4559
Parking *ample*

Landlord *Stephen Hughes*
Brewery *Charrington*
🍺 *Charrington IPA; Worthington Best Bitter; Toby Bitter; Guinness; Carling Black Label.*

Accommodation *30 bedrooms* **£A G1**
Check-in all day

Its position on the A235 Brighton Road makes the Windsor Castle a convenient place to stay. The three bars have heavy patterned wallpaper and button-back velour seating, while the bedrooms are in a modern extension with a separate entrance. The choice is between double, single or twin-bedded rooms, all with beige and cream schemes, lightwood furniture providing desk/dressing table space, and modern tiled bathrooms. Children welcome overnight.

Credit Access, Amex, Diners, Visa

CUCKFIELD — King's Head

South Street RH17 5JY `FOOD` `B&B`
Area Map 6 D3 *West Sussex*
Haywards Heath (0444)
454006
Parking *limited*

Bar food *11 am–11 pm, Sun 12–3 & 7–10.30*

Landlord *Peter Tolhurst*
Free house
🍺 *King & Barnes Sussex Bitter, Festive; Harvey Best Bitter; Ruddles County; Holsten.*

A popular and unspoilt village pub which is very much the local meeting place. Banknotes of all currencies decorate one intimate, low-ceilinged bar, while the spacious, panelled public bar leading out to the beer garden offers darts and pool. Simple bar snacks including fish pie, cauliflower cheese, sandwiches and filled rolls are available, but the big attraction here is the excellent food served in the rustic beamed restaurant (12.30–2 & 7.30–10), where booking is always required. Thick slices of lovely home-made bread accompany rich, satisfying soups or a lighter terrine of goat's cheese and walnuts, while a typical main course might be a hearty dish of guineafowl in red wine sauce with stir-fried cabbage. Portions are most generous, and the service friendly and attentive.

Typical dishes Macaroni cheese £2 Chicken curry £2.50

Accommodation *9 bedrooms* **£B G2**
Check-in all day

Simply furnished, good-sized bedrooms are kept beautifully warm and all but one offer private facilities. TVs, tea-makers, direct-dial telephones and duvets are standard throughout. Garden and play area. Children welcome overnight.

Credit Access, Amex, Visa

DARRINGTON — Darrington Hotel

Great North Road, Nr `B&B`
Pontefract WF8 3BL
Map 4 D3 *West Yorkshire*
Pontefract (0977) 791458
Parking *ample*

Landlords *Mavis & Robert Kerry*
Brewery *Younger* ➳
🍺 *Younger's IPA, Scotch; Newcastle Bitter; Harp; Beck's Bier; McEwan's Lager.*

Accommodation *26 bedrooms* **£B G1**
Check-in all day

High standards of accommodation make this substantial 1930s pub alongside the A1 a popular stopover. Most bedrooms have smart dark wood furniture as well as pretty fabrics and wallpaper, while all offer neat modern private facilities, hairdryers, trouser presses, TVs and tea-makers. Downstairs, drinks can be enjoyed in the comfortably relaxing atmosphere of Tod's Bar or in the peaceful little cocktail bar. A sauna and solarium are available for residents' use. Patio. *No dogs.*

Credit Access, Amex, Diners, Visa

DARTINGTON   Cott Inn

Nr Totnes TQ9 6HE   `FOOD`
Map 9 C2 *Devon*   `B&B`
Totnes (0803) 863777
Parking *ample*

Bar food *12–2 & 6.30–9.30 (Sun from 7)*

Landlords *Stephen & Gillian Culverhouse*
Free house
🍺 *Bass; Plympton 'Cott' Bitter; Ansells Bitter; Guinness; Carlsberg Hof.* 🍷 ⊖

Two major claims to fame are the 150-foot thatched roof and a licence that dates from 1320. Mrs Yeadon has handed the reins to her daughter and son-in-law, who are keeping up the inn's excellent reputation. The lunchtime buffet, supplemented by sandwiches and ploughman's platters, remains a very popular feature, offering roasts, sauced meat dishes, game pie, fresh fish and salads. It is a tempting selection, and the temptation continues with home-made sweets like raspberry Pavlova, lemon meringue gâteau or a Dutch apple tart that comes loaded with clotted cream. Steaks feature on the evening blackboard menu and more elaborate fare can be sampled in the dining room.

Typical dishes Spinach & salmon roulade £2.95 Turkey escalope with cranberries £3.95

Accommodation *5 bedrooms* **£C G2**
Check-in all day

Improvements have been made in the cottage-style bedrooms; there are five rooms, two with en suite facilities and three sharing a bathroom. Sound insulation is not advanced, so the rooms can be a bit noisy while the bar is in action. *No children under ten overnight. No dogs.*

Credit Visa

DARTMOUTH   Cherub Inn

13 Higher Street TQ6 9RB   `FOOD`
Map 9 C2 *Devon*
Dartmouth (080 43) 2571
Parking *difficult*

Bar food *12–2 & 7–10*

Landlords *Craig Carew-Wootton, Sally Carew-Comyns & Bob Bennet*
Free house
🍺 *Blackawton Bitter; Flowers IPA, Original; Bass; Heineken; Stella Artois.* 🍷 ⊖

Dating from 1380, this back-street pub near the quay is the oldest building in Dartmouth. A timber-framed frontage leads to a small bar with exposed beams and low ceilings. Fish features strongly on the menu, from smoked salmon mousse to fresh scallops, grilled shark and John Dory. Other dishes might be celery hearts with ham, lasagne or cauliflower cheese. Conclude with brandy and orange syllabub.
Typical dishes Cherub smokie £2.50 Seafood pasta £4.20

Credit Access, Visa

DARTMOUTH   Royal Castle Hotel

The Quay TQ6 9PS   `B&B`
Map 9 C3 *Devon*
Dartmouth (080 43) 4004
Parking *limited*

Landlords *Mr & Mrs Nigel Way*
Free house
🍺 *Courage Best Bitter; Bass; Marston Pedigree; Stella Artois; Carling Black Label; Heineken.* 🍷

Accommodation *23 bedrooms* **£C G1**
Check-in all day

Handsome Regency windows, overlooking the quay, conceal the Tudor heart of this finely restored hostelry. The Harbour bar, popular with locals, has a pub feel, while the Galleon bar is more spacious, beamed and sports a weaponry display. Light, original bedrooms have period furnishings, four have four-posters and several enjoy river views. TVs, telephones, tea-makers and modern bath or shower rooms. Children welcome overnight.

Credit Access, Visa

DEDHAM   *Marlborough Head*

Mill Lane CO7 6DH
Map 8 E2 *Essex*
Colchester (0206) 323124
Parking *limited*

Bar food *12–2 & 7–9.30*

Landlords *Brian & Jackie Wills*
Brewery *Ind Coope*
🍺 *Adnams Bitter; Benskins Best Bitter;
John Bull Bitter; guest beer; Guinness;
Löwenbräu.* ✆

Set in glorious Constable country, this delightfully unspoilt 15th-century pub offers an extensive choice of honestly prepared, daily-changing snacks in its heavily beamed bars. Traditionalists will plump for favourite ploughman's, quiche, steaks and jacket potatoes, while for the more adventurous there are such treats as Aga-roasted bacon steak with peaches, poached monkfish with crab sauce or vegetarian ravioli in spicy tomato sauce. Leave room for dessert – perhaps chocolate pâté with praline sauce or loganberry soufflé. Roast lunch available on Sunday. Garden, patio and outdoor play area.

Typical dishes Garlic chicken in filo pastry £4.50 Minted lamb with apricots and pine kernels £4.25

Accommodation *4 bedrooms* £C G2
Check-in by arrangement

Sloping floors, beams and rough plaster walls add to the character of the four spacious, simply furnished bedrooms (two with shower only). Electric blankets help keep out the cold, and all have TVs and tea-makers. *No children overnight. No dogs.*

DERSINGHAM   *Feathers Hotel*

Manor Road PE31 6LN
Map 8 E1 *Norfolk*
Dersingham (0485) 40207
Parking *ample*

Landlords *Tony & Maxine Martin*
Brewery *Charrington*
🍺 *Adnams Bitter; Charrington IPA;
Stones Bitter; Carling Black Label;
Tennent's Extra.*

Accommodation *6 bedrooms* £C G3
Check-in all day

The Sandringham Estate and pleasant woodland walks are both within easy reach of the Martins' stone-built pub. The mellow, oak-panelled main bar overlooks a large, attractive garden complete with a children's play area and solid wooden tables for summer drinks; horse brasses decorate the cheerful public bar. The six good-sized bedrooms are furnished with modern free-standing pieces and share two bathrooms. All have TVs, tea-makers and radio-alarms. Children welcome overnight.

Credit Access, Visa

DEVIZES   *Bear Hotel*

Market Place SN10 1HS
Map 10 A3 *Wiltshire*
Devizes (0380) 2444
Parking *limited*

Bar food *12–2 (Sun till 2.30) & 7–11*

Landlords *Keith & Jackie Dickenson*
Brewery *Wadworth*
🍺 *Wadworth 6X. IPA; Guinness;
Heineken; Löwenbräu.* ✆

In the centre of town overlooking the market place, this renowned West Country coaching inn has a distinguished history stretching back over 300 years. Long-serving landlords Keith and Jackie Dickenson are welcoming hosts in the cosy, low-beamed main bar where enjoyable light snacks are served. Choose from freshly cut sandwiches, giant meat rolls and ploughman's with cheese, ham or sausages, or opt for a blackboard special such as turkey and vegetable casserole or macaroni proven-çale. Buffet lunches featuring soup, salads, cold cuts and pies are available in the Lawrence Room. Good puddings like chocolate sponge with custard or apple and mincemeat tart round things off nicely.

Typical dishes Turkey and ham pie £2.75 Coffee and walnut pudding £1.40

Accommodation *25 bedrooms* **£A G1**
Check-in all day

Refurbished bedrooms have a charming, cottage appeal with their floral fabrics and sturdy furnishings (including three fourposters). Centrally heated and provided with TVs, hairdryers and direct-dial telephones, all now offer neat en suite facilities. Children welcome overnight.

Credit Access, Diners, Visa

DEVIZES   *Moonrakers*

29 Nursteed Road SN10 3AJ   B&B
Map 10 A3 *Wiltshire*
Devizes (0380) 2909
Parking *ample*

Landlord *Mr V.W. Gafney*
Brewery *Wadworth*
🍺 *Wadworth IPA, 6X, Northgate Bitter; Heineken; Löwenbräu.* 🍷

Accommodation *5 bedrooms* **£D G2**
Check-in all day

Homely overnight accommodation is provided at this mock-Tudor inn standing less than a mile from Devizes town centre. The five simple, well-kept bedrooms share two public bathrooms and all have their own shower cabinets as well as TVs, teamakers and cosy duvets. An open fire crackles beneath a copper-hooded fireplace in the plush lounge bar, while the more modest public bar houses a pool table. Garden for summer sipping. Children welcome overnight.

DODDISCOMBSLEIGH   *Nobody Inn*

Nr Exeter EX6 7PS   FOOD B&B
Map 9 C2 *Devon*
Christow (0647) 52394
Parking *ample*

Bar food *12–2 & 7–10*

Landlords *Mr & Mrs Bolton & Mr Borst-Smith*
Free house
🍺 *Bass; Flowers IPA; Eldridge Pope Royal Oak; Guinness; Stella Artois.* 🍷 ☺

A heart-of-the-village pub which oozes character from its log-burning inglenook to some medieval glass. Walls are stained ochre from tobacco smoke, ceilings are low and beamed and the bars are full of dark, quiet corners. Outside presents a view over well-tended gardens. Inside an incredible 210 whiskies are on offer. These are admirably complemented by a fine selection of over 30 Devon cheeses, all unpasteurised and including goats' and ewes' milk varieties. The speciality here, naturally enough, is a platter of cheese slices, each one labelled and accompanied by a simple salad and bread or biscuits. This fascinating bias somewhat overshadows the rest of the bar snacks.

Typical dishes Potted shrimps £2.60 Selection of Devon cheeses £2.50

Accommodation *7 bedrooms* **£C G2/3**
Check-in all day

Upstairs there are four simply furnished and homely bedrooms. Another three are available in a Georgian manor house 150 yards away, all with en suite bathrooms. Accommodation closed second week January *No children under 14 overnight. No dogs.*

Credit Access, Visa

DORCHESTER-ON-THAMES   *George Hotel*

High Street OX9 8HH   `B&B`
Map 10 B2 *Oxfordshire*
Oxford (0865) 340404
Parking *ample*

Closed *1 wk Xmas*

Landlady *Karen Bradbury*
Free house
🍺 *Morland Bitter; Brakspear Bitter; Heineken.* 🍷

Accommodation *17 bedrooms* **£A G1**
Check-in all day

The George is reputedly one of the oldest inns in the country, and it stands opposite a medieval abbey. The bar is smart and well-kept with open fireplace, comfortable sofas and fresh flower displays. Nine good-sized bedrooms with exposed beams and period furniture are in the pub itself; the rest, in a converted stable block, are more modern in style. All rooms provide TVs, radio-alarms, tea-makers and en suite facilities. Children welcome overnight. Accommodation closed one week Christmas.

Credit Access, Amex, Diners, Visa

DORNEY   *Palmer Arms*

Village Road, Nr Windsor   `FOOD`
SL4 6QW
Map 10 C3 *Buckinghamshire*
Burnham (0628) 666612
Parking *ample*

Bar food *12–2 & 6–10 (Sun from 7)*

Landlords *Neil & Dawn Brookfield*
Owner *Regent Inns*
🍺 *Bass; Charrington IPA; Mitchells & Butlers Mild; Tennent's Extra; Guinness; Carling Black Label.* 🍷 ⊝

First-rate bar food draws a large clientele here. The regularly-changing blackboard menu offers an extensive and imaginative range of dishes; you might start with fresh herring roes simply sautéed with lemon and move on to strips of tender beef with green peppers and onions, rounding off an enjoyable meal with home-made cherry fool. Garden.
Typical dishes Chicken avocado £4.75 Mushroom & bacon in garlic £1.95

Credit Access, Visa

DOWLISH WAKE   NEW ENTRY   *New Inn*

Nr Ilminster TA19 0NZ   `FOOD`
Map 9 C1 *Somerset*
Ilminster (0460) 52413
Parking *ample*

Bar food *12–2 & 7–10, Sun 12–2.30 & 7–9*

Landlords *Thérèse Boosey & David Smith*
Free house 🍷
🍺 *Butcombe Bitter; Wadworth 6X; Theakston Old Peculier; Holsten; Carlsberg.*

At the southern end of a little village known as the headquarters of perry cider making lies a small, stone-walled pub. Inside is a hospitable bar with traditional furnishings and hop-covered beams. Swiss-born Thérèse Boosey offers excellent bar snacks and à la carte menu. Soup, sandwiches, omelettes and cheese are staple fare, along with the famous local Bellew spicy sausages, fish dishes, duck and Swiss specialities such as charbonnade and steak fondue.
Typical dishes Raclette £4.50 Fresh fruit pavlova £1.65

DOWNHAM MARKET   NEW ENTRY   *Cock Tavern*

43 Lynn Road PE38 9NP   `FOOD`
Map 8 E1 *Norfolk*
Downham Market (0366) 385 047
Parking *ample*

Bar food *12–2 & 7–9.30*
No bar food *Tues eve*

Landlords *Roger & Julie Hassell*
Owner *Brent Walker*
🍺 *John Smith's Bitter; Flowers Original; Guinness; Heineken; Stella Artois.* 🍷

A small, neatly kept pub run with notable warmth and enthusiasm. The single bar can get quite crowded, especially at lunch-time, as word of Julie Hassell's good honest cooking gets around; the menu is largely conventional, with splendid soups, cold meat platters, Cromer crabs, fresh fish from Grimsby, steak and kidney pudding and curried vegetables. Brown rice is always used, and crisp sautéed potatoes make a change from ubiquitous chips.
Typical dishes Cottage pie £2.55 Bean casserole with garlic bread £2.95

DRAGONS GREEN   George & Dragon

Nr Shipley, Horsham   **A**
RH13 7JE
Area Map 6 C3 *West Sussex*
Coolham (040 387) 320
Parking *ample*

Landlords *Mr & Mrs Barber*
Brewery *King & Barnes* 🍺
🍺 *King & Barnes Sussex Bitter, Festive,
Old Ale (winter), J.K. Lager; Holsten
Export.*

A serious spot for lovers of a good pint, best
found by following the signs from the A272.
The pub dates from the 17th century, and
the low ceiling and even lower beams add a
lot to the atmosphere and a little to the
possibility of a headache. A log fire burns in
the inglenook, and horse brasses hang from
walls and timbers. The scene shifts in
summer to a pleasant, neatly kept garden
well supplied with tables and chairs.

---

*Any person using our name to obtain
free hospitality is a fraud.*

*Proprietors, please inform Egon Ronay's Guides
and the police.*

DRAYTON   NEW ENTRY   Roebuck

Nr Banbury OX15 6EN   **FOOD**
Map 10 B1 *Oxfordshire*   **B&B**
Banbury (0295) 730542
Parking *ample*

Bar food *12–2 & 7–9.30*
No bar food *Mon & Sat eves*

Landlords *Michael & Elizabeth Brown*
Free house
🍺 *Hook Norton Best Bitter; Marston
Pedigree; Adnams Extra; Guinness;
Carling Black Label.* 🍷 ☕

Standing next to the A423 about a mile
from Banbury is an attractive 16th-century
stone pub which has built up a strong local
following for its excellent food. The low-
beamed bars with their rough, painted
walls and solid wooden tables provide a
cosily atmospheric setting for everything
from triple-decker sandwiches and flavoursome ham and prawn chowder to spicy
chicken curry, salmon and cucumber pie or
vegetarian cracked wheat and walnut casserole. Daily specials might include tender
lamb hotpot with minty dumplings and
lovely fresh vegetables, and there are
pleasant sweets like lemon meringue pie or
apple strudel to finish. Traditional Sunday
roast lunch available.

Typical dishes Chicken or pork satay
£3.85 Beef and Guinness pie £3.50

Accommodation *2 bedrooms* **£D G2/3**
Check-in all day

Two neat, well-kept bedrooms, one with
exposed beams and a sloping ceiling, have
pretty floral fabrics and up-to-date furniture. They have a functional shower room
and are both equipped with remote-control
TVs, tea-makers and magazines.
Accommodation closed one week Christmas. *No children overnight. No dogs.*

DUDDINGTON   *Royal Oak Hotel*

High Street, Nr Stamford   FOOD
PE9 3QE   B&B
Map 7 C1 *Northamptonshire*
Duddington (078 083) 267
Parking *ample*

Bar food *12–2 & 7–10.30 (Sun till 10)*

Landlords *William & Rosa Morgado*
Free house
◗ *Greene King Abbot Ale; Tetley Bitter; Ansells Bitter; Kronenbourg 1664; Skol.*

The bar is modern, but by no means without character, due in part to plush banquette seating, lots of greenery and well-lit prints of Victorian scenes. At one end of the bar a winter fire burns; at the other an area is set up for eating, with smartly laid tables and waitress service. The food is home-made and unpretentious, with popular choices including baked salmon (always a decent fish choice), lasagne, steaks and stroganoff. Soup and sandwiches cope with lighter appetites, and there is a traditional roast lunch on Sunday. A garden and patio are available for taking refreshment under the sun.

Typical dishes Lasagne verdi £3.50
Fillet steak stuffed with Stilton £8.50

Accommodation *5 bedrooms* **£C G1**
Check-in all day

Decent-sized bedrooms, attractively done out in pastel shades, have antique-style reproduction pieces, Victorian prints and very comfortable beds with brass bedsteads. TVs, phones and tea-maker alarm clocks are standard, and the bathrooms are carpeted and fully tiled. Children welcome overnight. *No dogs*.

Credit Access, Visa

DUMMER   *The Queen*

Nr Basingstoke RG22 2AD   FOOD
Map 7 C3 *Hampshire*
Dummer (025 675) 367
Parking *limited*

Bar food *12–2.30 & 6.30–10*

Landlords *John & Jocelyn Holland*
Brewery *Courage*
◗ *Courage Best Bitter, Directors; John Smith's Bitter; Kronenbourg 1664; Foster's; Hofmeister.* ▼ ⊖

If you didn't know that you were in the village where the Duchess of York grew up, a visit to the Queen would soon enlighten you! Several rooms have been opened up to make one bar area, with beams and fireplaces. Salads and sandwiches (including enormous double-deckers) are generous and imaginative, and hot dishes such as lasagne, spare ribs, lemon sole and steaks are choices on the printed menu.
Typical dishes Poussin à la Queen £5.95
Double-decker toasted sandwich £3.95

Credit Amex, Visa

DUNCHURCH   NEW ENTRY   *Dun Cow Hotel*

The Green, Nr Rugby   B&B
CV22 6NJ
Map 7 B2 *Warwickshire*
Rugby (0788) 810233
Parking *ample*

Landlords *Richard & Carole Ryan*
Free house
◗ *Mitchells & Butlers Brew XI, Mild; Bass; Guinness; Tennent's Lager; Carling Black Label.*

Accommodation *21 bedrooms* **£A G1**
Check-in all day

Standing at a crossroads in the town centre, this attractive Georgian coaching inn retains considerable period charm in its two delightful bars. Open fires warm the heavily beamed Smoke Room and cosy little oak-panelled cocktail bar, and there is an intimate lounge with wooden settles and winged armchairs. Spacious bedrooms, including six pretty cottage rooms, boast fine old furnishings (two have four-posters) as well as TVs, telephones and well-equipped bath or shower rooms.

Credit Access, Amex, Diners, Visa

DUNSFOLD   *Sun Inn*

The Common GU8 4LE   FOOD
Area Map 6 B2 *Surrey*
Dunsfold (048 649) 242
Parking *ample*

Bar food *12–2.15 (Sun till 2) & 7–10
(Sun till 9.30)*

Landlady *Mrs Dunne*
Brewery *Friary Meux*
🍺 *Friary Meux Bitter; Ind Coope Burton
Ale; Gales HSB; Guinness; Skol.* ⊖

A charming setting on the village green, a
Georgian facade and, behind it, the exposed
beams and brickwork of a 17th-century
barn give the Sun Inn plenty of appeal
before you even contemplate the blackboard menu. Soup, pâté, whitebait and
spinach roulade are typical starters, with
traditional, filling main courses to follow.
Simple desserts include cheesecake and
treacle tart. Garden.
Typical dishes Steak & kidney pie £3.50
Deep-fried brie £2.75

Credit Access, Amex, Diners, Visa

DUNWICH   *Ship Inn*

St James Street IP17 3DT   FOOD
Map 8 F2 *Suffolk*   B&B
Westleton (072 873) 219
Parking *ample*

Bar food *12–2 & 7.30–9.30* ⊃

Landlords *Stephen & Ann Marshlain*
Free house
🍺 *Adnams Bitter, Broadside, Old (winter
only); Greene King Abbot Ale;
Kronenbourg; Foster's.*

Looking out across salt marshes to the sea,
the Marshlains' simple pub has a suitably
nautical air, with a cheery wood-burning
stove in the cosy bar and locally caught fish
dominating the blackboard menu. Huge
portions of fresh fried fish and crisp chips
satisfy the heartiest of appetites while other
hot choices include soups (try curried
parsnip), lasagne or steak and kidney pie. A
cold lunchtime buffet features home-cooked
ham, quiches and smoked mackerel pâté to
enjoy with tasty salads, while ploughman's
come with prawns as well as traditional
cheese. Old-fashioned treacle tart or bread
and butter pudding for afters. Evening
meals available in the restaurant.

Typical dishes Plaice and chips £3
Cottage pie £2.25

Accommodation *4 bedrooms* £D G3
Check-in by arrangement

A fine Victorian staircase leads to the
homely bedrooms made snug with duvets
and double glazing. All have tea-makers
and washbasins and share a carpeted
bathroom and neat shower room. Separate
breakfast room available. Garden and
patio.

EAST DEREHAM   *King's Head Hotel*

Norwich Street NR19 1AD   B&B
Map 8 E1 *Norfolk*
East Dereham (0362) 693842
Parking *ample*

Landlords *Mr & Mrs R. Black*
Brewery *Norwich*
🍺 *Norwich Bitter; Ruddles Best Bitter;
Webster Yorkshire Bitter; Guinness;
Holsten Export; Carlsberg.*

Accommodation *15 bedrooms* £C G1
Check-in all day

Locals fill the bar, which looks out onto a
bowling green edged with flowerbeds and a
pretty patio which are both attractive
summer features here. The inn was built in
the 17th century, and has been modernised
to provide comfortable bedrooms in a
converted stable block as well as in the
main building. All are centrally heated and
offer TVs, tea-makers and direct-dial telephones, as well as good en suite bath/
shower rooms. Children welcome
overnight.

Credit Access, Amex, Diners, Visa

EAST DOWN   NEW ENTRY   *Pyne Arms*

Barnstaple EX11 4LX   `FOOD`
Map 9 B1 *Devon*
Shirwell (027 182) 207
Parking *ample*

Bar food *12–2 & 7–9.45 (Sun till 9.30)*

Landlords *Jurgen & Elizabeth Kempf*
Free house ☎
☛ *Flowers IPA; Whitbread Best Bitter, Trophy; Guinness; Heineken; Stella Artois.* ▮

Leave the A39 at Arlington and follow the lane that winds to this little pebbledash pub. Jurgen Kempf's lengthy menu caters equally well for lovers of seafood – grilled or smoked trout, red mullet, scampi, four ways with mussels – and for carnivores, with a wide choice of beef, chicken and veal (note the 100% pure veal and pork German sausage). There is a children's room (no under-5s) and a garden.
Typical dishes Moules marinière £3.55
Whole fresh mullet in caper sauce £3.95

EAST HADDON   *Red Lion*

Nr Northampton NN6 8BU   `B&B`
Map 7 C2 *Northamptonshire*
Northampton (0604) 770223
Parking *ample*

Landlords *Mr & Mrs Ian Kennedy*
Brewery *Charles Wells*
☛ *Wells IPA, Noggin; Guinness; Kellerbräu; Wells Red Stripe.*

Accommodation *3 bedrooms* £C G3
Check-in all day

Peaceful overnight accommodation is guaranteed here in lovely countryside a few miles from junction 18 of the M1. Cottagy, well-kept bedrooms with pretty floral wallpapers, traditional furnishings and homely additions like candlewick bedspreads and ornaments share a spotless public bathroom. Residents can also relax in the comfortable chintzy TV lounge, or enjoy a drink in the softly lit bar with its pewter mugs, guns and brassware. Children welcome overnight. *No dogs.*

Credit Access, Diners, Visa

EASTERGATE   *Wilkes Head*

Nr Chichester PO20 6UT   `FOOD`
Area Map 6 B4 *West Sussex*
Eastergate (0243) 543380
Parking *ample*

Bar food *12–2 (Sun till 1.30) & 7–9.30*

Landlords *David & Christine Morris*
Brewery *Friary Meux*
☛ *Friary Meux Bitter; Ind Coope Burton Ale; King & Barnes Sussex Bitter; Guinness; Skol; Löwenbräu.* ☻

If you are off to Goodwood or Fontwell races drop in at this friendly unspoilt pub. Christine Morris' no-nonsense, honest food is full of flavour, while husband David fills the two lived-in, homely bars full of cheer. Savour the good ground beef lasagne with garlic bread by the river in the garden or a spinach and mushroom version with flagstones underfoot. Soups, pâté and sandwiches as well, and jam roly poly if you still have room.
Typical dishes Ploughman's £1.75
Cottage pie £1.95

EASTLING   *Carpenter's Arms*

Nr Faversham ME13 0AZ   `FOOD`
Area Map 5 C2 *Kent*
Eastling (079 589) 234
Parking *ample*

Bar food *12–2.30 (Sun till 1.30) & 6.30–10.30* ☎
No bar food *Sun eve*

Landlord *M.A. O'Regan*
Brewery *Shepherd Neame*
☛ *Shepherd Neame Master Brew Bitter, Abbey Ale, Mild; Beamish Stout; Hurlimann; Steinbock.* ☻

You will have to drive carefully down the scenic narrow lanes of the Kent countryside to reach this unspoilt pub, with its low beams and inglenook fireplace. Bar food is also plain and simple, ranging from thick soups, pizzas, hamburgers and sandwiches to the specials such as beef in Guinness and cider, game in season or steak, kidney and oyster pie. Outdoor drinking in the garden in summer.
Typical dishes Fillet steak £8.50 Half-pound burger £3.50

Credit Access, Visa

ECCLESHALL   NEW ENTRY   *St George Hotel*

Castle Street ST21 6DF   `B&B`
Map 7 A1 *Staffordshire*
Eccleshall (0785) 850300
Parking *ample*

Landlords *Anton & Cheryl Hyland*
Free house
🍺 *Ind Coope Burton Ale; Tetley Bitter;
Ansells Bitter, Mild; Löwenbrau;
Castlemaine XXXX.*

Accommodation *10 bedrooms* **£A G1**
Check-in all day

The Hylands have carefully restored their
250-year-old coaching inn which enjoys a
central crossroad position in Eccleshall.
The oak-beamed bar with its opaque glass
'smoke room' panel and red-brick inglenook
is full of character, and there is also a
relaxing little lounge. Cottage-style bedrooms, many with open fires, exposed
beams with vaulted ceilings and canopied
or four-poster beds, are thoughtfully
equipped and all have private facilities.
Children welcome overnight.

Credit Access, Amex, Diners, Visa

EDBURTON   *Tottington Manor*

Nr Henfield BN5 9LJ   `FOOD`
Area Map 6 D4 *West Sussex*   `B&B`
Steyning (0903) 815757
Parking *ample*

Bar food *12–2.30 (Sun till 3) & 7–9.30* ✖

Landlords *David & Kate Miller*
🍺 *King & Barnes Sussex Bitter; Adnams
Broadside; Fullers London Pride; Bateman
XXXB; Murphy Stout; JK Lager.* ⊖

Accommodation *5 bedrooms* **£C G1**
Check-in all day

Dating from 1604, this is a peaceful and
attractive country inn where Kate and
David Miller, with their pleasant staff, work
hard to achieve high standards for both food
and accommodation. The bar is simple,
almost rustic, with a cosy fire and a gaggle of
cats and dogs. Bar food is varied and very
well cooked, whether it is spicy mulligatawny soup, chargrilled chicken in a peanut
sauce, salmon mousse or cider-baked ham.
Sandwiches come plain or toasted, and, if
you want a rich sweet, chocolate torte fits the
bill admirably. One little niggle – why UHT
cream with the coffee? There is also a more
formal restaurant.

Typical dishes Sausages with red cabbage £3.80 'Prince of Wales' Welsh rarebit
£3.40

Recently decorated bedrooms are pretty in
creams, apricots and pinks, with good
sturdy furniture. All rooms are warm,
comfortable and well appointed, and a
thoughtful range of toiletries is provided in
the neat, practical bath/shower rooms.
Residents can also relax in the lounge, a
striking half-timbered room with a massive
inglenook.

Credit Access, Amex, Diners, Visa

EFFINGHAM   *Plough*

Orestan Lane KT24 5SW   `FOOD`
Area Map 6 C1 *Surrey*
Bookham (0372) 58121
Parking *ample*

Bar food *12–2 & 6.45–9.30*
No bar food *Sun eve*

Landlords *Lynn & Derek Sutherland*
Brewery *Courage*
🍺 *Courage Best Bitter, Directors;
Guinness; Hofmeister; Foster's.* 🍷 ⊖

A friendly, family-run pub with a smartly
rustic interior and a nice line in tasty bar
food. Cheesy cod and prawn mornay,
crusty-topped chicken and leek pie and a
splendid seafood thermidor are typically
imaginative main courses, while lighter
bites include cold meat salads and lunchtime sandwiches, filled jacket potatoes
(evenings only) and such richly irresistible
sweets as 'death by chocolate' (sponge and
mousse gâteau). Garden and play area.
Typical dishes Steak and kidney pie
£3.25 Treacle tart £1

ELLISFIELD
Fox

**Green Lane, Nr
Basingstoke RG25 2QW** `FOOD`
Map 7 C3 *Hampshire*
Herriard (025 683) 210
Parking *ample*

Bar food *12–2 & 7.30–9.30*
No bar food *all Mon*

Landlords *Mr R. Bull & Mrs G. Dickinson*
Free house
🍺 *Wadworth 6X; Bunce's Best; Gales HSB;
Marston Pedigree; Hall & Woodhouse
Badger Best; Kronenbourg 1664.* 🍴 ⊖

To get to the Fox, you will have a delightful
drive through narrow country lanes, and it
is well worth the effort. Sandwiches, salads,
filled jacket potatoes and Greek dips with
pitta bread make up the standard menu,
and blackboard specials range from salmon
steak and fillet steak to spicy beef casserole,
pork and apple in cider or Neapolitan pasta.
Cooking is enjoyably honest and
unpretentious.
Typical dishes Steak and kidney casserole £4.25 Vegetarian tagliatelle £3.75

ELSTED
Three Horseshoes

Nr Midhurst SU29 0JX `FOOD`
Area Map 6 A3 *West Sussex*
Harting (073 085) 746
Parking *ample*

Bar food *10–2 (Sun till 2.15) & 6.30–9.30*

Landlords *Ann & Tony Burdfield*
Free house
🍺 *Ballard's Best Bitter; Ringwood Old
Thumper; Fullers London Pride; Bateman
Best Bitter; Brakspear Bitter; Gales
HSB.* ⊖

Bowed walls, terracotta-tiled floors,
gnarled beams and mellow stained plasterwork paint a picture of rural charm in a
welcoming pub dating from 1500. The food
is as hearty and rustic as the surroundings:
thick carrot soup with hunks of brown
bread, jacket potatoes, cauliflower cheese,
vegetable curry, treacle tart. Fish is a
speciality, particularly at weekends, delivered very fresh from Selsey – try plaice or
maybe fried clams.
Typical dishes Steak & kidney pie in
Guinness £4.50 Cheesy leek bake £2.75

ELTERWATER
Britannia Inn

Nr Ambleside LA22 9HP `B&B`
Area Map 1 D3 *Cumbria*
Langdale (096 67) 210
Parking *ample*

Landlord *David Fry*
Free house
🍺 *Hartley XB; Marston Pedigree; Jennings
Bitter; Guinness; Carling Black Label;
Tennent's Extra.*

Accommodation *10 bedrooms* £C G2
Check-in all day

Over 400 years old, this mellow Lakeland
hostelry on the pretty village green is a
favourite with locals and walkers alike. The
beamed main bar and slate-floored snug
have a welcoming, lived-in air, and there is
a chintzy lounge for residents' use. Modest
accommodation is provided by ten simply
appointed bedrooms, all of which have TVs
and tea-makers. Four offer en suite facilities
and the others share two modern bathrooms. Children welcome overnight.

Credit Access, Visa

EMPINGHAM
White Horse

2 Main Street, Nr Oakham `B&B`
L15 8PR
Map 7 C1 *Leicestershire*
Empingham (078 086) 221
Parking *ample*

Landlords *Robert, Andrew & Helen Reid*
Brewery *John Smith*
🍺 *John Smith's Bitter; Courage Directors;
Guinness; Hofmeister; Foster's;
Kronenbourg 1664.*

Accommodation *12 bedrooms* £C G2
Check-in all day

The main bar here houses the largest log
fire in Rutland, and the pub, near Rutland
Water, offers good overnight accommodation. Eight individually decorated, en
suite bedrooms in the converted stables
feature attractive floral fabrics and stripped
pine furniture. Remaining main-house
rooms are full of character and share two
neat public bathrooms. Tastefully modernised public areas for drinking include the
Orange room, a lounge and a quiet intimate
bar. Children welcome overnight.

Credit Access, Amex, Diners, Visa

ESKDALE   Bower House Inn

Holmrook CA19 1TD   `FOOD`
Area Map 1 B4 *Cumbria*   `B&B`
Eskdale (094 03) 244
Parking *ample*

Bar food *12–2 & 6.30–9.30 (Sun from 7)*

Landlords *Mr & Mrs D.J. Connor*
Free house
🍺 *Hartley XB; Younger's Scotch;*
Theakston Best Bitter; Guinness; Harp.

Built as a farmhouse in the 17th century, this traditional Lakeland inn enjoys a tranquil setting amid the unspoilt beauty of Eskdale. Derek and Beryl Connor offer a warm welcome in the cosy beamed bar with its polished darkwood furniture and crackling log fire. Eat here or in the pretty restaurant, choosing from such imaginative offerings as garlic snails or creamy courgette soup served with home-made wholemeal bread followed by, say, quail with tarragon sauce, swordfish portugaise or wild duck with Cumberland sauce. Salads, sandwiches and ploughman's are always available and pleasant sweets include lemon mousse and apple crumble.

Typical dishes Pheasant Theodora £5
Sticky toffee pudding £1.20

Accommodation *23 bedrooms* **£B G2**
Check-in all day

Best bedrooms are in the converted barn and garden cottage annexes and offer modern furnishings, colour TVs and excellent carpeted bathrooms. Older rooms in the main building are simpler but tastefully appointed and share two public bathrooms. A comfortable lounge is available for residents' use. Children welcome overnight. *No dogs.*

Credit Access, Visa

ETON   Christopher Hotel

110 High Street SL4 6AN   `B&B`
Map 10 C3 *Berkshire*
Windsor (0753) 852359
Parking *limited*

Landlord *Trevor Rule*
Free house
🍺 *Brakspear Bitter; Marston Pedigree;*
Courage Best Bitter; Guinness; Stella
Artois; Heineken. 🍷

Accommodation *34 bedrooms* **£A G1**
Check-in all day

Keeping up with the Joneses – Windsor Castle, Eton College and old father Thames – has led this former coaching inn to undergo a facelift. Bedrooms, above a brasserie, are lavishly furnished with rich fabrics and gleaming tiled bathrooms. Most rooms, housed in a motel-style block, are also very comfortable, and their tired darkwood look is being brightened. Friendly staff serve an indifferent breakfast – grisly and gristly chargrilled gammon with lukewarm coffee! Children welcome overnight.

Credit Access, Amex, Diners, Visa

ETTINGTON   Houndshill

Banbury Road CV37 7NS   `B&B`
Map 10 B1 *Warwickshire*
Stratford-upon-Avon (0789) 740267
Parking *ample*

Landlord *Mr D.S. Martin*
Free house
🍺 *Davenports Traditional; McEwan's*
Export; Younger's No. 3; Beck's Bier;
McEwan's Lager.

Accommodation *8 bedrooms* **£C G1**
Check-in all day

High standards of accommodation are provided by the friendly Martin family at their substantial inn on the A422 Banbury Road to Stratford. The eight comfortable, spacious bedrooms are most appealing with their pretty floral fabrics and old pine furniture. Discreetly double-glazed, all offer direct-dial telephones and excellent bath/shower rooms. Children are welcome overnight and there is a play area in the garden.

Credit Access, Visa

EWEN
Wild Duck Inn

Nr Cirencester GL7 6BY **B&B**
Area Map 4 B3 *Gloucs*
Kemble (0285) 770364
Parking *ample*

Landlord *Martin Pulley*
Free house ☎
🍺 *Waduorth 6X; Bass; Worthington Best Bitter; Guinness; Carling Black Label; Tennent's Pilsner.*

Accommodation *10 bedrooms* **£A G1**
Check-in all day

Dating back to 1563, this mellow Cotswold-stone inn enjoys a peaceful village setting. The beamed bar is a cosy, convivial spot with its welcoming log fire, rugs on polished boards and old grandfather clock, while the residents' lounge retains its original Elizabethan inglenook. Most of the neat, well-kept bedrooms are in an extension and have fitted white furniture, tea-makers and compact private bathrooms. A spacious suite and two four-poster rooms are also available. Delightful garden.

Credit Access, Amex, Diners, Visa

EWHURST GREEN
White Dog Inn

Nr Robertsbridge TN32 5TD **FOOD**
Area Map 5 B5 *East Sussex* **B&B**
Staplecross (058 083) 264
Parking *ample*

Bar food *12–3 & 7–10* ☎

Landlords *Tina Rainbow & Richard Hayward*
Free house
🍺 *Charrington IPA, Toby; Bass; Guinness; Tennent's Lager; Carling Black Label.* ⊖

Accommodation *6 bedrooms* **£D G2**
Check-in all day

Enjoying a lovely village setting near the parish church, with fine views over the Rother Valley, this old tile-hung pub boasts a heated swimming pool in its pleasant garden. Inside, a huge inglenook dominates the attractive beamed bar, where the new chef offers a most interesting blackboard menu. Follow smoked salmon pâté, crispy whitebait or garlic snails with, say, an impressively well spiced Indonesian beef curry served with home-made tomato chutney, pickles and poppadums. There is always a good choice of fish and vegetable dishes, plus steaks, chicken and lamb in various imaginative sauces, while home-made sweets include treacle tart and sherry trifle. The traditional Sunday lunch here is quite a feast.

Typical dishes Lamb in cream and garlic sauce £6.25 Jam pudding £1.50

Good-sized bedrooms are individually decorated in a neat and simple style and all have private facilities as well as TVs, telephones and tea-makers. Pretty country views are a bonus.

Credit Amex, Visa

EXFORD
Crown Hotel

Nr Minehead TA24 7PP **B&B**
Map 9 C1 *Somerset*
Exford (064 383) 554
Parking *ample*

Landlord *Mr P. J. Mohan*
Free house
🍺 *Usher Country Bitter; Webster Yorkshire Bitter; Holsten Export; Carlsberg Pilsner. No real ale.*

Accommodation *17 bedrooms* **£A G1**
Check-in all day

A favourite of the huntin', fishin' and shootin' set, the 17th-century Crown stands by the green in a lovely Exmoor village. The comfortable lounge and rustic bar have plenty of traditional charm, while pretty bedrooms of varying sizes are individually furnished and boast excellent carpeted modern bathrooms. Thoughtful touches range from fresh fruit and a welcoming glass of sherry to hot water bottles, tea-makers and hairdryers. Children welcome overnight.

Credit Access, Amex, Visa

EYAM *Miners Arms*

S30 1RG `B&B`
Map 4 D4 *Derbyshire*
Hope Valley (0433) 30853
Parking *ample*

Closed *Mon*

Landlords *Mr & Mrs Peter Cooke & Mr & Mrs Paul Morris*
Free house
🍺 *Stones Bitter; Wards Best Bitter; Tennent's Pilsner.*

Accommodation *6 bedrooms* **£D G3**
Check-in all day

Run by the Cookes for over 26 years, this pleasant 17th-century inn stands in an ancient village within the Peak District National Park. Original leaded light windows combine with mock-Tudor beams to smartly traditional effect in the comfortable bars. Simply appointed bedrooms all offer tea-makers and TVs and three bedrooms in the main building share the family bathroom; annexe rooms have en suite facilities. Accommodation closed three days Christmas. *No children under 12 overnight. No dogs.*

EYAM *Rose & Crown*

S30 1QW `B&B`
Map 4 D4 *Derbyshire*
Hope Valley (0433) 30858
Parking *ample*

Closed *Mon lunch*

Landlords *Mason family*
Free house
🍺 *Stones Bitter; Tetley Bitter; Bass Mild; Skol; Carling Black Label.* No real ale.

Accommodation *3 bedrooms* **£D G3**
Check-in by arrangement

The Masons offer modest accommodation at modest prices. Red draylon banquettes flank cream woodchip walls in the main bar. A pool table pockets the floor space of another room while a real fire crackles with the regulars in the public bar in winter. Beds with draylon padded headboards don duvets in the three pleasant bedrooms decked in chipboard and laminate. All have shower cubicles and share a respectable bathroom and separate toilet. TVs and tea-makers. Garden with play area, and patio. Children welcome overnight. *No dogs.*

FAIRFORD *Bull Hotel*

Market Place **GL7 4AA** `B&B`
Area Map 4 C3 *Gloucs*
Cirencester (0285) 712535
Parking *ample*

Landlord *M. Klein*
Brewery *Arkell*
🍺 *John Arkell Bitter, Best Bitter, Kingsdown Ale; Guinness; Carling Black Label; Stella Artois.*

Accommodation *21 bedrooms* **£B G2**
Check-in all day

It was a monks' chanting house in the 15th century, and later a coaching stop, and is now beautifully maintained throughout. Equestrian prints and cartoons are a feature of the comfortable, low beamed bar, peaceful residents' lounge and breakfast room in the converted stables. Sloping floors, oak beams and traditional furnishings add to the period feel of spacious bedrooms, which all offer tea-makers and baby-listeners. Most have private facilities. Children welcome overnight. *No dogs.*

Credit Access, Amex, Diners, Visa

FALMOUTH *The Pandora Inn*

Restronguet Creek, Mylor `FOOD`
Bridge **TR11 5ST**
Map 9 A3 *Cornwall*
Falmouth (0326) 72678
Parking *ample*

Bar food *11–2.30 & 6.30–10 (12.15–2.15 & 7–9.30 in winter), Sun 12–2 & 7–9.30* 🍴

Landlords *Roger & Helen Hough*
Brewery *St Austell*
🍺 *Bass; St Austell Tinners Ale, Bosun, HSD; Carlsberg Export.* 🍴 ☺

Especially popular in summer, this charming old thatched pub has a patio and pontoon on the creek, plus three cosy, characterful bars filled with maritime mementos. Local fish dominates the menu, with choices like smoked haddock bake, crab thermidor and smoked salmon quiche; there are also huge Cornish pasties, sandwiches, ploughman's and sweets like sticky treacle tart. Buffet brunch Sundays.
Typical dishes Ham and leek au gratin £3.25 Moules marinière £3.25

Credit Access, Visa

FARINGDON   *Bell Hotel*

Market Place SN7 7HP `B&B`
Area Map 4 D3 *Oxfordshire*
Faringdon (0367) 20534
Parking *ample*

Landlord *William Dreyer*
Brewery *Wadworth* ☙
☞ *Wadworth 6X; Old Timer (winter only),*
Northgate Bitter; Guinness; Harp;
Löwenbräu.

Accommodation *11 bedrooms* **£C** G1/2
Check-in all day

Larger-than-life landlord William Dreyer
was a shipbuilder and a long-time regular
here before crossing the counter about 12
years ago. The inn is a 16th-century posting
house, and the stained walls, rustic furniture and hunting prints do much to preserve the past. Bedrooms, with pretty
colour schemes and floral fabrics, include a
splendid beamed attic room with a huge
bath. Eight rooms have private facilities,
the others share. Good breakfast, but
service can be slow.

Credit Access, Amex, Diners, Visa

FAUGH   *String of Horses*

Heads Nook, Carlisle `FOOD`
CA4 9EG `B&B`
Map 3 B1 *Cumbria*
Hayton (022 870) 297
Parking *ample*

Bar food *11.30–2.30 & 5.30–10.15,*
Sun 12–3 & 7–10.15

Landlords *Ann & Eric Tasker*
Free house
☞ *Theakston Best Bitter; Younger's*
Scotch; Murphy Stout; Guinness; Carlsberg
Hof; Beck's Bier. No real ale.

Accommodation *14 bedrooms* **£A** G1
Check-in all day

A 17th-century building tucked away in a
sleepy village, the String of Horses has
plenty of old world atmosphere. The bars
have oak beams, polished brasses, log fires,
wood panelling and oak settles and there is
also a separate restaurant with lacy tablecloths and tapestry-hung walls. In the main
bar you will find a range of pub food on
offer with, at lunchtimes, a cold buffet table
featuring assorted cold meats and salads.
Start with perhaps soup and move on to
sweet and sour pork or a home-made curry,
the speciality of the house.

Typical dishes Beef goulash £3.95 Shoe-
ring pastry £1.50

Bedrooms are well equipped and decorated
in sumptuous style, some having reproduction Louis XIV furniture, one boasting a
four-poster. High point is the glitzy bathrooms with gold-plated fitments, top quality toiletries and, in two, sunken baths.
Five rooms have showers only but these are
equally luxurious. Patio. Children welcome
overnight.

Credit Access, Amex, Diners, Visa

FELIXSTOWE   *Ordnance Hotel*

1 Undercliff Road West `B&B`
IP11 8AN
Map 8 F2 *Suffolk*
Felixstowe (0394) 273427
Parking *ample*

Landlord *Adrian Boone*
Brewery *Tolly Cobbold*
☞ *Tolly Cobbold Best Bitter, 4X; Guinness;*
Hansa, Export; Labatt's. ☙

Accommodation *16 bedrooms* **£C** G2
Check-in all day

Chintzy sofas wallow in the sunny residents' lounge, and 'lizards' can also enjoy
drinks on the terrace. All are contained in
the solid 19th-century hotel which boasts
handsome features including a heavy
wood-panelled bar. Refurbishment is
adding a family suite and five rooms
decorated à la Laura Ashley. Other homely,
spotless bedrooms have traditional furniture. Around half have en suite facilities;
the others share two functional bathrooms.
Children welcome overnight. *No dogs.*

Credit Access, Amex, Diners, Visa

FEN DRAYTON
Three Tuns

High Street CB4 5SJ   A
Map 8 D2 *Cambridgeshire*
Swavesey (0954) 30242
Parking *ample*

Landlords *Michael & Eileen Nugent*
Brewery *Greene King* ⌖
⍟ *Greene King IPA, Abbot Ale, KK Mild;*
Guinness; Harp; Kronenbourg 1664.

A thatched riverside pub dating from the 15th century and oozing old world charm. Pretty windowboxes and hanging baskets make the most of the exterior in summer, and there is a neatly maintained garden to the rear. In winter, fires crackle in the large inglenook fireplaces, casting reflections on the oak tables and chairs, polished copperware and assorted bric-a-brac. Local events based on the pub include darts matches and an annual sunflower seed growing competition.

Credit Access, Visa

FENNY BENTLEY
Bentley Brook Inn

Nr Ashbourne DE6 1LF   B&B
Map 4 D4 *Derbyshire*
Thorpe Cloud (033 529) 278
Parking *ample*

Landlords *David & Jeanne Allingham*
Free house
⍟ *Marston Pedigree; Worthington Best*
Bitter; Bass; Guinness; Carling Black Label;
Tennent's Extra.

Accommodation *8 bedrooms* £C G2
Check-in all day

Set back from the junction of the A515 and B5056, this handsome old half-timbered inn stands amid extensive acreage within the Peak District National Park that includes 250 yards of Bentley Brook trout stream. Existing main-house bedrooms (the three best have en suite bathrooms and woodland views) are to be joined by newly created rooms in an adjacent cottage. Homely residents' lounge and mellow bar-lounge. Promised redecoration throughout will be welcome. Children welcome overnight.

Credit Access, Visa

We welcome bona fide recommendations
or complaints on the tear-out pages at the back
of the book for readers' comments.

They are followed up by our professional team,
but do complain to the management on the spot.

FITTLEWORTH
Swan

Lower Street, Nr   B&B
Pulborough RH20 1EW
Area Map 6 B3 *West Sussex*
Fittleworth (079 882) 429
Parking *ample*

Landlord *Rod Aspinall*
Owners *Berni Chef & Brewer Hotels*
⍟ *Webster Yorkshire Bitter; Ruddles*
County, Best Bitter; Guinness; Holsten
Export; Carlsberg. ⍨

Accommodation *10 bedrooms* £C G2
Check-in all day

Luxuriate in the peaceful beauty of this 14th-century inn's lovely garden (with play area). Inside a log fire dominates the bar with its display of policemen's truncheons and brass and copper trinkets hung from beams. Villagers enjoy darts in the small public bar. Laura Ashley style bedrooms have modern bathrooms and all amenities including trouser presses. Three share two smart bathrooms. Indifferent breakfast in an attractive panelled restaurant. Children welcome overnight. *No dogs.*

Credit Access, Amex, Diners, Visa

FLETCHING   *Griffin Inn*

TN22 3SS
Area Map 6 E3 *East Sussex*
Newick (082 572) 2890
Parking *ample*

`FOOD`
`B&B`

Bar food *12–2.15 (Sun till 2) & 7–9, Sat
11.30–2.30 & 7–9.30* ✎
No bar food *Sun eve*

Landlord *David Groundwater*
Free house
🍺 *Hall & Woodhouse Tanglefoot; Harvey
Best Bitter; Ruddles Best Bitter;
Charrington IPA; Carlsberg; Holsten
Export.* 🍷 ⊖

Accommodation *3 bedrooms* **£C G2**
Check-in all day

David Groundwater is the welcoming new
host at this mellow 16th-century pub
opposite the village church in the picturesque high street. Oak beams, panelling and a
copper-canopied fireplace create a cosy
atmosphere in the long bar, while on sunny
days the landscaped garden and patio make
a delightful setting for some honest, home-
cooked fare. The appetising selection
ranges from straightforward offerings like
soup and pâté, steak, lamb cutlets and
grilled Dover sole to the more unusual –
perhaps avocado pie with a garlic crust
followed by veal à la crème or monkfish
with garlic and cashew nuts. Puddings are
more traditional (treacle tart, apple pie).

Typical dishes Beef stroganoff pancake
£4.50 Beef and Guinness pie £5.25

Three brand new bedrooms, all with original beams and four-posters, are tastefully
decorated and furnished, the one en suite
room boasting a huge open fireplace and
hearthside settee. Thoughtful touches
range from wicker chairs to pot-pourri. *No
dogs.*

Credit Access, Amex, Visa

FONTHILL BISHOP   *King's Arms*

Nr Salisbury SP3 5SH
Area Map 7 D2 *Wiltshire*
Hindon (074 789) 523
Parking *ample*

`FOOD`
`B&B`

Bar food *12–2 & 7–10* ✎

Landlords *Andrew & Sarah MacDonald*
Free house
🍺 *Wadworth 6X, IPA; Wiltshire
Stonehenge Best Bitter; John Smith's
Yorkshire Bitter; Tuborg; Spaten Gold.* 🍷 ⊖

Accommodation *4 bedrooms* **£D G3**
Check-in all day

A smart little red-brick pub (converted from
an old farm building) standing by the
roadside offers value for money and good
eating in a comfortable dining area with
waitress service. A blackboard announces
the day's specials, starting perhaps with
avocado and crab then moving on to beef
bourguignon served with a salad garnish
and baked potato. A printed menu offers
soup, sandwiches and steaks – including
the mighty 10oz sirloin, cooked in garlic
butter and accompanied by onion rings,
mushrooms, tomatoes and chips galore –
and there are home-made desserts such as
cheesecake and fruit crumble. Sunday
lunch is popular, and there is a children's
menu.

Typical dishes Steak and mushroom pie
£3.50 Lasagne £3.50

Two new bedrooms have recently been
added and the four rooms share a couple of
good-sized, well-appointed bathrooms.
Simple free-standing furniture and matching fabrics are used throughout and all offer
TVs and washbasins. Garden.

FORD   NEW ENTRY   *Dinton Hermit*

Nr Aylesbury HP17 8XH   `FOOD`
Map 10 C2 *Buckinghamshire*
Aylesbury (0296) 748379
Parking *ample*

Bar food *12–2 & 7–9.30*
No bar food *Sun & Mon*

Landlords *John & Jane Tompkins*
Brewery *Aylesbury*
📖 *ABC Best Bitter; Bass; Tetley Bitter;
Guinness; Carlsberg.* ⊖

A 15th-century stone pub named after John
Briggs, clerk to one of the judges who
condemned Charles I to death. The two bars
have a fair amount of character, but the real
draw is the hearty home cooking. Good
honest fare is typified by a meal of vegetable soup, succulent gammon with cauliflower cheese and a fruit pie. Friendly,
cheerful waitress service.
Typical dishes Saucy mushrooms £1.95
Pork chop in cider with apples £4.50

FORD   *White Hart at Ford*

Nr Chippenham SN14 8RP   `B&B`
Area Map 4 A5 *Wiltshire*
Castle Combe (0249) 782213
Parking *ample*

Landlords *W.P. & J.E. Futcher*
Free house ☙
📖 *Wadworth 6X; Marston Pedigree;
Smiles Exhibition; Fullers ESB; Stella
Artois; Dansk LA.* 🍷

Accommodation *11 bedrooms* £B G2
Check-in all day

Nestling beside a trout stream overlooking
the Weavern valley, this fine 16th-century
inn offers character and comfort galore.
Dark wood panelling and furniture, an open
fire and soft lighting create a mellow mood
in the three bars, or you can enjoy a well-
kept pint on the summer terraces. Delightful bedrooms (some with four-posters) in
the original building and converted stables
all have good private facilities as well as
TVs, radios and tea-makers. Swimming
pool available.

Credit Access, Visa

FORDWICH   NEW ENTRY   *Fordwich Arms*

Nr Canterbury CT2 0DB   `FOOD`
Area Map 5 E2 *Kent*
Canterbury (0227) 710444
Parking *ample*

Bar food *12–2 & 6–10*
No bar food *Sun*

Landlords *John & Julia Gass*
Brewery *Whitbread*
📖 *Fremlins Bitter; Flowers Original; guest
beer; Guinness; Heineken; Stella Artois.* ⊖

A solid, Tudor-style village pub with
mellow, comfortable bars and a neatly kept
beer garden beside the river Stour. Favourite snacks like soup, salads and sandwiches, filled jacket potatoes and ploughman's platters are supplemented by more
substantial blackboard offerings such as
paprika beef and nut roast with herby onion
sauce. Avoid the lifeless microwave pastry
dishes. Finish with hot cherry and hazelnut
cake. Good English cheeseboard.
Typical dishes Bacon pudding £3.85
Plaice with smoked salmon mornay £3.95

FORTY GREEN   *Royal Standard of England*

Beaconsfield HP9 X11   `A`
Map 10 C2 *Buckinghamshire*
Beaconsfield (049 46) 3382
Parking *ample*

Landlord *Alan Wainwright*
Free house ☙
📖 *Marston Pedigree, Owd Rodger;
Eldridge Pope Royal Oak; Guinness; Stella
Artois; Carlsberg Hof.* 🍷

Granted its title and coat of arms in 1651 by
Charles II, who sheltered here after the
Battle of Worcester, this splendid pub is one
of our oldest free houses, with a history
dating back over 900 years. Many of the
magnificent interior oak beams have nautical origins, including the massive carved
transom from an Elizabethan ship, which
now forms part of the entrance hall. A truly
atmospheric setting for a drink. Sadly, the
food is no longer good.

FOSSEBRIDGE   *Fossebridge Inn*

Nr Cheltenham GL54 3JS
Area Map 4 B2 *Gloucs*
Fossebridge (028 572) 310
Parking *ample*

FOOD
B&B

Bar food *12–2.30 & 6.30–9.30 (Fri & Sat till 10, Sun from 7)* ☎

Landlords *Hugh & Suzanne Roberts & Mr & Mrs A. Rork*
Free house
🍺 *Marston Pedigree, Best Bitter; Guinness; Carlsberg Pilsner; Stella Artois.* ▮ ☺

Accommodation *12 bedrooms* **£A G1**
Check-in all day

A Tudor coaching inn originally occupied the site of this attractive inn centred around a Georgian house on the banks of the river Coln. Imaginative snacks are served in the Bridge Bar, a most characterful setting with its Yorkstone floors, exposed limestone walls and inglenook fireplaces. Cornish mussels in cream and white wine or langoustines with garlic mayonnaise are among the starters, while main courses range from roast pigeon sauced with port wine to poached Dart salmon hollandaise and warm salad of smoked pheasant. Sticky toffee pudding and hazelnut meringue are typical desserts, and there are some fine English farmhouse cheeses. Traditional Sunday lunch menu.

Typical dishes Bacon and walnut salad £3.95 Rack of lamb £7.95

Airy, individually decorated bedrooms (including four in an annexe) are smartly furnished and equipped with TVs, telephones, tea-makers and hairdryers. All have up-to-date private facilities and many enjoy lovely views over the garden and river. Residents have the use of a peaceful, relaxing lounge in the main house.

Credit Access, Amex, Diners, Visa

FOTHERINGHAY   *Falcon*

Nr Peterborough PE8 5HZ
Map 8 D1 *Northamptonshire*
Cotterstock (083 26) 254
Parking *ample*

FOOD

Bar food *12.15–2 & 7–9.45 (Sun till 9)*
No bar food *Mon eve*

Landlords *Alan & Jill Stewart*
Free house
🍺 *Greene King IPA, Abbot Ale; Adnams Bitter; Elgood Bitter; Guinness; Carlsberg.* ☺

A conservatory and a beautifully kept garden provide alternatives to the traditional bars of the Stewarts' popular Victorian pub. The quality of the food accounts for a loyal mealtime following, with plenty of variety: baked spiced grapefruit, potted trout or salami salad to start, then maybe moussaka, roast pheasant, barbecued spare ribs or poached plaice fillets. Cold cuts, smoked fish and grills and always something for vegetarians.
Typical dishes Steak & kidney pie £3 Roast duckling £4.80

FOVANT   *Cross Keys Hotel*

Nr Salisbury SP3 5JH
Area Map 7 E2 *Wiltshire*
Fovant (072 270) 284
Parking *ample*

B&B

Landlady *Pauline Story*
Free house ☎
🍺 *Wadworth 6X; Hook Norton Best Bitter; Carlsberg Hof; Heineken.*

Accommodation *4 bedrooms* **£D G3**
Check-in all day

An old coaching inn on the A30 dating in part from 1485, the Keys has seen a lot more than weekend traffic go by. It stands beneath the Fovant Emblems – regimental badges carved in the chalk hill by World War One soldiers. Naturally enough it has ceilings that will not tolerate top hats. A grandfather clock keeps time, local craft objects decorate the walls. Four modest cottage bedrooms, rough-walled and white-painted, are warm. Bathroom and shower are shared. *No dogs.*

Credit Visa

FOVANT   **Pembroke Arms**

Nr Salisbury SP3 5JH   `B&B`
Area Map 7 E2 *Wiltshire*
Fovant (072 270) 201
Parking *ample*

Landlords *Mr & Mrs John Clinch*
Free house
🍺 *Flowers Original; Fullers London Pride;
Guinness; Carlsberg; Castlemaine XXXX.*

Accommodation *2 bedrooms* **£D G3**
Check-in all day

Formerly the shooting lodge of the Earl of
Pembroke, now a creeper-covered Georgian
pub, all the Pembroke's past is currently
relegated to its collection of World War One
memorabilia. A certain sombreness reigns,
the bars simple, the only luxury a large
open fire and a warm welcome from new
owners Mr and Mrs Clinch. Two bedrooms
are now available and another is planned.
The one inspected was smart, comfortable
and well-heated. Bathroom facilities are
shared with the owners. Garden. Children
welcome overnight. *No dogs.*

FOWLMERE   **Chequers Inn**

High Street, Nr Royston   `FOOD`
SG8 7SR
Map 10 D1 *Cambridgeshire*
Fowlmere (076 382) 369
Parking *ample*

Bar food *12–2 & 7–10*

Landlord *Norman Rushton*
Brewery *Tolly Cobbold*
🍺 *Tolly Cobbold Original Bitter; Guinness;
Hansa.* ❢ ⊖

When Samuel Pepys spent a night here in
1659, the inn was already a popular traveller's rest. Its period charm largely survives,
and it still goes into many diaries as a good
place for refreshment. Soup, garlic mushrooms, lasagne, plaice and chicken cordon
bleu show the span of bar food, and there
are also delicious espresso coffee, fine wines
by the glass and excellent cheeses.
Typical dishes Escalope of trout with
herb sauce £4.75 Coq au vin £4.20

Credit Access, Amex, Diners, Visa

FOWNHOPE   **Green Man Inn**

Nr Hereford HR1 4PE   `B&B`
Map 6 E3 *Hereford & Worcs*
Fownhope (043 277) 243
Parking *ample*

Landlords *Arthur & Maggie Williams*
Free house
🍺 *Hook Norton Best Bitter; Marston
Pedigree; Samuel Smith's Old Brewery
Bitter; Guinness; Hofmeister.*

Accommodation *15 bedrooms* **£C G2**
Check-in all day

A solid, black-and-white roadside inn
which dates back in part to 1485. The
roomy main bar welcomes with a log fire
and a wealth of beams. All the bedrooms
are beautifully kept; courtyard rooms small
and cheerful, those in the main building a
little larger; a couple of old rooms remain,
one with beams, creaking floor and four-
poster bed. All have TVs, dial-out phones,
clock-radios, hairdryers, trouser presses
and private facilities. Children welcome
overnight.

Credit Access, Visa

FRADLEY   **Fradley Arms Hotel**

Nr Lichfield WS13 8RD   `B&B`
Map 7 B1 *Staffordshire*
Burton-on-Trent (0283) 790186
Parking *ample*

Landlords *Mr & Mrs R. K. Taylor*
Free house
🍺 *Darley Thorne Best Bitter; Ansells Best
Bitter, Mild; Worthington Best Bitter;
Carlsberg; Löwenbräu.*

Accommodation *6 bedrooms* **£C G2**
Check-in all day

Standing beside the busy A38, this family-
run inn makes a very convenient overnight
stop and is especially popular with business visitors. The six double-glazed bedrooms have been freshly decorated with
lemon wallpaper and matching fabrics and
all offer neat carpeted bathrooms as well as
TVs, tea-makers and telephones. Downstairs, there is a peaceful residents' lounge
overlooking the garden and a convivial bar
sporting smart new banquette seating.
Children welcome overnight.

Credit Access, Amex, Diners, Visa

FRAMFIELD   *Barley Mow*

Eastbourne Road TN22 5QL   `FOOD`
Map 8 D4 *East Sussex*
Framfield (082 582) 234
Parking *ample*

Bar food *12–2 & 7–10*
No bar food *Sun eve*

Landlords *Andrew & Ramsay Walder*
Brewery *Phoenix*
🍺 *King & Barnes Festive; Webster Yorkshire Bitter; Watney Mild, Special; Guinness; Carlsberg.*

Honest home cooking matches the simple, homely appeal of a welcoming country pub alongside the A22. Follow hearty pea and ham soup with a cold meat platter, cauliflower cheese or steak and kidney pie served with bubble and squeak as a tasty alternative to chips. Jacket potatoes, ploughman's and French sticks filled with cheese, hot gammon or local sausages are popular snacks, and there is fruit pie for afters. Traditional Sunday lunch.
Typical dishes Moussaka £3.45 Fish pie £3.25

FRAMPTON MANSELL   *Crown Inn*

Stroud GL6 8JB   `B&B`
Area Map 4 A3 *Gloucs*
Frampton Mansell (028 576) 601
Parking *ample*

Landlord *Mr Redmond*
Free house
🍺 *Wadworth 6X; Archers Village Bitter; Younger's Scotch; Worthington Best Bitter; Beck's Bier; Carlsberg.*

Accommodation *12 bedrooms* £A G1
Check-in all day

A fine old village pub in a quiet setting just off the A419 from Stroud to Cirencester. Inside, the place oozes rural charm, with exposed Cotswold stone walls, open fires and beamed ceilings. The stylish accommodation is in a purpose-built block to the rear, where guests can make themselves comfortable in attractive rooms with pastel schemes, contemporary fabrics, darkwood fitted furniture, brass light fittings and smart en suite bathrooms. Children welcome overnight. Accommodation closed 2–4 weeks over Christmas.

FRAMSDEN   NEW ENTRY   *Dobermann*

The Street, Nr Stowmarket   `FOOD`
IP14 6HG
Map 8 F2 *Suffolk*
Helmingham (047 339) 461
Parking *ample*

Bar food *12.15–2 & 7.15–10,
Sun 12.15–2.30 & 7.15–9.30*

Landlady *Mrs S.M. Franklin*
Free house
🍺 *Greene King IPA; Adnams Broadside, Mild; Dobermann Bitter; Murphy Stout; Carlsberg Export.* ⊖

Once named the Greyhound, now the Dobermann for reasons incautious customers may discover should they chance their arm over the bar, this is a delightful part-thatched village inn. Its namesakes have their pictures on the walls and prize rosettes above the bar. There is a decent selection of capably cooked food on offer from home-made pâté or local game pie to beef in red wine and pepper sauce. Garden.
Typical dishes Steak and mushroom pie £5.50 Fresh country vegetable soup £1.50

FREELAND   NEW ENTRY   *Shepherds Hall Inn*

Witney Road OX7 2HQ   `B&B`
Area Map 4 E2 *Oxfordshire*
Freeland (0993) 881256
Parking *ample*

Landlords *Liz & David Fyson*
Free house ☂
🍺 *Whitbread Poacher; Wethered SPA; Flowers IPA; Stella Artois; Heineken.*

Accommodation *6 bedrooms* £D G2
Check-in all day

Originally a 13th-century shelter for shepherds and drovers and once known as the 'Shepherds All', the green-shuttered inn today offers plain and practical accommodation. The bar is simple, with wheelbacked chairs, and a collection of plates adorns the walls. Six bedrooms (three of which are in an annexe) are clean, comfortable and modern in style. The annexe rooms have neat tiled shower rooms, and the pub rooms have private bathrooms. Garden and children's play area.

Credit Visa

FRILFORD HEATH   *Dog House*

Nr Abingdon OX13 6QY   `B&B`
Area Map 4 F3 *Oxfordshire*
Oxford (0865) 390830
Parking *ample*

Landlord *Clive Hagger*
Brewery *Morland*
🍺 *Morland PA Bitter, Best Bitter;*
Guinness; Heineken; Stella Artois.

Accommodation *19 bedrooms* **£A G2**
Check-in all day

A pleasant 300-year-old tile-hung inn which commands a lovely view over the Vale of the White Horse. The bar is spacious, and incorporates a central stone fireplace with a real winter fire. Nine new rooms have recently been added, and all nineteen now have en suite facilities and free-standing pine furniture. Older rooms have woodchip walls; newer ones are more individual with floral wallpaper or pastels with stencil designs. All have TVs, telephones and hairdryers. Children welcome overnight.

Credit Access, Amex, Diners, Visa

FULKING   *Shepherd & Dog*

Nr Henfield BN5 9LU   `FOOD`
Area Map 6 D4 *West Sussex*
Poynings (079 156) 382
Parking *limited*

Bar food *12–2 & 7–9.30*
No bar food *Sun eve*

Landlord *Mr Bradley-Hole*
Brewery *Phoenix*
🍺 *King & Barnes Festive Bitter; Ruddles Best Bitter, County; Webster Yorkshire Bitter; Guinness; Holsten Export.* ⊖

The rural setting of this attractive pub is truly splendid, and inside there is one long bar with polished tables and fresh flowers. A varied selection of bar meals is offered, from lasagne, beef bourguignon, rack of lamb with apricot sauce and stuffed mushrooms to moules marinière, steaks and coquilles St Jacques. Unfortunately the cooking and service are not up to previous very high standards. Garden and play area.
Typical dishes Seafood gratin £3.95 Beef & Guinness pie £5.95

Credit Access, Visa

GIBRALTAR   *Bottle & Glass*

Nr Aylesbury HP21 8TY   `FOOD`
Map 10 C2 *Buckinghamshire*
Aylesbury (0296) 748488
Parking *ample*

Bar food *12–2.15 & 7–10*
No bar food *Sun eve* ⊠

Landlords *David & Heather Berry*
Brewery *ABC*
🍺 *ABC Best Bitter; Burton Ale; Murphy Stout; Löwenbräu; Skol.* 🍷 ⊖

David and Heather Berry offer excellent eating in friendly, informal surroundings at an attractive old pub on the A418. Tasty lunchtime offerings might include vegetarian stuffed peppers or succulent seafood crumble, while evenings bring more elaborate dishes such as creamy chicken with mango purée or pork fillet with Stilton and honey sauce. Fine cheeses and rich desserts to finish. *No children after 9 pm.*
Typical dishes Chicken curry £4.75 Fillet steak with horseradish butter £6.95

Credit Access, Amex, Diners, Visa

GLEMSFORD   NEW ENTRY   *Black Lion*

CO10 7PS   `FOOD`
Map 8 E2 *Suffolk*
Aylesbury (0296) 748379
Parking *ample*

Bar food *12–2 & 7–10, Sun 7.30–9.30*

Landlords *Michael & Anna Maria Kelvin*
Brewery *Greene King*
🍺 *Greene King IPA, Abbot Ale; Guinness; Kronenbourg 1664; Harp.*

An agreeable, basically unspoilt pub with pre-Tudor origins. The welcome in the beamed bars is warm and friendly, and while Michael Kelvin looks after front of house his wife Anna Maria does good work in the kitchen. Fresh, often local, ingredients go into familiar fare such as garlic prawns, seafood mornay, cold meat platters and game pie. The more adventurous could shell out for a dish of Suffolk snails.
Typical dishes Suffolk beef £5.25 Suffolk snails £3.25

GODALMING   NEW ENTRY   *Ram Cider House*

Cattershall Cross GU7 1LW   A
Area Map 6 B1 *Surrey*
Godalming (048 68) 21093
Parking *ample*

Landlord *Malcolm Evans*
Free house
🍺 *Bulmers Special Cider, Original, Traditional, Strongbow Special, West Country, No. 7.*

Exclusively a cider pub, the Ram offers more than two dozen varieties of that pleasing brew. It is a small, unpretentious place dating from the 16th century, and in addition to the two little bars there is plenty of outside seating on the broad patio or under fruit trees in the pretty garden, through which a stream runs. The Ram is a bit off the beaten track – Cattershall Cross is signposted off the A3100 Guildford to Godalming road.

GOLDSBOROUGH   *Bay Horse Inn*

Nr Knaresborough HG5 8NW   B&B
Area Map 2 F4 *North Yorks*
Harrogate (0423) 862212
Parking *ample*

Landlady *June Marks*
Brewery *Whitbread* 🌀
🍺 *Whitbread Trophy, Trophy Traditional, Castle Eden; Guinness; Stella Artois; Heineken.*

Accommodation *5 bedrooms* **£D G3**
Check-in by arrangement

A delightful, well maintained 450-year-old inn, quietly situated off the A59. It is spotless inside with gleaming copper-topped tables and furnishings in muted autumnal colours. Summer windowboxes and an award-winning garden complete the setting for the simple rooms in the annexe. All have washbasins, TVs, duvets and tea-makers, and the two public bathrooms are pristine. The rooms are small but the service and housekeeping are impeccable. *No children under five overnight. No dogs.*

Credit Access, Visa

GOMSHALL   *Black Horse*

Station Road, Nr Guildford   B&B
GU5 9NP
Area Map 6 C1 *Surrey*
Shere (048 641) 2242
Parking *ample*

Landlord *Mr A. W. Savage*
Brewery *Young*
🍺 *Young Bitter, Special, Winter Warmer (winter only); Beamish Stout; Young London Lager.* 🍷

Accommodation *4 bedrooms* **£C G2**
Check-in by arrangement

Standing on the A25 amid lovely country-side is a sturdy 17th-century inn full of traditional charm. Carved antique chairs, polished darkwood tables and a cheery coal fire add to the mellow character of the bar, while the four comfortable bedrooms all have attractive fabrics, electric blankets and tea-makers. They share a single public bathroom and a large, light residents' lounge with a TV up on the first floor. Children welcome overnight. *No dogs.*

Credit Access, Amex, Diners, Visa

GOSBERTON   *Five Bells*

Spalding Road PE11 4HL   B&B
Map 8 D1 *Lincolnshire*
Spalding (0775) 840348
Parking *ample*

Landlords *Mr & Mrs Woodhouse*
Brewery *Manns*
🍺 *Ansells Bitter, Mild; Tetley Bitter; Guinness; Castlemaine XXXX; Skol.*

Accommodation *2 bedrooms* **£D G3**
Check-in by arrangement

The Woodhouses offer a cheerful welcome at this simple pebbledash pub alongside the A16 on the Boston-Spalding road. There are just two bedrooms, bright and fresh with simple white furnishings, duvets and a shared bathroom, as well as TVs and tea-makers. Downstairs, the public bar has a pool table while the main bar is rather smarter and decorated with much brass and copperware. Garden and play area. Children welcome overnight. *No dogs.*

Credit Access

GOUDHURST   NEW ENTRY   *Star & Eagle*

High Street TN17 1AL   B&B
Area Map 5 A4 *Kent*
Goudhurst (0580) 211512
Parking *ample*

Landlords *Michel & Karin Dimet*
Brewery *Whitbread*
🍺 *Flowers Original; Fremlins Bitter;
Guinness; Stella Artois; Heineken.*

Accommodation *11 bedrooms* **£A G1**
Check-in all day

Behind the splendid timbered facade vintage charm and modern comfort blend harmoniously in a fine 14th-century hostelry. Beams, bricks, vaulted stonework and inglenooks make great appeal in the public rooms, while creaking floors and odd angles are the order of the day in the bedrooms. These vary in size and shape; the majority are furnished in pine, though the four-poster room has some antiques. Nine rooms have carpeted bathrooms en suite. Children welcome overnight.

Credit Access, Amex, Visa

GREAT CHISHILL   *Pheasant Inn*

Nr Royston SG8 8PT   A
Map 10 D1 *Hertfordshire*
Royston (0763) 838535
Parking *ample*

Closed *Mon lunch*

Landlords *Denis & Marshella Ryan*
Free house
🍺 *Younger's IPA, Tartan Bitter; Adnams Bitter; Tolly Cobbold Original; McEwan's Lager; Carlsberg Hof.* ☕

Racing is the main theme here, with landlord Denis Ryan himself an ex-jockey, and his son Willy presently riding. Photographs of the latter in action cover the walls, and there are plenty of plants and fresh flowers. It is shooting country here, too, hence the presence of some stuffed pheasants. Heavy ornate carved chairs and benches combine with horsey bric-a-brac, statuettes and prints around the huge inglenook fireplace to create a really authentic feel for this 300-year-old pub.

Credit Access, Visa

GREAT RYBURGH   *Boar Inn*

Nr Fakenham NR21 0DX   B&B
Map 8 E1 *Norfolk*
Great Ryburgh (032 878) 212
Parking *ample*

Landlords *Jim & Margaret Corson*
Free house
🍺 *Tolly Cobbold Original; Wensum Bitter; Adnams Bitter; Guinness; Carlsberg.*

Accommodation *4 bedrooms* **£D G2**
Check-in all day

If you are looking for peaceful and quiet accommodation within handy reach of the Norfolk coastline, the Boar Inn, a whitewashed pub nestling in a sleepy village, is the place to go. On chilly nights a log fire crackles in the huge inglenook fireplace in the low-beamed bar and there are more beams upstairs in the cottage bedrooms. Each room has a washbasin, colour TV and reading material; they share a shower and toilet. Children welcome overnight.

Credit Access, Visa

GREAT TEW   *Falkland Arms*

OX7 4DB   B&B
Map 10 B1 *Oxfordshire*
Great Tew (060 883) 653
Parking *ample*

Closed *Mon lunch*

Landlord *John Milligan*
Free house
🍺 *Donnington Best Bitter; Wadworth 6X; Hook Norton Best Bitter; Hall & Woodhouse Tanglefoot; Beamish Stout.*

Accommodation *5 bedrooms* **£D G2**
Check-in by arrangement

A lovely and historic village is the tranquil setting for this marvellous old Cotswold stone inn. Flagstone floors, shuttered windows, heavy oak beams, an inglenook fireplace and high-backed settles characterise the intimate bars, where a huge collection of beer and cider mugs hangs from the ceiling. Upstairs, five delightfully cottagy little bedrooms (one with a four-poster, three with brass beds) all have central heating, duvets and tea-makers. Garden. *No dogs.*

GRETA BRIDGE   *Morritt Arms Hotel*

Nr Barnard Castle DU2 9SE   FOOD
Map 3 C2 *Co. Durham*   B&B
Teesdale (0833) 27232
Parking *ample*

Bar food *12–2 & 6–10 (Sun from 7)*

Landlords *John & David Mulley*
Free house
🍺 *Theakston Best Bitter; Younger's
Scotch; Newcastle Exhibition; Carlsberg
Pilsner.* ☺

A handsome, ivy-clad Georgian inn
situated in lovely countryside, the Morritt
Arms is a fine base for touring the local
beauty spots. Day rooms are unashamedly
old-fashioned, and one features murals of
Dickensian scenes. Lunchtime bar food
spans a simple selection of sandwiches,
pâtés, salads, ice creams and sweets, plus
hot specials like chicken curry or beef
provençale. In the evening, only soup and
sandwiches are served in the bar, the main
business moving to the restaurant (7.30–
8.45), where salmon mayonnaise, rack of
lamb with rosemary and pork cutlet with
apples and cider show the choice. A traditional roast Sunday lunch is also
available.

Typical dishes Ploughman's lunch £2.75
Steak & mushroom pie £4

Accommodation *23 bedrooms* **£B G2**
Check-in all day

Neat bedrooms are mainly quite modestly
furnished, though one sports a four-poster
and several have splendid brass beds. TVs,
tea-makers and trouser presses are
standard, and 16 rooms have private facilities. Staff are friendly enough, but some of
the younger ones can be a bit slapdash.

Credit Access, Amex, Diners, Visa

GRETNA   NEW ENTRY   *Gretna Chase Hotel*

Carlisle CA6 8JB   B&B
Map 3 B1 *Cumbria*
Gretna (0461) 37517
Parking *ample*

Landlord *John W. Hall*
Free house
🍺 *Younger's Scotch, Dark Mild; Guinness;
Beck's Bier; Harp.*

Accommodation *9 bedrooms* **£C G2**
Check-in all day

Patrons of the first marriage house over the
Scottish border used the nearby Gretna
Chase for stabling their horses. That function has long since ceased, but today's
honeymooners can install themselves in a
splendid four-poster suite. All rooms (with
TVs, but discreetly phoneless) feature quality furniture and fabrics, and most overlook gardens. There is a spacious Victorian
reception hall, plenty of bar space and a
little lounge. Accommodation closed January. Children welcome overnight. *No dogs.*

Credit Access, Amex, Visa

GRETTON   *Royal Oak*

Nr Winchcombe GL54 5EP   FOOD
Map 10 A1 *Gloucs*
Cheltenham (0242) 602477
Parking *ample*

Bar food *12–2 & 7–9.30* 🍴

Landlords *Bob & Kathy Willison*
Free house
🍺 *Wadworth 6X; Courage Directors; John
Smith's Yorkshire Bitter; Guinness;
Kronenbourg 1664; Foster's.* 🍷 ☺

The Great Western Railway runs past the
bottom of the garden, and the pub itself is a
well modernised, family-run concern in a
delightful setting. Imaginative, capably
prepared dishes are offered in the two
stylishly simple, rustic bars, with choices
like garlic mushrooms, mussels grilled with
Stilton, baked ham with cauliflower cheese
and lamb and apricot curry. Choose the
bread and butter pudding for afters.
Typical dishes Crab and mushroom pot
£2.50 Sweet and sour pork £3.50

Credit Visa

GRIMSTHORPE   Black Horse Inn

Nr Bourne PE10 0LY   `FOOD`
Map 8 D1 *Lincolnshire*   `B&B`
Edenham (077 832) 247
Parking *ample*

Bar food *12–1.45 & 7–9.30 (Sat till 10)*
Closed *Sun*

Landlords *Mr & Mrs K.S. Fisher*
Free house
☛*Cameron Traditional Bitter.*
No real ale. ☙

The Fishers' Georgian inn has a very distinctive style. It is well lived-in and slightly eccentric, but Joyce's sound cooking certainly makes it worth seeking out. Order in the pleasant beamed bar, then move through to the charming restaurant and sit at one of the old polished tables decorated with fresh flowers to enjoy your choice. Traditional English dishes range from a rather bland home-made vegetable soup and Stilton pâté to grilled Grimsby plaice, Lincolnshire pork sausages with tomato and a well-made steak, kidney and mushroom pie accompanied by perfect stovie potatoes and leeks in cream sauce. Sweets include honey meringue (ovenbaked on our visit), apple or treacle tart and a citrus sorbet, and good coffee to finish.

Typical dishes Fish hors d'oeuvre £4.25
Rack of lamb £4.95

Accommodation *4 bedrooms* **£B G3**
Check-in by arrangement

Four chintzy, good-sized bedrooms enjoy peaceful parkland views and offer a variety of thoughtful extras, including plants and radios in all rooms. Functional carpeted bathrooms (two en suite). Accommodation closed Christmas week. *No children under eight overnight.*

Credit Access, Amex, Visa

GRINDLEFORD   Maynard Arms Hotel

Nr Sheffield S30 1HP   `B&B`
Map 4 D4 *Derbyshire*
Hope Valley (0433) 30321
Parking *ample*

Landlord *Robert Graham*
Owner *Ptarmigan Hotels Ltd*
☛ *Stones Bitter, Best Bitter; Guinness; Tennent's Extra; Carling Black Label.*

Accommodation *13 bedrooms* **£A G1**
Check-in all day

Tastefully refurbished over the years, this early-Victorian inn provides comfortable and spacious overnight accommodation. Two of the three superior rooms available boast four-posters, while other rooms have attractive fabrics and wallpapers, plus good laminate furnishings. Most offer smart private bathrooms; and TVs, teamakers, radio alarms and trouser presses are standard throughout. There are two relaxing bars and a charming lounge. Children welcome overnight.

Credit Access, Amex, Diners, Visa

GUILDFORD   Rats Castle

80 Sydenham Road GU1 3SA   `FOOD`
Area Map 6 B1 *Surrey*
Guildford (0483) 572410
Parking *difficult*

Bar food *12–2 & 7–9.30*
No bar food *Sun eve*

Landlady *Brenda Heath*
Brewery *Friary Meux*
☛ *Friary Meux Bitter; Ind Coope Burton Ale; Guinness; Castlemaine XXXX; Löwenbräu.*

Tucked away in a side street near the town centre is an old flint pub which has been stylishly done out inside. A blackboard advertises the day's menu of open sandwiches, jacket potatoes or leeks wrapped in ham with cheese sauce for a light meal; more substantial dishes include chicken curry, swordfish steak, pizzas and lasagne. There are further choices in the evening, and enjoyable sweets include treacle tart.
Typical dishes Tagliatelle £3.30
Chocolate fudge cake £1.50

Credit Access

GUILDFORD   NEW ENTRY   *The Withies Inn*

Nr Compton, Withies Lane   FOOD
GU3 1JA
Area Map 6 B1 *Surrey*
Godalming (04868) 21158
Parking *ample*

Bar food *12–2 & 7.30–10*

Landlord *Brian Thomas*
Free house
🍺 *Charrington IPA; Bass; Guinness;*
Tennent's Lager.

Light snacks are served in the bar of this friendly, old-fashioned pub, with more substantial meals available in the 75-seat restaurant (12–2.30 & 7–9.30). Charcoal grills are a winter staple, while fish finds favour in the summer months. Other favourites include soups, well-filled sandwiches, oysters, steak, kidney and mushroom pie, rack of lamb and cold meat salads. A popular pub, so expect company.
Typical dishes Mushrooms provençale £3 Bookmaker sandwich £6

Credit Access, Amex, Diners, Visa

GUISBOROUGH   *Fox Inn*

10 Bow Street TS14 6BP   B&B
Map 4 D2 *Cleveland*
Guisborough (0287) 32958
Parking *limited*

Landlords *Mr & Mrs Williamson*
Brewery *Scottish & Newcastle*
🍺 *Scottish & Newcastle Exhibition;*
Younger's Scotch; McEwan's 80/-;
McEwan's Lager; Harp.
No real ale.

Accommodation *7 bedrooms* £D G3
Check-in all day

One of the two spotless bars is decked out in green plush to complement the copper-topped tables, and the other is similarly furnished but in red and with mock beams and rough plaster walls. The exterior is pebble-dashed, and the Williamsons make you welcome as soon as you step through the door. High standards of cleanliness extend to the bedrooms, simply furnished with lightwood units, TVs and tea-makers. Two public bathrooms serve all the rooms. *No dogs.*

Credit Access, Amex, Visa

GUISBOROUGH   *Moorcock Hotel*

West End TS14 6RL   B&B
Map 4 D2 *Cleveland*
Guisborough (0287) 32342
Parking *ample*

Landlord *Tom Wallace*
Brewery *Whitbread* 🍺
🍺 *Whitbread Trophy; Murphy Stout;*
Heineken; Stella Artois. No real ale.

Accommodation *6 bedrooms* £D G3
Check-in all day

On the outskirts of town, a modern red-brick pub offering functional overnight accommodation in six neatly fitted bedrooms. All have their own shower cubicle and TV, and share two public bathrooms. Tea and coffee-making facilities are available in a small kitchen attached to the residents' lounge, which also acts as a breakfast area. Downstairs is the large, split-level main bar (complete with fruit machines and a small dance floor), and a pine-furnished family room. Garden.

GUITING POWER   *Ye Olde Inne*

Winchcombe Road   FOOD
GL54 5UX
Area Map 4 C1 *Gloucs*
Guiting (045 15) 392
Parking *ample*

Bar food *12–2 & 7–9.30*

Landlords *Ken & Paula*
Thouless-Meyrick
Free house
🍺 *Wadworth 6X; Hook Norton Bitter;*
Theakston Best Bitter; McEwan's Export;
Guinness; Carlsberg Export. 🍏

The new owners are exceptionally friendly and courteous at their tiny old pub on the edge of an unspoilt village in a splendid rural setting. Plain but satisfying snacks range from ploughman's, steak and kidney pie, haddock in breadcrumbs and vegetable curry to Scandinavian specialities like marinated Danish herrings and frikadeller (a minced pork rissole) served with spicy red cabbage. Bread pudding is a favourite among desserts.
Typical dishes Pork chop in barbecue sauce £3.75 Lasagne £2.95

GUNNISLAKE — *Cornish Inn*

The Square PL18 9BW   `B&B`
Map 9 B2 *Cornwall*
Tavistock (0822) 832475
Parking *ample*

Landlords *Raymond & Christine Davey &*
John & Hilda McKinley
Free house
🍺 *St Austell Tinners Bitter; Hicks Special;*
Worthington Best Bitter; Guinness;
Carlsberg Export.

Accommodation *5 bedrooms* **£D G2**
Check-in all day

Whether you are on business or on holiday, this white painted village inn beckons you enticingly off the A390. A simple, spacious, spick and span bar awaits you with a cosy first-floor residents' lounge. Plain painted walls give a bright feel to the modest but comfortable rooms. Three have functional en suite bathrooms; two others with washbasins share a bathroom. All have colour TVs and tea-makers. Children welcome overnight. Patio.

Credit Access, Amex, Diners, Visa

---

*Changes in data sometimes occur
in establishments
after the Guide goes to press.*

*Prices should be taken as indications
rather than firm quotes.*

HALLATON — *Bewicke Arms*

1 Eastgate, Nr Market   `FOOD`
Harborough LE16 8UB
Map 7 C1 *Leicestershire*
Hallaton (085 889) 217
Parking *ample*

Bar food *12–2 & 7–9.45*

Landlords *Mr & Mrs N. A. Spiers*
Free house
🍺 *Ruddles County, Best Bitter; Webster*
Yorkshire Bitter; Guinness; Holsten Export.

A picturesque country village provides the setting for this pretty thatched pub, where the welcome is warm in the two little beamed bars. Blackboard specials supplement the printed menu, with choices like help-yourself leek soup accompanied by good crusty bread, piping hot vegetable lasagne, trout in white wine sauce, steaks and roast chicken. Rich sweets include butterscotch and walnut fudge cake.
Typical dishes Chicken Boursin £5.40
Swordfish steak £4.80

Credit Access, Visa

HALTWHISTLE — NEW ENTRY — *Milecastle Inn*

Old Military Road NE49 9NN   `FOOD`
Map 3 C1 *Northumberland*
Haltwhistle (0498) 20682
Parking *ample*

Bar food *12–2 & 6.30–9.30, Sun 7–9*

Landlords *Ralph & Margaret Payne*
Free house
🍺 *Ruddles Best Bitter, County; Webster*
Yorkshire Bitter; Guinness; Foster's;
Carlsberg Hof.

An ideal refuge in cold weather with its roaring fire and gentle lamplight, the Milecastle Inn is perched up high overlooking Hadrian's Wall. In the intimate restaurant (closed Mon, except Bank Hols, and Tues lunch) warming dishes such as venison, jugged hare and pheasant and claret pie are available in season. Good soup but disappointing desserts. Bar snacks include soup and pies.
Typical dishes Venison sausages £3.25
Steak & kidney pie £3.25

Credit Access, Diners, Visa

HAMSTEAD MARSHALL   NEW ENTRY   *White Hart Inn*

Nr Newbury RG15 0HW
Map 10 B3 *Berkshire*
Kintbury (0488) 58201
Parking *ample*

FOOD
B&B

Bar food *12–2.30 (Sun till 2) & 6.30–10 (Sun & Mon from 7)*

Landlords *Nicola & Dorothy Aromando*
Free house
🍺 *Wadworth 6X; Hall & Woodhouse Badgers Best; Guinness; Carlsberg; Stella Artois.* 🍷 ⊖

Accommodation *6 bedrooms* **£C G1**
Check-in all day

Italian dishes are a speciality here and you can enjoy them either in the oak-beamed bar or in the restaurant (the latter closed Sunday & Monday). Pasta, pizzas and omelettes make fine quickish snacks, while for a full meal you could follow garlicky stuffed mushrooms with herby roast suckling pig, rounding things off with chocolate and chestnut pudding. Note the very moreish home-baked bread with caraway seeds.

Typical dishes Spaghetti bolognese £3.95 Pork spare ribs £4.95

The whole place, including a very pretty garden, has a well-kept air, and this is especially true of the bedrooms, quietly situated in an old timbered barn. Two rooms are smallish singles, two decent-sized doubles and two large family rooms under the rafters; all are fresh, bright and inviting, with pine furniture, televisions, direct-dial phones and very smart, well-equipped bathrooms. Children accommodated overnight. The pub is within easy reach of the A4 and M4 (junction 13 or 14).

Credit Access, Amex, Diners, Visa

HANBURY   NEW ENTRY   *Eagle & Sun*

Nr Droitwich WR9 7DX
Map 7 B2 *Hereford & Worcs*
Droitwich (0905) 770130
Parking *ample*

FOOD

Bar food *11.30–1.45 & 7–9.45*
No bar food *Sun*

Landlord *Kevin Plant*
Brewery *Mitchells & Butlers*
🍺 *Bass; M & B Springfield; Guinness; Carling Black Label; Tennent's Extra.* ⊖

The bar lacks nothing in comfort, but the large canalside garden is *the* place to enjoy a summer snack. Inside or out, you can tuck into home-made pâté, lasagne, an omelette or maybe chicken princess. Steaks are popular, along with specials like swordfish steak with an excellent prawn, mushroom and cream sauce (sounds good enough to sharpen any appetite!).
Typical dishes Mediterranean prawns flamed in brandy £4.20 Loin of pork with rosemary & barbecue sauce £3.85

HANWELL   NEW ENTRY   *Moon & Sixpence*

Nr Banbury OX17 1HW
Map 10 B1 *Oxfordshire*
Wroxton St Mary (0295) 730544
Parking *ample*

Bar food *12–2*
No bar food *eves*
Closed *Sat, Sun & Mon lunches & 2 wks July*

Landlords *Leonard & Gillian DeFelice*
Free house
🍺 *Flowers IPA, Original; Heineken.* ⊖

Standing in a village whose origins date back to Anglo-Saxon times, this delightful 17th-century pub offers simple but appetising bar lunches from Tuesday to Friday, plus more elaborate meals in its attractive split-level restaurant (also open 7–10 pm Monday to Saturday). Snacks such as chicken curry, lasagne, tortellini and steak and kidney pie are all popular, while the à la carte menu features some imaginative vegetarian specials (note stir-fry mangetout with almonds) amongst Italian-inspired meat and seafood dishes.

Typical dishes Lemon sole £9.95 Fresh poached salmon £9.95

Accommodation 3 bedrooms £D G2
Check-in by arrangement

The three spotlessly kept bedrooms combine pretty pine furnishings with a light decor and floral fabrics. Extremely well equipped, all provide tea-makers, hairdryers, trouser presses and bathrobes, as well as fresh fruit. They share an excellent bathroom (with separate shower) and a lounge offering TV and video. A kitchen is also available, complete with well-stocked fridge and washing machine. Children welcome overnight.

Credit Access, Visa

HAROME   *Star Inn*

Nr Helmsley YO6 5JE   FOOD
Area Map 3 B3 *North Yorks*
Helmsley (0439) 70397
Parking *ample*

Bar food 12–1.45
No bar food *eves*

Landlord *Peter Gascoigne-Mullett*
Free house
🍷*Cameron Traditional Bitter; Theakston Best Bitter, Old Peculier; Carlsberg Hof.* ☯

Set in a peaceful Yorkshire village, this delightful thatched pub has a pretty garden and cosy beamed bar where a limited selection of lunchtime snacks can be enjoyed. There is a different soup every day, while freshly made sandwiches range from exotic curried chicken or prawns with cottage cheese and mayonnaise to traditional ham, roast beef and cheese. Daily hot dishes are available in the restaurant.
Typical dishes Smoked salmon sandwich £2.80 Beef in mushroom sauce £3.75

HARRIETSHAM   *Ringlestone Inn*

Nr Maidstone ME17 1NX   A
Area Map 5 B2 *Kent*
Maidstone (0622) 859207
Parking *ample*

Landlord *Michael Millington-Buck*
Free house
🍷*Fremlins Bitter; Ringlestone Bitter; guest beer; Murphy Stout; Stella Artois; Heineken.*

Sup a pint of real ale and imbibe the 400-year-old atmosphere of this splendid country inn. Tricky to locate, but worth finding tucked away by the Pilgrim's Way, it was a hostel in Henry VIII's day. The low beamed ceilings and brick floors reverberate with history and intricately carved settles and an awesome oak dresser take pride of place. Try one of a score of country wines in the pleasant garden.

Credit Access, Amex, Diners, Visa

HARROGATE   *West Park Hotel*

19 West Park HG1 1BL   B&B
Area Map 2 F5 *North Yorks*
Harrogate (0423) 524471
Parking *ample*

Landlord *Mr Riolfo*
Brewery *Tetley*
🍷*Tetley Bitter, Mild; Guinness; Skol; Castlemaine XXXX; Löwenbräu.* 🍷

Accommodation 17 bedrooms £C G2
Check-in all day

Quietly situated overlooking the greenery of the Stray, yet close to the town centre, this attractive inn with its welcoming landlord and staff is a delightful place to stay. Good-sized bedrooms (most with private bathroom) have direct-dial telephones and TVs. All are bright, modern and spotlessly kept. Downstairs, the main bar boasts a splendid ornate ceiling and there is a neat little cocktail bar with stylish banquette seating. Children welcome overnight. *No dogs.*

Credit Access, Amex, Diners, Visa

HASLEMERE   *Crowns*

Weyhill GU27 1BX   `FOOD`
Area Map 6 A2 *Surrey*
Haslemere (0428) 3112
Parking *ample*

Bar food *12–2.30 & 7–10.30*

Landlady *Brenda Heath*
Brewery *Friary Meux*
🍺 *King & Barnes Sussex Bitter; Ind Coope Burton Ale; Tetley Crown Special; Guinness; Castlemaine XXXX; Löwenbräu.* 🍷 ☻

Brenda Heath offers a splendid range of freshly prepared dishes based on top-quality ingredients at her busy, food-orientated pub. The bar has rattan furniture, shelves of books and attractive prints on the walls, while the blackboard menu has something for everyone – from oak-smoked trout with raspberry and dill sauce to plain grilled lemon sole, lamb fillet with rosemary and redcurrant to cheesy leek pie. Traditional favourites like ploughman's, jacket potatoes, salads and steaks are also well represented, and to finish there are fine cheeses and really lovely desserts such as brandy truffle cheesecake or walnut and caramel tart. On Thursday, Friday and Saturday evenings part of the pub becomes a restaurant with red-checked table cloths and a separate printed menu offering dishes like roast duck and poached salmon with lemon sauce. Traditional Sunday lunch available. Garden.

Typical dishes Deep-fried whitebait £2.50 Baked avocado with crab £3.50 Creole Jambalaya £4.65 Peppered chicken £5.45

Credit Access, Visa

HASTINGWOOD COMMON   *Rainbow & Dove*

Nr Harlow CM17 9JX   `A`
Map 10 D2 *Essex*
Harlow (0279) 415419
Parking *ample*

Landlords *Tony & Joyce Bird*
Brewery *Ind Coope*
🍺 *John Bull Bitter; Tetley Bitter; Guinness; Skol; Löwenbräu.* No real ale.

The Rainbow and Dove epitomises everything good about a small country pub despite its close proximity to junction 7 of the M11. Hanging fuchsias festoon the frontage in summer while at the back a putting green keeps customers attentively involved. This outdoor bustle contrasts with a low-beamed and darkly lit interior, winking with polished horse brasses and busy with a jug collection in pottery, copper and pewter. Garden and patio.

HATHERLEIGH   *George Hotel*

Market Street, Nr   `B&B`
Okehampton EX20 3JN
Map 9 B2 *Devon*
Okehampton (0837) 810454
Parking *ample*

Landlords *Veronica Devereux & John Dunbar-Ainley*
Free house ☻
🍺 *Bass; Whitbread Trophy; Wadworth 6X; Guinness; Stella Artois; Tennent's Export.*

Accommodation *11 bedrooms* £B G2
Check-in all day

Six miles north of Dartmoor is a cob and thatch inn that was originally a monks' retreat. The cobbled courtyard and low beamed ceilings preserve period charm, and the place is at its liveliest on Mondays and Tuesdays (market days), when all the bars see action. There are three of them, plus a tiny cocktail bar and a comfortable oak-furnished lounge. Bedrooms, most with en suite facilities, are in traditional style; some have four-posters. TVs and dial-out phones have been installed. Garden.

Credit Access, Visa

HAWKSHEAD   NEW ENTRY   *Drunken Duck Inn*

Barngates LA22 0NG   `B&B`
Area Map 1 D4 *Cumbria*
Hawkshead (096 66) 347
Parking *ample*

Landlords *Peter & Stephanie Barton*
Free house ☙
🍺 *Jennings Bitter; Tetley Bitter; Marston's Pedigree; Theakston Old Peculier; Murphy Stout; Labatt's.*

Accommodation *10 bedrooms* **£B G1**
Check-in all day

A lively, friendly inn at the pretty heart of the Lake District. The jokey new name might mislead some, but there are no game machines and noise is restricted to clinking glasses and drinkers' chatter. Refurbishment of the old building by younger generation owners has tidied up without losing the essential character of the place. New bedrooms have 'old-fashioned' decor; their en suite bathrooms are tiled and carpeted, though a little unfinished, lacking towel rails and shelves. Terrace.

Credit Access, Visa

HAWKSHEAD   *Queen's Head*

LA22 0NS   `FOOD`
Area Map 1 D4 *Cumbria*   `B&B`
Hawkshead (096 66) 271
Parking *difficult*

Bar food *12–2 & 6.15–9.30* ☙

Landlord *Mr Merrick*
Brewery *Hartley*
🍺 *Hartley XB, Mild; Robinson Best Bitter; Guinness; Stella Artois; Heineken.* ⊖

Accommodation *14 bedrooms* **£C G2**
Check-in all day

Dating back to Elizabethan times, this pretty, white-painted pub enjoys an attractive Lakeland village setting. Deceptively small from the outside, it opens out into two panelled bar areas resplendent with brass and copper and, to the rear, a neat dining room. An extensive bar menu offers a great variety of snacks, from soup and sandwiches to Cumberland sausages and steaks or ratatouille and macaroni. Good cheeses, including Wensleydale and Blue Shropshire, accompany the ploughman's and there is a choice of simple sweets. Traditional Sunday lunch available.

Typical dishes Curried cauliflower soup £1.10 Beef and mushroom pie £4.50

Low beams and simple furnishings characterise the main-house bedrooms, four of which have neat private bathrooms. Cottage rooms provide en suite facilities and include two new bedrooms (one with a four-poster) decorated on a Beatrix Potter theme. TVs and telephones are standard, and residents have the use of a plushly comfortable lounge. *No children under eight overnight. No dogs.*

Credit Access, Amex, Visa

HAYDON BRIDGE   NEW ENTRY   *General Havelock Inn*

Ratcliffe Road NE47 6ER   `FOOD`
Map 3 C1 *Northumberland*
Haydon Bridge (043 484) 376
Parking *ample*

Bar food *12–2*
No bar food *eves & lunch Sun–Tues*
Closed *All Mon & Tues lunch*

Landlords *Ian & Angela Clyde*
Free house
🍺 *Tetley Bitter, Mild; Castlemaine XXXX.*

A barn-style rear extension houses the excellent restaurant (12–1.30 & 7.30–9), whose patio doors lead out onto a little terrace beside the rushing River Tyne. Inside, local art combines with exposed stonework, bric-a-brac and pine dressers. The menu's emphasis is on local fresh ingredients, especially fish – try the delicious poached salmon. Soups, dressed crab, whiskied mussels or home-made terrine to start, followed by spiced fillet of pork, roast sirloin or king prawns. Lunchtime bar snacks are simpler versions of the same.

HAYTOR VALE   Rock Inn

Nr Newton Abbot TQ13 9XP   FOOD
Map 9 C2 *Devon*   B&B
Haytor (036 46) 305
Parking *ample*

Bar food *11–2 & 7–9.30* ☕

Landlord *Christopher Graves*
Free house
🍺 *Eldridge Pope Royal Oak, Dorset Original IPA; Bass; Guinness; Labatt's.* ☺

Dating back nearly 300 years, this sturdy pub stands in a tiny village below Haytor, the best known of the Dartmoor tors. Its characterful beamed bar and adjoining rooms make an attractive and extremely popular setting for a wide variety of well-prepared snacks. If all that fresh country air has made you ravenous, tuck into a substantial hot dish such as rabbit pie, flavoursome venison in red wine, smoked haddock crumble or chicken curry. Lighter alternatives include sandwiches, salads, Cheddar or Stilton ploughman's, jacket potatoes and soup, together with such sweets as treacle tart and chocolate fudge pudding. Traditional roast Sunday lunch available.

Typical dishes Steak & kidney pie £3.65
Beef curry £3.65

Accommodation *9 bedrooms* **£A G1/2**
Check-in all day

Nine well-kept bedrooms are attractively decorated and furnished in individual style (one boasts a four-poster) and most have private bath or shower rooms. Tea and coffee making facilities, TVs and direct-dial telephones are standard throughout. Garden. *No dogs.*

Credit Access, Amex, Visa

HECKINGTON   NEW ENTRY   Nag's Head

34 High Street NG34 9QZ   B&B
Map 4 E4 *Lincolnshire*
Sleaford (0529) 60218
Parking *ample*

Landlords *Bruce & Georgina Pickworth*
Brewery *Manns*
🍺 *Ruddles County, Best Bitter; Webster Yorkshire Bitter; Guinness; Foster's.*

Accommodation *4 bedrooms* **£D G3**
Check-in all day

In the centre of a village by the Lincolnshire Fens, the Nag's Head offers agreeable overnight accommodation. The atmosphere is warm and relaxing in the bar. Other day rooms have been rearranged, the upstairs dining room now being a resident's lounge. Four simple little bedrooms have quaintly old-fashioned furniture, pretty floral wallpaper, TVs and tea-makers. All have washbasins; the bathroom is shared. Enjoyable breakfasts. Children welcome overnight.

Credit Amex, Diners

HELFORD   Shipwright's Arms

Nr Helston TR12 6JX   FOOD
Map 9 A3 *Cornwall*
Manaccan (032 623) 235
Parking *difficult*

Bar food *12–1.30 & 7–9*
No bar food *Sun eve (winter)*

Landlords *Brandon Flynn & Charles Herbert*
Brewery *Cornish*
🍺 *John Devenish Dry Hop Bitter, Dark Mild, Cornish Original Bitter; Newquay Steam Bitter; Guinness; Heineken.* 🍷 ☺

The location, on the banks of the Helford Estuary, is quite stunning, and the approach to the thatched hostelry is so narrow that it is restricted to pedestrians in summer. Salads, lasagne and steak and kidney pudding are typical lunchtime dishes, supplemented in the evenings by such delights as crab and lobster, seasonal fresh fish and a good rich beef bourguignon. Sweets are limited but mainly home-made.

Typical dishes Garlic mushrooms £2
Fresh lobster salad £8.50

HELMSLEY   *Feathers Hotel*

Market Place YO6 5BH   `B&B`
Area Map 3 B3 *North Yorks*
Helmsley (0439) 70275
Parking *ample*

Landlords *Feathers family*
Free house ☎
🍺 *Theakston Best Bitter; Cameron
Traditional Bitter; McEwan 80/-;
Carlsberg Hof.* 🍷

Accommodation *18 bedrooms* **£C G2**
Check-in all day

On the stylish market square is a busy,
family-run inn made up from a tiny 15th-
century cottage and an elegant 18th-
century house. Simply appointed bedrooms
offer TVs and tea-makers and most have
functional bathrooms (those without are
provided with washbasins and share two
public bathrooms). The lounge bar features
attractive locally carved furniture and there
is a cheerful, beamed public bar as well as a
first-floor residents' lounge. Accommodation closed from Christmas to 1 January.

Credit Access, Amex, Diners, Visa

HENLEY-ON-THAMES   *Argyll*

Market Place RG9 2ZA   `FOOD`
Map 10 C3 *Oxfordshire*
Henley-on-Thames (0491) 573400
Parking *ample*

Bar food *12–2*
No bar food *eves*

Landlords *Ray & Veronica Boswell*
Brewery *Morland*
🍺 *Morland Best Bitter, Bitter, Mild; Stella
Artois; Heineken.* ⊖

Mullioned windows with panes of coloured
glass offset dark panelling and polished
tables inside a well-kept black-and-white
pub in the centre of the town. Buffet-style
food includes a large home-cooked ham
sliced to order, quiches, pâté and roast of
the day. Select your own salad accompaniments. Hot dishes might be steak and
kidney pie, curry or a casserole, and there is
trifle among other simple sweets.
Typical dishes Lancashire hotpot £3.80
Chicken & gammon pie £3.60

HENLEY-ON-THAMES   *Little Angel*

Remenham Lane,   `FOOD`
Remenham RG9 2LS
Map 10 C3 *Oxfordshire*
Henley-on-Thames (0491) 574165
Parking *ample*

Bar food *12–2 & 7–10 (Sun till 9.30)*

Landlord *Paul Southwood*
Brewery *Brakspear*
🍺 *Brakspear Bitter, 4X Old; Guinness;
Heineken.* 🍷 ⊖

Imaginative bar food in a characterful
setting is the winning combination at a fine
old pub just over the bridge on the A423.
The monthly-changing menu ranges from
home-made soup and garlic mushrooms on
toast to chicken with cashew nuts, moules
marinière and rump steak with chilli sauce.
More elaborate meals in the restaurant (12–
2 & 7.30–10), and a traditional roast lunch
on Sundays.
Typical dishes Chicken and prawn foo
yung £5 Calf's liver and bacon £7.50

Credit Access, Amex, Diners, Visa

HENTON   *Peacock*

Nr Chinnor OX9 4AH   `B&B`
Map 10 C2 *Oxfordshire*
Kingston Blount (0844) 53519
Parking *ample*

Landlord *Mr H.S. Good*
Free house
🍺 *Brakspear Bitter; Hook Norton Best
Bitter; Murphy Stout; Carlsberg.*

Accommodation *12 bedrooms* **£C G1**
Check-in all day

A lovely 600-year-old thatched inn in a
sleepy village just off the B4009. Peacocks
roam the grounds, and inside the bar is
spotless and comfortable. The residents'
lounge and the nearest bedrooms are all in
an extension built by the landlord with care
and pride. The bedrooms are smart, warm
and equipped to a high standard with
direct-dial telephones, radio-alarms, hairdryers, tea-makers and remote control TVs.
All have carpeted en suite bathrooms.
Children welcome overnight.

Credit Access, Amex, Visa

HETTON   NEW ENTRY   *Angel Inn*

Nr Skipton BD23 6LT   `FOOD`
Area Map 2 C4 *North Yorks*
Skipton (075 673) 263
Parking *ample*

Bar food *12–2 (Sun till 2.30) & 6–10*

Landlord *Denis Watkins*
Free house
🍺 *Theakston Best Bitter, XB, Old Peculier; Timothy Taylor Landlord; Beck's Bier; Slalom Lager.* ☺

A popular, well-kept pub whose bar decor includes fresh flowers, attractive pictures and sepia photographs. The bar menu is extensive, and on Friday a special fish menu widens the choice with dishes like a platter of lobster, prawns and salmon with an avocado garnish and a light, garlicky dressing. Summer pudding is a favourite sweet. Excellent local farmhouse cheeses. Also a restaurant, open evenings (Monday to Saturday) and Sunday lunch.

Typical dishes Gravadlax £3.50 Poached salmon beurre blanc with dill £5.95

HEYDON   NEW ENTRY   *King William IV*

Chrishall Road SG8 8PW   `A`
Map 10 D1 *Cambridgeshire*
Chrishall (0763 838) 773
Parking *ample*

Landlady *Mary Kirkham*
Free house 🛏
🍺 *Greene King IPA; Adnams Bitter; Ruddles County; Guinness; Kronenbourg 1664.*

Unremarkable on the outside, but an Aladdin's Cave within, this ancient pub just 20 minutes' drive from Cambridge literally overflows with amazing memorabilia. Heavy beams, rustic tables suspended by chains from the ceiling, and a blazing log fire provide the background for a collection that embraces giant bellows, a plough, cast-iron cauldrons, stuffed animals in glass cases – even a copper font with a gothic-style wooden lid for impromptu christenings! Family room and patio.

Credit Access, Amex, Diners, Visa

Any person using our name to obtain
free hospitality is a fraud.

Proprietors, please inform Egon Ronay's Guides
and the police.

HIMLEY   *Crooked House*

Coppice Mill, Nr Dudley   `A`
DY3 4DA
Map 6 E2 *West Midlands*
Dudley (0384) 238583
Parking *ample*

Landlords *Gary & Dawn Ensor*
Brewery *Banks's*
🍺 *Banks's Bitter, Dark Mild, Hanson's Black Country Bitter; Kronenbourg 1664; Harp.*

A pub that has even the soberest of customers reeling! The 250-year-old building was a Victorian victim of mining subsidence, with the result that the walls and the quarry-tiled floors are at crazy angles. The oddest feature of all is tables where bottles apparently roll uphill – you can try it out for a small contribution to charity. Besides the main bar there is a lounge bar, a conservatory seating area and tables out on the front terrace by a stream.

HINDON   *Lamb at Hindon*

Nr Salisbury SP3 6DP
Area Map 7 D2 *Wiltshire*
Hindon (074 789) 573
Parking *ample*

Bar food *12–2 & 7–10*

Landlords *Mr A.J. Morrison & John Croft*
Free house
👄 *Wadworth 6X, IPA; Webster Yorkshire Bitter; Guinness; Carlsberg Export.* 🍺 ⊖

FOOD
B&B

Once well known as a smugglers' haunt, and later a popular coaching inn, the Lamb dates back to the 17th century. Bay windows in the stone facade, large open fireplaces and a fine old staircase recreate the original look, and across the street in this unspoilt village is a raised garden area for summer drinking. A favourite with the locals is the roast of the day, and at lunchtimes on certain days there is a cold buffet. Sandwiches, ploughman's, beef curry, fisherman's pie and salmon coulibiac all share a place on the menu. Hot fruit pie to follow. Children's outdoor play area.

Typical dishes Game casserole £3.75 Fresh salmon fish cakes £4.75

Accommodation *16 bedrooms* **£C G2**
Check-in all day

Smart rooms with pretty fabrics and carpets, with furnishings ranging from traditional to modern, all have TVs, direct-dial telephones, radio intercoms and tea-makers. Eleven are en suite and the others share three public bathrooms. Some of the floors slope quite dramatically. Children welcome overnight. *No dogs.*

Credit Access, Amex, Visa

HOLT   *Old Ham Tree*

Nr Trowbridge BA14 6PY
Map 10 A3 *Wiltshire*
North Trowbridge (0225) 782581
Parking *ample*

Bar food *12–2 & 7–10*

Landlords *John & Carol Francis*
Free house
👄 *Wadworth 6X; Marston Pedigree; Ash Vine Bitter; Guinness; Carlsberg Hof.* ⊖

FOOD
B&B

Whither the old ham tree? The 18th-century inn of that name stands seemingly unconcerned keeping an eye instead on the village green. This and other such rural conundrums may be pondered on or ignored in favour of a pint and a perusal of the menu in the beamed but otherwise unfussy bar. The spectacular is eschewed in favour of the reliable here. Typical of the short daily-changing menu is chicken and leek soup, braised liver and onions or lamb cutlets with. home-made puddings like Bakewell tart or date and walnut sponge. Lighter appetites are appeased with sandwiches, plain or toasted.

Typical dishes Steak and Guinness pie £3.25 Chicken with avocado and cream sauce £3.25

Accommodation *4 bedrooms* **£D G3**
Check-in all day

The four centrally heated bedrooms are clean and airy, white-walled with matching furniture. Duvets have pretty floral covers. The rooms share a modern carpeted and clean bathroom. TV lounge above the bar is available to residents. Children welcome overnight.

Credit Access, Diners, Visa

HOLTON   *Old Inn*

Nr Wincanton BA9 8AR   A
Area Map 7 B3 *Somerset*
Wincanton (0963) 32002
Parking *ample*

Landlords *Lou & Lin Lupton*
Free house
🍺 *Greene King Abbot Ale; Butcombe
Bitter; Guinness; Carlsberg Hof.* 🍺

A pleasant spot to pause for a drink, in a
peaceful setting not far from the A303, the
Old Inn is locally popular. It dates from the
17th century and in the bar beams, paved
floor, a log-burning stove, upholstered
wooden settles and refectory tables keep a
traditional feel. An interesting feature is a
collection of key-rings hanging from the
ceiling by the counter. There is a garden for
taking refreshment in the summer sun.

Credit Access, Visa

HOLYWELL   *Ye Olde Ferryboat Inn*

Nr St Ives, Huntingdon   B&B
PE17 3TG
Map 8 D2 *Cambridgeshire*
St Ives (0480) 63227
Parking *ample*

Landlord *Richard Jeffrey*
Free house ☕
🍺 *Greene King IPA, Bitter, Abbot Ale;
Guinness; Carling Black Label; Tennent's
Extra.*

Accommodation *5 bedrooms* £C G2
Check-in all day

An inn with a thousand-year history, on
many occasions rebuffing the angry floods
of the Ouse, the Ferryboat has seen its
owner of twenty years disembark and is
now boarded by a new proprietor. Particular
features of note are the old black beams, the
sun terrace, affording splendid views, and a
particularly charming panelled alcove off
the main bar. At present, there are five neat
bedrooms, two en suite, adequate for overnight, but major plans are afoot. Garden. *No
children under 14 overnight. No dogs.*

Credit Access, Amex, Diners, Visa

HOLYWELL GREEN   *Rock Inn Hotel*

Nr Halifax HX4 9BS   B&B
Map 3 C3 *West Yorkshire*
Halifax (0422) 79721
Parking *ample*

Landlord *Robert Vinsen*
Free house
🍺 *Theakston Best Bitter, XB; Younger's
IPA; Guinness; Slalom Lager, Pilsner.*

Accommodation *18 bedrooms* £B G2
Check-in all day

Enjoying a peaceful rural setting, yet conveniently near junction 24 of the M62, this
carefully modernised pub converted from a
row of 17th-century cottages has a warmly
welcoming air. Open fires, beams and
original stonework walls characterise the
bars, while pine-ceilinged bedrooms in a
rear extension are contrastingly modern. All
have white fitted furniture and brightly tiled
shower rooms, as well as TVs, radios, direct-
dial telephones, drinks trays and trouser
presses. Children welcome overnight.

Credit Access, Amex, Diners, Visa

HONILEY   NEW ENTRY   *Honiley Boot Inn*

Nr Kenilworth LV8 1NP   B&B
Map 7 B2 *Warwickshire*
Kenilworth (0926) 484234
Parking *ample*

Landlord *Roger Thomas*
Brewery *Whitbread*
🍺 *Flowers IPA; Whitbread Mild; Guinness;
Heineken; Stella Artois.*

Accommodation *10 bedrooms* £D G3
Check-in all day

Important developments at this 15th-
century coaching inn by the A4177 include
a smart new nightclub. Bedrooms are quite
modest, but comfortable enough and very
clean, with white walls and furniture. TVs,
tea-makers and trouser presses are
provided, and the ten rooms share two
spotless bathrooms and separate showers.
The bars mix modern and period features,
and you will also find a well-equipped
children's outdoor play area, a garden and a
patio.

HOPE

Poachers Arms

Castleton Road s30 2RD `FOOD`
Map 4 D4 *Derbyshire* `B&B`
Hope Valley (0433) 20380
Parking *ample*

Bar food *12–2 & 6–10 (Sun from 7)*

Landlords *Gladys & David Bushell*
Free house
🍺 *John Smith's Bitter; Courage Directors; Guinness; Foster's.* ⊖

Accommodation *7 bedrooms* £C G1
Check-in all day

Copper-topped tables, beams, plaster walls and a pair of stuffed fox heads set the scene at Mrs Bushell's and son David's ship-shape pub in the Peak District National Park. A vast choice of bar food is served seven days a week. Home-baked ham, home-made bread rolls and a huge serving of Hungarian goulash made with tender meat feature alongside fish crumble, garlic mushrooms, steaks, Roman lamb and tortellini. Vegetarians are well catered for.

Typical dishes Steak and kidney pie £3.85 Roast lamb £3.95

Varying sized bedrooms can be very large with spacious bathrooms equipped with corner baths, bidets and showers. Walls may be plain white woodchip or patterned. Furniture ranges from utilitarian laminate and cheap reproduction to the odd antique. All rooms have en suite modern bathrooms, direct dial phones, TVs and tea-makers. Children welcome overnight.

Credit Access, Amex, Diners, Visa

Our inspectors never book in the name of Egon Ronay's Guides.

They disclose their identity only if they are considering an establishment for inclusion in the next edition of the Guide.

HOPESGATE

NEW ENTRY

Stables Inn

Nr Minsterley SY5 0EP `FOOD`
Map 6 D2 *Shropshire*
Worthen (074 383) 344
Parking *ample*

Bar food *12–1.45 & 7–8.45*
No bar food *eves Sun–Wed*
Closed *all Mon*

Landlords *Denis & Debbie Harding*
Free house
🍺 *Bass; Woods Special; Marston Pedigree; Beamish Stout; Marston Pilsner; Carlsberg.* ⊖

Take the signposted road off the A488 south of Minsterley to find this delightfully rustic and remote pub. Once inside, you face the pleasant task of choosing from the blackboard menu: everything is fresh and tasty, from soups and pâtés to curries, casseroles and crumbles, with bread and butter pudding an excuse to indulge further. Best to book in the evening (Thurs–Sat).

Typical dishes Beery beef & vegetable pie £3.90 Tomato & aubergine bake on walnut & garlic rice £3.50

HORNINGSEA   Plough & Fleece

High Street CB5 9JG   `FOOD`
Map 8 D2 *Cambridgeshire*
Cambridge (0223) 860795
Parking *limited*

Bar food *12–2 (Sun till 1.45)* & *7–9.30*
No bar food *Sun & Mon eves*

Landlords *Joyce & Ken Grimes*
Brewery *Greene King*
● *Greene King IPA, Abbot Ale; Harp;*
Kronenbourg 1664.

Two cosy bars provide an informal setting to enjoy traditional bar snacks. Lunchtimes see sandwiches, pies and stews, with traditional English puddings to finish, while evenings bring a more elaborate range of dishes from Romany rabbit to individual beef Wellington. Arrive early at lunchtime to beat the crowds. Limited menu Sunday lunchtime. Garden.
Typical dishes Suffolk ham hotpot £3.70 Welsh fish pie £4.50

Credit Access, Visa

HORN'S CROSS   Hoops Inn

Nr Bideford EX39 5DL   `B&B`
Map 9 B1 *Devon*
Horn's Cross (023 75) 222
Parking *ample*

Landlords *Marjorie & Derek Sargent*
Free house ☻
● *Marston Pedigree; Flowers Original;*
Wadworth 6X; Stella Artois; Heineken.

Accommodation *13 bedrooms* £C G2
Check-in all day

White cob walls and a reed-thatched roof make a pretty sight at an ancient inn (under new ownership) less than a mile from the coast. The well-appointed bar features light oak furniture, an open fireplace and a glass-covered well. There is also a family room and a very comfortable and traditional lounge. Five bedrooms in the original part have much more character than those in the purpose-built block, but the latter have TVs and private shower rooms. Garden.

Credit Access, Amex, Diners, Visa

HORRINGER   Beehive

The Street IP29 5SD   `FOOD`
Map 8 E2 *Suffolk*
Horringer (028 488) 260
Parking *ample*

Bar food *12.15–2* & *7.15–10*
No bar food *Sun eve*

Landlords *Gary & Diane Kingshott*
Brewery *Greene King*
● *Greene King Abbot Ale, IPA;*
Kronenbourg 1664; Harp. ♥

Once an old beer house, this charming village pub today offers good eating in its cosy, convivial little bars. Blackboards display the day's fresh fish specials – perhaps grilled Dover sole or cheese-topped oysters with cream and prawns – while from the printed menu come snacks like hot chilli mushrooms and smoked haddock hash. Butterscotch meringue pie or fresh fruit pavlova to finish. Patio.
Typical dishes Spaghetti napoletana £3.25 Cheese and broccoli bake £3.25

HORSEBRIDGE   NEW ENTRY   Royal Inn

Nr Tavistock PL19 8PJ   `FOOD`
Map 9 B2 *Devon*
Milton Abbot (082 287) 214
Parking *ample*

Bar food *12–2* & *7–10 (Sat till 10.30)*
No bar food *Sun eves*

Landlords *Terry & June Wood*
Free house
● *Horsebridge Heller, Best, Tamar; Bass;*
Guinness; Tennent's Extra. ✆

Three excellent reasons for a detour to Terry Wood's informal pub are to look at the ancient Tamar Bridge, to sample the Horsebridge Ales (brewed by a son) and to tuck into a bar meal prepared by Terry's wife June. Her repertoire runs from ploughman's with herby home-baked bread to chilli, curry, beef bourguignon and Aylesbury pie made with pressed duck breast, duck liver and mushrooms. Imaginative salads, no chips, ample sweets.
Typical dishes 'Nutter's roast' £2.75 Plaice florentine £3.70

HORTON   *Horton Inn*

Cranborne, Nr Wimborne   `FOOD` `B&B`
BH21 5AD
Area Map 7 E4 *Dorset*
Witchampton (0258) 840252
Parking *ample*

Bar food *12–2 & 7–10* ☙

Landlord *Nicholas Caplan*
Free house
🍺 *Ind Coope Burton Ale; Wadworth 6X; Courage Best Bitter; John Smith's Bitter; Kronenbourg 1664; Foster's.* 🍷

Accommodation *5 bedrooms* £C G2
Check-in all day

Find this attractively refurbished 18th-century inn at a crossroads on the B3078, surrounded by the downlands of southern Dorset. Young resident proprietor Nicholas Caplan is a hard-working and enthusiastic host, and there is good eating to be had in the convivial bar or, in fine weather, the garden and patio. The regular menu offers traditional snacks like soup, sandwiches and ploughman's as well as more substantial steaks, grills and fish dishes. Listed on the blackboard are daily specials such as seafood pancakes, cannelloni or trout with almonds, with perhaps hazelnut meringue or cream-filled profiteroles to finish. Traditional roast lunch on Sundays.

Typical dishes Fisherman's pie £3.75 Lasagne £2.65

The five bright, fresh bedrooms are extremely spacious and offer comfortable easy chairs as well as TVs and tea-makers. Two rooms have large, well-equipped bathrooms en suite, while the rest share a public bathroom. There is a separate lounge for residents' use on the first floor.

Credit Access, Visa

HORTON-IN-RIBBLESDALE   *Crown Hotel*

Nr Settle BD24 0HF   `B&B`
Area Map 2 B3 *North Yorks*
Horton-in-Ribblesdale (072 96) 209
Parking *limited*

Landlords *Richard & Norma Hargreaves*
Brewery *Theakston*
🍺 *Theakston Best Bitter, XB, Mild; Guinness; Matthew Brown Slalom Lager.* 🍷

Accommodation *10 bedrooms* £D G3
Check-in all day

A genuine Yorkshire welcome awaits visitors to this most unpretentious of pubs, a limestone building standing right on the Pennine Way, near the river Ribble. This is walking country par excellence, and walkers join local characters for a chat in the beamed bars; residents can join in, or watch TV in one of the homely lounges. Bedrooms are smallish, clean and quite modest, with modern utility furniture; most have shower cubicles. Two cottages are suitable for families. Children welcome overnight. Garden and play area.

HUBBERHOLME   *George Inn*

Kirk Gill, Nr Skipton   `B&B`
BD23 5JE
Area Map 2 C3 *North Yorks*
Kettlewell (075 676) 223
Parking *ample*

Landlords *John Frederick & Marjorie Forster*
Free house ☙
🍺 *Younger's No 3, Scotch; Harp; Beck's Bier.*

Accommodation *4 bedrooms* £D G3
Check-in all day

A marvellously peaceful place to stay, right on the banks of the river Wharfe. The bar is charming and quite small, with burnished copper-topped tables. The floor is flagged, the walls of thick stone, and there is an open-range fireplace – an ideal spot for a drink and a chat. The room adjacent is similar (but no bar; children allowed). Overnight accommodation comprises four well-kept rooms with whitewashed stone walls, modern white furniture and washbasins. They share a bathroom. *No children under eight overnight.*

HUNGERFORD   *John O'Gaunt Inn*

21 Bridge Street RG17 0NH [FOOD] [B&B]
Map 10 B3 *Berkshire*
Hungerford (0488) 83535
Parking *ample*

Bar food *12–2 & 7–9.30*
No bar food *Sun eve*

Landlords *Jane Wratten & David Ricketts*
Free house
🍺 *Courage Best Bitter; Wadworth 6X; Wiltshire Old Grumble; Guinness; Foster's; Kronenbourg 1664.* 💵 ⊖

Standing at the bottom end of town next to a bridge over the Kennet and Avon canal, this spruce pink and green inn offers simple but delicious snacks in appealing surroundings. Weathered beams, bare wood floors and pine seating characterise the three interconnecting bars, where dishes from the blackboard menu can be enjoyed. Choose from flavoursome home-made soup and lovely French bread sandwiches, freshly caught fish or perhaps a juicy, well-hung steak served with carefully cooked seasonal vegetables. The choice of sweets is limited, but watch out for the featherlight, currant-studded Norwegian bread and butter pudding. Traditional roast lunch available on Sundays.

Typical dishes Cottage pie £2.45 Lasagne £2.85

Accommodation *3 bedrooms* **£C G2**
Check-in by arrangement

The three neatly furnished bedrooms are bright and clean, with pretty matching duvet covers and curtains. One room boasts a fine brass-headed bed and has its own en suite bathroom, while the other two have private shower room. Good hearty cooked breakfasts. Patio. *No dogs.*

Credit Access, Visa

HUNTINGDON   *Old Bridge Hotel*

1 High Street PE18 6TQ [FOOD]
Map 8 D2 *Cambridgeshire*
Huntingdon (0480) 52681
Parking *ample*

Bar food *10.30–2.30 & 6–11*

Landlord *Raymond Waters*
Free house
🍺 *Ruddles County; Tolly Cobbold Bitter; Paine's XXX; Kestrel* 💵 ⊖

Here the bar menu steals its ideas from all sorts of cuisine – tagliatelle Genovese, stir-fried fillet of beef with fresh beansprouts, lamb tikka masala and Gruyère cheese fritters show the scope. Sound cooking and first-class ingredients abound, the fish of the day being particularly recommended, as are the freshly-made trolley puddings. Also of note is the terrace right by the river Ouse.

Typical dishes Pigeon pie £6.25 Hamburger with relish £5.45

Credit Access, Amex, Diners, Visa

ICKHAM   NEW ENTRY   *Duke William*

Nr Canterbury CT1 1QP [FOOD]
Area Map 5 E2 *Kent*
Canterbury (0227) 721308
Parking *ample*

Bar food *12–2 & 7–10, Sun 12–3 & 7–9*
Pub closed *Mon lunch (except Bank Hols)*

Landlords *Mr & Mrs A.R. McNeil*
Free house
🍺 *Young Special; Fuller London Pride; Adnams Bitter; Shepherd Neame Master Brew Bitter; Guinness; Steinbock.*

Staff and resident cats alike offer a warm welcome at this comfortable old village pub near the A257. Simple, satisfying snacks such as Lincolnshire sausages, ploughman's and poached haddock can be enjoyed in the front bar, while the restaurant menu has a wide choice of meat and fish dishes served either plain or elaborately sauced. Irresistible chocolate and walnut cups feature among tempting sweets.

Typical dishes Battered cod £2.75 Steak & kidney pie £3.95

Credit Access, Amex, Diners, Visa

ILMINGTON   Howard Arms

Lower Green, Nr Shipston- **FOOD**
on-Stour CV36 4LX
Map 10 A1 *Warwickshire*
Ilmington (060 882) 226
Parking *ample*

Bar food *11.45–2 (Sun 12–1.30) &
6.45–9.45*
No bar food *Sun eve*

Landlords *David & Sarah Russon*
Brewery *Whitbread*
🍷 *Flowers Best Bitter, Original; Guinness;
Heineken, Stella Artois.* 🍷 ⊖

The enthusiastic Russons work hard to
produce consistently enjoyable meals at
their well-run village pub. Eat in the
pleasantly traditional bar or restaurant,
choosing from a weekly-changing menu
that runs from flavoursome soups, smoked
mackerel pâté and ploughman's to, say,
sautéed kidneys with mushrooms or sole
Florentine. Nice sweets like Dutch apple
meringue pie to finish.
Typical dishes Stuffed chicken breast
£4.95 Roast rack of lamb £5.50

Credit Access, Visa

IVY HATCH   The Plough

Nr Sevenoaks TN15 0NL **FOOD**
Area Map 6 F1 *Kent*
Plaxtol (0732) 810268
Parking *ample*

Bar food *12–2.30 & 7–9.30*
No bar food *Sun eve*

Landlady *Mrs Ginzler*
Free house
🍷 *Ind Coope Bitter; Bateman XXX, XB;
Larkins Bitter; guest beer; Löwenbräu.* 🍷 ⊖

Candles at night and the light from a log fire
reflecting in polished dark wood furniture
make for a wonderfully romantic atmosphere at this late 18th-century country inn.
Chef-patron Mrs Ginzler's cooking more
than matches its surroundings and her
authentic dishes include rich, velvety fish
soup, featherlight mussel and asparagus
flan, hearty oxtail stew and simple but
delicious liver and bacon. In the pretty
conservatory restaurant, more formal
menus range from tender pink pigeon
breast with a honey and grape sauce to
splendid local venison cooked with juniper
berries in a game sauce or rack of lamb with
apricot and rosemary sauce, all served with
lovely sliced potatoes in cream cheese.
Sweets such as bread and butter pudding or
crème brûlée are available in both the bar
and restaurant. Restaurant closed Sunday
evening and Monday lunchtime; less choice
of bar food Sunday lunch.

Typical dishes Ratatouille & garlic bread
£2.50 Game casserole £6.50 Salade tiède
£4.50 Pissaladière £3.95

Credit Access, Visa

KENLEY   Wattenden Arms

Old Lodge Lane CR3 5JR **FOOD**
Map 10 D3 *Surrey*
01-660 8638
Parking *ample*

Bar food *12–2.30 & 7–9*

Landlords *Joan & Ron Coulston*
Brewery *Charrington*
🍷 *Charrington IPA; Bass; Worthington
Best Bitter; Stones Bitter; Tennent's Extra;
Carling Black Label.* 🍷 ⊖

The Coulstons have cared for this splendid
village pub for over 25 years and offer
appetising bar snacks as traditionally
British as the portraits of royals past and
present crowding the panelled walls.
Hearty favourites such as roast beef and
Yorkshire, grilled kippers and sausage, egg
and chips stand alongside excellent home-
cooked meats for sandwiches and salads,
with spotted dick or bread pudding for
afters. Sandwiches only on Sunday. Patio.
Typical dishes Steak pudding £4
Apple pie £1

KESWICK   *Pheasant Inn*

Crosthwaite Road CA12 5PP   `B&B`
Area Map 1 C1 *Cumbria*
Keswick (076 87) 72219
Parking *limited*

Landlords *D.G. & M. Wright*
Brewery *Jennings*
🍺 *Jennings Bitter; Tetley Bitter; Guinness; Ayingerbräu.*

Accommodation *3 bedrooms* **£D G3**
Check-in all day

Locals and fell walkers alike love this homely little inn standing just off the A66, about a mile from the centre of Keswick. A coal fire warms the sturdily traditional bar, whose walls are decorated with a colourful collection of cartoons, and there is a patio for summer drinking. Three neat, simply appointed bedrooms all have washbasins, individual heating and tea-makers. They share a modern carpeted bathroom well stocked with soft towels. Children welcome overnight.

KEYSTON   *The Pheasant*

Nr Bythorn, Huntingdon   `FOOD`
PE18 0RE
Map 8 D2 *Cambridgeshire*
Bythorn (080 14) 241
Parking *ample*

Bar food *12–2 & 6–10, Sun 12–1.30 & 7.15–9.30*

Landlord *Bill Bennett*
Free house
🍺 *Tolly Cobbold Bitter; Ruddles County; Adnams Bitter; Stella Artois; Carlsberg.* 🍷

Food and wine are taken very seriously at this stylish thatched village pub run with flair and panache by chef-patron Bill Bennett. Imaginative and keenly priced wines by the glass and bottle accompany such delicious daily-changing specials as deeply flavoured leek soup, piquant chicken and vegetable stir-fry and beautifully fresh crab mornay. Excellent puddings, too, from nursery offerings to rich crêpes.
Typical dishes Steak and kidney pie £4.95 Whole grilled trout £5.95

Credit Access, Amex, Diners, Visa

KILVE   *Hood Arms*

Nr Bridgwater TA5 1EA   `FOOD`
Map 9 C1 *Somerset*   `B&B`
Holford (027 874) 210
Parking *ample*

Bar food *11.30–2 & 6.30– 10, Sun 12–1.30 & 7–9.30*

Landlords *Robbie Rutt & Neville White*
Free house
🍺 *Flowers Original; Marston Pedigree; Whitbread Best Bitter; Guinness; Heineken; Stella Artois.* ⊖

Accommodation *5 bedrooms* **£B G2**
Check-in by arrangement

The bars are traditional, with beams, brasses and a stone fireplace, and the landscaped garden and patio are pleasant spots when the sun comes out. The landlords extend a warm welcome, and service is both friendly and efficient. The bar menu, available lunchtime and evening every day, ranges from soup, sandwiches, ploughman's platters and salads to a blackboard list of daily hot dishes, which might include chicken scrumpy or haddock and broccoli mornay. It is well worth leaving a gap for one of the good sweets, perhaps mincemeat crumble or the popular treacle tart.

Typical dishes Cauliflower, celery & Stilton bake £3.20 Bread & butter pudding £1.10

Four of the variously-sized bedrooms have en suite facilities (one shower/wc only). Furniture is simple but quite smart, fabrics attractive, and a good range of accessories comprises heaters, TVs, trouser presses, clock-radios and kettles. Breakfast on our last visit was adequate but by no means exciting. *No children under seven overnight.*

Credit Access, Visa

KINETON
Halfway House

Nr Guiting Power,   `B&B`
Cheltenham GL54 5UG
Area Map 4 C1 *Gloucs*
Guiting Power (045 15) 344
Parking *ample*

Landlords *Derek & Jean Marshall*
Brewery *Donnington*
Donnington Best Bitter, SBA; Carlsberg Pilsner.

Accommodation *3 bedrooms* £D G3
Check-in all day

In a hamlet overlooking the picturesque Windrush valley, the Marshalls' 17th-century stone inn offers a warm welcome and simple but spotlessly kept accommodation. Light and airy, the three bedrooms are simply furnished, all have washbasins and share a bathroom and smart modern shower room. The cosy bar (children welcome lunchtimes only) and pretty garden with play area provide attractive drinking spots for all seasons. Accommodation closed one week Christmas. *No children under 14 overnight. No dogs.*

KINGSCLERE
NEW ENTRY   Swan Hotel

Swan Street, Nr Newbury   `FOOD`
RG15 8PP   `B&B`
Map 10 B3 *Berkshire*
Newbury (0635) 298314
Parking *ample*

Bar food *12–2 & 7–9.30*

Landlord *Geoffrey Buckle*
Free house
Courage Best Bitter, Directors; John Smiths Yorkshire Bitter; Foster's; Kronenbourg 1664.

Accommodation *10 bedrooms* £A G1
Check-in all day

The immaculately kept bar is a fine setting for enjoying food that is far superior to everyday pub fare. Short, seasonally changing menus propose an interesting variety of dishes: try a bowl of soup, poached salmon with mixed leaves or a splendid seafood terrine to start, then maybe vegetable-filled breast of chicken, lightly cooked calf's liver served on rösti with a simple herb butter or bahmi goreng – a popular Indonesian dish with noodles, chicken and prawns. Sweets are much too tempting to resist, and our blackberry parfait put the finishing touch on a top-quality bar meal.

Typical dishes Terrine of fresh sea fish £3.25 Poached wild salmon (main course) £5.95 Bahmi goreng £5.75 Blackberry parfait £2.45

Ten delightful bedrooms with pretty floral fabrics and fine period furniture have a fresh, light feel. TVs, dial-out phones and tea-makers are standard, along with little extras like fruit and sherry. All rooms have smart modern en suite facilities (two shower/wc only). Children welcome overnight. Accommodation closed 23 Dec–15 Jan.

Credit Access, Amex, Diners, Visa

KINGSCOTE
Hunters Hall Inn

Nr Tetbury   `FOOD`
Map 10 A2 *Gloucs*
Dursley (0453) 860393
Parking *ample*

Bar food *12–2 & 7–9.45, Sun 12–2.30 & 7–9.30* ⮳

Landlords *Sandra & David Barnett-Roberts*
Free house
Bass; Hook Norton Best Bitter; Marston Pedigree; Toby Bitter; Carling Black Label; Tennent's Extra.

A lunchtime buffet display featuring succulent cold meats, quiches and fresh salads draws the crowds to this congenial 16th-century pub on the A4135. Hot dishes from the blackboard might include poached salmon, spaghetti bolognese and grilled chicken wings. The bars, with low beamed ceilings, flagstoned floors and sturdy wooden furnishings, have a well-loved feel. Children are especially well looked after.
Typical dishes Savoury beef crumble £3.75 Yorkshire grill £6.75

Credit Access, Amex, Diners, Visa

KINGSKERSWELL   NEW ENTRY   *Barn Owl*

Aller Mills TQ12 5AW   FOOD
Map 9 C2 *Devon*
Kingskerswell (080 47) 2130
Parking *ample*

Bar food *12–2 & 7–10*

Landlords *Derek & Margaret Warner*
Free house
🍷 *Janners Old English Ale; Courage Best Bitter; John Smith's Yorkshire Bitter; Guinness; Kronenbourg 1664; Foster's.* 🍷

A former farmhouse next to the A380 has been transformed into a pub of real character. Black beams, flagstoned floors and fine oak panelling distinguish the three interconnecting rooms where lunchtime dishes such as crisply fried cod, spicy chilli and individual steak and kidney pies are offered alongside sandwiches, ploughman's and filled jacket potatoes. More elaborate evening meals in the barn restaurant.

Typical dishes Chicken marengo £3.25 Liver and bacon casserole £3.20

Credit Access, Visa

KINGSTEIGNTON   *Old Rydon Inn*

Rydon Road, Nr Newton   FOOD
Abbot TQ12 3QG
Map 9 C2 *Devon*
Newton Abbot (0626) 54626
Parking *ample*

Bar food *12–2 & 7–10*

Landlords *Hermann & Miranda Hruby*
Free house
🍷 *Bass; Wadworth 6X; Janner's Ale; Worthington Best Bitter; Tennent's Extra.* 🍷 ⊖

Hermann Hruby produces some of the best pub food in the south west, so a diversion off the A380 to his former farmhouse is very worthwhile. The old cider loft forms part of the main bar, where you might well sit on an upturned beer cask at your cramped table. A blackboard menu spells out tempting dishes from all round the world: chicken and barley soup, brandied herb pâté, rabbit casserole and pork in a Malayan peanut sauce are typical items, and there is usually plenty of fish to choose from. A medley of seafood, which includes salmon, prawns, mussels and a crab claw, comes in a tarragon-flavoured white wine sauce; served with boulangère potatoes and fresh vegetables, it is a tasty, good-value plateful. Sweets keep up the high standards, so it is hard not to be greedy at the thought of Austrian apple pancakes or chocolate meringue torte with clotted cream. Separate from the bar is a comfortable lounge that leads through to the pub's restaurant.

Typical dishes Cauliflower & prawns gratinée £3.50 Tortellini in gorgonzola sauce £3.25 Beef, mushroom & Stilton pie £3.40 Nasi goreng £3.65

KINGSTON   *Juggs*

Nr Lewes BN7 3NT   FOOD
Area Map 6 E4 *East Sussex*
Brighton (0273) 472523
Parking *ample*

Bar food *12–2 & 6–9.30 (Sun from 7)* ⌣

Landlords *Andrew & Peta Browne*
Free house
🍷 *Harvey Best Bitter; King & Barnes Sussex Bitter, Old Ale, Festive; Guinness; Tennent's Extra.* ⊖

Two tiny cottages have been made into a picturesque little inn that simply oozes character, particularly in the low-ceilinged main bar with its rough black timbers, rustic benches and yellowed walls. The bar snacks are entirely in keeping – honest, unassuming fare like sausages, spaghetti bolognese, salt beef sandwiches and an excellent steak and kidney pudding. Jugg Special is pitta bread with ham, tomato, mushrooms and cheese.

Typical dishes Jugg Special £2.95 Home-made ice cream £1.25

KINTBURY   *Dundas Arms*

Nr Newbury NY7 6HG
Map 10 B3 *Berkshire*
Kintbury (0488) 58263
Parking *ample*

FOOD
B&B

Bar food *12–2*
No bar food *Sun & eves*

Landlords *Dalzell-Piper family*
Free house
🍺 *Morland Bitter; Eldridge Pope
Dorset IPA; Guinness; Stella Artois;
Carlsberg.* 🍷 ⊖

A lovely inn by the banks of the Kennet and
Avon canal, dating from the late 18th
century, and run for over 20 years by the
Dalzell-Piper family. In the tastefully traditional bar, where one wall completely
covered with blue-patterned plates
provides a splash of colour amidst the dark
wood, lunchtime snacks are served. Sandwiches, ploughman's and soup are sup-
ported by crab au gratin, smoked salmon
quiche, thick, juicy gammon steaks and a
traditional steak and kidney pie served
with fresh vegetables. A small selection of
sweets might include chocolate brandy
cake or bread and butter pudding. The
patio is a popular spot for summer lunches.

Typical dishes Steak & kidney pie £4.45
Seafood platter £4.25

Accommodation *5 bedrooms* **£A G1**
Check-in all day

A converted stable block houses five strikingly decorated bedrooms with sliding
picture windows leading on to a riverside
terrace. Solidly furnished, all the good-sized
rooms have TVs, tea-makers, lots of magazines and modern bathrooms. An outside
table and chairs are provided for each room
on the terrace. There is also a residents'
lounge. Children welcome overnight.

Credit Access, Amex, Diners, Visa

KIRK LANGLEY   *Meynell Arms Hotel*

Nr Derby DE6 4NF
Map 7 B1 *Derbyshire*
Kirk Langley (033 124) 515
Parking *ample*

B&B

Landlord *John Richards*
Brewery *Bass* ⌇
🍺 *Bass; Worthington Best Bitter; Mitchells
& Butlers Mild; Carling Black Label.* 🍷

Accommodation *10 bedrooms* **£C G2**
Check-in all day

A useful overnight stopping place on the
A52 Derby to Ashbourne road. It is a
Georgian manor house dating from 1776
and its appeals are largely traditional.
Helpful staff provide friendly service in the
two bars, one on either side of the entrance
hall. Floral fabrics adorn the neat little
bedrooms, which all offer wardrobes and
writing desks, telephones and TVs, tea-
makers and bedside radios. There are two
four-poster rooms. Front rooms are double-
glazed, rear ones enjoy meadow views.

Credit Access, Amex, Diners, Visa

---

*We welcome bona fide recommendations
or complaints on the tear-out pages at the back
of the book for readers' comments.*

*They are followed up by our professional team,
but do complain to the management on the spot.*

KIRKBY STEPHEN   *King's Arms Hotel*

Market Street CA17 4QN
Map 3 C2 *Cumbria*
Kirkby Stephen
(0930) 71378
Parking *ample*

Bar food *12–1.45 & 7–8.45*

Landlords *Jenny Reed & Keith Simpson*
Brewery *Whitbread*
🍺 *Whitbread Trophy Cask; Flowers Best
Bitter; Castle Eden Ale; Murphy Stout;
Heineken.* ⊖

In the small, convivial bar of the King's
Arms, with its open fire and panelled walls,
you can find a limited range of dishes such
as shepherd's pie, steak and kidney pie and
chicken curry. Those wanting a more
imaginative meal should head for the
dining room at lunchtime, where in a pretty
setting of dark polished tables, red napkins,
fresh flowers and an oak sideboard a wider
variety of food is served. Fresh fish, steaks,
roasts and salads are all on offer, with a
good selection of English and continental
cheeses to follow and sweets from the
trolley. Booking is essential for the traditional roast lunch on Sundays.

Typical dishes Lasagne £2.65 Chilli con
carne £2.65

Accommodation *9 bedrooms* **£C G2**
Check-in all day

Upstairs there is a residents' lounge with
TV and nine traditional bedrooms with
patterned carpets, lacy bedspreads and
solid period furniture. Three have en suite
facilities, the remaining six sharing three
public bathrooms. All have direct dial
phones.   Garden.   Children   welcome
overnight.

Credit Access, Visa

KIRKBYMOORSIDE   *George & Dragon*

Market Place YO6 6AA
Area Map 3 C2 *North Yorks*
Kirkbymoorside (0751)
31637
Parking *ample*

Bar food *12–1.30*
No bar food *eves*

Landlords *Mr & Mrs Curtis & Mr & Mrs
Austin*
Free house
🍺 *Theakston Best Bitter; Younger's
Scotch; Guinness; Carlsberg Hof.* ⊖

Two purposes are served here – that of a
country-town pub in an old cobbled market
square, and also that of a simple hotel. Set in
lovely gardens, the 13th-century pub
provides a short bar snack menu which
includes open and closed sandwiches, a
soup, and three specials such as chicken
curry or nut cutlets with apricot sauce. A
good choice of sweets – apple pie, raspberry
cheesecake or peach gâteau. Traditional
Sunday lunch is served in the bar.

Typical dishes Steak & kidney pie £3
Roast beef and Yorkshire pudding £3

Accommodation *24 bedrooms* **£B G2**
Check-in all day

At the rear of the inn are a converted
granary and an old vicarage in which you
will find the twenty-four unfussy bedrooms, perfect for a peaceful stay. Some
overlook the gardens, and all have white
melamine furniture, direct-dial telephones
and tea-makers. All but two have functional
en suite bathrooms and TVs. *No children
under five overnight. No dogs.*

Credit Access, Visa

Prices given are as at the time of our research and thus may change.

KNAPP   NEW ENTRY   *Rising Sun*

Nr Taunton TA3 6BG   FOOD
Map 9 C1 *Somerset*
Taunton (0823) 490436
Parking *ample*

Bar food *12–2 & 6.30–10*
No bar food *Sun eve, Tues lunch & all
Mon*

Landlords *Peter & Claire Morgan*
Free house
● *Golden Hill Exmoor Ale; Bass; Guinness;
Tennent's Extra; Carling Black Label.*

A pretty, white-painted cottage pub, the
Sun caters more for eaters than drinkers. It
has been partly renovated and completely
refurbished, leaving beams and inglenook
pristine. Sandwiches are available only at
lunchtime. Otherwise a good choice of
meals always includes vegetarian dishes
and a children's menu. Crab soup is excellent, steak and kidney casserole tender and
tasty.
Typical dishes Rib-eye steak £5.75
Home-made lasagne £3.50

Credit Access, Visa

KNIGHTWICK   *Talbot Hotel*

Nr Worcester WR6 5PH   FOOD
Map 6 E3 *Hereford & Worcs*   B&B
Knightwick (0886) 21235
Parking *ample*

Bar food *12–2 & 6.30–9.30,
Sun 12–1.30 & 7–9*

Landlord *Mr D. Hiles*
Free house
● *Bass; Flowers IPA, Original; Banks's
Bitter; Guinness; Heineken.* ⊖

Take the turning by the bridge over the
river Teme, just off the A44, to find the
Talbot, a sturdy, white-painted inn. The
spacious beamed bar is divided by a central
fireplace, one side of which is a huge wood-
burning stove, the other open. Fresh fish
dominates the imaginative blackboard
menu, with choices like turbot béarnaise,
monkfish and haddock, while alternatives
range from pork with mustard and cheese
to casseroled Welsh rabbit and devilled
lentil pie. To finish, try the home-made St
Clements ice cream or sticky date and toffee
sponge. Service remains on the relaxed side.

Typical dishes Caribbean chicken £4.95
Venison steak Napoleon £6.50

Accommodation *10 bedrooms* £C G3
Check-in all day

Bedrooms in the main building are full of
character with their oak beams and sloping
floors, but three have no private facilities
and share a functional bathroom. Neat and
cottage extension rooms with simple fitted
furnishings have the bonus of en suite
bathrooms, and all offer tea-makers and
radio-alarms. There is a homely residents'
lounge with TV. Children welcome
overnight.

Credit Access, Visa

KNOWLE   *Greswolde Arms Hotel*

High Street, Nr Solihull   B&B
B93 0LL
Map 7 B2 *West Midlands*
Knowle (0564) 772711
Parking *ample*

Landlord *Mr I.P. Hartley*
Brewery *Allied*
● *Ansells Bitter, Mild; Ind Coope Burton
Ale; Tetley Bitter; Skol; Castlemaine
XXXX.*

Accommodation *18 bedrooms* £C G2
Check-in all day

Popular with business visitors to the
nearby National Exhibition Centre, this
busy little pub makes a convenient and
comfortable overnight stop. While only six
bedrooms offer private facilities (the other
dozen share four public bathrooms), accessories are good, with trouser presses, hairdryers, direct-dial telephones, TVs and tea-
makers all standard. There is a pleasant
residents' lounge. Accommodation closed
three days Christmas. Children welcome
overnight. *No dogs.*

Credit Access, Amex, Diners, Visa

LACOCK   NEW ENTRY   *Carpenters Arms*

Church Street SN15 2LB   `B & B`
Map 10 A3 *Wiltshire*
Lacock (024 973) 203
Parking *limited*

Landlord *Mr Duhig*
Brewery *Ushers* ⌣
🍺 *Ushers Best Bitter; Ruddles County;
Guinness; Carlsberg; Holsten.*

Accommodation *3 bedrooms* £C G3
Check-in by arrangement

An ancient stone-built inn located in the heart of a delightful village, its mellow charms still remain after sympathetic refurbishment. The cosy bars are a pleasant spot for a quiet drink, with their low-beamed ceilings, flagstoned or wooden floors, rough stone walls and rustic pine furnishings. Upstairs, the three good-sized bedrooms are smartly furnished in period style, with quilts. All offer tea-makers and en suite shower rooms. Patio.

Credit Access, Visa

LACOCK   *Red Lion at Lacock*

High Street SN15 2LQ   `FOOD`
Map 10 A3 *Wiltshire*   `B & B`
Lacock (024 973) 456
Parking *ample*

Bar food *12.15–2.30 & 6.30–10
(Sun from 7)*

Landlord *Mr J.S. Levis*
Brewery *Wadworth*
🍺 *Wadworth 6X, IPA; Guinness;
Heineken; Labatt's.* ⊖

Accommodation *3 bedrooms* £C G3
Check-in all day

A fine old red-brick inn close to Lacock abbey and in the centre of a National Trust village, the Red Lion is less straight-laced than it sounds. Beams and open fires may be par for the course but the stuffed game birds are decidedly more eccentric. A cage for a live bird stands empty and one looks anxiously for him on the blackboard menu! The choice might include duck, leek and mushroom soup or duck terrine with damsons, then perhaps pheasant in red wine. The spicy lamb – in a good sauce with mushrooms and peppers and accompanied by bubble and squeak – is enjoyable.

Typical dishes Duck and orange in cognac £5.60 Salmon steak in herbs and butter £5.75

Antiques replace the displayed birds on the stairs leading to three modest but comfortable bedrooms, one with private bathroom. By early 1990, there will be five en suite rooms. A handsome walnut bed-head embellishes one room. *No children under ten overnight.*

We publish annually so make sure you use the current edition.

LANCASTER   *Farmers Arms*

Penny Street LA1 1WX   `B & B`
Map 3 B3 *Lancashire*
Lancaster (0524) 36368
Parking *difficult*

Landlord *Mr J.E. Keenan*
Brewery *Thwaites* ⌣
🍺 *Thwaites Bitter, Best Mild; Guinness;
Carlsberg Export; Tuborg.*

Accommodation *15 bedrooms* £C G3
Check-in all day

Business people value the decent overnight accommodation provided by this unpretentious pub opposite a canal, and it is often busy during the week. Staff are very cheerful, with a warm Lancastrian welcome for guests, and the bars bustle bright. Good housekeeping is particularly evident in the bedrooms, five of which have private facilities en suite (the rest share three well-kept public bathrooms). Colour TVs in all rooms. Decent grilled tomatoes for breakfast. *No dogs.*

Credit Access, Visa

LANCING *Sussex Pad Hotel*

Old Shoreham Road
BN15 0RH
FOOD
B&B
Area Map 6 C4 *West Sussex*
Brighton (0273) 454647
Parking *ample*

Bar food *11 am–10 pm, Sun 12–3 & 7–10*

Landlords *Mr & Mrs W. Pack*
Free house
🍺 *Tetley Bitter; John Bull Bitter; Guinness; Castlemaine XXXX; Löwenbräu.*
No real ale. 🍷 ⊖

A substantial, superior roadside inn on the A27, standing between Lancing College's grandiose chapel, which juts out of the South Downs, and Shoreham airport. Light aircraft taking off and landing can be watched from the restaurant (12–2 and 7–9.45), in which speciality fish dishes are a treat and an excellent-value three-course set lunch is offered. In the bar (a sweep of red plush banquette seating with matching carpet and curtains) the all-day snacks are just as good. Leek and potato soup, dressed crab, oysters, lobster, moules marinière, steak and kidney pie, shepherd's pie, ploughman's and salads are all freshly made and delicious. Sweets are conventional but all home-made.

Typical dishes Crab salad £6.25 Fresh salmon sandwich £2.55

Accommodation *6 bedrooms* **£C G1**
Check-in all day

The six spacious and comfortable bedrooms are each named after a famous Grande Marque champagne, and are trimly furnished and always spotless. All are en suite, with TVs, tea-makers, telephones and hairdryers. More desk space would be better for business travellers. Children welcome overnight.

Credit Access, Amex, Diners, Visa

Changes in data sometimes occur in establishments after the Guide goes to press.

Prices should be taken as indications rather than firm quotes.

LEAMINGTON SPA NEW ENTRY *Slug & Lettuce*

32 Clarendon Avenue
CV32 4RZ
FOOD
Map 7 B2 *Warwickshire*
Leamington Spa (0926) 883342
Parking *ample*

Bar food *12–2.15 & 7–10*

Landlord *Vincent Thomas*
Brewery *Courage*
🍺 *Courage Best Bitter, Directors, John Smith's Yorkshire Bitter; Guinness; Kronenbourg 1664; Foster's.* 🍷 ⊖

Slug and Lettuce establishments have prospered by spotting a gap in the market and filling it with good food. They bring the chic of wine bars to pubs and now Leamington boasts its own, at the top of the town. Starters include a skillet of eggs and bacon with black pudding, and main courses chicken breast with avocado and garlic, and fresh salmon fishcakes.

Typical dishes Tagliatelle neapolitana £3.25 Chicken breast with avocado and garlic £4.50

Credit Access, Visa

LEDBURY — Feathers Hotel

High Street HR8 1DF
Map 6 E3 *Hereford & Worcs*
Ledbury (0531) 2600
Parking *limited*

FOOD
B&B

Bar food *12–2 & 7–9.30 (Sun till 8.30)*

Landlord *Tim Wingrove*
Free house
◗ *Bass; Mitchells & Butlers Brew XI; Springfield Bitter; Guinness; Carling Black Label.* ⊖

Accommodation *11 bedrooms* **£A G1**
Check-in all day

The Feathers' strident black and white plumage pushes apart the architectural mix of stucco fronts and Cotswold stone of the high street. Stylish refurbishment of this Elizabethan hostelry has created a genteel ambience – popular with the county set. Hops hover overhead from beams, and the food bar, Fuggles, is named after a famous Herefordshire hop grower. The handwritten menu and blackboard daily specials offer mostly traditional English fare – Ledbury sausages and mash, rich hot game pie, lamb cutlets and very garlicky bread. Cooking is careful and pleasant though erring on the bland.

Typical dishes Venison casserole with herb dumpling £3.95 Home-made fish cakes and spicy sauce £3.75

Smart, imaginatively designed bedrooms, though not large, are packed full of character with sloping floors, half-timbering and bold wallpapers and furnishings. There is one four-poster. Compact, modern en suite bathrooms, TVs, telephones, tea-makers and double glazing are standard. There is an elegant breakfast room. Children welcome overnight.

Credit Access, Amex, Diners

LEDBURY — Verzons Country House Hotel

Trumpet, Nr Ledbury
HR8 2PZ
Map 6 E3 *Hereford & Worcs*
Trumpet (053 183) 381
Parking *ample*

B&B

Landlords *Edward & Carolyn Henson & Robin Pollock*
Free house
◗ *Marston Pedigree; Hook Norton Best Bitter; Guinness; Carlsberg.*

Accommodation *10 bedrooms* **£B G3**
Check-in all day

A former 18th-century farmhouse, this fine red brick inn on the A438 boasts a splendid facade, majestic staircase and spacious rooms. Seven bedrooms, inexpensively decorated with white melamine furniture, have simple en suite bathrooms. The other three smaller rooms at the rear share two very functional bathrooms. Investment would dispel the faded air and exploit the potential of the building. Garden and play area. Children welcome overnight.

Credit Access, Amex, Diners, Visa

LEDBURY — Ye Olde Talbot Hotel

New Street HR8 2DX
Map 6 E3 *Hereford & Worcs*
Ledbury (0531) 2963
Parking *limited*

B&B

Landlords *Terry & Pauline Ryan*
Free house
◗ *Ansells Bitter; Burton Ale; Guinness; Skol; Löwenbräu.* ▼

Accommodation *5 bedrooms* **£D G3**
Check-in all day

The 16th-century building with its striking half-timbered exterior is being excellently maintained both inside and out. You enter through a massively heavy oak door into the neat and simple bar, and a darkly old-fashioned dining room, used for guests' breakfast, is also a fine feature. In keeping with the age of the pub, the charming bedrooms are small with low doorways, low beamed ceilings and pretty bedspreads. Two are en suite. Children welcome overnight. *No dogs.*

Credit Access, Visa

LEEDS   NEW ENTRY   *Whitelocks*

Turks Head Yard,   `FOOD`
Briggate LS1 6HB
Map 4 D3 *West Yorkshire*
Leeds (0532) 453950
Parking *difficult*

Bar food *12–2.30 (Sun till 2) & 5.30–8*
No bar food *Sun eve*

Landlord *Fred Cliff*
Brewery *Younger*
🍺 *Younger's Scotch, No. 3, IPA; Guinness; McEwan's Lager.*

Tucked away down a narrow alley in the city centre, this marvellous old pub attracts an appreciative crowd for its traditional home-made fare. Sandwiches spread with dripping, Cornish pasties and beef hotpot are typical of the hearty bar snacks, while in the restaurant uniformed waitresses serve splendid roasts and Yorkshire pudding with rich onion gravy. Children's menu available. Patio.
Typical dishes Meat and potato pie £2
Beef sandwich with dripping 95p

Credit Access, Amex, Visa

LEEK   *Three Horseshoes Inn*

Blackshaw Moor ST13 8TW   `B&B`
Map 3 C4 *Staffordshire*
Blackshaw (053 834) 296
Parking *ample*

Landlord *Mr W.R. Kirk*
Free house
🍺 *McEwan's Tartan 80/-, Export; Younger's Scotch, Dark Mild; Guinness; Beck's Bier; McEwan's Export.* 🍷

Accommodation *6 bedrooms* £D G2
Check-in all day

A large mock-Tudor style pub located on the A53 north of Leek. Inside there is a public bar with pool table as well as the main bar which is decorated with horse brasses and plates and furnished with wheelback chairs and green banquettes. Traditional free-standing period furniture characterises the bedrooms which have floral curtains and candlewick bedspreads. All have showers, TVs and tea-makers, and share two public bathrooms. Accommodation closed one week Xmas.

Credit Access, Amex, Diners, Visa

LEIGH-ON-MENDIP   *Bell Inn*

Nr Bath BA3 5QQ   `A`
Area Map 7 B1 *Somerset*
Mells (0373) 812316
Parking *ample*

Landlord *Mr C. I. Jackson*
Free house
🍺 *Wadworth 6X; Devenish Wessex; Guinness; Carling Black Label.*

The Bell is a listed 17th-century pub in a peaceful little village. Nothing special outside, but delightful inside, with fresh flowers, patterned plates and gleaming brasses adding to the charms of the softly lit main bar with its exposed stone walls, black beams and high-backed oak settles. A wood-burning stove in the inglenook fireplace is a delightfully cosy attraction in winter and there is a pleasant garden for fine-weather drinks. Children welcome lunchtimes only.

LENHAM   NEW ENTRY   *Dog and Bear Hotel*

The Square, Nr Maidstone   `B&B`
ME17 2PG
Map 8 E3 *Kent*
Maidstone (0622) 858219
Parking *ample*

Landlord *Mr R. A. Hedges*
Brewery *Shepherd Neame*
🍺 *Shepherd Neame Master Brew Bitter, Best Bitter; Guinness; Hurlimann Sternbräu; Steinbock.* 🍷

Accommodation *21 bedrooms* £B G1
Check-in all day

Vigorous refurbishment has restored this attractive coaching inn dating from 1602 to its former glories. Splendid oak beams combine with a new, up-to-date decor and comfortable seating in the bar, and there is a welcoming little foyer-lounge, too. Centrally heated bedrooms with darkwood furniture and bright contemporary fabrics all have direct-dial telephones, TVs and neatly kept en suite bathrooms. Staff are something of a let-down. Children welcome overnight.

Credit Access, Visa

LEOMINSTER   *Royal Oak Hotel*

South Street HR6 8JA   `B&B`
Map 6 E3 *Hereford & Worcs*
Leominster (0568) 2610
Parking *ample*

Landlord *Gregory Surrey*
Free house
🍺 *Hook Norton Best Bitter; Wadworth 6X;
John Smith's Bitter; Bass Special; Carling
Black Label; Tennent's Extra.*

Accommodation *18 bedrooms* **£C G2**
Check-in all day

This former Georgian coaching inn offers
straightforward accommodation in the
centre of town. The Oak Bar sports original
oak panelling, beams bearing copper pans,
and log fires in winter— which also warm
the snug Acorn Bar. There is one four-
poster room; the other bedrooms – several
singles included – are functional, clean and
on the small side. They have inexpensive
furniture of varying colours and styles,
pleasant en suite bathrooms, tea-makers
and radios. Children welcome overnight.

Credit Access, Amex, Diners, Visa

LEVINGTON   *Ship*

Nr Ipswich IP10 0LQ   `FOOD`
Map 8 F2 *Suffolk*
Nacton (047 388) 573
Parking *ample*

Bar food *12–2*
No bar food *eves*

Landlords *Len & Jo Wenham*
Brewery *Tolly Cobbold*
🍺 *Tolly Cobbold Bitter, XXXX; Guinness;
Hansa.* ⊖

Views over the Orwell estuary and a
nautical ambience are the more noticeable
attractions here. There is a healthy slant to
the regularly changing dishes chalked up
on the blackboard. A typical choice might
read: brazil nut loaf with tomato sauce,
wholemeal steak and kidney pie, chicken
and broccoli lasagne. Excellent English
cheeses and good puddings, too. Cold food
includes an array of ploughman's (all there
is on Sundays).
Typical dishes Home-smoked ham £3.95
Homity pie £3.50

LINCOLN   *Wig & Mitre*

29 Steep Hill LN2 1LU   `FOOD`
Map 4 E4 *Lincolnshire*
Lincoln (0522) 535190
Parking *ample*

Bar food *8 am–midnight*

Landlords *Valerie & Michael Hope*
Brewery *Samuel Smith*
🍺 *Samuel Smith's Old Brewery Bitter,
Museum Ale; Ayingerbräu.* ▼

You will find the 14th-century Wig & Mitre
in the heart of medieval Lincoln. Downstairs in the bar the menu changes twice
daily, and upstairs the restaurant offers full
meals all day as well. Service is efficient and
the cooking careful. Bar food includes
soups, pâtés, warm liver parfait with grape
sauce to start, vegetable chilli, Stilton in
puff pastry in tomato and basil sauces and
lamb's liver in garlic to follow.
Typical dishes Braised ox tongue £3.85
Cream of fennel soup £1.45

Credit Access, Amex, Diners, Visa

LINCOLN   *Woodcocks*

Burton Lane End, Saxilby   `B&B`
Road LN1 2RD
Map 4 E4 *Lincolnshire*
Lincoln (0522) 703000
Parking *ample*

Landlord *Richard Costall*
Free house
🍺 *Manns Mild; Webster Yorkshire Bitter;.
Guinness; Holsten Export; Carlsberg;
Foster's.*

Accommodation *8 bedrooms* **£C G1**
Check-in all day

The music satellite channel bops over the
large TV screen attracting a young crowd
to these tranformed cottages three miles
outside Lincoln. Framed posters, wrought-
iron tables and an abundance of greenery
are also found in the conservatory-style
cocktail bar. Pine complements pastel decor
in bedrooms equipped with satellite TV,
telephones and en suite bathrooms. Suntrap
patio and garden leading down to a canal.
Children's outdoor play area. Children
welcome overnight.

Credit Access, Visa

LINTON   *Bull Inn*

The Hill ME17 4AN   `FOOD`
Area Map 5 A3 *Kent*
Maidstone (0622) 743612
Parking *ample*

Bar food *12–2 & 7–10 (Sun, Mon
& Tues till 9)*
No bar food *Sun Jan–Feb*

Landlord *David Brown*
Brewery *Whitbread*
*Flowers Best Bitter, Original; Fremlins
Bitter; Guinness; Stella Artois; Heineken.*

If you love fresh fish, this is the pub for you.
Delivered regularly from Rye, Hastings and
Folkestone, the choice includes plaice, haddock, cod, brill and huss, either grilled or
fried in a good, light batter. Other dishes on
the menu are Scotch salmon, dressed crab,
sautéed monkfish, fisherman's pie and
skate wings. Lasagne, steak and kidney pie
or shepherd's pie for those who really don't
want fish.
Typical dishes Fresh local trout £6 Cod
& chips £3.35

Credit Access, Visa

---

*Our inspectors never book in the name of
Egon Ronay's Guides.*

*They disclose their identity only if they are
considering an establishment for inclusion
in the next edition of the Guide.*

LINWOOD   NEW ENTRY   *High Corner Inn*

Nr Ringwood BH24 3QY   `FOOD`
Area Map 7 F4 *Hampshire*
Ringwood (0425) 473973
Parking *ample*

Bar food *12–2 & 6.30–10, Sun 12–1.45
& 7–10*

Landlords *Lin & Roger Kernan*
Free house
*Wadworth 6X; Flowers Original;
Pompey Royal; Guinness; Carlsberg Hof;
Stella Artois.*

High Corner Inn is a little cluster of white
pebbledash buildings down a rough track
deep in the heart of the New Forest. The
beamy bars and the forest garden are very
agreeable settings for sampling a range of
dishes that includes soup, grilled sardines,
savoury pies, omelettes and sherry trifle.
The lunchtime choice is limited on Sunday,
but an all-day carvery compensates.
Typical dishes Steak, kidney & mushroom pie £3.95 Venison sausage platter
£2.25

Credit Access, Amex, Diners, Visa

LITTLE BEDWYN   NEW ENTRY   *Harrow Inn*

Nr Marlborough SN8 3JP   `FOOD`
Map 10 B3 *Wiltshire*
Marlborough (0672) 870871
Parking *ample*

Bar food *12–1.45 & 7–9.30*
No bar food *Sun & Mon eves Oct–Mar*
Pub closed *Mon lunch (except Bank Hols)*

Landlords *Jacki & Richard Denning*
Free house
*Hook Norton Best Bitter; Marston
Pedigree; Guinness; Carling Black Label;
Carlsberg Hof.*

Landlord Richard Denning runs the village
post office from the back of this solid red-
brick pub; so, after buying your stamps,
visit the welcoming bar for some of landlady Jacki's sustaining snacks. Blackboards announce the day's choice —
perhaps devilled sardine pâté followed by
sweet and sour lamb, ratatouille crumble or
beef and prune casserole, with light, moist
chocolate roulade for afters.
Typical dishes Chicken curry £3.75
Baked trout £4.35

Credit Access, Visa

LITTLE COMPTON   *Red Lion Inn*

Nr Moreton-in-Marsh
GL56 0RT
Map 10 B1 *Gloucestershire*
Barton on the Heath
(060 874) 397
Parking *ample*

FOOD
B&B

Bar food *12–2 (Sun till 1.15) & 7–8.45
(Sat till 9.30)*

Landlords *Sarah & David Smith*
Brewery *Donnington*
🍺 *Donnington BB, SBA; Carlsberg Hof,
Pilsner.* 🍷 ☕

David and Sarah Smith run their charming
16th-century village inn with warmth and
pride, offering good plain cooking to match
the simple surroundings of exposed stone
walls, beams and sturdy wooden furnishings. Follow thick, spicy mulligatawny
soup or mushrooms in garlic butter with a
huge helping of moist pheasant casserole
served with a baked potato and fresh
vegetables, a chargrilled swordfish steak or
splendid grill featuring rump steak cut
from the joint to your own specification.
Ploughman's platters and filled granary
rolls make lighter bites and there are sweets
like Scotch whisky trifle and raspberry
meringue.
Typical dishes Beef with green peppercorn sauce £4.25 Chicken with Stilton and
ham sauce £4.25

Accommodation *3 bedrooms* **£D G3**
Check-in by arrangement

Upstairs, the three spotless bedrooms overlooking the attractive garden share a spacious carpeted bathroom, and each has its
own washbasin and tea-making facilities.
Two rooms feature original beams and one
has open stone walls. Garden and play area.
No children under eight overnight. No dogs.

Credit Access, Visa

LITTLE LANGDALE   *Three Shires Inn*

Nr Ambleside LA22 9NZ
Area Map 1 D3 *Cumbria*
Langdale (096 67) 215
Parking *ample*

FOOD
B&B

Bar food *12–2 & 6.30–8.45 (Sun from 7)*

Landlords *Mr and Mrs Neil Stephenson*
Free house
🍺 *Webster Yorkshire Bitter; Wilsons
Original Bitter, Special Mild; Guinness;
Carlsberg.* ☕

Walkers love this friendly pub both for its
splendid lakeland setting and its hearty
snacks served in the slate-walled public bar
or the cosy carpeted lounge. Lunchtime
brings sustaining soups, brown bread
sandwiches, salads and ploughman's, as
well as hot main dishes like Cumberland pie
or grilled sirloin steak with mushrooms and
tomato. The choice widens at night (try
garlic prawns followed by roast chicken or
the day's vegetarian special), and a children's menu also becomes available. Sweets
might be hazelnut roulade or strawberry
malakoff.

Typical dishes Baked trout and almonds
£4.50 Steak and kidney pie £3.50

Accommodation *11 bedrooms* **£A G2**
Check-in all day

Light, airy bedrooms with sprigged cotton
curtains and white furniture enjoy lovely
views and either have their own neat,
modern bathroom or share two spotless
public ones. All offer tea-makers, and there
is a chintzy TV lounge and comfortable bar
for residents' exclusive use. Garden and
patio. Accommodation closed Monday to
Thursday (November and December),
Christmas and last three weeks January. *No
dogs.*

LITTLE MILTON   NEW ENTRY   *Lamb Inn*

Nr Oxford OX9 7PU   `FOOD`
Map 10 B2 *Oxfordshire*
Great Milton (0844) 279527
Parking *ample*

Bar food *12–2 & 7–10* 🍽

Landlords *David & Ruth Bowell*
Brewery *Halls*
🍺 *Ind Coope Burton Ale; Tetley Bitter; Skol; Löwenbräu.* ℮

Conveniently placed for Oxford and the M40 on the A329, the 17th-century Lamb offers travellers rustic, characterful bars and good home cooking. A standard menu featuring pâté, sandwiches and simple hot dishes like fried plaice and steaks is supplemented by more elaborate blackboard specials such as smoked quail, venison in red wine and pork fillet in sherry sauce. Enjoyable sweets include chocolate pot.
Typical dishes Beef and Guinness casserole £4.65 Kidneys Dijonnaise £4.65

Credit Diners

LITTLE WASHBOURNE   *Hobnails Inn*

Nr Tewkesbury GL20 8NQ   `FOOD`
Map 10 A1 *Gloucs*
Alderton (024 262) 237
Parking *ample*

Bar food *12–2 & 7–10.30* 🍽

Landlords *Mr & Mrs S. Farbrother & Mrs R.C. Fletcher*
Brewery *Whitbread Flowers*
🍺 *Flowers Original, IPA, Best Bitter, P.A.; Guinness; Heineken.*

Stop here for a filling snack if you find yourself on the A438 a few miles east of Tewkesbury. Plainly decorated and simply furnished, there is warmth in the welcome and pride in the home cooking. Filled Scottish baps are the speciality, and the menu lists forty different and generous fillings from steak and onion to cider cake and cheese. Specials are also on offer, and the home-made sweets are good.
Typical dishes Gammon, egg & mushroom bap £3.35 Brandied peaches £2.25

Credit Access, Diners, Visa

LIVERPOOL   *Philharmonic Dining Rooms*

36 Hope Street L1 9BX   `A`
Map 3 B4 *Merseyside*
051-709 1163
Parking *ample*

Landlord *Mr Draper*
Brewery *Tetley Walker*
🍺 *Tetley Bitter; Burtonwood Bitter; Jennings Bitter; Guinness; Castlemaine XXXX.*

The Philharmonic is without doubt one of Liverpool's most unusual and attractive pubs, a thankfully preserved monument to Victorian style and opulence. The main bar is the focal point, and its mosaic tiles, carved mahogany, rosewood panelling and engraved glass make a splendid picture. A jukebox and fruit machine do not help the atmosphere, but the decor is truly memorable. Almost as remarkable are the washrooms, done out in pink marble, with more mosaic tiles.

LLANYMYNECH   NEW ENTRY   *Bradford Arms*

Nr Oswestry SY22 6EJ   `FOOD`
Map 6 D2 *Shropshire*
Oswestry (0691) 830582
Parking *ample*

Bar food *12–2 & 7–10*
Closed *Mon (except Bank Hols) & 3 wks mid-Oct–Nov*

Landlords *Anne & Michael Murphy*
Free house
🍺 *Marston Pedigree; Burton Bitter; Stella Artois; Marston Pilsner.* ℮

In the heart of the village, the friendly, well-run Bradford Arms offers above-average eating in its spotless, comfortably traditional bar. Arrive early to ensure a seat and then tuck in to, say French onion soup, garlic mushrooms or tasty curried egg, followed perhaps by pork with apricots, beef stifado or home-roasted ham salad. Appealing desserts include blackberry and almond pie. Patio.
Typical dishes Stuffed aubergines £3.50 Salmon and mushroom gratin £4.50

LODSWORTH   NEW ENTRY   *Halfway Bridge Inn*

Nr Petworth GV28 9VP   `FOOD`
Area Map 6 A3 *West Sussex*
Lodsworth (079 85) 281
Parking *ample*

Bar food *12–2 & 6–9.45, Sun 12.30–1.30
& 7–9.15*

Landlord *Rex Colman*
Free house
🍺 *Fremlins Bitter; Wadworth 6X; Flowers
Original; Guinness; Stella Artois;
Heineken.* 🍷 ⊖

The bar and stylish restaurant serve an
identical choice of tasty food at a comfortable, smart pub halfway between Midhurst and Petworth. Soup, smoked mackerel pâté, crab salad, filled baked potatoes,
steaks and stuffed duckling show the range,
and treacle and nut tart is one of several
tempting sweets. Sunday lunch offers traditional roast beef and Yorkshire pudding.
Typical dishes Leek & potato soup with
crusty bread £1.40 Roast rack of lamb
£4.50

Credit Access, Visa

LONG MELFORD   *Crown Inn Hotel*

Hall Street CO10 9JN   `B&B`
Map 8 E2 *Suffolk*
Sudbury (0787) 77666
Parking *ample*

Landlords *Mr & Mrs Heavens*
Free house
🍺 *Adnams Bitter; Mauldons Bitter; Greene
King IPA; Guinness; Carlsberg Export.* 🍷

Accommodation *12 bedrooms* £C G1
Check-in all day

New owners have raised the standard of
accommodation at this historic inn dating
back to 1620. Bedrooms in the original
building and converted coach house are
individually decorated and furnished with
smart darkwood pieces (including one four-
poster). All now offer en suite facilities, and
extras include hairdryers, trouser presses
and direct-dial telephones, as well as TVs
and tea-makers. The open-plan bar is airy
and comfortable. Children welcome overnight. Garden and play area.

Credit Access, Amex, Diners, Visa

LONGFRAMLINGTON   *Granby Inn*

Nr Morpeth NE65 8DP   `B&B`
Map 3 C1 *Northumberland*
Longframlington (066 570) 228
Parking *ample*

Landlady *Mrs A. Bright*
Brewery *Bass*
🍺 *Stones Best Bitter; Bass; Guinness;
Carling Black Label.*

Accommodation *6 bedrooms* £C G2
Check-in all day

Flower-filled windowboxes make this
lively pub a riot of colour in the summer
months, and inside the high standards of
cleanliness are everywhere evident in the
gleaming polished surfaces. In the main
building the bedrooms are small, neat and
modern and all except one are en suite.
Some individual chalets in the garden
incorporate a small sitting area, fridge and
en suite facilities. Accommodation closed
ten days Christmas. *No children under eight
overnight. No dogs.*

Credit Access, Amex, Visa

LONGLEAT   *Bath Arms*

Horningsham BA12 7LY   `FOOD`
Area Map 7 C1 *Wiltshire*   `B&B`
**Maiden Bradley (098 53)
308**
Parking *ample*

Bar food *12–2 & 6–10 (Sun 7–9)*

Landlords *Joe, Beryl & Paul Lovatt*
Free house
🍺 *Wadworth 6X; Bass; Eldridge Pope
Dorchester Bitter; Usher Best Bitter;
Hacker-Pschorr Lager; Holsten.* ⊖

Like the rest of the village, the Bath Arms is
owned by the Longleat estate and it
provides a convenient watering hole for
visitors emerging from the safari park. The
small lounge bar boasts decorative plates,
old photographs and horse brasses, and
outside there is a pretty, sheltered garden
with a dozen tables for al fresco eating.
There is also a comfortable public bar and a
restaurant with a separate menu seating
about 40. The bar food offers some imaginative choices on the blackboard menu with
pheasant and wild duck in season and

plenty of fresh fish dishes; our inspector enjoyed an excellent fish chowder. Cheeses include Cheddar, Stilton and cambozola.

Typical dishes Steak & kidney pie £3.95 Lasagne £3.50

Accommodation *6 bedrooms* **£B G1**
Check-in all day

The bedrooms have painted walls and chintzy fabrics; four have en suite bathrooms while the other two, which are never let separately, have an interconnecting door and share an en suite bathroom. All have TV and beverage facilities. Children welcome overnight.

Credit Access, Diners, Visa

LOWDHAM   *Springfield Inn*

Old Epperstone Road   `B&B`
NG14 7B2
Map 7 C1 *Nottinghamshire*
Nottingham (0602) 663387
Parking *ample*

Landlords *Peter & Jenny Repetto*
Brewery *John Smith*
🍺 *John Smith's Bitter; Chestnut Mild; Courage Best Bitter; Guinness; Foster's Hofmeister.* 🍷

Accommodation *12 bedrooms* **£B G1**
Check-in all day

High standards of housekeeping and comfort prevail here, in a converted private house set back from the A6097 amid acres of green fields. Mock beams adorn the handsomely furnished main bar and relaxing lounge bar with its collection of water jugs. Most of the 12 attractively refurbished bedrooms have pretty floral soft furnishings and simple white units, while all offer good private facilities plus TVs, direct-dial telephones, radio-alarms and tea-makers. Garden. Children welcome overnight. *No dogs.*

Credit Access, Amex, Visa

LOWER PEOVER   *Bells of Peover*

Nr Knutsford WA16 9PZ   `A`
Map 3 C4 *Cheshire*
Lower Peover (056 581) 2269
Parking *ample*

Landlords *Mr & Mrs Barker*
Brewery *Greenall Whitley* ⌘
🍺 *Greenall Whitley Bitter, Mild; Guinness; Grünhalle, Export Gold; Labatt's.*

Toby jugs of all sizes and features make quiet but amusing company in the snug, where this ancient inn's only bar counter is located. The main room houses a motley collection of old tables and chairs, copper and brass ornaments and decorative blue plates. You will find the pub – its outside covered in creepers, its door almost hidden by a venerable wisteria – by the church, at the end of a cobbled lane off the B5081. Garden.

Credit Access

LOWER WIELD   *Yew Tree Inn*

Nr Alresford SO24 9RX   `FOOD`
Map 7 C3 *Hampshire*
Preston Candover (025 687) 224
Parking *ample*

Bar food *12–2 & 7–9.30*
No bar food *Sun eve, all Mon (except Bank Hols)*

Landlords *M. & A. Ferguson*
Free house
🍺 *Bass; Gales HSB; Bunces Best Bitter; Marston Pedigree; Guinness; Stella Artois.*

Signposted off the B3046 at Preston Candover, this cosy whitewashed pub with exposed beams provides a convivial atmosphere in which to eat. The short, varied blackboard menu features such unusual treats as a beautifully presented avocado and smoked salmon salad followed by succulent lamb with basil and tomato. Simpler but equally appealing dishes include chicken liver pâté, juicy sirloin steak and chicken and ham pie.
Typical dishes Steak and kidney pie £4.25 Sole with prawns and chives £8.50

LOWESWATER · Kirkstile Inn

Nr Cockermouth CA13 0RV [B&B]
Area Map 1 B2 *Cumbria*
Lorton (090 085) 219
Parking *ample*

Landlord *Kenneth Gorley*
Free house ☙
🍺 *Jennings Bitter; Younger's Scotch, Tartan Bitter; Guinness; McEwan's Lager.*

Accommodation *10 bedrooms* **£C G2**
Check-in all day

A very quaint little inn in a quiet Lakeland valley which has everything – lakes, mountains, pastures and forest. The beamed bars attract locals and climbers alike, and they are made pleasing by pot plants, wooden tables and settles and a Buttermere slate shove-ha'penny board. The compact bedrooms are clean and functional, with simple furniture, individual heaters, duvets and tidy bathrooms with good towels and soaps; there is also a cosy residents' lounge and a dining room.

Credit Access

LOWICK GREEN · Farmers Arms

Nr Ulverston LA12 8DT [FOOD] [^B&B]
Area Map 1 D5 *Cumbria*
Greenodd (022 986) 277
Parking *ample*

Bar food *12–2 & 6–10 (Sun 7–9.30)*

Landlords *Mr & Mrs A. Lockwell*
Brewery *Scottish & Newcastle*
🍺 *Younger's No. 3, Scotch; Guinness; Harp; Beck's Bier.* 🍷 ☺

Accommodation *11 bedrooms* **£C G2**
Check-in all day

Although the restaurant menu looks fairly predictable, the food itself is full of flavour, and while you eat you can appreciate the excellent art collection on display around you. Black beams and diamond-paned windows give a traditional aura for enjoying home-made soup, pâté, grilled lemon sole or steak chasseur followed by rich sherry trifle. If you've less time and money to spend, opt for the excellent bar snacks offered in this original 14th-century farmhouse, which range from particularly good sandwiches to chilli con carne and smoked mackerel.

Typical dishes Steak, kidney & stout pie £2.95 Stilton pâté £2.30

The bedrooms, seven of which are en suite, are reached via an old narrow staircase, and all have pine furniture, duvets, TVs and tea-makers. Mattresses are well-sprung and the housekeeping is immaculate. Apart from the warren of bars and the charming lounge, you can also sit on the front patio or in the garden at the back.

Credit Access, Amex, Visa

LUDLOW · Angel Hotel

Broad Street SY8 1NG [B&B]
Map 6 E3 *Shropshire*
Ludlow (0584) 2581
Parking *ample*

Landlords *Mr & Mrs J. M. Hargreaves*
Free house
🍺 *Flowers Original, IPA; Younger's No 3; Guinness; Stella Artois; Heineken.*

Accommodation *17 bedrooms* **£B G1**
Check-in all day

A handsome, half-timbered coaching inn on an equally picturesque street. The spacious lounge bar features luxurious, richly patterned armchairs, polished brass ornaments and pot plants. Fine carved oak furnishings grace the restful bedrooms, two of which have lovely bay windows looking out onto Broad Street. All the rooms offer TVs, tea-makers, radio-alarms, telephones and hairdryers, plus good carpeted modern bathrooms with showers. Children welcome overnight.

Credit Access, Amex, Diners, Visa

LUTTERWORTH   Denbigh Arms Hotel

High Street LE17 4AD   `B&B`
Map 7 C1 *Leicestershire*
Lutterworth (045 55) 3537
Parking *ample*

Landlord *Simon Pyle*
Free house
🍺 *Marston Pedigree, Premium; Stella Artois; Marston Pilsner.*

Accommodation *34 bedrooms* £A G1
Check-in all day

A Georgian town-centre inn with a traditional coaching-inn frontage and a modern rear extension, just a few minutes' drive from junction 20 of the M1. The single bar is smart and comfortable, with light panelled walls, pine furniture and ceiling fans, and the lounge is decorated in homely pastel shades. The pine theme is continued into the good-sized cottagy bedrooms, whose private modern bathrooms all have bath and shower, and a bidet wherever possible. *No dogs.*

Credit Access, Amex, Diners, Visa

LYDDINGTON   Marquess of Exeter

Nr Uppingham LE15 9LT   `B&B`
Map 7 C1 *Leicestershire*
Uppingham (0572) 822477
Parking *ample*

Landlord *Mr N.L. Martin*
Free house
🍺 *Ruddles County, Best Bitter; Bateman Best Bitter, XXXB; Carlsberg Hof.*

Accommodation *17 bedrooms* £A G1
Check-in all day

In a peaceful village surrounded by lovely countryside, this thatched 16th-century coaching inn is full of period charm. The low-beamed bars with their brass-topped tables, oak furniture and inglenook fireplace are splendidly traditional – a contrast to the good-sized bedrooms (including two suites) in a separate modern annexe which offer many extras as well as private facilities. Accommodation closed 27 to 30 December. Children welcome overnight. *No dogs.*

Credit Access, Amex, Diners, Visa

LYDFORD   Castle Inn

Nr Okehampton EX20 4BH   `FOOD`
Map 9 B2 *Devon*   `B&B`
Lydford (082 282) 242
Parking *ample*

Bar food *12–2.30 & 6–9.30 (Sun from 7)* ☙

Landlords *David & Susan Grey*
Free house
🍺 *Courage Best Bitter, Directors; Bass; Guinness; Kronenbourg 1664; Foster's.* 🍷☙

In a quiet Devon village next to the castle remains, this splendid 16th-century pink-washed pub simply bursts with period character. The Foresters' Bar, where meals are served, is especially attractive with its low, lamp-lit beams, decorative plates and huge Norman fireplace, while the friendly Tinners' Bar houses a unique collection of antique stallion posters. Blackboards announce appetising daily specials such as chicken and leek soup, popular suet crust steak and kidney pie and beef curry, and there is always an attractive lunchtime buffet featuring quiches, cold meats and colourful salads. Nice sweets, too, like tangy lemon syllabub or strawberry cheesecake. On sunny days, eat in the lovely garden complete with children's playground.

Typical dishes Somerset chicken £3.50 Steak & kidney pie £3.95

Accommodation *8 bedrooms* £D G2
Check-in all day

Beams and sloping floors add to the homely charms of the comfortable bedrooms, which have traditional furnishings and a pleasant floral decor. Three have simple bath or shower rooms, and the others share a neat bathroom. All offer TVs and tea-makers.

Credit Access, Visa

LYNDHURST   *Waterloo Arms*

Pikes Hill SO43 7AY   `FOOD`
Map 7 B4 *Hampshire*
Lyndhurst (042 128) 3333
Parking *ample*

Bar food *12–2 & 7–9*
No bar food *Sun–Tues eves* ✆

Landlords *Nick & Sue Wateridge*
Brewery *Whitbread*
🍺 *Marston Pedigree; Strong Country Bitter; Flowers Original; Murphy Stout; Stella Artois; Heineken.*

Rustic charm goes beyond architecture and artefacts here. The Waterloo Arms is three centuries old, thatched on top and hung with hunting paraphernalia inside – flintlocks, spears, fishing rods – and their 'Waterloo Doorstops' in the summer season are a throwback to pre-sliced-bread days. Everything edible goes between thick slices of granary bread. Hot dishes, too, and more choice in the evening. Garden.
Typical dishes Lasagne and salad £2.25 Beef and beer stew £2.25

LYNMOUTH   NEW ENTRY   *Rising Sun*

The Harbour EX35 6EQ   `B&B`
Map 9 B1 *Devon*
Lynmouth (0598) 53223
Parking *limited*

Closed *Jan*

Landlord *Hugo Jeune*
Free house
🍺 *Usher Country Bitter, Triple Crown; Guinness; Carlsberg; Holsten Export.*
No real ale.

Accommodation *16 bedrooms* £A G1
Check-in all day

Hugo Jeune has spent a great deal of money in lovingly restoring his 14th-century thatched pub and adjacent cottages which climb steeply up the slope from the Lynmouth breakwater. The bedrooms boast individual decor, stylish fabrics, pine furniture, colour TV, direct-dial phones and spotless bathrooms; and the top cottage, where Shelley spent his honeymoon in 1812, has been decked out for modern newly-weds. *No children under five overnight. No dogs.*

Credit Access, Amex, Visa

LYONSHALL   *Royal George Inn*

Nr Kington HR5 3JN   `B&B`
Map 6 D3 *Hereford & Worcs*
Lyonshall (054 48) 210
Parking *ample*

Landlords *Mr & Mrs Allen*
Brewery *Whitbread*
🍺 *Flowers Original, IPA; Whitbread Best Bitter; Guinness; Stella Artois.*

Accommodation *5 bedrooms* £D G3
Check-in all day

A friendly black and white inn dating back to 1600, offering a choice of three bars, including the cosy beamed lounge and rather more rough and ready public bar where horse harnesses and dried hops add to the rustic atmosphere. The third bar has a popular pool room attached. Cosy bedrooms are simply furnished with functional pieces and share a bathroom and shower. All offer TVs, tea-makers and telephones. Garden and play area. Children welcome overnight. *No dogs.*

Credit Access, Visa

MAIDENSGROVE   *Five Horseshoes*

Nr Henley-on-Thames   `FOOD`
RG9 6EX
Map 10 B2 *Oxfordshire*
Nettlebed (0491) 641282
Parking *ample*

Bar food *12–2 (Sun till 1.30) & 7–10 (Mon, Fri & Sat till 9.30)*
No bar food *Sun eve*

Landlords *Graham & Mary Cromack*
Brewery *Brakspear*
🍺 *Brakspear Bitter, Special; Guinness; Heineken; Stella Artois.* 🍷 ⊖

The Cromacks' creeper-clad, 17th-century pub still draws the crowds, but cooking standards have unfortunately slipped slightly. Follow home-made soup or one of five different pâtés with chicken Kiev, seafood lasagne, calf's liver, poached whole trout or a daily special such as venison in red wine. Snacks include pancakes, and filled jacket potatoes, with chocolate cheesecake for afters.
Typical dishes Deep-fried mushrooms £3.50 Stir-fried beef £5.95

Credit Visa

MALTON   Green Man Hotel

Market Street YO17 0LY   `B&B`
Area Map 3 C4 *North Yorks*
Malton (0653) 692662
Parking *ample*

Landlords *John & Liz Barwick*
Free house
🍷 *Cameron Traditional Bitter, Tetley Bitter; Guinness; Hansa Export; Castlemaine XXXX.*

Accommodation *27 bedrooms* £C G2
Check-in all day

A family-run hostelry, located in the town centre market place, which boasts an impressive foyer-lounge featuring exposed beams and a huge inglenook. Locally carved furniture decorates the oak-panelled bar, while the spacious Fleece Bar has a smart, more modern appeal. Redecoration has brightened the modestly fitted bedrooms, all of which offer TVs, tea-makers and direct-dial telephones. Most have private bath or shower rooms.

Credit Access, Amex, Visa

MANCHESTER   NEW ENTRY   Lass O'Gowrie

36 Charles Street M1 7DB   `FOOD`
Map 3 C4 *Greater Manchester*
061-273 6932
Parking *limited*

Bar food *11.30–2 (Sat till 2.30), Sun 12–2*
No bar food *eves*

Landlords *Joe & Vi Fylan*
Brewery *Whitbread*
🍷 *Lass Bitter, Strong; Chesters Best Bitter; Murphy Stout; Stella Artois; Heineken.* ⊖

It is beautifully kept throughout, from the gleaming exterior tilework to the tasteful bar (all stripped floorboards, sturdy wooden furniture and sepia photographs), and also attracts with excellent beer brewed on the premises and generously served food. During the week, hot meals feature moussaka, spicy meatballs or shepherd's pie, while on Saturdays and Sundays only a splendid ploughman's is available. Coffee, but no sweets.

Typical dishes Mince and onion pie £1.90 Ham and vegetable platter £2.10

MANCHESTER   Royal Oak

729 Wilmslow Road,   `FOOD`
Didsbury M20 0RH
Map 3 C3 *Greater Manchester*
061-445 3152
Parking *difficult*

Bar food *12–2*
No bar food *eves, all Sat & Sun*

Landlord *Arthur Gosling*
Brewery *Marston*
🍷 *Marston Pedigree, Burton Bitter, Mild, Lager; Heineken.* ⊖

Quantity and quality of cheese draw people here, for Arthur Gosling has a passion for it. At lunchtime the bar counter is piled high with a huge selection of English and French cheeses. Sadly, however, you can only sample one type. It comes in an enormous slice with plenty of delicious wholemeal bread. Bowls of onion and beetroot accompany, and doggy bags are on hand for those who cannot do their portions justice.

Typical dishes Cheese platter £1.90 Pâté platter £1.90

MARHAMCHURCH   Bullers Arms

Nr Bude EX23 0HB   `B&B`
Map 9 B2 *Cornwall*
Widemouth Bay (028 885) 277
Parking *ample*

Landlords *Chris & Keith Nesbitt*
Free house ☙
🍷 *Wadworth 6X; Greene King Abbot Ale; Worthington BB; Devenish Cornish Original; Guinness.*

Accommodation *6 bedrooms* £C G3
Check-in all day

The Hunter's Bar, with its wall-mounted trophies over the stone fireplace, is the focal point of this large pub named after Sir Redvers Buller, a hero of the Boer War. Redecoration is taking place, which is very welcome, and the accommodation consists of four self-catering flatlets, and two en suite double bedrooms which can be let either as self-catering or with full hotel services. The flatlets contain sitting room with TV, breakfast alcove and fitted kitchen, two bedrooms and a bathroom.

Credit Access, Visa

MARKET DRAYTON   *Corbet Arms Hotel*

High Street TF9 1PY   B&B
Map 6 E2 *Shropshire*
Market Drayton (0630) 2037
Parking *ample*

Landlords *John & Cynthia Beckett*
Free house ☻
🍺 *Mitchells & Butlers Springfield Bitter; Stones Bitter; Guinness; Carling Black Label; Carlsberg.*

Accommodation *12 bedrooms* £C G2
Check-in all day

Comfortable overnight accommodation, and a warm welcome in the open-plan bars, is guaranteed at this creeper-clad coaching inn standing in the centre of town. Spacious bedrooms with modern fitted units and attractively co-ordinating fabrics offer TVs, tea-makers and direct-dial telephones, while all but two have carpeted private bathrooms. Low-ceilinged rooms on the top floor are especially characterful, and there is a delightful residents' lounge featuring handsome winged armchairs.

Credit Access, Amex, Diners, Visa

MARKET WEIGHTON   *Londesborough Arms*

High Road YO4 3AH   B&B
Map 4 E3 *Humberside*
Market Weighton (0430) 872219
Parking *ample*

Landlord *Simon Usher*
Brewery *Cameron*
🍺 *Cameron Traditional Bitter, Strongarm; Guinness; Castlemaine XXXX; Hansa.*

Accommodation *14 bedrooms* £D G3
Check-in all day

New manager Simon Usher inherits a degree of fading grandeur here and hopes, with help from his brewers, to stop the rot. It is a red-brick Georgian hotel with possibilities for style and comfort. Though there is no lounge for residents, three good bars provide options – the Bradley Bar commemorating the town's 18th-century patron. Front bedrooms with double glazing are best, although all have TVs and direct-dial telephones. Bathrooms are en suite but little else. Children welcome overnight.

Credit Access, Amex, Diners, Visa

MARSHSIDE   *Gate Inn*

Nr Canterbury CT3 4EB   FOOD
Area Map 5 E1 *Kent*
Chislet (022 786) 498
Parking *ample*

Bar food *11–2.30 & 6–11, Sun 12–3 & 7–10.30* ☻

Landlord *Christopher John Smith*
Brewery *Shepherd Neame*
🍺 *Shepherd Neame Master Brew Bitter, Master Brew Best Bitter, Master Brew Old Ale; Steinbock.*

The setting is a pure delight, with ducks and geese on a pond in the pretty little garden. The pub itself is suitably rustic and totally unpretentious, the atmosphere lively and happy. A log fire warms the bars, whose walls are hung with old photographs of the village. Cooking is down-to-earth, with hearty soups, ploughman's, raised pies, hotpots (meat and vegetarian) and a splendid bread pudding among the favourites.
Typical dishes Black pudding sandwich 90p Hotpot £2.85

MAYFIELD   *Rose & Crown*

Fletching Street T20 6TE   FOOD
Area Map 6 F3 *East Sussex*
Mayfield (0435) 872200
Parking *ample*

Bar food *12–2 & 7–10 (Sun till 9)*

Landlords *Richard & Claudette Leet*
Free house
🍺 *Adnams Bitter; Harvey Best Bitter; Faust; Young London Lager.* ☻

Standing alongside the original London to Brighton road – now a quiet village lane – is a friendly, white-painted inn dating back over 500 years. Inside, a huge log fire warms the low beamed bar, where the locals gather for old-fashioned pub games like shove ha'penny, and to enjoy the varied and capably prepared bar food. Consult the blackboard for the day's choice, starting perhaps with creamy crab mousse or country broth, then moving on to swordfish steak with herb and garlic butter, sausages provençale or tasty sweet and sour pork on brown rice. Ploughman's lunches and vegetarian specials are always featured, and sweets include sticky banoffi pie.

Typical dishes Chicken curry mayonnaise £2.65 Vegetable crumble £2.95

Accommodation *2 bedrooms* **£B G1**
Check-in by arrangement

Two immaculately kept bedrooms provide extremely comfortable overnight accommodation. Smart pine furnishings and stylish fabrics add to the appeal of uneven walls and blackened beams, and one room boasts its own small lounge. Both have TVs and spotless carpeted bathrooms. Children welcome overnight. *No dogs.*

Credit Visa

MEDMENHAM   NEW ENTRY   *Dog & Badger*

Nr Marlow SL7 2HE   `FOOD`
Map 10 C3 *Buckinghamshire*
Henley-on-Thames (0491) 571362
Parking *ample*

Bar food *12–2.30 (Sun till 2.15) & 7–9.30*

Landlords *Bill & Beryl Farrell*
Brewery *Whitbread*
🍺 *Wethered Bitter, SPA; Flowers Original; Winter Royal (winter only); Guinness; Stella Artois.*

Historical associations with this 16th-century timbered pub include Nell Gwynne and Sir Francis Dashwood. Inside it is all black beams, brasses and red plush, an atmospheric ambience for enjoying particularly good shortcrust pastry, fried cod or plaice, filled jacket potatoes and coffee and walnut gâteau. Steaks are a popular item on the restaurant menu (7–10, Sun till 9.30).
Typical dishes Jacket potato with mushrooms & bean sprouts £2.25 Haddock au gratin £4.50

Credit Access, Amex, Diners, Visa

MELLOR   *Millstone Hotel*

Church Lane, Nr Blackburn `B&B`
BB2 7JR
Map 3 C3 *Lancashire*
Mellor (025 481) 3333
Parking *ample*

Landlord *Richard Robinson*
Free house
🍺 *Thwaites Best Bitter; Guinness; Carlsberg.* 🍷

Accommodation *19 bedrooms* **£A G1**
Check-in all day

In the centre of Mellor village you will find a warm stone inn which offers a friendly and efficient welcome. The oak-panelled, low-ceilinged bar lounge immediately inside the entrance is a favourite haunt of the locals in the evenings, and its polished wood tables and high-backed chairs certainly make it a pleasant spot. Well-equipped, spotlessly clean bedrooms have good fitted units, pretty floral fabrics and decent carpeted bathrooms (ten with shower only).

Credit Access, Amex, Diners, Visa

MELMERBY   *Shepherds Inn*

Nr Penrith CA10 1HF   `FOOD`
Map 3 B2 *Cumbria*
Langwathby (076 881) 217
Parking *ample*

Bar food *11–2.30 & 6–9.45, Sun 12–2 & 7–9.45* ☻

Landlords *Martin & Christine Baucutt*
Brewery *Marston*
🍺 *Marston Burton Bitter, Pedigree, Owd Roger, Merrie Monk; Guinness.* 🍷 ☺

A lovely Lakeland building in a pretty village setting, but sadly the interior is a little gloomy and soulless. The bar is one long area with a pool table and games machine at one end and, at the other, an open fireplace. Acceptable food is on offer, with a mixture of dishes to please both those wanting hearty, plain fare and those wishing for something a little different.
Typical dishes Spinach & feta filo parcel £3.90 Cumberland sausage hotpot £3.60

Credit Access, Amex, Visa

MERE   *Old Ship Hotel*

Castle Street BA12 6JE   `B&B`
Area Map 7 C2 *Wiltshire*
Mere (0747) 860258
Parking *ample*

Landlord *Philip Johnson*
Brewery *Hall & Woodhouse*
🍺 *Hall & Woodhouse Badger Best, Badger Export; Guinness; Hofbräu Export, Royal.*

Accommodation *24 bedrooms* **£B G2**
Check-in all day

Until 1682 the home of Sir John Coventry, MP, whose banishment from court led to the expression 'sent to Coventry', this sturdy coaching inn exudes old-world charm. Winter log fires warm the beamed bar and there is a snug, peaceful residents' lounge. Annexe bedrooms have practical units and modern bathrooms, while those in the main building are more traditional in style (one boasts a four-poster). All offer TVs, tea-makers and direct-dial telephones. Children welcome overnight.

Credit Access, Visa

METAL BRIDGE   *Metal Bridge Inn*

Nr Gretna CA6 4HG   `B&B`
Map 3 B1 *Cumbria*
Rockcliffe (022 874) 206
Parking *ample*

Landlord *Mr R.R. Frazer*
Brewery *Younger* ☻
🍺 *Younger's Tartan, IPA; McEwan's Export, Lager.*

Accommodation *4 bedrooms* **£C G2**
Check-in all day

An extremely picturesque location on the edge of the River Esk is the main attraction of the Metal Bridge Inn, a white-painted house with red granite outbuildings in a tiny hamlet. Four en suite bedrooms in the main house have views over the estuary, and their pine furniture and floral curtains give them a pleasantly rural air. They are well-equipped with TVs, trouser presses and beverage facilities; the neat bathrooms have hairdryers. Patio.

Credit Access, Amex, Visa

METHERELL   *Carpenters Arms*

Nr Callington PL17 8BJ   `B&B`
Map 9 B2 *Cornwall*
Liskeard (0579) 50242
Parking *ample*

Landlords *Douglas & Jill Brace*
Free house ☻
🍺 *Worthington Best Bitter; Whitbread Poacher; Guinness; Carling Black Label; Stella Artois; Tennent's Pilsner.*

Accommodation *2 bedrooms* **£D G3**
Check-in all day

Perhaps the first recorded instance of moonlighting, the Carpenters Arms was built between times by carpenters working on Cotehele Manor in 1433. Inside it is fairly much as was – low beams, rough stone walls and flagstone floors. Settles and wheelback chairs are old enough to keep the bar suitably atmospheric. A more modern lounge is rather soulless by comparison. Above this two simple bedrooms share a functional shower room. Family area. Accommodation closed one week Christmas.

MIDDLEHAM   *Black Swan*

Market Place DL8 4NP   `B&B`
Area Map 2 D2 *North Yorks*
Wensleydale (0969) 22221
Parking *ample*

Landlords *Kenneth & Margaret Burton*
Free house
🍺 *Theakston Best Bitter, Old Peculier; Tawny Bitter; John Smith's Bitter; Guinness; Carlsberg Hof.*

Accommodation *7 bedrooms* **£D G2**
Check-in all day

A string of racehorses trots through the centre of this rugged stone-built village every morning, setting the theme for pictures in the bar of the crowded, haphazard 17th-century pub. Bedrooms are neatly squeezed in, up odd staircases and down passages in a modernised back section. Thick walls and tiny windows create an intimate feel and the two largest rooms contain four-posters. All have TVs, tea-makers, duvets and en suite bathrooms. *No children under ten overnight.*

Credit Access, Visa

MIDDLETON STONEY — Jersey Arms

Nr Bicester OX6 8SE   `B&B`
Area Map 4 F1 *Oxfordshire*
Middleton Stoney (086 989) 234
Parking *ample*

Landlords *Donald & Helen Livingston*
Free house
🍺 *Younger's Scotch, IPA; Harp.* 🍷

Accommodation *16 bedrooms* £A G1
Check-in all day

High standards prevail here, in a 16th-century Cotswold-stone inn. Excellent bedrooms (including two de-luxe rooms with sitting areas and three suites) in the main building and converted cottages are comfortable and spacious, with quality furnishings and carpeted private bathrooms. Thoughtful extras include mineral water, hairdryers and trouser presses, and room service is also available. The bar is friendly, and there is a cosy residents' lounge. Children welcome overnight. *No dogs.*

Credit Access, Amex, Diners, Visa

MIDHURST — Angel Hotel

North Street GU27 9DN   `B&B`
Area Map 6 A3 *West Sussex*
Midhurst (073 081) 2421
Parking *ample*

Landlord *Mr K. Yardley*
Owner *Gales*
🍺 *Gales HSB, BBB; Guinness; Carlsberg.* 🍷

Accommodation *17 bedrooms* £B G1
Check-in all day

A 16th-century former coaching inn with comfortable and in some cases very atmospheric bedrooms. The smart, darkly panelled entrance hall and reception give immediate evidence of period charm and good housekeeping, continued in the beamed bars. Some more superb panelling marks the way to front bedrooms, where exposed beams, sloping floors and heavy old furnishings give great character. Rear rooms have a more contemporary look. Children welcome overnight.

Credit Access, Amex, Diners, Visa

MILDENHALL — Bell Hotel

High Street IP28 7EA   `B&B`
Map 8 E2 *Suffolk*
Mildenhall (0638) 717272
Parking *ample*

Landlord *Mr J.A. Child*
Free house
🍺 *Greene King Abbot Ale; Adnams Bitter; Younger's Scotch; Guinness; Carlsberg Pilsner.*

Accommodation *17 bedrooms* £B G1/2
Check-in all day

The Child family have been at the Bell for nearly sixty years adding familial longevity to the pub's fire-blackened beams, uneven surfaces and old panelling. Collage pictures adorn the walls made up of photos of many past visitors to the pub. There is a family room beyond the bar and, in fine weather, drinks can be taken in the courtyard. Unfussy bedrooms are neat and comfortable. Most have private facilities and offer TVs, tea-makers and direct-dial phones.

Credit Access, Amex, Diners, Visa

MILTON — Jolly Brewer

5 Fen Road CB4 4AD   `FOOD`
Map 8 D2 *Cambridgeshire*
Cambridge (0223) 860585
Parking *ample*

Bar food *12–2 & 7–9*
No bar food *Mon eve*

Landlords *Chris & Ange Costard*
Brewery *Tolly Cobbold*
🍺 *Tolly Cobbold Original, Bitter, Best Bitter; Guinness; Hansa Export; Labatt's.*

An appealing, unpretentious pub with low-beamed ceilings, pine and darkwood tables and jugs of flowers on the windowsills. There is a good range of food which includes salads, stews, pasta and pies, with sweets such as cherry flan and bread and butter pudding. The speciality, though, is pork satay with peanut sauce, mixed salad, French bread and garlic herb butter. Children are offered indoor and outdoor play areas. Garden.
Typical dishes Lasagne £3.45 Dutch treat £2.25

MILTON ABBAS
Hambro Arms

Nr Blandford Forum   `B&B`
DT11 0BP
Area Map 7 C5 *Dorset*
Milton Abbas (0258) 880233
Parking *ample*

Landlord *Ken Baines*
Brewery *Devenish*
🍺 *John Devenish Dry Hop, Wessex;*
Guinness; Newquay Steam Pils.

Accommodation *2 bedrooms* **£C G1**
Check-in by arrangement

The thatched whitewashed appearance of
the 18th-century Hambro Arms completes
the picturesque scene of a fine village street.
The two bedrooms (one boasts a four-
poster) have been attractively refurbished
with pretty wallpapers and fabrics, good-
quality unit furniture and ample comforts,
from tea-makers, mini-bars and chocolates
to remote-control TVs, radio-alarms and
magazines. Both now offer well-equipped
modern bathrooms. Patio. *No children
under ten overnight. No dogs.*

Credit Access, Diners, Visa

MILTON COMBE
Who'd Have Thought It

Nr Yelverton PL20 6HP   `FOOD`
Map 9 B2 *Devon*
Yelverton (0822) 853313
Parking *ample*

Bar food *12–2 & 7–9.30*

Landlords *Gary Rager & Keith Yeo*
Free house
🍺 *Wadworth 6X; Palmer Bitter;*
Blackawton Bitter; Golden Hill Exmoor Ale;
Eldridge Pope Royal Oak; Heineken. ⊖

A 16th-century pebbledash pub which
gained its name when a long-ago owner
was finally granted a licence. Ancient
settles, foxes' heads and posting horns
adorn the unpretentious bars. The blackboard menu lists about twelve hot and cold
dishes such as duck with orange or curry;
also available are basket meals, grills,
salads and the usual pub fare. Sunday
lunch is more limited. Garden, terrace.
Typical dishes Steak & kidney pie £3.50
Steak in red wine £4.95

MINSTER LOVELL
Old Swan Hotel

Nr Witney OX8 5RN   `B&B`
Area Map 4 E2 *Oxfordshire*
Witney (0993) 775614
Parking *ample*

Landlord *Mr A.R. Taylor*
Brewery *Hall's & West Oxfordshire*
Brewery 🍺
🍺 *Tetley Bitter; Ind Coope Burton Ale;*
Löwenbräu.

Accommodation *10 bedrooms* **£A G1**
Check-in all day

An ancient half-timbered inn of Cotswold
stone close to the Windrush river, the Old
Swan has many typical and traditional
features. There are three lounges with
polished flagstone floors and open log fires.
Upstairs bedrooms are a good size for such
an old place, and a four-poster fits cosily
into one of them. Dark wood furniture and
small windows lend a cottage feel. Bathrooms are en suite with good toiletries.
Garden. *No children under 12 overnight. No
dogs.*

Credit Access, Amex, Diners, Visa

MOBBERLEY
NEW ENTRY   Bird In Hand

Knoll Green WA16 7BN   `FOOD`
Map 3 C4 *Cheshire*
Mobberley (0565) 873149
Parking *ample*

Bar food *12–2 & 7–9.30*
No bar food *Sun & Mon eves*

Landlord *A. R. Bentley*
Brewery *Samuel Smith*
🍺 *Samuel Smith Old Brewery Bitter,*
Museum Ale, Dark Mild; Ayingerbräu.

A neat black-and-white pub, formerly a
couple of old cottages, offering an enjoyable
selection of home-made snacks in four or
five pretty little rooms. Generously garnished sandwiches, salads and ploughman's are freshly prepared and attractively
presented, while hot dishes include battered
haddock, Welsh rarebit and mild chicken
curry served on wholegrain rice. Sandwiches only Sunday lunchtime. Patio.
Typical dishes Ham open sandwich
£2.50 Chilli con carne £3.75

Credit Access, Visa

MOLESWORTH   _Cross Keys_

Nr Huntingdon PE18 0QF   `B&B`
Map 8 D2 _Cambridgeshire_
Bythorn (080 14) 283
Parking _ample_

Landlady _Frances Mary Bettsworth_
Free house
☛ _Adnams Bitter; Younger's Tartan; McEwan's Export; Guinness; Carlsberg._

Accommodation _9 bedrooms_ **£D G2**
Check-in all day

Skittles, darts and billiards are all enjoyed by the locals at their unpretentious, 200-year-old pub which has a relaxed and friendly atmosphere. Best of the bedrooms (in a modern block to the rear) are warm, quiet and comfortable, while those in the original house have more character but are smaller and plainer. All rooms now offer en suite bathrooms, as well as TVs and tea-makers. Garden and play area. Children welcome overnight.

MONKSILVER   _Notley Arms_

Nr Taunton TA4 4JB   `FOOD`
Map 9 C1 _Somerset_
Stogumber (0984) 56217
Parking _ample_

Bar food _12–2 & 7–9.30, Sun 12–1.45 & 7–9_ ☙
No bar food _first 2 wks Feb_

Landlords _Alistair & Sarah Cade_
Brewery _Usher_
☛ _Ruddles County; Usher Best Bitter; Webster Yorkshire Bitter; Guinness; Holsten Export._

A friendly little village pub with a stream running along its pretty garden. A warm welcome awaits in the L-shaped bar with its log-burning stove, rustic wooden furnishings, beams and light classical music. The food is undoubtedly the star of the show, and the excellent blackboard menu is available lunchtime and evening seven days a week. Regular dishes take in soups, ploughman's platters, home-made pasta and pitta stuffed with lamb, beef or cheese. These are supplemented by four or five hot dishes, which on our last visit included superb red-roast pork served with rice and stir-fried vegetables, smoked haddock pancake and a vegetarian croustade with leeks, mushrooms and tomatoes. The owners Sarah and Alistair Cade have an excellent reputation in pub management.

Typical dishes Chinese red-roast pork with stir-fried vegetables £4.25 Tagliatelle with ham, cheese and mushrooms £2.75 Pitta bread with lamb, garlic and salad £2.25 Oliver's chocolate pudding £1.25

_Changes in data sometimes occur
in establishments
after the Guide goes to press._

_Prices should be taken as indications
rather than firm quotes._

MONTACUTE *Kings Arms Inn*

TA15 6UU
Area Map 7 A3 *Somerset*
Martock (0935) 822513
Parking *ample*

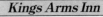
FOOD
B&B

Bar food *12–2 & 7.30–10*
(Sun till 9.30) ☙

Landlord *Mr S.D. Price*
Free house
🍺 *Bass; Gibbs Mew Wiltshire Bitter;*
Worthington Best Bitter; Guinness;
Carlsberg. ⊖

The new owners run a very friendly ship in this mellow 16th-century inn, whose public areas include a comfortable bar-lounge, half of which also serves as a breakfast room and buffet bar. The dining room is very pretty in pink and white, and here a full restaurant menu is available (12–2 & 7.30–9, except Sun eve), with dishes like salmon with parsley butter, pork Normandy and venison among the main courses. The lunchtime buffet, with cold meats and salads, is a popular attraction, and other favourites run from well-seasoned tomato soup and cream-baked smoked haddock to chicken curry and a fine selection of sweets, all home-made.

Typical dishes King's smokey £3.50 Stilton ploughman's £1.95

Accommodation *11 bedrooms* **£A G1**
Check-in all day

Eight of the bedrooms (those at the back) have been refurbished, and the remaining rooms are next in line. Rooms are generally quite compact – the exceptions being two honeymoon rooms, one with a four-poster – but adequately equipped. The newly decorated rooms feature attractive locally-made mahogany furniture. Bathrooms are mostly modern and tiled.

Credit Access, Amex, Visa

MORETON-IN-MARSH *Redesdale Arms Hotel*

High Street GL56 0AW
Map 10 A1 *Gloucs*
Moreton-in-Marsh (0608) 50308
Parking *ample*

B&B

Landlords *Michael C. Elvis & Patricia M. Seedhouse*
Free house
🍺 *Bass; Courage Best Bitter, Directors;*
Charringtons IPA; Beck's Bier; Foster's.

Accommodation *20 bedrooms* **£A G1**
Check-in all day

Fine Queen Anne panelling teamed with a handsome flagstone floor make the spacious Archway Bar of this lovely old Cotswold-stone inn a splendid setting for a quiet drink. Residents can also relax in the restful, leafy conservatory lounge. Stylish, individually decorated bedrooms (including six in an annexe and three luxury suites with patios) all have carpeted private facilities as well as tea-makers, trouser presses, radio-alarms and hairdryers. Children welcome overnight. *No dogs.*

Credit Access, Visa

MORETONHAMPSTEAD *White Hart Hotel*

The Square TQ13 8NF
Map 9 C2 *Devon*
Moretonhampstead (0647) 40406
Parking *limited*

B&B

Landlord *Peter Morgan*
Free house ☙
🍺 *Bass; Flowers IPA; Tetley Bitter; Ansells*
Bitter; Guinness; Carlsberg Export. 🍷

Accommodation *20 bedrooms* **£B G1**
Check-in all day

A fine traditional inn, one of the friendliest in the area. This is due largely to likeable landlord Peter Morgan, who is very proud of his inn's 300-year history of hospitality. The beamed bar, where an open fire adds its cheery glow, houses all sorts of bric-a-brac, and there is a comfortable lounge. TVs and radios (but no phones) are provided in the spotless bedrooms, all of which have private facilities. *No children under ten overnight.*

Credit Access, Amex, Diners, Visa

MORVAL   Snooty Fox Hotel

Nr Looe PL13 1PR   B&B
Map 9 B2 *Cornwall*
Widegates (050 34) 233
Parking *ample*

Landlords *P.A. & S.T. Faulkner
& R.W. Rix*
Free house
🍺 *Courage Best Bitter, Directors; Marston
Pedigree; Guinness; Stella Artois;
Carlsberg.*

Accommodation *5 bedrooms* £C G2
Check-in all day

Set on the top of a windswept hill some 3½
miles north-west of Looe on the A387, the
Snooty Fox consists of a charming original
pub and a new extension which houses the
public bar. The bedrooms are reached via a
rather inconvenient spiral staircase and are
named after some months of the year. All
have en suite facilities, TVs and tea-
makers. A good base for exploring the
lovely Cornish countryside. Children's
playpark in the grounds. Children welcome
overnight.

Credit Access, Visa

MOULTON   Black Bull Inn

Nr Richmond DL10 6QJ   FOOD
Area Map 2 E1 *North Yorks*
Barton (032 577) 289
Parking *ample*

Bar food *12–2*
No bar food *eves & Sun*
Restaurant closed *Sat lunch & Sun*

Landlords *Mr & Mrs G.H. Pagendam*
Free house
🍺 *Theakston Best Bitter, Old Peculier;
McEwan's 80/-; Guinness; Carlsberg
Hof.* ⊖

A popular village pub where the lunchtime
bar restaurant becomes a seafood restaurant at night (12–2 & 7–10.15; no bookings),
and you can also eat in a converted Pullman
coach or pretty conservatory. Light snacks
could be garlic mushrooms, ploughman's
and barbecued spare ribs. Main dishes
might include pan-fried monkfish in pepper
sauce, with delicious orange liqueur pancakes to finish. *No children under seven.*
Typical dishes Leek and potato soup £1
Salmon and asparagus quiche £3.25

Credit Access, Amex, Visa

MUCH WENLOCK   NEW ENTRY   Talbot Inn

High Street TF13 6AA   FOOD
Map 6 E2 *Shropshire*   B&B
Much Wenlock (0952)
727077
Parking *ample*

Bar food *9–2 & 7–10, Sun 12–2.30
& 7–8.30*

Landlord *Tim Lathe*
Free house
🍺 *Ruddles Best Bitter; Webster Yorkshire
Bitter; Guinness; Budweiser;
Carlsberg.* 🍷 ⊖

Dating from 1360 and originally known as
the Abbot's Hall, the Talbot is a black-and-
white timbered inn which formed part of
the almonry to Wenlock Priory in the 15th
century. Today, a pretty little courtyard
leads into the well-kept, heavily beamed bar
decorated with fresh flowers and plants;
this is the scene for some appetising,
speedily served snacks. At lunchtime, the
choice embraces soup, omelettes, filled
jacket potatoes and sirloin steak, while in
the evening there are more elaborate dishes
such as smoked salmon mousse followed
by herby lamb cutlets with garlic butter, or
plaice in a white wine sauce with prawns.
Highly recommendable sweets include a
perfectly cooked apple and blackberry pie.

Typical dishes Scampi provençale £6.95
Apple crumble £1.25

Accommodation *6 bedrooms* £C G1
Check-in all day

Immaculate bedrooms in the main building
and sympathetically converted malthouse
contrast honey-pine furnishings with plain
walls and pristine white duvet covers. All
have TVs and tea-makers, plus gleaming
private bathrooms. There is a pleasant little
breakfast room and a residents' lounge.
Children welcome overnight. *No dogs.*

Credit Access, Visa

NASSINGTON   *Black Horse Inn*

Nr Peterborough PE8 6QU   `FOOD`
Map 8 D1 *Northamptonshire*
Stamford (0780) 782324
Parking *ample*

Bar food *12–1.45 & 7–10, Sun 12–2
& 7–9.30*

Landlord *Thomas Guy*
Free house
🍺 *Greene King IPA; Adnams Bitter;
Young Special; Guinness; Harp;
Kronenbourg 1664.*

Friendly staff are bright as the firelight
glinting in the horse brasses here, the Black
Horse being a standard, well-maintained
village pub centred on its enormous stone
fireplace. A blackboard menu changes
daily and specialises in fish, such as
swordfish, scallops and plaice. Alligator
steaks are unusual, but the printed menu
less so – e.g. roast duckling with peaches,
beef stroganoff.
Typical dishes Lemon sole £6.95 Stir-
fried pork £7.25

Credit Access, Amex, Diners, Visa

NAUNTON   *Black Horse*

Nr Cheltenham GL54 3AD   `FOOD`
Area Map 4 C1 *Gloucs*   `B&B`
Guiting Power (045 15) 378
Parking *ample*

Bar food *12–1.30 & 6.30–9.30
(Sun from 7)*

Landlords *Adrian & Jennie Bowen-Jones*
Brewery *Donnington*
🍺 *Donnington Best Bitter, SBA; Carlsberg
Hof.* 🍷 ☻

The setting is a typical Cotswold village
sunk deep in beautiful countryside. Flagstones, beams and simple furniture exude
rural charm in the main bar while the
lounge offers a smaller, snugger retreat.
Plain, popular bar snacks start with half a
pint of smoked prawns, home-made soup or
chicken liver pâté. The printed menu
features ten main courses including seafood
platter with fried haddock, plaice, scampi
and scallops and fine home-cooked cold
ham. Vegetarians can ruminate on spring
vegetables au gratin or vegetable lasagne.
Blackboard specials may include carbonnade of beef. Chocolate truffito or pear
frangipane sweeten the ending.

Typical dishes Scotch beef steaks £7.50
Lasagne £3.50

Accommodation *3 bedrooms* **£D G3**
Check-in by arrangement

Unfussy, modestly furnished bedrooms
provide comfortable accommodation. The
rooms have washbasins and tea and coffee
making facilities. All share a public bathroom. Patio. *No children under 14 overnight. No dogs.*

Prices given are as at the time of our research and thus may change.

NEEDINGWORTH   *Pike & Eel Hotel*

Overcote Lane, Nr St Ives   `B&B`
PE17 3TW
Map 8 D2 *Cambridgeshire*
St Ives (0480) 63336
Parking *ample*

Landlords *John & Nicola Stafferton*
Free house ☙
🍺 *Bass; Adnams Bitter; Greene King IPA,
Abbot Ale; Guinness; Kronenbourg 1664.*

Accommodation *12 bedrooms* **£C G3**
Check-in all day

Gardens beside the river Ouse make this
much-extended 17th-century inn a popular
spot for summer sipping. On cooler days,
the welcome is warm in the cosy lounges
and mellow bar, where armchairs and
copper-topped tables add a homely note.
Cheerful, well-kept bedrooms (three with
modern private bathrooms) all have washbasins, writing areas, TVs and tea-makers.
A further 24 en suite bedrooms were being
built at the time of our visit. *No dogs.*

Credit Access, Amex, Diners, Visa

NETTLETON   NEW ENTRY   *Nettleton Arms*

Nr Chippenham SN14 7NP   `B&B`
Map 10 A3 *Wiltshire*
Castle Combe (0249) 782783
Parking *ample*

Landlords *Lesley & Les Cox & Cynthia & Jim Harvey*
Free house
🍺 *Wadworth 6X; Flowers Original; Guinness; Stella Artois; Heineken.*

Accommodation *4 bedrooms* **£D G2**
Check-in all day

Ancient timbers and a minstrels' gallery testify to the inn's considerable age, but there has also been a good deal of refurbishment and general updating. A medieval barn was recently converted into four comfortable, well-laid-out bedrooms, the two upstairs keeping some old rafters. Plaster walls, floral curtains and practical modern furnishings are standard, and all rooms have TVs, direct-dial phones and good en suite bathrooms with tubs and showers. Children welcome overnight.

Credit Access, Amex, Visa

NEWNHAM   NEW ENTRY   *George*

44 The Street ME9 0LL   `FOOD`
Map 8 E3 *Kent*
Eastling (079 589) 237
Parking *limited*

Bar food *12–2 & 7.30–10*
No bar food *Sun eve & all Mon*

Landlords *Ann & Simon Barnes*
Brewery *Shepherd Neame*
🍺 *Shepherd Neame Master Brew Bitter, Best Bitter, Mild; Steinbock; Hurlimann; Beamish Stout.*

Fine rugs on polished wooden floors, candlelit tables, a piano and splendid flower arrangements provide the civilised background for an imaginative range of snacks here at an attractive tile-hung 16th-century pub. Daily specialities such as wild mushroom salad, guineafowl with chestnuts in a wine sauce and creamy fish pie supplement regular treats like rack of lamb, chicken en croûte and home-made desserts. Garden and play area.
Typical dishes Seafood stuffed courgettes £2.75 Pork and apple pudding £4.25

NEWTON   *Queens Head*

★   ★

Nr Cambridge CB2 5PG   `FOOD`
Map 10 D1 *Cambridgeshire*
Cambridge (0223) 870436
Parking *limited*

Bar food *12–2.30 & 6–10.30, Sun 12–2 & 7–10*

Landlords *David & Juliet Short*
Free house
🍺 *Adnams Bitter, Old (winter only); Palmer Tally Ho (Xmas only); Tuborg Gold; Guinness.* ☻

Cambridge dons and local farm workers form part of the interesting cross-section of clientele here in the simple, stone-tiled bars. They come for the friendly, honest atmosphere, unmarred by gimmickry, and for the Shorts' refreshingly straightforward approach to food, that has remained unchanged over the past 26 years. It is all very simple – soup, sandwiches and baked potatoes at lunchtimes, soup and cold platters in the evening – but the standard is first-rate. Thick, flavour-packed soup comes in a mug with a spoon and hunk of granary bread. The cut-to-order sandwiches are probably the best pub sandwiches in Britain, being filled with tender rare beef, succulent ham, farmhouse Cheddar or smoked salmon, and baked potatoes served with cheese or butter make a decidedly tasty addition or alternative. In the evening, cold platters of beef, salmon and pâté are available.

Typical dishes Soup of the day £1.30 Cold ham platter £2.50 Roast beef sandwich £1.20 Baked potato with cheese £1.30

We publish annually so make sure you use the current edition.

NEWTON   *Red Lion Inn*

Nr Sleaford NG34 OEE   `A`
Map 8 D1 *Lincolnshire*
Folkingham (052 97) 256
Parking *ample*

Landlords *Bill & Gaenor Power*
Free house
🍺 *Bateman XB; Webster Yorkshire Bitter; Guinness; Carlsberg.*

Twenty-two dedicated years of looking after their charming little 17th-century pub in a remote rural setting off the A52 have not diminished the warmth of the Powers' welcome. An open fire burns in the softly lit main bar, where copper, brass and dark wood all gleam with polish, and stuffed animal heads decorate the exposed brick walls. An adjoining cottage is being converted to provide up to six en suite bedrooms. Patio.

Any person using our name to obtain free hospitality is a fraud.

Proprietors, please inform Egon Ronay's Guides and the police.

NORTH CERNEY   *Bathurst Arms*

Nr Gloucester GL7 7BZ   `FOOD`
Area Map 4 B2 *Gloucs*   `B&B`
North Cerney (028 583) 281
Parking *ample*

Bar food *12–2 & 6.45–9.45 (Sun 7–9.30)*

Landlords *Freddie & Caroline Seward*
Free house
🍺 *Hook Norton Best Bitter; Wadworth 6X; Smiles Best Bitter; Flowers Original; Guinness; Foster's.* ᕮ

Standing alongside the A435, this 17th-century former coaching inn retains considerable period charm in its delightfully rustic, flagstone-floored bar. Consult the blackboard for the constantly changing selection of dishes, ranging from hearty soups to appetising main courses like pan-fried duck breast with mushroom sauce, tuna and butter bean bake or pork chop with cider and apricot sauce. There are sandwiches and salads, too, plus sweets (treacle tart, apple pie) and a good cheeseboard to finish. Traditional roast for Sunday lunch. Hospitable owners Freddie and Caroline add to the welcoming atmosphere in the bar.

Typical dishes Bibury fish cakes with lobster sauce £4.25 Bathurst mixed grill £5.75

Accommodation *7 bedrooms* **£D G2**
Check-in by arrangement

Seven light, pretty bedrooms, each named after a different flower, are furnished in a variety of attractive styles (one room boasts a four-poster). TVs, tea-makers, direct-dial telephones and duvets are standard throughout and all but two rooms have carpeted bath/shower rooms. Riverside garden.

Credit Access, Visa

NORTH DALTON　　　　　　　　*Star Inn*

Nr Driffield YO25 9UX
Area Map 3 D5 *Humberside*
Middleton-on-the-Wolds
(037 781) 688
Parking *ample*

FOOD
B&B

Bar food *12–2 (Sun till 3) & 7–10*

Landlords *Kathryn & Phillip Mason*
Free house
🍺 *Tetley Bitter; John Smith's Yorkshire Bitter, Chestnut Mild; Carlsberg.* 🍷 ☻

Once at the heart of the Yorkshire wolds, now, somewhat prosaically, merely in Humberside, the Star has relinquished nothing but its county nomenclature. The pub stands by the village pond, its best bedrooms overlooking it to the parish church. At this roadside end is the traditional bar, while at the further, extended one, is a 'Victorian Parlour' incorporating a cocktail bar. From a safe soup or pâté and garlic bread start, the menu ventures out to Bengal Tiger (curry), Starlight Catch (fish pie) and Hopping Mad (rabbit casserole) before being brought to a sticky end with toffee pudding. Sunday lunch is served here. Garden. Patio.

Typical dishes Tuscan tagliatelle £3.45 Banana split £1.20

Accommodation *7 bedrooms* £B G1
Check-in by arrangement

A tasteful conversion of the stables has left their outer Georgian style intact with cottage-like interiors and reproduction furniture. Bedrooms sizes are adequate with good facilities – colour TVs, radio cassettes, direct-dial telephones and mini-bars – and are all en suite. *No children overnight. No dogs.*

Credit Access, Visa

NORTH PETHERTON　　　　　　*Walnut Tree Inn*

Fore Street, Nr Bridgwater
TA6 6QA
Map 9 C1 *Somerset*
North Petherton (0278) 662255
Parking *ample*

B&B

Landlords *Mr & Mrs Goulden*
Free house ☻
🍺 *Wadworth 6X; Golden Hill Exmoor Ale; Guinness; Castlemaine XXXX; Löwenbräu.* 🍷

Accommodation *28 bedrooms* £A G1
Check-in all day

A delightfully mellow bar with much gleaming copper and dark wood provides a focal point for village social life at a little 18th-century inn. Efficient staff welcome overnight guests, offering a choice of spacious, individually decorated executive rooms (including eight newly built ones) with sitting area, hairdryers and trouser presses, or smaller but equally comfortable standard rooms. Well-kept private bathrooms throughout. Accommodation closed three days Christmas. *No dogs.*

Credit Access, Amex, Diners, Visa

NORTH WOOTTON　　　　　　　*Crossways Inn*

North Wootton, Nr Shepton
Mallet BA4 4EU
Area Map 7 A1 *Somerset*
Pilton (074 989) 237
Parking *ample*

B&B

Landlords *John & Cynthia Kirkham*
Free house ☻
🍺 *Wadworth 6X; Bass; Webster Yorkshire Bitter; Guinness; Carling Black Label.*

Accommodation *17 bedrooms* £D G2
Check-in by arrangement

The Crossways Inn overlooks Glastonbury Tor across the historic Vale of Avalon. It is an 18th-century cider house enjoying a peaceful setting amidst lovely unspoilt countryside. Well-kept bedrooms are pleasantly decorated with floral fabrics and all have good thick carpets and duvets as well as hairdryers, trouser-presses, TVs and teamakers. Compact modern en suite facilities throughout. There is a homely little lounge for residents' use. *No children under three overnight. No dogs.*

Credit Access, Visa

NORTON   NEW ENTRY   *Hundred House Hotel*

Nr Shifnal TF11 9EE
Map 6 E2 *Shropshire*
Norton (095271) 353
Parking *ample*

FOOD
B&B

Bar food *12–2 & 6.30–9.30 (Sun 7–9)*

Landlords *Henry, Sylvia & David Phillips*
Free house
🍺 *Heritage Bitter; Marston Pedigree;*
Flowers Original; Murphy Stout; Wethered
Winter Royal; Stella Artois. ⊖

Accommodation *9 bedrooms* **£A G1**
Check-in all day

The mellow brick building, with a 13th-century barn in the car park, is a jumble of ages and styles. Real fires warm the bar, where bunches of flowers and herbs hang from the beams. Friendly girls serve, and one of the landlords is always around. Bar snacks cover a fair range, from ploughman's platters and cold meat salads to sautéed chicken livers and mushrooms, herb-filled trout, beef casserole and char-grilled steaks. From the restaurant menu comes a splendid steak and pheasant pie with tender, succulent meat, tasty gravy and melt-in-the-mouth pastry. Vegetarian dishes, delicious sweets.

Typical dishes Spaghetti bolognese £3.25 Steak & pheasant pie £8

Outshining even the food and the decor are the lovely bedrooms, with really pretty soft furnishings, convertible beds for children and no end of thoughtful extras. Most rooms have padded swing seats hanging from the timbers – great fun for youngsters. Dial-out phones, TVs. Garden.

Credit Access, Amex, Visa

NORTON   NEW ENTRY   *Vine Tree*

Nr Malmesbury SN16 0BZ
Map 10 A3 *Wiltshire*
Malmesbury (0666) 837654
Parking *ample*

FOOD

Bar food *12–2.30 & 7–10.30 (Sun till 10)*

Landlords *Brian & Tina Mussell*
Free house
🍺 *Wadworth 6X; Fullers London Pride;*
Vine Tree Bitter; Guinness; Beck's Bier. ⊖

Brian and Tina Mussell run their delightful country pub in an affable and informal way that has won them many friends. Tina's cooking is a big attraction, and her blackboard menus are of more than usual interest, with dishes as diverse as battered king prawns with a sweet and sour dip, roast duck, jugged hare, beef kebabs and shark steaks. Jacket potatoes and open sandwiches provide quicker snacks.
Typical dishes Carbonnade of beef £5.95 Chicken in red wine £5.95

Credit Access, Visa

NORTON ST PHILIP   NEW ENTRY   *George Inn*

Nr Bath BA3 6LH
Map 7 A3 *Avon*
Falkland (037 387) 224
Parking *limited*

A

Landlord *Michael Moore*
Brewery *Wadworth*
🍺 *Wadworth 6X, Devizes Bitter; Guinness;*
Harp; Löwenbräu.

Built at the end of the 14th century, the George saw service as the Duke of Monmouth's headquarters before the Battle of Sedgemoor in 1685. The black-and-white beamed building is one of the finest surviving medieval inns in the land, and visitors will sense the atmosphere and happenings of yesteryear in the four splendid bars and little galleried courtyard. Michael Moore, the inn's highly personable landlord, has been at the helm for 25 years.

NOTTINGHAM — Ye Olde Trip to Jerusalem Inn

Brewhouse Yard, Castle Road, NG1 6AD `A`
Map 7 C1 *Nottinghamshire*
Nottingham (0602) 473171
Parking *difficult*

Landlords *Janet & Ernie Marshall*
Free house
🍺 *Marston Pedigree; Samuel Smith's Old Brewery Bitter; Ruddles Best Bitter; Wards Sheffield Best Bitter; Carling Black Label.*

The family of landlady Janet Marshall (née Ward) has held the licence at this renowned inn for over 100 continuous years. Originally a brewhouse for Nottingham Castle, and a public house since 1189, the 'Trip' was a favourite resting place for crusaders en route to Jerusalem. Today's visitors will find ample character behind the 16th-century facade in the honeycomb of passages, rooms and cellars literally carved out of the porous rock on which the castle stands. Courtyard.

NUNNEY — George Inn

11 Church Street, Nr Frome BA11 4LW `B&B`
Area Map 7 C1 *Somerset*
Nunney (037 384) 458
Parking *ample*

Landlords *Mr & Mrs J. S. B. Lewis*
Free house ⭘
🍺 *Butcombe Bitter; Bunce's Best Bitter; Bass; Guinness; Holsten; Carling Black Label.*

Accommodation *11 bedrooms* **£C G2**
Check-in all day

Nunney is a picturesque village with a brook, an old church and a moated ruined castle. The George is a traditional inn dating back to the 14th century, white-painted, with a pretty walled garden. The bars have a cosy, rustic appeal, while bedrooms of various shapes are modestly furnished apart from one four-poster room. Some overlook the garden, some the castle; all have private bath or shower, dial-out phones, TVs and tea-makers.

Credit Access, Amex, Diners, Visa

NUNTON — NEW ENTRY — Radnor Arms

Nr Salisbury SP5 4HS `FOOD`
Area Map 7 F3 *Wiltshire*
Salisbury (0722) 29722
Parking *ample*

Bar food *12–2 (Sun till 1.30) & 7–9.30*

Landlords *Richard & Lesley Penny*
Brewery *Hall & Woodhouse* ⭘
🍺 *Hall & Woodhouse Badger Best, Tanglefoot; Guinness; Hofbräu Export, Royal.* ⊖

An unpretentious little ivy-clad pub serving honest, hearty fare like ploughman's platters, jacket potatoes, casseroles and fried dishes. Specials of the day could be liver and bacon pâté, stuffed courgettes and half a pint of prawns. Steaks extend the evening choice and Sunday lunch includes a traditional roast (bookings only). This is one of the fairly few pubs with a special toilet for wheelchair-users.
Typical dishes Beef & horseradish casserole £3.95 Treacle tart £1.20

OAKWOODHILL — Punchbowl Inn

Nr Ockley RH5 5PU `FOOD`
Area Map 6 C2 *Surrey*
Oakwoodhill (030 679) 249
Parking *ample*

Bar food *12–2 (summer till 2.30) & 7–10* ⭘

Landlords *Rob & Shirley Chambers*
Free house
🍺 *King & Barnes Sussex Bitter; Young Special; Hall & Woodhouse Badger Best; guest beer; Guinness; Carlsberg.* ⊖

Moss and lichen encrust the stone slates that roof this 600-year-old tile-hung pub. Inside, there are worn flagstones and two cartwheels in the huge inglenook. The rarely changing menu features nicely cooked sweet and sour crispy duck, steak and kidney pie, and ham, egg and chips as well as sandwiches and ploughman's. Soup only on Sunday, Monday and Tuesday nights. Excellent rhubarb crumble for afters.
Typical dishes Chicken & sweetcorn soup £1.25 Chicken curry £3.50

Credit Diners, Visa

OCKLEY   King's Arms

Stane Street RH5 5TP   FOOD
Area Map 6 C2 *Surrey*   B&B
Dorking (0306) 711224
Parking *ample*

Bar food *12–2 & 7–9.30* ⚖

Landlords *Mary Kates Doyle & family*
Free house
🍺 *King & Barnes Sussex Bitter; Hall &
Woodhouse Badger Best; Fullers ESB;
Guinness; Carlsberg Pilsner.* ⊖

The Doyle family will give you a friendly
welcome at their 300-year-old roadside pub,
which has two small traditional bars with
dark beams, horsebrasses, shining copperware and oak furniture as well as a more
spacious family room which opens onto the
patio and well-kept gardens. The bar menu
covers such items as soup, taramasalata,
sandwiches, traditional steak and kidney
pie, salads and moussaka, with good fresh
vegetables to accompany main dishes.
Home-made desserts include lemon gâteau
and sherry trifle. More elaborate dishes are
offered in the restaurant (closed Sunday
evening), such as duck with honey and
black pepper or lamb with wild mushrooms, garlic and red wine; traditional
Sunday lunch here too.

Typical dishes Steak & kidney pie £3
Plaice & chips £3.20

Accommodation *5 bedrooms* **£A G1**
Check-in by arrangement

Three of the five bedrooms have private
facilities (two with shower only) and are
quite small; the two older rooms at the front
share a public bathroom. All have kettles,
and are situated over the bars which can be
noisy at certain times.

Credit Access, Amex, Visa

ODIHAM   George Hotel

High Street RG25 1LP   B&B
Map 10 C3 *Hampshire*
Odiham (0256) 702081
Parking *ample*

Landlords *Peter & Moira Kelsey*
Brewery *Courage*
🍺 *Courage Best Bitter, Directors; John
Smith's Bitter; Guinness; Kronenbourg
1664.*

Accommodation *15 bedrooms* **£A G1**
Check-in all day

The choice of accommodation continues to
improve at this historic inn. As well as the
characterful main-building bedrooms with
their low beams and antique furnishings
(including one four-poster), there are six
attractive rooms in the converted coach
house, plus a further three doubles in a
former barn. Accessories throughout are
thoroughly modern, and all rooms have
private facilities. Farming artefacts decorate the flagstoned bar, while the residents'
lounge features exposed stonework.

Credit Access, Amex, Diners, Visa

OLD DALBY   Crown Inn

Debdale Hill, Nr Melton   FOOD
Mowbray LE14 3LE
Map 7 C1 *Leicestershire*
Melton Mowbray (0664) 823134
Parking *ample*

Bar food *12–2 & 6–9.45 (Mon till 8.30)*
No bar food *Sun eve* ⚖

Landlords *Salvatore Inguanta & Lynne
Bryan*
Free house
🍺 *Marston Pedigree; Ruddles County;
Adnams Bitter; Theakston XB.* 🍷 ⊖

Tucked away down a lane in the village
centre, this 200-year-old converted farmhouse is today the home of some enjoyable,
often ambitious cooking. Cosy, antique-
furnished bars provide the setting, while
the choice embraces sirloin steak sandwiches, Cumberland sausage with sage and
onion sauce and pastry-wrapped chicken in
a creamy lemon and tarragon sauce. Evening menu available in the restaurant.
Garden.

Typical dishes Welsh rarebit £2.25 Noisettes of lamb £6.95

OLLERTON   *Dun Cow*

Chelford Road WA16 8RH   `FOOD`
Map 3 C4 *Cheshire*
Knutsford (0565) 3093
Parking *ample*

Bar food *12–2 (Sun till 1.45) & 6.30–9.30*
No bar food *Mon, Tues & Sun eves*

Landlord *Mr G. Tilling*
Brewery *Greenall Whitley*
🍺 *Greenall Whitley Original, Local Bitter,
Mild; Guinness; Grünhalle, Export.* 🍷 ⊖

Landlord Geoff Tilling provides simple
meals in the bars of his beamed and horse-
brassed pub. You might start with vegetable soup with crusty bread, followed by
lamb and leek pie, cauliflower cheese, meat
loaf, a filled jacket potato or sandwiches. On
Sunday, only sandwiches are available in
the bar, but a traditional roast is served in
the restaurant. Terrace.
Typical dishes Turkey & nut pie £2
Cauliflower cheese & mushroom pancakes
£2

OMBERSLEY   *Kings Arms*

Nr Worcester WR9 0EW   `FOOD`
Map 10 A1 *Hereford & Worcs*
Worcester (0905) 620142
Parking *ample*

Bar food *12.15–2.15 & 6–9.30 (Fri & Sat
till 9), Sun 12–8.30*

Landlord *Chris Blundell*
Brewery *Mitchells & Butlers*
🍺 *Bass; Mitchells & Butlers Brew XI,
Springfield Bitter; Guinness; Carling Black
Label; Tennent's Extra.* ⊖

Bent with age and oozing with character,
the Kings Arms is a lovingly kept black-
and-white inn (*circa* 1411) which provides a
delightful setting in which to enjoy some
excellent food. Delicious soups (try lettuce
and green pea or nutty parsnip) might
precede broccoli and cauliflower mornay,
popular turkey and leek pie or an unusual
breadcrumb-topped   macaroni   cheese.
Finish with old-fashioned rhubarb crumble
or spicy apple cheesecake.
Typical dishes Haddock and prawn casserole £3.95 Chilli beef chowder £3.95

*We welcome bona fide recommendations
or complaints on the tear-out pages at the back
of the book for readers' comments.*

*They are followed up by our professional team,
but do complain to the management on the spot.*

ORFORD   *King's Head Inn*

Front Street, Nr   `B&B`
Woodbridge IP12 2LW
Map 8 F2 *Suffolk*
Orford (0394) 450271
Parking *ample*

Landlords *Alistair & Joy Shaw*
Brewery *Adnams*
🍺 *Adnams Bitter; Murphy Stout;
Castlemaine XXXX.*

Accommodation *6 bedrooms* £D G3
Check-in by arrangement

Standing in the shadow of the village
church and windswept graveyard, the
Shaw family's 13th-century pub is steeped
in smuggling history. A huge inglenook
fireplace warms the low-ceilinged bar,
while up under the eaves are the equally
characterful bedrooms with their exposed
beams and sloping floorboards. Three have
been refurbished and all offer TVs and tea-
makers; they share two neat public bathrooms. Accommodation closed January.
Children welcome overnight.

Credit Diners, Visa

OSWALDKIRK   *Malt Shovel Inn*

Nr Helmsley YO6 5XT   `FOOD`
Area Map 3 B3 *North Yorks*   `B&B`
Ampleforth (043 93) 461
Parking *ample*

Bar food *12–2 & 7–9.30*
No bar food *Sun eve & all Mon
& Tues in winter* ☜

Landlords *Brian & Kay Hughes*
Brewery *Samuel Smith*
🍷 *Samuel Smith's Old Brewery Bitter,
Draught Stout; Ayingerbräu, Pils.* ♟ ⊖

An early 17th-century manor has been
converted into a lovely old pub which
retains many original features. The tap
room (ideal for children) boasts a huge
inglenook and lofty ceiling, and roaring log
fires warm the two little bars. Imaginative
snacks are carefully prepared and attractively presented, with choices like deep-fried
Brie with cranberry sauce or prawns and
mushrooms in garlic butter followed by
lasagne, a substantial granary bread sandwich or daily special such as cheesy
vegetable bake served with potato and an
excellent mixed salad. More elaborate evening choices include trout with almonds and
beef in beer, with locally made puddings
(try the banana and butterscotch pie) to
finish.

Typical dishes Ginger and celery soup
£1.50 Chicken curry in a cottage loaf £3.50

Accommodation *3 bedrooms* **£D G3**
Check-in by arrangement

A fine oak staircase leads to the three good-
sized bedrooms, in which sloping floors and
ceilings add to the charm. Spotlessly kept
and simply appointed, all offer electric
blankets, washbasins and tea-makers and
share a functional public bathroom.
Accommodation closed 24–26 December.

OVER STRATTON   *Royal Oak*

South Petherton TA13 5LQ   `FOOD`
Map 7 A4 *Somerset*
South Petherton (0460) 40906
Parking *ample*

Bar food *12–2 & 7–10 (Sun till 9.30)* ☜

Landlords *Derek & Claire Blezard*
Free house
🍷 *Wadworth 6X; Butcombe Bitter; Hook
Norton Best Bitter; Murphy Stout; Stella
Artois.* ♟ ⊖

Although difficult to track down, the Royal
Oak is welcoming once found. Derek and
Claire Blezard's thatched pub is also ideal
for families in summertime, as outside there
is a barbecue, garden, trampoline and
children's play apparatus. The regularly
changing menu, incorporating children's
and vegetarian dishes, provides a range
from simple pancakes and burgers to
salmon pie and beef in stout.
Typical dishes Squid in lemon mayonnaise £2.95 Lamb in Greek pastry £5.95

Credit Access, Visa

OVINGTON   *Bush Inn*

Nr Alresford SO24 0RE   `A`
Map 7 C4 *Hampshire*
Alresford (0962) 732764
Parking *ample*

Landlords *Mr & Mrs G. M. Draper*
Free house
🍷 *Wadworth 6X; Strong Country Bitter;
Gales HSB; guest beer; Stella Artois.* ♟

Tucked away down a winding, wooded
country lane off the A31 is the Bush, a
delightful rose-covered old pub in a picturesque setting by the tranquil river Itchen.
The rustic, softly lit bars with their copper
pans, old hunting prints and giant antique
bellows beside the roaring log fire create a
relaxing atmosphere for enjoying a pint of
traditional ale or cider. Children welcome in
the bar lunchtimes only. Garden for summertime drinking.

PELYNT   *Jubilee Inn*

Nr Looe PL13 2JZ   `B&B`
Map 9 B2 *Cornwall*
Lanreath (0503) 20312
Parking *ample*

Landlord *Mr F. E. Williams*
Free house
🍺 *Jubilee Original; Tetley Bitter, Falstaff;*
Guinness; Carlsberg; Löwenbräu.

Accommodation *9 bedrooms* **£C G1**
Check-in all day

Originally the Axe Inn, this friendly, pink-painted pub patriotically changed its name in 1887 to commemorate Queen Victoria's Jubilee. A collection of Victorian china decorates the characterful lounge bar, and there is a simpler, flagstone-floored public bar. Good-sized bedrooms are pleasantly furnished in period style and all offer neat private bathrooms, direct-dial telephones and TVs. A homely lounge is available for residents' use and the large rear garden has a play area. Children welcome overnight.

Credit Access, Visa

PEMBRIDGE   *New Inn*

Market Square HR6 9DZ   `B&B`
Map 6 D3 *Hereford & Worcs*
Pembridge (054 47) 427
Parking *ample*

Landlady *Jane Melvin*
Brewery *Whitbread*
🍺 *Flowers Original, IPA, PA; Guinness;*
Stella Artois.

Accommodation *6 bedrooms* **£D G3**
Check-in by arrangement

Overlooking the tiny covered village market, the timbered New Inn dates from 1311; bulging walls, heavy beams and sloping floors throughout testify to its antiquity. The two bars are delightfully rustic, especially the public with its huge open fire, flagstoned floor and enormous wooden settle. Equally atmospheric bedrooms are modest but well kept and include a particularly light, spacious front-facing room with an en suite shower; remaining rooms share two public bathrooms. Children welcome overnight.

PENDOGGETT   *Cornish Arms*

St Kew, Bodmin PL30 3HH   `B&B`
Map 9 B2 *Cornwall*
Bodmin (0208) 880263
Parking *ample*

Landlords *Paul Stewart & Mervyn Gilmour*
Free house 🍺
🍺 *Bass; Pendoggett Special; St Austell*
Duchy; Worthington Best Bitter; Carlsberg
Hof, Pilsner. 🍷 ☺

Accommodation *7 bedrooms* **£B G2**
Check-in all day

On the B3314 in a hamlet about a mile from the sea, this popular and lovingly kept 17th-century inn has a delightfully rustic appeal. Gleaming brassware and traditional china ornaments decorate the shiny slate-floored bars, and there is a chintzy residents' lounge where guests like to take their morning coffee and afternoon tea. Warm, comfortable bedrooms are solidly furnished in white Regency style and five have neat en suite bathrooms. *No children under five overnight.*

Credit Access, Visa

---

*Our inspectors never book in the name of
Egon Ronay's Guides.*

*They disclose their identity only if they are
considering an establishment for inclusion
in the next edition of the Guide.*

PENSAX   Bell Inn

Nr Abberley WR6 6AE   `FOOD`
Map 7 A2 *Hereford & Worcs*
Great Witley (0299) 896677
Parking *ample*

Bar food *12–2 & 7–10 (Sun till 9.30)* ☙

Landlords *John & Christine Stroulger*
Free house
☛ *Hook Norton Best Bitter; Timothy Taylor Landlord; Ruddles County; Foster's; Tennent's Extra; Carlsberg Pilsner.*

On the edge of Pensax amid fine rolling countryside is a delightfully unspoilt, friendly pub offering consistently good bar snacks carefully prepared by landlady Christine Stroulger. Follow ginger chicken wings or her excellent French onion soup with beef in Guinness, grilled trout and almonds, a juicy steak or vegetable lasagne. Enterprising sweets include hot blackcurrant meringue and apricot syllabub. Children welcome in the dining room. Garden.
Typical dishes Mariner's pie £4.75 Broccoli and Stilton quiche £3.60

PERRANUTHNOE   NEW ENTRY   *Victoria Inn*

Nr Penzance TR20 9NP   `FOOD`
Map 9 A3 *Cornwall*   `B&B`
Penzance (0736) 710309
Parking *ample*

Bar food *12–2 & 6.30–9.30 (Sun from 7)*
No bar food *Sun eve in winter* ☙

Landlords *Julia & Chris Martin*
Brewery *Courage*
☛ *Courage Best Bitter, Directors; John Smith Yorkshire Bitter; Guinness; Kronenbourg 1664.*

Officially described as a safe house for the clergy, and equally welcoming to families and dogs, the Victoria is a super little pub just off the A394. Julia Martin does good work in the kitchen, and among much maritime memorabilia patrons tuck into favourites like 10oz sirloin and gammon steaks, filled jacket potatoes and daily specials such as chicken curry with side dishes of chutney, coconut and banana. There are also dishes for vegetarians, with a short selection of sweets to round things off.

Typical dishes Smoked chicken breast salad £3.95 Jacket potato with ham and coleslaw £2.95

Accommodation *2 bedrooms* £C G2
Check-in by arrangement

Two smallish pine-fitted bedrooms have their own WCs, showers and washbasins, and there is just room for a kettle, a luggage stand and a chair. A TV set sits in the residents' lounge, and a payphone is provided in the hall. Rooms overlook a rear terrace, and sandy beaches are just moments away.

Prices given are as at the time of our research and thus may change.

PETER TAVY   Peter Tavy Inn

Nr Tavistock PL4 9NN   `FOOD`
Map 9 B2 *Devon*
Mary Tavy (082 281) 348
Parking *ample*

Bar food *12–2.15 & 7–9.45* ☙

Landlords *Janice & Phil Hawkins*
Free house
☛ *Wadworth 6X; Bass; Eldridge Pope Royal Oak; Guinness; Hofmeister; Foster's.* ♟ ☕

The 15th-century building started life as a home for masons, and graduated through a smithy to a coaching house. Now it is just a lovely Devon village pub serving enjoyable snacks with a wholefood slant. Vegetable moussaka, homity pie and cauliflower croustade are typical, as are cashew nut fingers and wholemeal pasties and quiches. Sweets such as date and walnut loaf, fruit pie or honey and oat flan to follow. Extended evening choice. Garden.
Typical dishes Chilli con carne £3.15 Vegetable lasagne £3.15

PETWORTH   *Angel*

Angel Street GU28 0BG   `B&B`
Area Map 6 B3 *West Sussex*
Petworth (0798) 42153
Parking *ample*

Landlords *Brian & Anne Pellant*
Free house 🛏
🍺 *Webster Yorkshire Bitter; Ruddles Best Bitter, County; Guinness; Foster's; Holsten Export.*

Accommodation *3 bedrooms* £D G3
Check-in by arrangement

Bowed walls, exposed beams, head-cracking doorways and wildly sloping floors all testify to the Angel's antiquity, and the jumble of the centuries is particularly apparent in the bedrooms. These rooms are quite modest in their appointments; all three have washbasins and share two modern, carpeted bathrooms. In the bar, tapestry-covered stools and benches, Windsor chairs and horse brasses create a fairly standard old-world look. Garden.

Credit Access, Diners, Visa

PETWORTH   *Welldiggers Arms*

Pulborough Road GU28 0HG   `FOOD`
Area Map 6 B3 *West Sussex*
Petworth (0798) 42287
Parking *ample*

Bar food *12–2 & 6–10, Sun 12–2 & 7–10*

Landlords *Mr & Mrs E.H. Whitcomb*
Free house
🍺 *Young Bitter, Special; Ruddles County; Young London Lager; Carlsberg; Budweiser.* 🍷 ☻

This is very much a food pub, and the bar and snug are nearly always busy. Oysters, crab soup, red mullet and lemon sole typify an excellent seafood choice, and there are casseroles, game and properly hung steaks for meat-eaters, plus a vegetarian special. Note well-kept hand-pulled beers, good wines and a decanted vintage port (just right for the farmhouse Stilton).
Typical dishes Courgette casserole £2.95 Roast duck & apple sauce £7.50

Credit Access, Amex, Diners, Visa

PEWSHAM   NEW ENTRY   *Lysley Arms*

Nr Chippenham SN15 3RU   `FOOD`
Map 10 A3 *Wiltshire*
Chippenham (0249) 652864
Parking *ample*

Bar food *12–2 (Sun till 1.30) & 6.30–10 (Sun till 9.30)* 🛏

Landlords *Geoff & Ann Needham*
Free house
🍺 *Bass; Wadworth 6X; Guinness; Tennent's Extra; Carling Black Label.*

Spot the stone roof and the colourful flower beds as you drive along the A4 east of Chippenham. Inside it is just as attractive, with beams, chintz and winter log fires. The blackboard menu combines familiar fare with more imaginative choices like vegetables au gratin or medallions of pork with plums. Good vegetables, decent sweets and a special menu for children (who also have an outside play area).
Typical dishes Chicken country style £5.95 Chocolate roulade £1.50

Credit Access, Amex, Diners, Visa

PHILLEIGH   *Roseland Inn*

Nr Truro TR2 5NB   `FOOD`
Map 9 A3 *Cornwall*
Portscatho (087 258) 254
Parking *ample*

Bar food *12–1.45 & 6.30–9 (Sun from 7)*
No bar food *eves (Sept–May)*

Landlord *Desmond Sinnott*
Brewery *Cornish Brewery Company*
🍺 *John Devenish Dry Hop, Cornish Original; Guinness; Cornish Pils; Heineken.* ☻

Ornaments, pictures and plaques with a seafaring theme decorate the bars in an immaculately-kept village inn, whose history goes back three centuries. The rural setting in a Cornish village is a delightful one for sampling the uncomplicated bar snacks which range from pasties, ploughman's and steak and kidney pie to smoked mackerel or salade niçoise, as well as salads and sandwiches. Chocolate biscuit cake or fruit crumble to follow.
Typical dishes Egg & prawn mayonnaise £3.50 Quiche £3

PICKHILL   Nag's Head

Nr Thirsk YO7 4JG   `B&B`
Area Map 2 F2 *North Yorks*
Thirsk (0845) 567391
Parking *ample*

Landlords *Raymond & Edward Boynton*
Free house
🍺 *Theakston Best Bitter, Old Peculier;*
Tetley Bitter; Younger's Scotch; Guinness;
Löwenbräu.

Accommodation *17 bedrooms* £D **G2**
Check-in all day

Deep in Herriot country just five minutes
from the A1 stands a much modernised and
extended village pub offering simple but
comfortable accommodation. More up-to-
date rooms are also available in a newly
converted house next door, and in a nearby
cottage. All have radios, tea-makers, TVs
and fresh fruit and are decorated in the
same style. Bathrooms (one public, the rest
en suite) are clean and functional. Things
can get a bit noisy at night in the lively bar.
Children welcome overnight.

Credit Access, Visa

PITTON   Silver Plough

Nr Salisbury SP5 1D2   `FOOD`
Area Map 7 F2 *Wiltshire*
Farley (0722 72) 266
Parking *ample*

Bar food *12–2 & 7–10* ☙

Landlords *Michael Beckett, Charles*
Manktelow & Paul Parnell
Free house
🍺 *Wadworth 6X; Flowers Original;*
Courage Best Bitter; Guinness;
Heineken. 🍷 ☺

Lovers of fine food flock to this attractively
converted farmhouse, where superb cooking can be enjoyed in a cosily rustic setting.
His regularly changing printed menu
features such delights as light, subtly
flavoured chicken and saffron mousse,
fresh pasta with fish and shellfish, juicy,
chargrilled steaks and pastry-wrapped beef
and foie gras served with a rich red wine
sauce. Consult the blackboard for splendid
seasonal game and seafood specialities,
including perhaps marinated Orkney
herrings with Madeira or pheasant and
chicken pâté followed by moist sea bass
with prawns and capsicums,wild duck with
cassis sauce or monkfish in puff pastry with
tomato and saffron. Accompanying vegetables and salads are first-rate, home-made
ice-creams and plum tart feature among the
desserts and there is a fine English cheeseboard. English country wines and champagne available by the glass. Traditional
Sunday lunches. Garden.

Typical dishes Dorset mussels £3.75
Suckling pig with honey and ginger sauce
£9.50 Salmon with basil sauce £8.50 Prune
and brandy ice-cream £1.75

Credit Access, Amex, Diners, Visa

PLYMOUTH   NEW ENTRY   Unity

Eastlake Street PL1 8BD   `FOOD`
Map 9 B2 *Devon*
Plymouth (0752) 262622
Parking *ample*

Bar food *12–2.30*
No bar food *eves*

Landlady *Mrs M. Law*
Brewery *Halls*
🍺 *Halls Plympton Best; John Bull Bitter;*
Tetley Bitter; Guinness; Castlemaine
XXXX; Löwenbräu.

Find this busy little pub just off the main
pedestrianised area – a convenient location
for that most convenient of lunches, the
sandwich. Choose your filling from a tempting display of home-cooked beef and ham,
prawns and tuna in mayonnaise, plus
excellent Cheddar and Stilton, and a delicious wholegrain 'doorstep' will be rapidly
assembled. Jacket potatoes and a couple of
hot specials like tasty bacon and vegetable
bake complete the selection.
Typical dishes Lasagne £2.50 Tuna
sandwich £1.95

POCKLINGTON   *Feathers Hotel*

56 Market Place YO4 2AH   B&B
Area Map 3 C5 *Humberside*
Pocklington (0759) 303155
Parking *ample*

Landlord *Mr K.F. Suttle*
Brewery *Younger*
🍺 *Younger's Scotch, No. 3, IPA; Beck's Bier; McEwan's Lager.*

Accommodation *12 bedrooms* **£C G1**
Check-in all day

Popular with the locals, who enjoy a drink in the spacious, welcoming bar, this pebble-dash pub on the market place also has decent overnight accommodation. The six main-house bedrooms of varying sizes have a traditional appeal (one boasts a half-tester), while the remaining six, across the car park, are in a chalet style. All offer hairdryers, trouser presses, tea-makers and smart private facilities. Residents have the use of a homely TV lounge. Children welcome overnight. *No dogs.*

Credit Access, Amex, Diners, Visa

POLKERRIS   NEW ENTRY   *Rashleigh Inn*

Nr Fowey PL24 2TL   FOOD
Map 9 B2 *Cornwall*
Par (072 681) 3991
Parking *ample*

Bar food *12–2.30 & 7–10.30 (Sun till 9.45)*

Landlady *Kate Harrower*
Free house
🍺 *St Austell Hicks Special, Tinners Bitter, Duchy Bitter; Guinness; Stella Artois.* ⊖

From the large bay window of the bar there are magnificent views over St Austell and Mevagissey bays. Local photographs are highlighted on the walls of the main bar, where a good bar menu is available. Specials might be chicken Maryland, lasagne or sirloin steak, while the staples of home-made soup, sandwiches, salads and ploughman's make use of fresh local sea-food. Sandwiches served all day in summer. **Typical dishes** Chef's fish pie *£4.50* Prawns in garlic & herbs *£6.25*

Credit Access, Amex, Visa

PONTEFRACT   NEW ENTRY   *Parkside Inne*

Park Road WF8 4QD   B&B
Map 4 D3 *West Yorks*
Pontefract (0977) 709911
Parking *ample*

Landlord *Charles Birdsall*
Free house
🍺 *Whitbread Trophy Bitter, Castle Eden; Younger's Scotch; Murphy's Stout; Guinness; Stella Artois.*

Accommodation *19 bedrooms* **£C G1**
Check-in all day

If you enjoy attending race meetings, this is the place for you, as it is directly opposite the racecourse, near junction 32 of the M62. A spacious conservatory area has recently been added to the bar, lending character with its oak beams and old-fashioned bar counter. The bedrooms are neat, compact, modern and attractively decorated with matching fabrics. TVs, telephones, mini-bars and tea-makers are standard, as are excellent en suite bathrooms. Children welcome overnight.

Credit Access, Amex, Diners, Visa

POOLE   NEW ENTRY   Antelope Hotel

The Old High Street   B&B
BH15 1BP
Area Map 7 E5 *Dorset*
Poole (0202) 672029
Parking *limited*

Landlords *Loreno & Nanette Gallai*
Owner *Lansbury Hotels*
🍺 *Whitbread Best Bitter; Fremlins Bitter; Flowers Original; Guinness; Stella Artois; Heineken.* 🍷

Accommodation *21 bedrooms* **£A G1**
Check-in all day

An inn of historical and architectural inter-est just a stone's throw from the quay. The neo-Georgian brick facade includes an 18th-century 'wine and spirit vaults' shop fron-tage, while inside are original 15th-century timbers and fireplaces. Back bedrooms are the biggest and quietest, but front rooms have more period feel. All are very well equipped, with en suite bathrooms, TVs, direct-dial phones, hairdryers and trouser presses. Children welcome overnight. *No dogs.*

Credit Access, Amex, Diners, Visa

POOLE   *Inn in the Park*

Pinewood Road,   `B&B`
Branksome Park BH13 6JS
Area Map 7 E5 *Dorset*
Bournemouth (0202) 761318
Parking *limited*

Landlords *Alan & Paula Potter*
Free house
🍺 *Wadworth 6X, IPA; Ringwood Best
Bitter; Younger's Tartan Bitter; Guinness;
Stella Artois.*

Accommodation *6 bedrooms* **£C G2**
Check-in by arrangement

Near Branksome Dene Chine and the sea, a
substantial Victorian house which looks
more like a guest house from the outside.
Inside, however, is more pubby, with a fine
collection of postage stamps and cigarette
cards on the walls. Bright, well-kept bedrooms with simple furnishings and floral or
candlewick bedspreads are all provided
with TVs, tea-makers and easy chairs. Four
have private facilities. Accommodation
closed Christmas week. Children welcome
overnight. *No dogs.*

Credit Access, Visa

PORLOCK WEIR   *Anchor Hotel & Ship Inn*

Nr Minehead TA24 8PB   `B&B`
Map 9 C1 *Somerset*
Porlock (0643) 862636
Parking *ample*

Landlords *Pandy Sechiari & Donald
Wade*
Free house 🛏
🍺 *Usher Best Bitter, Triple Crown; Golden
Hill Exmoor Ale; Guinness; Foster's;
Holsten.*

Accommodation *26 bedrooms* **£B G2**
Check-in all day

The thatched 16th-century Ship Inn and
adjacent 19th-century Anchor Hotel command a lovely setting overlooking a small
harbour, with views across the Bristol
Channel to the Welsh coast. The Ship Inn
has a little residents' bar incorporating 600-
year-old beams taken from a shipwreck. All
the light, good-sized bedrooms offer TVs,
tea-makers and direct-dial telephones; 20
have private facilities and many enjoy sea
views. Ship Inn accommodation closed
Christmas to Easter.

Credit Access, Amex, Visa

PORT GAVERNE   *Port Gaverne Hotel*

Nr Port Isaac PL29 3SQ   `B&B`
Map 9 B2 *Cornwall*
Bodmin (0208) 880244
Parking *ample*

Pub closed *mid-Jan to end-Feb*

Landlords *Frederick & Marjorie Ross*
Free house 🛏
🍺 *St Austell Hicks Special; Whitbread Best
Bitter; Guinness; Stella Artois.*

Accommodation *19 bedrooms* **£A G1**
Check-in all day

Set in a sheltered cove is a charming 17th-
century inn which has been run for over 20
years by Freddie and Midge Ross. The best
of the cheerful en suite rooms have dormer
windows and sea views. Extras include
morning tea and complimentary newspaper brought to your room. A Club Bar
and balconied lounge are available for
residents' use and there are two cosy,
popular pub bars. Self-catering cottages are
also offered. Accommodation closed mid-
January to end-February.

POWERSTOCK   *Three Horseshoes Inn*

Bridport DT6 3TF   `FOOD`
Area Map 7 A5 *Dorset*   `B&B`
Powerstock (030 885) 328
Parking *ample*

Bar food *12–2 & 7–10 (Sat till 11),
Sun 12–3 & 7–9*
No bar food *Sun eve (winter)*

Landlord *Mr P.W. Ferguson*
Brewery *Palmer*
🍺 *Palmer BB, Traditional Best, Tally Ho;
Guinness; Eldridge Pope Faust
Pilsener.*

The thatch of the original pub (rebuilt in
1906) is today recalled in the thatched
canopy over the bar counter. Here blackboards in the pine-boarded bar list the
lengthy and imaginative choice of snacks
available, from spicy parsnip soup, sliced
salt beef with horseradish and bowls of
steaming mussels to baked lamb chops,
grilled sausages with onion compôte and
sirloin steak. Fish is something of a speciality, with up to a dozen varieties appearing
daily when the market allows (we noted
seafood pancakes with prawn sauce and

monkfish with onions, wine and cream), and there are also salads and vegetarian dishes such as nut roast and vegetable lasagne.

Typical dishes Ratatouille pancake £2.95 Dorset trifle £2.50

Accommodation *4 bedrooms* £C G2
Check-in by arrangement

Four simple, centrally heated bedrooms with traditional furniture, candlewick bedspreads and tea-makers provide homely overnight accommodation, and two have en suite bathrooms. Lovely views of the surrounding countryside are a bonus. Children welcome overnight.

Credit Access, Amex, Visa

RAMSBURY · Bell at Ramsbury

Market Square, Nr Marlborough SN7 2PE
Area Map 4 D4 *Wiltshire*
Marlborough (0672) 20230
Parking *ample*

`FOOD`

Bar food *12–2 (Sun till 1) & 7–9.30*
No bar food *Sat eve* ✆

Landlady *Mrs W. Marshall*
Free house
🍺 *Wadworth IPA, 6X; Younger's Tartan Bitter; Marston Pedigree; Guinness; Carlsberg Export.*

This unassuming whitewashed pub in the middle of Ramsbury offers a pleasant, convivial atmosphere in its neatly decorated bars. Pictures of the old village, once dominated by a huge oak tree, line the walls, and there is a smart little restaurant whose beams continue the character of the main bar. In addition, a rear garden provides an excellent alfresco eating and dining area. Food is taken seriously here, and the new chef's menu and daily specials provide abundant variety. Many dishes, including baked field mushrooms with garlic and parsley, hot stuffed tomatoes and salade niçoise, may be ordered as starters or main courses. Savoury pies are a great feature and come in several versions, from potato-topped fish to chicken and broccoli, cidery pork and Hungarian veal. The daily special we sampled was splendid chargrilled salmon with a creamy tomato and tarragon sauce.

Typical dishes Cheddar ploughman's £2.95 Baked field mushrooms (main course) £2.95 Steak & kidney pudding £3.65 Rich chocolate truffle cake £1.75

Credit Access, Amex, Diners, Visa

RATTERY · Church House Inn

South Brent TQ10 9LD
Map 9 B2 *Devon*
Buckfastleigh (0364) 42220
Parking *ample*

`FOOD`

Bar food *12–2 & 7–9.30 (Sun till 9)*

Landlords *Mr & Mrs B. Evans*

Free house
🍺 *Courage Directors, Best; John Smith's Bitter; Guinness; Kronenbourg 1664.* 🍷 ✆

Framed on a wall of this atmospheric inn is a list of parish priests of nearby St Mary's Church going back to 1199; parts of the inn are probably even older. Beams, brasses and ancient inglenooks create a very traditional setting for enjoying good bar food. Fresh soups, ploughman's, salad platters and fry-ups (one for vegetarians) are all popular choices, along with home-cooked specialities like steaks and fresh quiches.
Typical dishes Chicken Wensleydale £4.25 Vegetarian pancakes £3.95

Credit Access, Visa

RAVENSTONEDALE   **Black Swan**

Nr Kirkby Stephen
CA17 4NG   `FOOD` `B&B`
Area Map 2 A1 *Cumbria*
Newbiggin on Lune (058 73) 204
Parking *ample*

Bar food *12–2 & 6–9.15 (Sun from 7)*
Closed *all Jan*

Landlords *Gordon & Norma Stuart*
Free house
🍺 *Younger's Scotch; Hartley Bitter;*
Carlsberg Pilsner; Hofmeister; Holsten
Pils. 🍷 ⊖

Spectacular Lakeland scenery surrounds this peaceful old village inn, whose cosy lounge bar with its copper-topped tables, stone walls and rich red carpet is an attractive place in which to enjoy some simple, wholesome snacks. Good thick vegetable soup garnished with freshly made croûtons, flavoursome pâté and ploughman's with local cheeses, apple and fine bread make excellent light bites, while for something more substantial there is home-baked ham, Cumberland sausage with spiced apple sauce and grilled salmon. More elaborate meals are available in the restaurant.

Typical dishes Steak and kidney pie £2.95 Sticky toffee pudding 90p

Accommodation *13 bedrooms* **£C G2**
Check-in all day

Four new bedrooms have joined the nine existing rooms, which range from solidly traditional to pine-furnished and decorated in floral cottage style. Tea-makers, magazines and hairdryers are provided, and all but two rooms have their own compact modern bathroom. The comfortable upstairs residents' lounge has a TV and plenty of reading matter. Garden. Children welcome overnight.

Credit Access, Amex, Visa

READING   NEW ENTRY   **Railway Tavern**

31 Greyfriars RG1 1PA   `FOOD`
Map 10 C3 *Berkshire*
Reading (0734) 590376
Parking *difficult*

Bar food *12–2 & 6–9*
No bar food *Sat & Sun eves*

Landlords *Derek & Lynda Moir*
Brewery *Hall's*
🍺 *John Arkell BB; Wadworth 6X; Ind*
Coope Burton Ale; John Bull Bitter;
Guinness; Castlemaine XXXX.

The bulk of the menu at this railway-themed pub is a selection of platters, including Stilton, Cheddar, sardines, cockles, turkey and beef. Hot meals are on the schedule, too, and their spicy sausage toad-in-the-hole is a good, full-flavoured dish; you might alternatively go for an omelette, chilli or spaghetti bolognese. Nearly everything is home-made, including warming soups in the winter.

Typical dishes Steak & kidney pie £2.50 Sausage in French bread 90p

Credit Access, Visa

RINGMORE   **Journey's End Inn**

Nr Bigbury-on-Sea TQ7 4HL   `B&B`
Map 9 B3 *Devon*
Bigbury-on-Sea (0548) 810205
Parking *ample*

Landlords *D. Brinkhurst & N.A.A. Abdali*
Free house ⛄
🍺 *Butcombe Bitter; Golden Hill Exmoor*
Ale; Wadworth 6X; Guinness; Carlsberg;
Löwenbräu.

Accommodation *3 bedrooms* **£C G3**
Check-in by arrangement

An ale house since the reign of the first Elizabeth, the Journey's End actually traces back much further, to about 1300. The bars are full of old-world charm and good beer, and the owners have completely refurbished the bedrooms, making use of Victorian pine furniture. Rooms have TVs but no phones. Other improvements include new toilets, a conservatory and the resurfacing of the car park. *No children under 14 overnight. No dogs.*

Credit Access, Amex, Visa

RIPLEY   NEW ENTRY   *Seven Stars*

New Ark Street GU23 6DL   `FOOD`
Map 10 C3 *Surrey*
Guildford (0483) 225128
Parking *ample*

Bar food *12–2 & 7–9*
No bar food *Sun eve* ☙

Landlord *Rodney Dean*
Brewery *Friary Meux*
🍺 *Ind Coope Burton Ale; Friary Meux Best; Tetley Bitter; Gales HSB; Castlemaine XXXX; Löwenbräu.* ⊖

Just to the north of Ripley on the B367 is the Seven Stars, a pleasant pebble dash pub, which is run in friendly fashion by Rodney Dean. An open fire adds winter warmth to the bar, where speciality home-baked pizzas are supplemented by blackboard dishes such as moist pork and apple plait, chilli or creamy mushroom crumble. Salads, sandwiches and ploughman's provide lighter bites, while Sunday lunch brings a traditional roast. Garden.
Typical dishes Mexican hat dance pizza £2.80 Moussaka £3.30

---

*Changes in data sometimes occur
in establishments
after the Guide goes to press.*

*Prices should be taken as indications
rather than firm quotes.*

RIPON   *Unicorn Hotel*

Market Place HG4 1BP   `B&B`
Area Map 2 F3 *North Yorks*
Ripon (0765) 2202
Parking *ample*

Landlords *Mr & Mrs D.T. Small*
Free house ☙
🍺 *Taylor Landlord; John Smith's Yorkshire Bitter; Tetley Bitter; Younger's Scotch; Guinness; Carlsberg Hof.*

Accommodation *33 bedrooms* **£A G1**
Check-in all day

Ivy-clad and ancient, this former posting house on the market place of historic 9th-century Ripon has immediate appeal. Slightly disappointing within, there is a choice of two lively and popular bars (one, named after the young resident ghost Tom Crudd, is decorated with striking murals depicting scenes of local life), and a relaxing residents' lounge upstairs. Functional bedrooms, all with modest en suite bathrooms, offer TVs, tea-makers and direct-dial telephones. Refurbishment would be welcome.

Credit Access, Amex, Diners, Visa

RISPLITH   *Black-a-Moor Inn*

Sawley, Nr Ripon HG4 3EW   `B&B`
Area Map 2 E4 *North Yorks*
Sawley (076 586) 214
Parking *ample*

Landlords *Mr & Mrs D.B. Campbell*
Free house
🍺 *Younger's Scotch, No 3; Tetley Bitter; Beck's Bier; McEwan's Lager; Castlemaine XXXX.*

Accommodation *6 bedrooms* **£D G2**
Check-in by arrangement

Perched up on the moors to the west of Ripon, this homely pub beside the B6265 makes a useful overnight stop. Prettily decorated bedrooms, including three with en suite facilities and colour TVs in a separate chalet-style building, all have tea-makers, duvets and simple free-standing furniture. Downstairs, the single bar is divided between a comfortable lounge area and more informal public end. Terrace. *No children under nine overnight. No dogs.*

ROCHESTER — Redesdale Arms Hotel

Nr Otterburn NE19 1TA
Map 3 C1 *Northumberland*
Otterburn (0830) 20668
Parking *ample*

FOOD
B&B

Bar food *12–3 (Sun till 2) & 7–9 (Sat till 10)*

Landlords *Hilda & Johnny Wright*
Free house
🍺 *Drybrough Heavy, Scotch; Tetley Bitter; Carlsberg.*

Standing alongside the A68, some 12 miles from the Scottish border, this mellow, stone-built coaching inn is part of the Northumbrian National Park and makes a good base for visitors exploring the region. Tapestry-style banquettes, wheelback chairs and copper-topped tables help make the bar an inviting spot in which to enjoy home-made snacks like warming lentil soup, well filled 'stottie' sandwiches, ploughman's and lasagne. More substantial dishes like steaks, flavoursome casseroles, local game and baked gammon in red wine sauce are also available and puddings include old-fashioned jam roly-poly.

Typical dishes Steak and kidney pie £4.20 Pheasant in red wine sauce £4.75

Accommodation *12 bedrooms* **£D G2**
Check-in all day

Traditionally furnished bedrooms (three with four-posters) range from fairly simple with white-painted walls to larger, prettier rooms featuring attractive wallpapers. All offer cosy duvets, tea-makers and TVs, and four have en suite facilities; the rest share two public bathrooms. Children welcome overnight.

Credit Access, Diners, Visa

ROMALDKIRK — Rose & Crown Hotel

Teesdale DL12 9EB
Map 3 C2 *Co. Durham*
Teesdale (0833) 50213
Parking *ample*

B&B

Landlords *David & Jill Jackson*
Free house 🛏
🍺 *Theakston Best Bitter, Old Peculier; Matthew Brown Bitter; Slalom Lager, Slalom 'D'.* 🍷

Accommodation *13 bedrooms* **£B G1**
Check-in all day

Find this hospitable 18th-century coaching inn next to the ancient church overlooking the village green. Pleasant overnight accommodation is provided by traditionally furnished main-house bedrooms, which include a number of characterful beamed suites on the top floor, and five smart chalet-style rooms in the courtyard block. Private bathrooms, TVs and direct-dial telephones are standard throughout, and the courtyard honeymoon room boasts a four-poster. There is a choice of two bars.

Credit Access, Amex, Diners, Visa

ROSEDALE ABBEY — NEW ENTRY — Milburn Arms Hotel

Nr Pickering YO18 8RA
Area Map 3 C2 *North Yorks*
Lastingham (075 15) 312
Parking *ample*

FOOD
B&B

Bar food *12–2 & 7–9.30 (Fri & Sat till 10)* 🛏

Landlords *Stephen & Frances Colling*
Free house
🍺 *Theakston Best Bitter, Old Peculier; Tetley Bitter; Guinness; Carlsberg Export.* 🍷

Rosedale, in the North Yorkshire moors, is largely unspoilt, and the Milburn Arms, in the centre of pretty Rosedale Abbey, fits in well. Both bar food and the accommodation are commendable, the welcome from landlords Stephen and Frances Colling most friendly. Beyond a garden at the front for outdoor drinking, the bar is long and low with beams and an open fire. Rugby and cricket prints and banquette seating provide extra character. An attractive family/function room is next door. There is food both at lunchtime and evenings from soups (their onion is French-style, dark and full flavoured) and 'Non-sexist Ploughperson's Lunch' to more substantial dishes with home-made puddings and good coffee to finish.

Typical dishes Mariner's hotpot £4.75 Country cottage pie £4.75

Accommodation *14 bedrooms* **£A G1**
Check-in all day

Bedrooms are either in the main building (more traditional and with showers only) or the new extension (floral fabrics and pine furniture). Annexe bathrooms are neat and modern.

Credit Access, Visa

ROSEDALE ABBEY   *White Horse Farm Hotel*

Nr Pickering YO18 8SE   B&B
Area Map 3 C2 *North Yorks*
Lastingham (075 15) 239
Parking *ample*

Landlords *Mr & Mrs H.J. Proctor*
Free house
🍺 *Tetley Bitter, John Smith's Bitter, Magnet; Guinness; Foster's.* 🍷

Accommodation *15 bedrooms* **£C G1**
Check-in all day

Its origins as a farm are still evident in the horsey knick-knacks displayed in the bar, and its position is enviable – high above the village of Rosedale Abbey with spectacular moor views. There are plans to refurbish the presently stark residents' lounge, but the bedrooms have already been tastefully redecorated to a high standard. All have en suite bath or shower rooms, TVs, and radio-alarms, and some command magnificent views. The food is most disappointing, however. Children welcome overnight.

Credit Access, Amex, Diners, Visa

ROTHERWICK   *Coach & Horses*

The Street, Nr Hook   FOOD
RG27 9BG
Map 10 B3 *Hampshire*
Hook (025 672) 2542
Parking *ample*

Bar food *12–2 & 7–10 (Sun till 9.45)*

Landlady *Mrs Terry Williams*
Free house
🍺 *Hall & Woodhouse Badger Best; Eldridge Pope Royal Oak; Arkells Kingsdown Ale; Marston's Pedigree; Ringwood Old Thumper; Faust Pilsner.* ☕

Winter log fires, beamed ceilings and a motley collection of old wooden chairs characterise this agreeable pub dating back over 450 years in parts. Well-kept real ales complement the bar snacks, like pizzas and meaty burgers, ham sandwiches, breaded sole, steaks and stir-fried chicken. On Friday and Saturday evenings (and exclusively for Sunday lunch) a carvery joins the menu; puddings available in the evenings only. Patio.
Typical dishes Rump steak £6.25 Hamburger £1.95

ROWHOOK   *Chequers Inn*

Nr Horsham RH12 3PY   FOOD
Area Map 6 C2 *West Sussex*
Horsham (0403) 790480
Parking *ample*

Bar food *12–2 & 7–10 (Sun till 9.30)* 🥂

Landlords *Mr G.M. & Mrs M.F. Culver*
Brewery *Whitbread*
🍺 *Flowers Original; Whitbread Strong Country Bitter; Fremlins Bitter; Guinness; Stella Artois; Heineken.*

The Flagstone Bar, with its uneven flagged floor, wood-burning stove and yellowed paintwork, is the most atmospheric of several in this agreeable 15th-century pub. At lunchtime, sandwiches, ploughman's and pâté provide quick snacks, with chicken and onion tagliatelle or ham and chips for something more substantial. Evening fare includes steaks and roast duck. This is a real regular's pub, with everyone seeming to know everyone else.
Typical dishes Mushrooms & bacon au gratin £2.95 Chinese spare ribs £3.50

RUCKHALL   *Ancient Camp Inn*

Nr Eaton Bishop HR2 9QX
Map 6 E3 *Hereford & Worcs*
Golden Valley (0981)
250449
Parking *ample*

Bar food *12–2 & 7–9.30*
No bar food *Sun eves & all Mon*

Landlords *Mr & Mrs D.W.T. Hague*
Free house
🍺 *Flowers Original; Wood Parish Bitter; John Smith's Yorkshire Bitter; Guinness; Heineken; Stella Artois.* ℮

Accommodation *4 bedrooms* **£C G1**
Check-in all day

Spectacular views can be enjoyed from the pretty front terrace here, at a delightful country inn perched atop a wooded escarpment, the site of an important iron age fort. Hand-made wooden furniture, flagstoned floors and open fires characterise the charmingly rustic public bar, while the tastefully appointed lounge bar is softly carpeted and features stripped pine and inviting sofas. Imaginative, carefully prepared snacks range from lettuce, dill and celery soup, garlic mushrooms and ploughman's with speciality English cheeses to first-class locally-made pasta (try the richly sauced cannelloni filled with ricotta and spinach), turkey paprika and sustaining oxtail casserole. Good sweets include iced coffee soufflé and lemon syllabub.

Typical dishes Greek shepherd's pie £3.95 Hazelnut torte £1.95

The four comfortable, spotlessly kept bedrooms are bright and cottagy, with duvets, modern white furniture, clock-radios and tea-makers. The mini-suite has its own bathroom, while the rest offer carpeted en suite shower rooms. Garden. *No children under eight overnight.*

Credit Access, Visa

RUNNING WATERS   *Three Horse Shoes*

Sherburn House, Nr Durham DH1 2SR
Map 4 D2 *Co. Durham*
091-372 0286
Parking *ample*

Landlords *Derek & Lesley Crehan*
Free house
🍺 *Vaux Samson; Lorimer Best Scotch; Wards Sheffield Best Bitter; Guinness; Stella Artois.*

Accommodation *6 bedrooms* **£C G1/2**
Check-in all day

Standing alongside the A181 a few miles south-east of Durham, this friendly pub is kept in spick and span order throughout. The two popular bars are comfortably rustic and there is a traditional lounge for residents' use upstairs. Prettily decorated bedrooms with simple modern furnishings all have duvets, tea-makers and radio-alarms. Original rooms offer shower cubicles only and share a smart carpeted bathroom, while three newer rooms have their own up-to-date facilities. Garden.

Credit Access, Amex, Diners, Visa

RUSTHALL   *Red Lion*

Nr Tunbridge Wells
TN4 8TW
Area Map 6 F2 *Kent*
Tunbridge Wells (0892) 20086
Parking *ample*

Bar food *12.30–2 & 7–10.30* ✲
No bar food *Sun*

Landlords *Barry & Eileen Cooter*
Brewery *Flowers*
🍺 *Whitbread Best Bitter, Dark Mild; Fremlins Bitter; Flowers Best Bitter; Stella Artois; Whitbread White Label.* 🍷 ℮

Eileen Cooter offers a good variety of appetising snacks at this friendly village pub with a characterful beamed public bar and rather plusher, carpeted second bar. Stick with traditional favourites such as soup, salads, sausages and sandwiches, or go for something more unusual like savoury meatballs in a vegetable-packed curry sauce. Less choice in the evening. Garden with play area. Children's menu.
Typical dishes Goujons of plaice and chips £2.50 Grilled gammon steak £2.75

SAFFRON WALDEN   *Eight Bells*

Bridge Street CB10 1BU
Map 10 D1 *Essex*
Saffron Walden (0799)
22790
Parking *ample*

Bar food *12–2.30 & 6.30–9.30 (Sat till 10, Sun from 7)* ☞

Landlords *Mr & Mrs R. Moore*
Brewery *Benskins*
🍺 *Benskins Best Bitter; Adnams Bitter; Ind Coope Burton Ale; Guinness; Castlemaine XXXX; Löwenbräu.* 🍷 ⊖

Accommodation *2 bedrooms* **£D G2**
Check-in all day

There is a solidly traditional look here, created by dark wood chairs, benches and plain tables with cream walls mellowed by age, exposed beams and natural brick. Two bars are divided effectively only by ancient upright wall timbers. An excellent wine list complements the imaginative bar menu, and an excellent range of cheeses for ploughman's is displayed at the bar, together with pickles, salads, bread, pâtés, quiches and pies. Dishes of the day might be calf's liver with bacon, hunter's pie (chicken, rabbit and pork), steaks, fresh fish or mushrooms thermidor with garlic bread. Children's menu. Garden and play area.

Typical dishes Saffron gilded chicken £5.45 Prawns thermidor £5.45

One bedroom is very spacious, half-timbered with white walls, two armchairs, a table and chairs and a washbasin; the other is slightly smaller but also well furnished in an old-fashioned style. Both have TVs and tea-makers, and they share a pleasant, carpeted bathroom. *No dogs.*

Credit Access, Amex, Diners, Visa

SAFFRON WALDEN   *Saffron Hotel*

High Street CB10 1AY
Map 10 D1 *Essex*
Saffron Walden (0799)
22676
Parking *limited*

Bar food *12–2 & 7–9.30*
No bar food *Sun*

Landlords *Craddock family*
Free house
🍺 *Greene King IPA; John Smith's Yorkshire Bitter; Younger's Tartan Bitter; Guinness; Carlsberg; Kronenbourg 1664; Taunton Dry Blackthorn Cider.* 🍷 ⊖

Accommodation *21 bedrooms* **£B G1/2**
Check-in all day

Ronald Craddock offers a good choice of honest, home-cooked dishes at his friendly town-centre pub. The spruced-up bar makes a comfortable setting for appetising daily-changing offerings such as cream of vegetable soup followed by trout with almonds, chicken escalope in cream and paprika, spaghetti bolognese or liver and bacon with new potatoes and peas. Portions are generous, so those with a smaller appetite might plump for the moist, deliciously flavoured ham and cheese quiche served with a crisp, fresh salad. Homely sweets like bread and butter pudding to finish.

Typical dishes Moules marinière £3.85 Steak, kidney and Guinness pie £4.50

A dozen of the rooms have been attractively modernised and boast splendid en suite bathrooms with marble-effect walls and gold-plated fittings; others have shower rooms only, and there are two immaculate carpeted public bathrooms for the remainder. TVs, tea-makers and direct-dial telephones are standard throughout and all have neat built-in furniture. Children welcome overnight.

Credit Access, Visa

ST AUSTELL   NEW ENTRY   *White Hart*

Church Street PL25 4AT   `B&B`
Map 9 B2 *Cornwall*
St Austell (0726) 72100
Parking *difficult*

Landlord *Mr D.E. Walker*
Brewery *St Austell*
🍺 *St Austell Tinners Ale, Duchy, Bosuns Bitter; Guinness; Carlsberg Hof.*

Accommodation *18 bedrooms* **£C G2**
Check-in all day

A convenient place to stay in the centre of St Austell, the White Hart offers attractive, comfortable accommodation. There is no separate residents' lounge as such; the public areas include a saloon bar with bright red velour banquettes and a polished wood bar counter. The bedrooms all have smart darkwood furniture, pink and plum decor, brass light fittings, telephones, hairdryers, beverage facilities and modern carpeted bathrooms. Accommodation closed 24–26 December.

Credit Access, Amex, Diners, Visa

ST MARGARET'S AT CLIFFE   *Cliffe Tavern*

High Street, Nr Dover   `B&B`
CT15 6AT
Area Map 5 F3 *Kent*
Dover (0304) 852749
Parking *ample*

Landlord *Christopher Waring Westby*
Free house ⌘
🍺 *Shepherd Neame Master Brew Bitter; Fremlins Bitter; Flowers Original; Guinness; Carlsberg Hof.*

Accommodation *12 bedrooms* **£C G2**
Check-in all day

Two rooms in the pub itself and ten in two separate cottages provide useful accommodation for travellers booked onto early-morning ferries, especially from Dover. The cottages and pub are weatherboarded and white-painted, and there are two bars and a walled beer garden at the back. The rooms are veering on the shabby in decor, but are reasonably well maintained. All en suite, bathrooms are clean and functional. A nice feature of each room is the solid green-leather-topped desk.

Credit Access, Amex, Diners, Visa

ST MAWES   *Rising Sun Inn*

The Square TR2 5DJ   `B&B`
Map 9 A3 *Cornwall*
St Mawes (0326) 270233
Parking *limited*

Landlords *John Milan & Frank Atherley*
Brewery *St Austell* ⌘
🍺 *St Austell BB, Hicks Special, Duchy; Guinness; Carlsberg Hof.* 🍷

Accommodation *12 bedrooms* **£A G1**
Check-in all day

Harbour views from the airy, comfortable residents' lounge and convivial main bar adjoining a flower-bordered terrace add to the attractions of this popular inn at the heart of village life. Overnight guests can relax in compact, stylishly furnished bedrooms decorated in pretty soft colours and provided with TVs, direct-dial telephones and tea-makers. Nine have excellent private facilities, others share a public bathroom. *No children under ten overnight.*

Credit Access, Amex, Visa

ST NEOTS   *Chequers Inn*

St Mary's Street,   `FOOD`
Eynesbury PE19 2TA
Map 10 C1 *Cambridgeshire*
Huntingdon (0480) 72116
Parking *ample*

Bar food *12–2 & 7–10 (Sun till 9)*

Landlords *David James & Ann Elizabeth Taylor*
Free house
🍺 *Paine XXX; Webster Yorkshire Bitter; Tolly Cobbold Original; Guinness; Carlsberg; Foster's. No real ale.*

A lovely old English country pub, where choosing whether to sit in the main bar with its roaring winter fires and highly polished dark furniture or to sink into the deep luxury of sofa and chairs in the small room leading to the restaurant is as difficult as selecting from the blackboard bar menu. Devilled whitebait, taramasalata, lasagne, chicken liver stroganoff, trout and lemon sauce . . . the list goes on.
Typical dishes Pasta & prawn mornay £3.60 Steak & mushroom pie £4.10

Credit Access, Amex, Diners, Visa

ST NEOTS   *Rocket*

Crosshall Road, Eaton Ford   `B&B`
PE19 4AG
Map 10 C1 *Cambridgeshire*
Huntingdon (0480) 72773
Parking *ample*

Landlady *Mrs V. Stephenson*
Free house
🍺 *Adnams Bitter; Greene King IPA; Benskins Best Bitter; John Arkell BB; Harp; Kronenbourg 1664.*

Accommodation *9 bedrooms* **£B G2**
Check-in all day

Despite its position at the junction of the A1 and A45, the Rocket's bedrooms are undisturbed by traffic and you can expect a comfortable overnight stay. The rooms, in the motel extension, are large and warm, with fitted units, colour TVs, tea/coffee-makers, direct-dial phones and well-fitted carpeted bathrooms with showers and baths. In the main building (once a farm-house) there is an oak-panelled bar featuring a collection of coronation mugs. Garden. Children welcome overnight.

Credit Access, Diners, Visa

SALISBURY   NEW ENTRY   *Coach & Horses*

39 Winchester Street   `FOOD`
SP1 1HG
Area Map 7 F2 *Wiltshire*
Salisbury (0722) 336254
Parking *difficult*

Bar food *10 am–10 pm (Sunday from 11)*

Landlords *Martin & Angie Cooper & Jeremy Bowers*
Brewery *Ushers* 🍺
🍺 *Ushers Best Bitter, Triple Crown; Ruddles County; Webster Bitter; Carlsberg; Holsten Export.* ❷

Many changes have taken place in its 500-year history, but the black-and-white timbered facade remains. There are several rooms and a pleasant garden in which to enjoy home-cooked fare running from tarragon-flavoured chicken broth and stuffed mushrooms to grills, burgers and some dishes from the European repertoire. Sweets include scrumpy, a moreish apple and cider cake. Garden and play area.
Typical dishes Skillet of prawns £1.95 Beef, Guinness and mushroom bake £2.75

Credit Access, Amex, Diners, Visa

SALISBURY   *Haunch of Venison*

1 Minster Street SP1 1TB   `A`
Area Map 7 F2 *Wiltshire*
Salisbury (0722) 22024
Parking *difficult*

Landlords *Antony & Victoria Leroy*
Brewery *Courage*
🍺 *Courage Directors, Best Bitter; John Smith's Bitter; Guinness; Kronenbourg 1664; Foster's.*

A pub of great antiquity and unspoilt character, very popular with tourists, who crowd into the tiny bar and the chop house above. Central feature of the bar is a mounted set of brass spirit taps, no longer functioning but still a talking point. Carved oak benches jut out of blackened stone walls alongside tables that look like upturned beer barrels. At the upper level ducking at the doorway is recommended, or heads could meet oak beams.

Credit Access, Amex, Diners, Visa

SALISBURY   *King's Arms*

9 St John Street SP1 2SB   `B&B`
Area Map 7 F2 *Wiltshire*
Salisbury (0722) 27629
Parking *ample*

Landlord *Mr R. N. Craven*
Owner *Chef & Brewer*
🍺 *Usher Best Bitter; Ruddles County; Holsten; Guinness; Carlsberg.*

Accommodation *15 bedrooms* **£B G1**
Check-in all day

You could have taken a room here when the place was 90 years old and still watched them start to build the cathedral. That makes the wattle-and-daub facade added in the early 1600s relatively modern. Beamed, panelled and sloping-floored, one is grateful for a bar to hold on to and an open fire to warm by. Varying-sized bedrooms, all en suite, share a high standard of comfort. Courtyard. Children welcome overnight. *No dogs.*

Credit Access, Amex, Diners, Visa

SAUNDERTON   Rose & Crown Inn

Wycombe Road, Nr Princes B&B
Risborough HP17 9NP
Map 10 C2 *Buckinghamshire*
Princes Risborough (084 44) 5299
Parking *ample*

Landlords *R.M. & J.G. Watson*
Free house
🍺 *Morland Bitter; Wethered Bitter;*
Morrell Varsity; Guinness; Stella Artois;
Heineken.

Accommodation *16 bedrooms* £B G1
Check-in all day

A grand square pianoforte dating back to
1840 is an unusual feature of the spacious,
oak-furnished bar at this large pub on the
A4010. Brightly decorated bedrooms
(including one reached by an outside staircase) with built-in units and two easy chairs
apiece all have compact en suite bathrooms,
as well as TVs, tea-makers and radio-
alarms. Garden. Accommodation closed
one week at Christmas. *No children under
eight overnight. No dogs.*

Credit Access, Amex, Diners, Visa

SCALES   NEW ENTRY   White Horse Inn

Threlkeld, Nr Keswick FOOD
CA12 4SY
Area Map 1 D1 *Cumbria*
Threlkeld (059 683) 241
Parking *limited*

Bar food *12–1.45 & 7.30–8.30*
(also 3–5 summer for teas)
No bar food *Mon–Thurs eves Nov to
Easter*

Landlords *Larry & Judy Slattery*
Free house
🍺 *Jennings Best Bitter; Guinness; Hansa.* ⊖

A friendly old whitewashed pub set amidst
stunning scenery, and a favourite of fell
walkers, which offers excellent eating in its
spotless bar. Lunchtime brings potted
shrimps, cheese and ham platters and
cottage pie, while candlelit evening meals
(booking essential) might begin with flavoursome vegetable soup, move on to
chicken breast in a mild curry sauce or
poached Borrowdale trout, and end with
mature local farmhouse cheese.
Typical dishes Broccoli and cheese flan
£2.95 Pork fillet with sherry sauce £6.95

SCOLE   Crossways Inn

Ipswich Road, Nr Diss FOOD
IP21 4DP   B&B
Map 8 F1 *Norfolk*
Diss (0379) 740638
Parking *ample*

Bar food *12–2.15 & 6–10, Sun 12–2
& 7–10*

Landlord *Peter Black*
Free house ☂
🍺 *Adnams Bitter; Guinness; Heineken;*
Stella Artois. 🍷

This 16th-century Norfolk pub is the scene
for some unusual cooking. Douglas Hamil-
ton-Dick is a widely travelled chef whose
extensive repertoire takes in dishes from
Singapore, Portugal and Greece. In the bar-
bistro or the restaurant proper, you can
enjoy such diverse creations as Kleftiko
(braised lamb) with Greek salad, cata-
planta (a Portuguese fish stew) and Mahmee
(a Singapore dish of noodles, chicken, fish
and pork). For more conventional appetites
there are steak and oyster pie, 100% pure
beef hamburgers and Dover sole. Finish
with sweet cherry pancakes. Excellent
wines chosen by Peter Black, who worked
in the wine trade before he became a
publican.

Typical dishes Kleftiko with Greek salad
£5.95 Steak & oyster pie £3.95

Accommodation *5 bedrooms* £C G2
Check-in all day

The standard of housekeeping in the bedrooms is high. They are smartly decorated
and have attractive modern furniture with a
potted plant in each room, a colour TV and
direct-dial telephone. They are all double-
glazed. Good breakfast. Peaceful garden.
No dogs.

Credit Access, Diners, Visa

SCOLE
Scole Inn

Nr Diss IP21 4DR   **B&B**
Map 8 F1 *Norfolk*
Diss (0379) 740481
Parking *ample*

Landlord *Keith Dunmur*
Free house
🍺 *Adnams Bitter, Broadside; Greene King Abbot Ale; Guinness; Carling Black Label; Tennent's Extra.* 🍷

Accommodation *24 bedrooms* **£A G2**
Check-in all day

A fine 17th-century listed building on the A140, which was built in 1655 by a wealthy wool merchant and later became a coaching inn. The bar area retains considerable period appeal with its handsome open fireplace, while splendidly proportioned bedrooms boast fine oil portraits and solid oak furnishings (including a four-poster and half-tester). Annexe rooms are smaller but quieter, and all offer adequate private bathrooms plus hairdryers and trouser presses. Children welcome overnight.

Credit Access, Amex, Diners, Visa

SEAHOUSES
Olde Ship Hotel

NE68 7RD   **B&B**
Map 2 D5 *Northumberland*
Seahouses (0665) 720200
Parking *ample*

Landlords *Alan & Jean Glen*
Free house 🍴
🍺 *McEwan's Scotch Bitter, 70/-, 80/-; Newcastle Exhibition, Bitter; Guinness; Beck's Bier.* 🍷

Accommodation *12 bedrooms* **£B G2**
Check-in all day

Built as a farmhouse in 1745, the Olde Ship is a truly delightful inn just above a tiny, picturesque fishing harbour. The landlords have filled it with character, and the nautical connection is evident in the splendid saloon bar – full of naval curios – and the leafy lounge gallery with its model ships. Bedrooms are warm, cosy and ship-shape, with simple, homely decor, TVs, books and tea-makers. Private facilities are mostly shower rooms. Garden. Accommodation closed November to March. *No dogs.*

SEAVIEW
Seaview Hotel

High Street PO34 5EX   **FOOD**
Map 7 C4 *Isle of Wight*   **B&B**
Isle of Wight (0983) 612711
Parking *ample*

Bar food *12–2 & 7–9.15*

Landlords *Nicholas & Nicola Hayward*
Free house
🍺 *Burt VPA; Whitbread Best Bitter; Guinness; Stella Artois; Heineken.* 🍷 ☺

In a pretty village setting, the Seaview overlooks the Solent from its nautically-themed front and some bedrooms. Very much the centre of village life, it also has a bar at the rear, and residents have a choice of ground-level and first-floor lounges (the latter non-smoking). The bar menu holds very few surprises, but cooking is competent and portions more than generous. Sandwiches, pizza and chicken wings with a garlicky peanut butter dip provide tasty quick snacks, while the seriously hungry could start with soup, pass on to grilled lamb chops and round things off with cheese and biscuits.

Typical dishes Hot crab ramekin £2.60 Vegetarian pasta £3.50

Accommodation *16 bedrooms* **£A G1**
Check-in all day

Though the bedrooms are small they match most on the island in terms of decor and general comfort. Antiques, en suite bathrooms and TVs they have; telephones they do not. The two newest bedrooms are at ground level, with patio access and room enough for a small family. Good housekeeping throughout. Children welcome overnight.

Credit Access, Amex, Visa

SEDGEFIELD   *Dun Cow Inn*

43 Front Street TS21 3AT   `B&B`
Map 4 D2 *Co. Durham*
Sedgefield (0740) 20894
Parking *ample*

Landlord *Geoff Rayner*
Free house
🍺 *McEwan's 80/-; Younger's No 3;*
Newcastle Bitter, Exhibition; Carlsberg
Hof. 🍷

Accommodation *6 bedrooms* **£C G2**
Check-in all day

An appealing old town-centre inn where standards of accommodation have been high under the care of Mr Rayner; we hope that his successor will show similar dedication. Six immaculate bedrooms in mock-rustic style with smart darkwood furniture and tapestry-weave fabrics all offer TVs, telephones, tea-makers and fresh fruit. They share three splendid bath/shower rooms, generously equipped and spotlessly kept. Downstairs, the spacious bar has comfortable red banquettes.

Credit Access, Amex, Diners, Visa

SEMLEY   *Benett Arms*

Nr Shaftesbury SP7 9AS   `FOOD`
Area Map 7 D3 *Wiltshire*   `B&B`
East Knoyle (074 783) 221
Parking *ample*

Bar food *12–2 & 7–10* 🍴

Landlord *Joseph Duthie*
Brewery *Gibbs Mew*
🍺 *Gibbs Mew Salisbury Best, Gibbs*
Premium Bitter; Guinness; Graf Arco;
Kronenbourg 1664. 🍷 ⊖

An agreeable, old-fashioned pub set in rolling countryside, with a genial landlord and a warm, welcoming atmosphere in the rustic bars. Down-to-earth bar snacks cover a good range and cater for varying appetites. Sandwiches, ploughman's platters and prawns with garlic mayonnaise are popular for lighter meals, while the seriously hungry could attack a plateful of gammon, pineapple, chips and peas or chilli con carne served on a bed of rice, and then call for sherry trifle, lemon meringue pie or banana split. On Sunday a traditional roast lunch is available. Children's room and outdoor play area.

Typical dishes Home-made venison pie with potatoes and fresh vegetables £3.80 Chocolate mousse with rum £1.50

Accommodation *5 bedrooms* **£C G2**
Check-in all day

Bedrooms, all kept in good order, are traditionally furnished in the main building, much more modern in the annexe. TVs, direct-dial phones and tea-making facilities are standard, and all rooms have en suite bath or shower rooms.

Credit Access, Amex, Diners, Visa

SENNEN COVE   *Old Success Inn*

Land's End TR19 7DG   `B&B`
Map 9 A3 *Cornwall*
Sennen (0736) 871232
Parking *ample*

Landlord *Mr F. Carroll*
Free house
🍺 *Bass; Worthington Bitter; Stones Bitter;*
Guinness; Carling Black Label; Tennent's
Extra.

Accommodation *11 bedrooms* **£B G2**
Check-in all day

Would-be surfers can study the Atlantic rollers coming in, as they drink or stay at the 17th-century fisherman's inn right on the sea front. Many of the comfortable bedrooms enjoy fine views and all have modern en suite bathrooms as well as solid pine furnishings (including one four-poster), attractive fabrics, hairdryers and tea-makers. The spacious residents' lounge is stylishly furnished and commands superb sea views. Children welcome overnight. *No dogs.*

Credit Visa

SHALDON   NEW ENTRY   *Ness House Hotel*

Marine Drive TQ14 0HP   `B&B`
Map 9 C2 *Devon*
Shaldon (0626) 873480
Parking *ample*

Landlord *Hylton Oliver*
Owner *Character Inns*
🍺 *Bass; Flowers Original; Eldridge Pope Royal Oak; Guinness; Heineken; Newquay Steam Pils.*

Accommodation *7 bedrooms* **£A G1**
Check-in all day

Built in 1810 and overlooking the Teign estuary and the town of Shaldon the inn here has retained its Regency exterior. A new block of bedrooms to the side pleasingly follows the classical lines. Inside there is a spacious open-plan bar and, at the back, a small simple lounge. New extension bedrooms are superior to those in the main house, having refrigerators, settees and access to a small terrace. The older rooms have laminated units and compact bathrooms. *No dogs.*

Credit Access, Amex, Diners, Visa

SHALFLEET   *New Inn*

Yarmouth Road PO30 4NS   `FOOD`
Map 7 B4 *Isle of Wight*
Isle of Wight (0983) 78314
Parking *ample*

Bar food *12–2 & 7–10 (12–2.30 & 7–10.30 Easter–Oct.)*

Landlord *Chris Vanson*
Brewery *Whitbread*
🍺 *Whitbread Pompey Royal; Flowers Original; Fremlins Bitter; Murphy Stout; Heineken; Stella Artois.*

Lovers of fresh seafood flock to this characterful pub with a cosy little bar and a separate room where fish enthusiasts can eat together. The shellfish platter is a real feast, while other choices from the blackboard might include prawn-stuffed rainbow trout, shark steak, lobster or Dover sole. Meat eaters can choose steak and lasagne, and there are sweets like apricot crumble for afters. Traditional Sunday lunches in winter. Garden.
Typical dishes Crab pie £4.95 Poached salmon £4.50

SHAMLEY GREEN   *Red Lion*

Nr Guildford GU5 0UB   `FOOD`
Area Map 6 B1 *Surrey*   `B&B`
Guildford (0483) 892202
Parking *ample*

Bar food *10.30–2.30 (Sun from 12) & 7–10.30*

Landlord *Ben Heath*
Brewery *Friary Meux*
🍺 *Friary Meux Best; Ind Coope Bitter, Burton Ale; Guinness; Löwenbräu.*

Accommodation *4 bedrooms* **£D G2**
Check-in all day

A few dolls and teddy bears can be found scattered about the cosy Doll's House carvery (not in operation Sunday and Monday evenings) at this appealing old pub on the village green. Ask them to move up while you tuck into, say, tasty topside of beef with good Yorkshire pudding, or choose something from the blackboard menu – perhaps creamy leek and Stilton soup, garlicky stuffed mussels or an excellent mixed meat platter. There are sandwiches too, and a selection of sweets such as chocolate roulade, bramble pudding and tarte au citron. Traditional Sunday lunch available.

Typical dishes Grilled stuffed mushrooms £2.95 Ham, egg and chips £3.65

Upstairs, the four freshly decorated bedrooms blend chintzy fabrics with antique furnishings and all have the ubiquitous dolls and teddies to keep you company. TVs are provided and the large, carpeted shared bathroom, with its old-fashioned tub and comfortable sofa, is indeed a splendid affair. The garden has a children's play area. Children welcome overnight.

Credit Access, Amex, Diners, Visa

SHAVE CROSS — Shave Cross Inn

**Marshwood Vale, Nr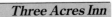
Bridport** DT6 6HW
Map 9 C2 *Dorset*
Broadwindsor (0308) 68358
Parking *ample*

Closed *Mon (except Bank Hols)*

Landlords *Bill & Ruth Slade*
Free house
🍺 *Hall & Woodhouse Badger Best; Bass; Eldridge Pope Royal Oak; Guinness; Carlsberg Export; Labatt's.* 🍷

Moss-covered thatch tops the charm on 13th-century stone walls here. The sun-trap garden has a goldfish pond and a thatch-covered wishing well. Inside corn dollies vie with horse brasses around the impressive inglenook fireplace. The two small flag-stoned rooms flank a single bar. Popular in summer with caravanners from an adjacent site, it is crowded on a wet day. Weathered garden tables and benches accommodate all, however, when the sun is out.

SHELLEY — Three Acres Inn

**Roydhouse, Nr
Huddersfield** HD8 8LR   **FOOD**
Map 4 D3 *West Yorkshire*   **B&B**
Huddersfield (0484) 602606
Parking *ample*

Bar food *12–2*
No bar food *eves*
Closed *Sat lunch*

Landlords *Derrick & Neil Truelove & Brian Orme*
Free house
🍺 *Tetley Bitter, Mild; Younger's Scotch; Guinness; Beck's Bier; Castlemaine XXXX.* ⊖

Accommodation *19 bedrooms* **£C G1**
Check-in all day

Look out for the nearby Cemley TV mast to guide you to this excellent stone-built pub set high up in the Pennines above Hudders-field. First-class lunchtime snacks can be sampled in the traditional beamed bar with its copper-hooded open fire and grand piano. The list encompasses soup (ideal potato and watercress), cold or warm salads, including chicken livers and smoked bacon in a creamy nutmeg dress-ing, decidedly upmarket sandwiches (try smoked salmon with a dill and coriander dressing), and a few hot dishes like sau-sages and mash with onion gravy. The restaurant serves more elaborate meals from 12 to 1.45 and 7 to 9.30.

Typical dishes Steak and onion sandwich £3.25 Grilled gammon and egg £5.25 Salad St Remo £3.95 Salad Veronique £3.95

Immaculate bedrooms (including ten new rooms in adjacent cottages) with pretty matching fabrics and free-standing pine furniture all have TVs, telephones, radio-alarms, trouser presses and tea-makers. Neat en suite bath/shower rooms through-out. Children welcome overnight. *No dogs.*

Credit Access, Amex, Diners, Visa

SHEPPERTON — Anchor Hotel

Church Square TW17 9JZ   **B&B**
Map 10 C3 *Middlesex*
Walton-on-Thames (0932) 221618
Parking *ample*

Landlord *John Goddard*
Free house
🍺 *Flowers Original; Eldridge Pope Dorset Original IPA, Royal Oak; Faust Export; Labatt's.*

Accommodation *29 bedrooms* **£A G1**
Check-in all day

Sympathetically restored after fire damage, the Anchor is a sturdy old inn overlooking a tiny square. It has occupied its Thames-side position for over 400 years. There is no residents' lounge, but the friendly bar with its authentic-looking linenfold panelling has ample charm and character. Attractive bedrooms on the first floor are double-glazed and cosy and all offer TVs, tele-phones and tea-makers, as well as compact shower rooms (one also has a bath). Child-ren welcome overnight.

Credit Access, Amex, Diners, Visa

SHEPPERTON   *King's Head*

Church Square TW17 9JY   `A`
Map 10 C3 *Middlesex*
Walton-on-Thames (0932) 221910
Parking *ample*

Landlord *Mr D. K. Longhurst*
Brewery *Courage*
🍺 *Courage Directors, Best Bitter;*
Guinness; Kronenbourg 1664; Foster's.

Reputed to have accommodated Nell Gwynne, the popular 300-year-old King's Head stands in a pleasant little square close to the Thames. Inside, much period charm and character is retained in the often crowded, low-ceilinged bars with their exposed beams, flagstoned floors and fine inglenook fireplace. A number of tiny, quieter rooms lead off from the main bar, while in summer there is a garden gazebo for sheltered drinking.

SHEPPERTON   *Warren Lodge*

Church Square TW17 9JZ   `B&B`
Map 10 C3 *Middlesex*
Walton-on-Thames (0932) 242972
Parking *limited*

Landlord *Douglas Gordon*
Free house
🍺 *Whitbread Tankard; Heineken.*
No real ale

Accommodation *49 bedrooms* £A G1
Check-in all day

A shady garden reaching down to the Thames is a popular spot for summer drinks at this 18th-century house in a picturesque little square. Comfortable seating is provided in both the cosy reception area and characterful bar (used primarily by residents). Six of the homely bedrooms are in the main house, the remainder divided between two extensions. TVs, tea-makers and hairdryers are standard, and most rooms offer private facilities. Children welcome overnight. *No dogs*.

Credit Access, Amex, Diners, Visa

SHEPTON MALLET   *Kings Arms*

Leg Square BA4 5LN   `B&B`
Area Map 7 B1 *Somerset*
Shepton Mallet (0749) 3781
Parking *ample*

Landlords *Drew & Jean Foley*
Brewery *Hall's*
🍺 *Hall's Harvest Bitter; Wadworth 6X;*
Ind Coope Burton Ale; Löwenbräu;
Castlemaine XXXX.

Accommodation *3 bedrooms* £D G3
Check-in all day

Check directions when booking at this 1660-built stone pub, as it is set in a quiet corner of town. Locally known as the 'Dusthole' from the days when it was a haunt of quarry workers, it contains low-beamed bars with open stone walls and some photographs of the area past and present. Free-standing furniture and duvets, washbasins and tea-makers are to be found in all three bedrooms, which share a bathroom and lounge.

SHIPLAKE   *Baskerville Arms*

Station Road, Nr Henley   `B&B`
RG9 3NY
Map 10 C3 *Oxfordshire*
Wargrave (073 522) 3332
Parking *ample*

Landlords *Derek & Janice Tomlin*
Brewery *Whitbread* ☎
🍺 *Wethered SPA, Bitter; Flowers Original;*
Murphys Stout; Stella Artois.

Accommodation *4 bedrooms* £D G3
Check-in by arrangement

A fine weeping willow dominates the patio garden of this red-brick pub near the Thames, making it a pleasant spot on sunny days for enjoying a traditional pint. Inside, the single bar is large and simply furnished, and a family room is available. For overnight guests, the four neat bedrooms have old-fashioned furnishings, armchairs and candlewick bedspreads; they share a carpeted bathroom with a separate shower unit.

SHIPSTON-ON-STOUR   **White Bear**

High Street CV36 4AJ   `B&B`
Map 10 B1 *Warwickshire*
Shipston-on-Stour (0608) 61558
Parking *ample*

Landlords *Suzanne & Hugh Roberts*
Brewery *Mitchells & Butlers* ☞
🍺 *Bass; Springfield Bitter; Guinness;*
Carling Black Label; Tennent's Pilsner. 🍷 ⊖

Accommodation *10 bedrooms* **£C G2**
Check-in all day

Standing right on the market place is a fine old pub dating back in parts to the 16th century. The two beamed bars, one warmed by a log-burning stove, are full of character, as are bedrooms in the oldest part of the building up a steep staircase. All ten rooms have private facilities and are comfortable and individual in style, offering TVs, tea-makers and, in most cases, cosy duvets. Patio. Children welcome overnight.

Credit Access, Amex, Diners, Visa

SHIPTON-UNDER-WYCHWOOD   **Lamb Inn**

High Street OX7 6DG   `FOOD`
Area Map 4 D1 *Oxfordshire*   `B&B`
Shipton-under-Wychwood
(0993) 830465
Parking *ample*

Bar food *12.15–2 & 7–10, Sun 12–1.30*
& 7.30–9
No bar food *Mon in winter*

Landlords *Hugh & Lynne Wainwright*
Free house
🍺 *Hook Norton Best Bitter; Wadworth 6X;*
Guinness. 🍷 ⊖

Accommodation *5 bedrooms* **£C G2**
Check-in all day

A delightful old Cotswold-stone inn, in which the splendidly rustic beamed bar with its exposed stone walls, polished wooden floor and sturdy furniture makes a fine setting for an interesting range of carefully prepared dishes. Game soup, avocado and orange mousse and smoked prawns are all delicious snacks or starters, while main courses might include fresh plaice, popular Cotswold pie or richly sauced game in season. Finish with lemon mousse or marmalade cheesecake. Cold buffet available in summer; limited choice of bar food Sunday lunchtime.

Typical dishes Chicken and mushroom fricassee £4 Braised pheasant £5.50.

Climb the steep stairs to reach the cosy, cottagey bedrooms, where pretty floral curtains and candlewick bedspreads contrast with plain painted walls and white furniture. All offer tea-makers, radios and carpeted modern bathrooms. Accommodation closed two weeks Feb–March. *No children under 14 overnight. No dogs.*

Credit Access, Amex, Diners, Visa

Any person using our name to obtain
free hospitality is a fraud.

Proprietors, please inform Egon Ronay's Guides
and the police.

SHIPTON-UNDER-WYCHWOOD   *Shaven Crown Hotel*

High Street OX7 6BA
Area Map 4 D1 *Oxfordshire*
Shipton-under-Wychwood
(0993) 830330
Parking *ample*

Bar food *12–2 & 7–9.30 (Sun till 9)*

Landlords *Brookes family*
Free house
🍺 *Hook Norton Best Bitter; Flowers Original, Best Bitter; Heineken.* ⊖

A 14th-century hospice built in Cotswold stone for the monks from Bruern Abbey is now a thriving village-centre pub full of historical atmosphere. There is an old gateway leading to the courtyard garden, and a medieval hall (which now operates as a residents' lounge) with stone walls and fireplace and high beamed ceilings. In the Buttery Bar highly enjoyable snacks are served, from garlic mushrooms or potato skins topped with cheese and bacon, as starters, to curried prawns, mushroom and walnut pancakes or delicious boboutie for main course. Sweets include chocolate and apple cake, marmalade pudding and treacle tart.

Typical dishes Steak & kidney pie £3.95 Spinach & bacon lasagne £3.85

Accommodation *9 bedrooms* **£A G2/3**
Check-in all day

Varying in size, the bedrooms are simply decorated and mainly furnished in period style with plain fabrics. Several would benefit from redecoration, and some work is already planned. Six rooms have functional en suite facilities, and the others are to be converted. All have TVs and tea-makers. No dogs.

Credit Access, Visa

SHIRLEY   *Saracens Head Hotel*

Stratford Road, Nr Solihull [B&B]
B90 3AG
Map 7 B2 *West Midlands*
021-744 1016
Parking *ample*

Landlord *M.D. Stevens*
Brewery *Allied*
🍺 *Ansells Best Bitter, Mild; Ind Coope Burton Ale; Guinness; Löwenbräu.*

Accommodation *34 bedrooms* **£B G1**
Check-in all day

A few minutes from junction 4 of the M42, on the A34 Birmingham to Stratford road, is a substantial purpose-built hotel in which all the bedrooms are very comfortable and well equipped. Pastel colour schemes, brass lamps, prints and lightwood units combine with en suite facilities, direct-dial telephones, tea-makers and effective double glazing to provide above-average accommodation. Major refurbishment of the cocktail bar and restaurant is under way. Pleasant and friendly service. *No dogs.*

Credit Access, Amex, Diners, Visa

SILK WILLOUGHBY   *Horseshoes*

Nr Sleaford NG34 8NZ   [FOOD]
Map 8 D1 *Lincolnshire*
Sleaford (0529) 303153
Parking *ample*

Bar food *12–2 & 7–10 (Sat till 10.30)*
No bar food *Sun eve*

Landlords *Jean & Francisco Cuñago*
Brewery *John Smith*
🍺 *John Smith's Bitter; Guinness; Kronenbourg 1664; Hofmeister; Foster's.*
No real ale. 🍷 ⊖

Jean and Francisco Cuñago offer an appetising selection of soundly prepared bar snacks at their red-brick pub alongside the A15. Consult the blackboards for the day's menu – perhaps cream of cauliflower soup or pâté, followed by halibut and prawns au gratin with fresh vegetables, goulash or a seafood pancake. Pleasant sweets like apricot flan or nicely made crème caramel round things off. Garden.

Typical dishes Chicken princesse £4.25 Lasagne £3.95

Credit Access, Visa

SKIDBY   Half Moon Inn

16 Main Street HU16 5TG   `FOOD`
Map 4 E3 *Humberside*
Hull (0482) 843403
Parking *ample*

Bar food *12–2 (Sun till 2.30) & 7–10*

Landlords *Peter Madeley & Di Parker*
Brewery *John Smith*
🍺 *John Smith's Bitter, Chestnut Mild;*
Guinness; Foster's; Kronenbourg 1664.
No real ale.

Chips with everything is not the stuff of the
Half Moon; its speciality is Yorkshire
puddings. These are mated with anything
from pheasant to venison, rabbit to minced
beef, and make delicious combinations.
They are also big enough to obscure the
approaching waitress. The pub itself is not
without idiosyncrasies having four little
bars and wooden pillar supports.
Typical dishes Yorkshire pudding with
beef £3.55 Home-made steak and kidney
pie £2.70

Credit Access, Visa

SLAIDBURN   Hark to Bounty Inn

Nr Clitheroe BB7 3EP   `B&B`
Area Map 2 A5 *Lancashire*
Slaidburn (020 06) 246
Parking *ample*

Landlady *Patricia M. Holt*
Brewery *Scottish & Newcastle*
🍺 *Theakston Old Peculier; Younger's No. 3;*
Guinness; Beck's Bier; McEwan's Lager.

Accommodation *8 bedrooms* £C G2
Check-in all day

Set in the heart of a picturesque village, this
characterful inn features a 13th-century
court room. The spacious lounge bar with
open fire and dark oak beams is as welcoming as the comfortable residents' lounge
with armchairs and TV. Bedrooms are
simply furnished and homely with duvets,
TVs, tea and coffee making facilities and
radios. All are equipped with modern
bathrooms, some with showers. Garden.
Children welcome overnight.

Credit Access, Amex, Diners, Visa

SLEIGHTS   Salmon Leap

Coach Road, Nr Whitby   `B&B`
YO22 5AA
Area Map 3 D1 *North Yorks*
Whitby (0947) 810233
Parking *ample*

Landlord *Adrian Linford Mee*
Brewery *Cameron*
🍺 *Cameron Traditional Bitter, Strongarm;*
Guinness; Cameron Hansa.

Accommodation *10 bedrooms* £D G2
Check-in all day

Modest improvements continue at this
homely pub close to the river Esk. The ten
compact bedrooms with new carpets and
attractive fabrics have been individually
decorated and all offer bedside cabinets and
tea-makers. Two rooms are suitable for
families and there are four small, shared
bathrooms. Residents have the use of a
first-floor lounge and there are three simple
bars, where fishermen and moorland
walkers often pause for refreshment. Children welcome overnight. *No dogs.*

SMARDEN   Bell

Bell Lane, Nr Ashford   `FOOD`
TN27 8PN   `B&B`
Area Map 5 B3 *Kent*
Smarden (023 377) 283
Parking *ample*

Bar food *12–2 (Sun till 2.30) & 6.30–10*
(Sun from 7, Sat till 10.30) 🍴

Landlord *Mr I.J. Turner*
Free house
🍺 *Fullers London Pride; Fremlins Bitter;*
Goachers Light Bitter; Theakston Best
Bitter, Old Peculier; Stella Artois. 🍷 🍵

A short drive from Smarden, this delightful
15th-century inn stands amid peaceful
Kentish countryside. Hop-festooned oak
beams and inglenook fireplaces provide a
charmingly rustic background in the three
flagstone-floored bars for a straightforward
choice of capably prepared snacks – accompanied by a range of fine real ales. Home-
made soup, pâté or clam fries might precede
a popular basket meal or mixed grill, pizza
or daily special such as Greek shepherd's
pie or lamb rogan josh served on a bed of
exemplary rice. Salads, sandwiches and

ploughman's are also available, and sweets include apple crumble and bread and butter pudding. Candlelight adds to the atmosphere in the evenings – which can get very busy.

Typical dishes Steak and kidney pie £3.75 Fish mornay £3.55

Accommodation *4 bedrooms* **£D G3**
Check-in by arrangement

A narrow outside spiral staircase leads to the four cottage bedrooms furnished in solid period style. All have duvets, TVs and tea-makers and share two up-to-date shower rooms. Continental breakfast is served in the rooms. Garden.

Credit Access, Visa

SMARDEN   *Chequers Inn*

Nr Ashford TN27 8QA   `FOOD`
Area Map 5 B3 *Kent*
Smarden (023 377) 217
Parking *ample*

Bar food *11–2 & 6.30–10. Sun 12–2 & 7–9.45*

Landlords *Frank & Frances Stevens*
Brewery *Courage*
🍺 *Courage Best Bitter, Directors; John Smiths Yorkshire Bitter; Guinness; Kronenbourg 1664; Foster's.* ✆

In the village centre, this characterful weatherboarded pub combines a warm welcome with some imaginative bar snacks. The selection ranges from simple favourites like pâté, ham, egg and chips or steak and kidney pie to more elaborate offerings such as mussel soup, swordfish provençale and stuffed quails. Puddings include sherry trifle and crème brûlée. Children's menu and play area.
Typical dishes Lamb cutlets with rosemary £4.75 Poussin with herb pâté £5.75

Credit Access, Visa

SNAINTON   *Coachman Inn*

Nr Scarborough YO13 9PL   `B&B`
Area Map 3 D3 *North Yorks*
Scarborough (0723) 85231
Parking *ample*

Landlord *Mr G. Senior*
Free house
🍺 *Cameron Traditional Bitter, Strongarm; Guinness; Hansa.*

Accommodation *12 bedrooms* **£C G2**
Check-in all day

The pub sign turn-off at the village entrance from Pickering leads you to a 200-year-old coaching inn flanked by paddocks and a verdant garden for summer drinking. The public and little lounge bars both have coal fires and sturdy wooden furniture. The bedrooms are spacious, plainly decorated in cream and white and simply furnished. All but one have basic en suite bathrooms, and TVs, tea-makers and extra heaters are standard. Cosy, old-fashioned residents' lounge. Children welcome overnight.

Credit Access, Amex, Diners, Visa

SNAPE   NEW ENTRY   *Golden Key*

Priory Road IP17 1SQ   `FOOD`
Map 8 F2 *Suffolk*
Snape (072 888) 510
Parking *ample*

Bar food *12–2 & 6.30–9, Sun 12–1.30 & 7–9*

Landlord *M. Kissick-Jones*
Brewery *Adnams*
🍺 *Adnams Bitter, Broadside, Old Ale (winter), Tally Ho (Xmas); Guinness; Carling Black Label.* 🍷 ✆

The key to success here is the simple, carefully prepared food served promptly and cheerfully in the beamed bar or at tables set outside. The blackboard menu holds few surprises, with things like quiches, cold cuts, salads, ploughman's and the favourite sausage, egg and onion pie. Finish with treacle and walnut tart or hot lemon cake. Take the side road off the A1094 Aldeburgh road.
Typical dishes Smoked haddock quiche £3.50 Hot lemon cake £1.50

SNETTISHAM   Rose & Crown Inn

Old Church Road, Nr   A
King's Lynn PE31 7LX
Map 8 E1 *Norfolk*
Dersingham (0485) 41382
Parking *ample*

Landlady *Margaret Trafford*
Free house ❧
🍺 *Adnams Bitter; Greene King IPA; Rose & Crown BB; Woodforde Wherry Best Bitter; Carling Black Label.* 🍷

A good local for the owners of Sandringham should they wander off the estate. More likely customers, though, are tired would-be royal-watchers sagging under the weight of telephoto lenses. Commiseration is made easy here with three bars encompassing a variety of traditional features from ingle-nook fireplace with a wood-burning stove to flagstone floors and oak beams. One bar has a collection of old farm implements (a suitable place for disappointed photographers to sling their hooks?).

Credit Access, Visa

SNITTERFIELD   NEW ENTRY   *Snitterfield Arms*

Nr Stratford-upon-Avon   B&B
CV37 0JH
Map 10 A1 *Warwickshire*
Stratford-upon-Avon (0789) 731294
Parking *ample*

Landlords *Glenys & Ron Crean*
Brewery *Whitbread*
🍺 *Flowers IPA, Original; Guinness; Stella Artois; Heineken.*

Accommodation *2 bedrooms* **£D G3**
Check-in all day

A handy base for visitors to Stratford-upon-Avon, the Snitterfield Arms is imbued with a cosy, welcoming air and a quiet country atmosphere. Plates and old photographs make an eye-catching display on the walls of the bar, and when the weather's kind the garden really comes into its own. The two homely, well-kept bedrooms are both provided with double and single beds; each has its own washbasin, but the bathroom serves both.

SONNING-ON-THAMES   *Bull Inn*

High Street RG4 0UP   FOOD
Map 10 C3 *Berkshire*   B&B
Reading (0734) 693901
Parking *limited*

Bar food *12–2*
No bar food *eves* ❧

Landlord *Mr D.T. Catton*
Brewery *Wethered*
🍺 *Wethered Bitter, SPA; Flowers Original; Heineken; Stella Artois.* ⊖

In a picture-postcard setting by the village church, the Bull is a quintessentially southern English old-world pub that dates from the 14th-century. Outside is very pretty – black and white gabling, climbing plants, flowers, wooden tables and chairs for alfresco sipping. Inside, there is one main bar with sturdy beams, gleaming brassware and inglenook – ablaze with logs in winter, filled with flowers in summer. Children's room lunchtime only. Bar food is served only at lunchtime and centres round a buffet highlighted by good cold meats and English cheeses. Steak and kidney pie and a hot chicken dish are also usually available, along with soup and home-made cheesecake.

Typical dishes Quiche & salad £3.20 Veal & ham pie £3.20

Accommodation *5 bedrooms* **£A G2**
Check-in by arrangement

The five bedrooms are stylishly old-fashioned, with white walls, beams and solid free-standing furniture; most of them overlook the courtyard and church. Mattresses are well sprung, and each room has a washbasin. They share a modest but pristinely clean bathroom. Accommodation closed one week Christmas. *No dogs.*

SOUTH DALTON   *Pipe & Glass*

West End HU17 7PN `FOOD`
Area Map 3 D5 *Humberside*
Market Weighton (0430) 810246
Parking *ample*

Bar food *12–2 & 7.15–10 (Sat from 7.30)*
No bar food *Sun eve*

Landlords *Mr & Mrs M. Crease*
Free house
🍷 *Webster Choice; Stones Bitter; Guinness; Foster's.* 🍷

A delightful garden complete with children's play area is a popular summer feature at a pub which also offers a choice of three bars and a restaurant. Hearty, daily-changing snacks are served in the beamed main bar, ranging from vegetable soup and a woodman's lunch with home-made pickles to sardines provençale and Yorkshire pudding with onion gravy. Note fresh fruit pavlova amongst the sweets.
Typical dishes Duck in orange £3.50 Chicken piri piri £3

Credit Access, Visa

---

*We welcome bona fide recommendations
or complaints on the tear-out pages at the back
of the book for readers' comments.*

*They are followed up by our professional team,
but do complain to the management on the spot.*

SOUTH HARTING   *White Hart*

Nr Petersfield GU31 5QB `FOOD`
Map 7 C4 *West Sussex*
Harting (073 085) 355
Parking *ample*

Bar food *11–2 (Sun from 12) & 7–10* 🍴
No bar food *Mon eve (winter)*

Landlords *Mr & Mrs Hayter*
Brewery *Friary Meux*
🍷 *Friary Meux Bitter; Ind Cooper Burton Ale; John Bull Bitter; Löwenbräu.* ⊖

A pleasant village pub with log fires, polished wooden tables and a decent choice of plain, fresh food. Steak and kidney or game pie is popular, with sweet and sour chicken or Dijon pork typical alternatives. Sandwiches, omelettes and cauliflower cheese provide quick snacks, while bread and butter pudding is a favourite sweet. Sunday always brings a roast beef and a fruit crumble. Children's rooms, menu and play areas. Garden.
Typical dishes Trout with mushroom sauce £3.95 Lasagne £3.75

SOUTH ZEAL   *Oxenham Arms*

Nr Okehampton EX20 2JT `B&B`
Map 9 B2 *Devon*
Okehampton (0837) 840244
Parking *ample*

Landlords *Jim & Pat Henry*
Free house 🛏
🍷 *St Austell Tinners Ale; Hicks Special; Flowers Best Bitter; Guinness; Stella Artois; Kronenbourg 1664.*

Accommodation *10 bedrooms* £C G2
Check-in all day

Enjoying a peaceful village setting just off the A30, this splendid creeper-clad inn was first licensed in 1477. Blackened beams, rough stone walls and an open fire add to the mellow charms of the bar, while the lounge boasts a huge fireplace and antique furnishings. Bedrooms (including two in a cottage opposite) are full of character with their sloping floors, beams and chintzy fabrics. Most have private facilities, and TVs, tea-makers and telephones are standard. Garden and play area.

Credit Access, Amex, Diners, Visa

SOUTHPOOL   NEW ENTRY   *Millbrook Inn*

Nr Kingsbridge TQ7 2RW   `FOOD`
Map 9 C3 *Devon*
Frogmore (054853) 581
Parking *difficult*

Bar food *11.45–2 & 6.45–9.30, Sun 12–2 & 7.30–9.30*

Landlords *Christine & Michael Jones*
Free house
🍺 *Bass; Worthington Best Bitter; Stones Bitter; Carling Black Label.*

Customers arrive at this small pub close to Salcombe estuary by boat when the tide is high. Millbrook stream also flows past the little terrace, a sunny spot for tucking into simple, unfussy snacks like succulent local crab and mackerel in salads and sandwiches, ploughman's and hot dishes such as soup and cottage pie. The two bars are comfortable and welcoming and there is a pretty, flower-bedecked patio.
Typical dishes Prawn salad £2.80 Quiche salad £1.95

SOUTHWOLD   *The Crown*

High Street IP18 6DP   `FOOD`
Map 8 F2 *Suffolk*   `B&B`
Southwold (0502) 722275
Parking *ample*

Bar food *12.30–2 & 7.30–9.30*

Landlord *Dudley Clarke*
Brewery *Adnams*
🍺 *Adnams Bitter, Old (winter only), Broadside; Guinness; Skol.* 🍷 ⊖

A very well restored 18th-century inn in a town which lies in the centre of an area of great natural beauty. Stylish throughout, the main bar has a high ceiling, high-backed wooden settles, pine tables and smart yellow walls. A great feature is the Cruover machine which enables an excellent range of wines to be served by the glass. This is well matched by the food on offer – baked catfish with fennel and ginger, salmon and sole roulade with garlic mayonnaise and aubergine fritters with pimento sauce are just a selection from the bar menu. Sweets include nectarine cheesecake and pineapple fritters with pomegranate and orange. There is also a restaurant.

Typical dishes Smoked trout mousse £3.90 Sautéed loin of pork £4.80

Accommodation *12 bedrooms* **£C G2**
Check-in all day

The bedrooms are unfussy and quite compact, with pine furniture and good modern bathrooms (nine en suite and three just across the corridor from their own rooms), and all are well heated. Children welcome overnight.

Credit Access, Amex, Visa

SPEEN   *Old Plow Inn*

Flowers Bottom HP17 0PZ   `FOOD`
Map 10 C2 *Buckinghamshire*
Hampden Row (024 028) 300
Parking *ample*

Bar food *12–2.15*
No bar food *eves*
Closed *Mon*

Landlords *Malcolm & Olivia Cowan*
Free house
🍺 *Marston Pedigree; Greene King Abbot Ale; Guinness; Stella Artois.* 🍷 ⊖

Once a forge, the 17th-century Old Plow boasts low-beamed ceilings and tiled floors in the well-maintained bars, where plenty of good food is supplied. While the restaurant is the main feature, the interesting bar menu offers such dishes as chilled tomato soup, pasta with prawns and tomato sauce and blackcurrant parfait.
Typical dishes Crispy duck with plum sauce £3.95 Avocado prawns £4.50

Credit Access, Amex, Visa

SPROUGHTON   NEW ENTRY   *Beagle*

Old Hadleigh Road, Nr   `FOOD`
Ipswich IP8 3AR
Map 8 E2 *Suffolk*
Cordock (0473) 86455
Parking *ample*

Bar food *12–2* ☙
No bar food *Sun & eves*

Landlord *Mr W.M. Freeth*
Free house
🍺 *Mauldon's Bitter; Adnams Bitter;*
Greene King IPA Bitter; Guinness; Beck's
Bier; Carlsberg. ℗

The Beagle takes a little bit of tracking down, so get directions in the village. Lunchtime victuals are fresh and satisfying, and staples like soup and various ploughman's platters are joined by daily specials such as cheese and vegetable pie or lamb chop in wine sauce. The splendid sheltered garden is a popular summer alternative to the roomy bar.
Typical dishes Lowestoft kipper with brown bread £2.35 Soup, bread, celery & Stilton £2.50

Credit Access, Visa

STAFFORD   *Swan Hotel*

46 Greengate Street   `B&B`
ST16 2JA
Map 7 A1 *Staffordshire*
Stafford (0785) 58142
Parking *ample*

Landlord *John Pointon*
Brewery *Ansells*
🍺 *Ind Coope Burton Ale; Ansells Bitter,*
Mild; Skol; Castlemaine XXXX.

Accommodation *32 bedrooms* **£A G1**
Check-in all day

Built on the site of monastic college buildings, this handsome town-centre coaching inn retains many original features – from the Jacobean-style reception area (located, like the car park, to the rear) to the original oak floorboards and beams in several of the bedrooms. All rooms offer fully-tiled private facilities, remote-control TVs, trouser presses and tea-makers: double-glazed front ones are largest. There are two attractive bars and a walled patio garden. Children welcome overnight.

Credit Access, Amex, Diners, Visa

STAMFORD   *Bull & Swan Inn*

St Martins PE9 2JL   `B&B`
Map 8 D1 *Lincolnshire*
Stamford (0780) 63558
Parking *ample*

Landlords *Mr & Mrs De Sadeleer*
Brewery *Cameron*
🍺 *Cameron Traditional Bitter, Strongarm;*
Tolly Cobbold Original; Guinness; Hansa,
Export.

Accommodation *6 bedrooms* **£C G2**
Check-in all day

The oldest part is 15th-century, and additions down the years end with up-to-date en suite shower facilities (only one room has a bath). Pretty flowered duvets and light paintwork and furniture create a neat, bright appearance; the best and biggest room takes character from its sloping floor and angled ceiling. Three cosy little bars have considerable old-world atmosphere, and the pub's friendly owners give the place a relaxed and welcoming feel. *No dogs.*

Credit Access, Amex, Diners, Visa

STAMFORD   *Crown Hotel*

All Saints Place PE9 2AG   `B&B`
Map 8 D1 *Lincolnshire*
Stamford (0780) 63136
Parking *ample*

Landlords *R.D. & E.W. McGahon*
Free house
🍺 *Ruddles County; Bass; Tennent's*
Pilsner; Carling Black Label.

Accommodation *18 bedrooms* **£C G2**
Check-in all day

One of the oldest inns in Lincolnshire, the Crown provides comfortable accommodation and a bright, friendly ambience. Floral fabrics are used for curtains and covers in the bedrooms, most of which have their own bathrooms. There are some pleasant water-colours of Stamford in the modest bar, along with a print of Daniel Lambert, renowned as Britain's fattest man, who expired on the premises. A print on the bar testifies to his enormousness. Children welcome overnight.

Credit Access, Amex, Diners, Visa

STAMFORD
George of Stamford

71 St Martin's High Street
PE9 2LB
Map 8 D1 *Lincolnshire*
Stamford (0780) 55171
Parking *ample*

Bar food *11 am–11 pm*

Landlords *Philip Newman-Hall & Ivo Vannocci*
Free house
Samuel Smith's Old Brewery Bitter; Ruddles Rutland Bitter; Beck's Bier.

FOOD
B&B

A massive gallows spanning the High Street marks this renowned old coaching inn, where first-class snacks are served throughout the day in the delightfully summery plant-filled garden lounge. A fine display of roast meats, poached fish (try the fillet of pike) and imaginative warm salads with pigeon, pheasant and smoked bacon makes up the tempting cold buffet, while hot alternatives range from flavoursome leek and potato soup to Lincolnshire sausages in red wine sauce and various savoury pancakes and pasta dishes. Don't miss the light, velvety chocolate mousse for dessert, and excellent selection of wines by the glass from the Cruover machine.

Typical dishes Seafood platter £11.95 Stir-fry vegetables in black bean sauce £4.85

Accommodation *47 bedrooms* **£A G1**
Check-in all day

Superb bedrooms are individually decorated with striking fabrics and quality furnishings (including four four-posters) and offer everything from hairdryers, trouser presses and radio-alarms to good towels and toiletries in their comfortably modern bathrooms. Children welcome overnight.

Credit Access, Amex, Visa

STANFORD DINGLEY
NEW ENTRY
Bull Inn

Nr Reading RG7 6LS
Map 10 B3 *Berkshire*
Bradfield (0734) 744409
Parking *ample*

Bar food *12–3 & 7.30–10*

Landlords *Pat & Trudi Langdon*
Free house
Bass; Charrington IPA; Eldridge Pope Dorset IPA; Tennent's Export; Carling Black Label.

FOOD

Stanford Dingley is a tranquil village in the heart of the Berkshire countryside, and its red-brick pub has its origins in the 15th century. Traditional bars are home to some good cooking – prawns à la crème or soups such as carrot and orange or Stilton, followed by 'drunken fish', vegetable lasagne, chicken provençale or a tender and well-flavoured beef stroganoff. Specials include chicken simla, ratatouille or beef goulash. Garden.
Typical dishes Fish pie £3.20 Trout with almonds £4.25

STANFORD DINGLEY
Old Boot Inn

Nr Bradfield RG7 6LS
Map 10 B3 *Berkshire*
Bradfield (0734) 744292
Parking *ample*

Bar food *12–2 & 6–10, Sun 12–1.30 & 7–9.30*

Landlord *Tony Howells*
Free house
Eldridge Pope Royal Oak; Guinness; Stella Artois.

FOOD

A spacious garden and patio are popular summer features of this 18th-century pub, which also has a cosy beamed bar where simple snacks are served. The lengthy menu ranges from sandwiches, salads and filled jacket potatoes to more substantial offerings – perhaps baked ham with eggs and mushrooms or braised liver and bacon. Sweets from the restaurant trolley and a traditional roast Sunday lunch also available.

Credit Access, Visa

STANTON ST JOHN
NEW ENTRY
Star Inn

Nr Oxford OX9 1EX   `FOOD`
Map 10 B2 *Oxfordshire*
Stanton St John (086 735) 277
Parking *ample*

Bar food *12–2 & 7–10* 🍴

Landlords *Nigel & Suzanne Tucker*
Brewery *Wadworth*
🍺 *Wadworth 6X, Farmers Glory, IPA; Hall & Woodhouse Tanglefoot; Guinness; Stella Artois.* ⊖

Dating from 1723, the Star was a butcher's shop and abattoir before assuming its current role of pleasant village hostelry. The period feel is largely intact, and the simple appeal of the bars is matched by an enjoyable, unpretentious menu: plain or toasted sandwiches, crispy garlic mushrooms, quiche, chicken Kiev. There is always a vegetarian main dish, plus daily specials like pork and cider casserole.
Typical dishes Cheesy tuna bake £3 Chicken, celery & almond pie £3

STANTON WICK
Carpenters Arms

Nr Pensford BS18 4BX   `FOOD`
Map 7 A3 *Somerset*   `B&B`
Compton Dando
(076 18) 202
Parking *ample*

Bar food *12–2 & 7–10*

Landlord *Nigel Pushman*
Free house
🍺 *Wadworth 6X; Bass; Butcombe Bitter; Guinness; Tennent's Extra; Stella Artois.* ⊖

Prettily sunk a few feet below the level of the road, this mellow country inn of honey-coloured stone was once a row of 17th-century miners' cottages. Inside, exposed stone walls, oak beams, open fires and wood-burning stoves characterise the traditional bars, while the Coopers' Parlour is an attractive setting for a wide range of snacks. Home cooked meats and fresh salads make up the cold buffet, while the hot selection ranges from filled jacket potatoes and ratatouille-stuffed pepper to lamb kebabs, plaice with parsley sauce and various grills. Home-made puddings are also available and a traditional Sunday lunch is served. More elaborate meals in the restaurant.

Typical dishes Mendip snails in garlic butter £2.75 Chicken chasseur £4.95

Accommodation *9 bedrooms* £C G2
Check-in all day

Cottagy bedrooms with their low ceilings, tiny windows set into thick walls and solid pine furnishings are both appealing and comfortable. Magazines, tea-makers and radio-alarms are provided and all have excellent modern bathrooms. Children welcome overnight. *No dogs.*

Credit Access, Amex, Diners, Visa

STAPLE FITZPAINE
Greyhound Inn

Nr Taunton TA3 5SP   `FOOD`
Map 9 C1 *Somerset*
Hatch Beauchamp (0823) 480227
Parking *ample*

Bar food *12–2 & 7–10*

Landlords *Steven & Audrey Watts*
Free house
🍺 *Golden Hill Exmoor Ale; Flowers IPA; Eldridge Pope Royal Oak; Murphy Stout; Stella Artois.* 🍷 ⊖

Unusual names characterise the extensive and varied menu here – Bailiffs Bag (fresh bream fillet), Famished Forester (ham and mushroom in cheese sauce, topped with an egg and cheese) and Hungry Monk (potato, onion, tomato, cheese and herb bake) are just a few. The pub itself is reached by driving down narrow country lanes off the A358, and inside you will find flagstoned floors and rustic furniture.
Typical dishes Devilled whitebait £1.95 Fettucine Alfredo £3.95

Credit Access, Visa

STARBOTTON — Fox & Hounds

Nr Kettlewell, Upper
Wharfdale BD23 5HY
Area Map 2 C3 *North Yorks*
Grassington (075 676) 269
Parking *ample*

Closed *Mon-Thurs lunch & all Nov-May*

Landlords *Bernard & Pam Garvie*
Free house
🍺 *Younger's Scotch; Theakston Best Bitter, Old Peculier; Carlsberg.*

A

Just what you would probably imagine a pub in a Yorkshire village to be like: stone-flagged floors, rough walls, simple wooden tables and wheelback chairs. Open fires in both rooms complete the picture of rural charm. The surroundings are delightful, and there are plenty of lovely walks for building up a thirst. Benches are set outside on the patio for enjoying an alfresco drink. The owners have plans to make two letting bedrooms available.

STAVELEY — Royal Oak

Nr Knaresborough HG5 9LD
Area Map 2 F4 *North Yorks*
Harrogate (0423) 340267
Parking *ample*

Bar food *12–2*
No bar food *eves*

Landlords *Mr & Mrs P. Gallagher*
Free house
🍺 *Theakston Best Bitter; Guinness; Slalom Lager.* 🍴

FOOD

Black and terracotta floor tiles balance with black painted woodwork to offset blue checked tablecloths, curtains and cushions in the warm and welcoming lounge bar. At lunchtime the restaurant offers the same menu as the bar, but there are more elaborate evening meals such as poached salmon or duck breast with port wine. Excellent pies, salads and sandwiches in the bar.
Typical dishes Game pie £4.20 Steak & kidney pie £3.95

Credit Access

STAVERTON — Sea Trout Inn

Nr Totnes TQ9 6PA
Map 9 C2 *Devon*
Staverton (080 426) 274
Parking *ample*

Landlord *Andrew M. Mogford*
Free house
🍺 *Hall's Harvest Bitter; Bass; Ruddles Best Bitter; Guinness; Löwenbräu; Castlemaine XXXX.*

Accommodation *6 bedrooms* £C G2
Check-in all day

B&B

A warm welcome heralds a pleasant stay at the Sea Trout, a country inn that is a particular favourite of fishermen. The fishing theme runs through the pub, some specimens mounted in showcases, others depicted in paintings or on plates. Neat, bright accommodation comprises a double bedroom with large carpeted bathroom en suite and five other rooms sharing two bathrooms. Plans are under way for an extra four bedrooms, and for all rooms to be en suite. Children welcome overnight.

Credit Access, Amex, Diners, Visa

STEEP — Harrow Inn

Nr Petersfield GU32 2DA
Map 7 C4 *Hampshire*
Petersfield (0730) 62685
Parking *limited*

Bar food *12–2 & 6.15–10, Sun 12–2.30 & 7–10*

Landlord *Eddie McCutcheon*
Brewery *Whitbread*
🍺 *Samuel Whitbread; Flowers Original; Strong Country Bitter; Guinness; Stella Artois.*

FOOD

Tucked away down small country lanes the Harrow is a gem of a rustic pub, still totally unspoilt. There are two small bars, one with a huge inglenook, long table and shelves of old books. In spring both bars are festooned with beautiful wild flower arrangements. Food is simple, home-made, and of good quality, especially the large china bowl of country soup or the herby Scotch egg. Fine long garden and patio for quiet alfresco eating.
Typical dishes Home-made soup and bread £1.20 Roast beef salad £5

STEEPLE ASTON   NEW ENTRY   Red Lion

Nr Oxford OX5 3RY   `FOOD`
Area Map 4 F1 *Oxfordshire*
Steeple Aston (0869) 40225
Parking *limited*

Bar food *12–2*
No bar food *Sun*

Landlord *Colin Mead*
Free house
🍺 *Wadworth 6X; Hook Norton Best Bitter;*
Hall & Woodhouse Tanglefoot; Tuborg. ⊖

Good plain cooking makes a stop off here in a village just off the A423 very worth while. Inside, the pub is quaint, with a splendid settle and stone fireplace complemented by Victorian-style prints. A short menu is displayed on a blackboard – soup, pâté or taramasalata to start, a casserole, fresh fish or above average sandwiches to follow. Sadly, low-flying jets from Upper Heyford can spoil the peace and quiet. Garden.
Typical dishes Moules marinière £2.60 Smoked salmon platter £3.90

Credit Access, Visa

STILTON   NEW ENTRY   Bell

Great North Road PE7 3RL   `FOOD`
Map 8 D1 *Cambridgeshire*
Peterborough (0733) 241066
Parking *ample*

Bar food *11–2.30 (Sun 12–3) & 6–9.30*
No bar food *Sun eve*

Landlords *L.A. & M.J. McGivern*
Free house
🍺 *Marston Pedigree; Tetley Bitter;*
Courage Directors; Greene King Abbot Ale;
Ind Coope Burton Ale; Skol.

In a village which gave its name to a cheese, it is hardly surprising that the chief pub in the main street should offer an outstanding selection. Prime Long Clawson Stilton is offered as a superb ploughman's, in Stilton and walnut pâté, and in the unforgettable Stilton and plum bread. Cheddar and red Leicester also feature on the short bar menu, as do local sausages, sprats in herbs and garlic, and vegetable soup.
Typical dishes Stilton soup £1.20 Lamb with beer dumplings £3.75

Credit Access, Amex, Visa

STOCKBRIDGE   Grosvenor Hotel

High Street SO20 6EH   `B&B`
Map 7 B4 *Hampshire*
Andover (0264) 810606
Parking *ample*

Landlords *Arlette & Graham Livett*
Owner *Lansbury Hotels*
🍺 *Strong Country Bitter; Whitbread Best*
Bitter; Wadworth 6X; Heineken; Stella
Artois.

Accommodation *25 bedrooms* £A G1
Check-in all day

A handsome pillared portico marks the entrance to a comfortable Georgian hotel near the river Test. Historic fly-fishing tackle used by the Houghton Fishing Club, whose headquarters lie upstairs, adorns the brightly lit bar, while the panelled dining room features etchings of famous race-horses. Bedrooms in the original building and converted stable block have mahogany furnishings, excellent carpeted private bathrooms and thoughtful extras like trouser presses and sewing kits. *No dogs.*

Credit Access, Amex, Diners, Visa

STOCKBRIDGE   NEW ENTRY   White Hart Inn

High Street SO20 6HF   `B&B`
Map 7 B4 *Hampshire*
Andover (0264) 810475
Parking *ample*

Landlord *Mr A.P. Curtis*
Free house
🍺 *Bass; Charrington IPA; Worthington*
Best Bitter; Guinness; Tennents Pilsner;
Carling Black Label. 🍷

Accommodation *14 bedrooms* £C G2
Check-in all day

An ancient inn of unusual appearance, the first-floor overhang creating a covered area for enjoying a drink outside (there is also a garden). Low beams, brick pillars and timber-laced walls give the bar the look of cosy old age, a charm that extends to main-house bedrooms. The stable block area provides alternative accommodation in simple motel style. Staff are courteous, and plenty of printed local information is available in reception. *No dogs.*

Credit Access, Visa

STOCKPORT   NEW ENTRY   *Red Bull*

14 Middle Hillgate SK3 1AW   `FOOD`
Map 3 C4 *Greater Manchester*
061-480 2087
Parking *limited*

Bar food *12–2.15 & 5–7.30*
No bar food *Sat eve & Sun*

Landlord *Brian Lawrence*
Brewery *Robinson*
🍺 *Robinson Best Bitter, Best Mild;*
Guinness; Einhorn; Tennent's Lager. ⊖

Landlord Brian Lawrence believes in robust cooking based on good fresh ingredients at his modest cream-painted pub. In the neat beamed bars short, regularly changing menus might offer hearty red bean and pepper soup or smoked mackerel pâté with olives as a snack or starter, with perhaps cidered beef and dumplings or halibut in a herby sauce to finish. Sandwiches, quiche and fine cheeses for light eaters, too.
Typical dishes Beef and burgundy pie £2.65 Roghan josh £2.55

STOKE-BY-NAYLAND   *Angel Inn*

Colchester CO6 4SA   `FOOD`
Map 8 E2 *Suffolk*   `B&B`
Colchester (0206) 263245
Parking *ample*

Bar food *12–2 & 6.30–9, Sun 12–1.30 & 7–9*

Landlords *Richard E. Wright & Peter G. Smith*
Free house
🍺 *Greene King Abbot Ale, IPA; Adnams Bitter; Kronenbourg 1664; Carlsberg.*

Soft lamplight glows in the windows of this solid, beautifully restored village inn. Inside, the bar is divided into two: a lounge bar with a brick fireplace and log-burning stove, exposed timbers and wooden furniture, and a real lounge with deep sofas, wing chairs and a grandfather clock. Fresh fish is a major feature of the menu, and there is a choice of halibut, grouper, Dover sole, grey mullet, salmon, brill and plaice in season. Also offered are chicken liver pâté, supreme of pigeon with mushrooms and bacon sauce, and lentil soup. A medley of fine fruits, lemon cheesecake or vanilla bavaroise to follow.

Typical dishes Pork en croûte £5.75 Fresh fish platter £5.95

Accommodation *6 bedrooms* **£C G1**
Check-in all day

Three bedrooms are reached from a small gallery over the restaurant and three new rooms are housed in an annexe. They are all of a decent size and individually decorated with a strong sense of style. En suite facilities, TVs and tea-makers are provided throughout. *No children under six overnight. No dogs.*

Credit Access, Amex, Diners, Visa

STOKE ST GREGORY   *Rose & Crown Inn*

Nr Taunton TA3 6EW   `FOOD`
Map 7 A4 *Somerset*   `B&B`
North Curry (0823) 490296
Parking *ample*

Bar food *12–2 & 7–10 (Sun till 9.30)*

Landlords *Ron & Irene Browning*
Free house
🍺 *Eldridge Pope Royal Oak, Dorchester IPA; Golden Hill Exmoor Ale; Guinness; Kronenbourg 1664.* ⊖

One of three pubs in a scattered village off the A361, the Rose & Crown is fronted by a pretty, flower-decked patio. Inside are cosy alcoves, dark beams, horse brasses and other ornaments – all adding up to a quaint, cosy picture. Regulars travel miles for scrumpy chicken, a great favourite among a good range of bar snacks posted on the blackboard. A tomato, onion and mushroom sauce accompanies an adult-size portion of chicken, with good chips on the side. Liver and onions, grilled skate and whole plaice are other main-course choices, while soup, sandwiches, ploughman's and salads provide lighter fare. Apple pie, crème caramel and home-made ice cream are popular sweets. Traditional Sunday lunch.

Typical dishes Scrumpy chicken £4.35 Chocolate mousse cake £1.50

Accommodation *3 bedrooms* **£D G3**
Check-in all day

Three modest bedrooms with modern fittings, TVs, radios and kettles share a bathroom fitted with a whirlpool bath. Children welcome overnight.

Credit Access, Visa

STONY STRATFORD   *Bull Hotel*

64 High Street MK11 1AQ `B&B`
Map 10 C1 *Buckinghamshire*
Milton Keynes (0908) 567104
Parking *ample*

Landlords *Paul Waring & Diane Chapman*
Brewery *Aylesbury*
🍺 *ABC Bitter; Wadworth 6X; Bass; Guinness; Löwenbräu; Skol.*

Accommodation *14 bedrooms* **£C G2**
Check-in all day

A massive wrought-iron pub sign landmarks this former coaching inn, which, with its neighbour, the Cock, coined the eponymous 'cock and bull' story. A refurbished lounge bar doubles as reception, while the simpler flagstoned Vaults bar attracts a younger crowd with live music at weekends (public toilet unsatisfactory). Accommodation is adequate for overnighters. Colourful curtains brighten smallish rooms with TVs. En suite bathrooms. Children welcome overnight. *No dogs.*

Credit Access, Visa

STONY STRATFORD   *The Cock Hotel*

72 High Street MK11 1AH `B&B`
Map 10 C1 *Buckinghamshire*
Milton Keynes (0908) 567733
Parking *ample*

Landlord *James Higgins*
Free house
🍺 *Adnams Bitter; Younger's Tartan, IPA; Guinness; Carlsberg.*

Accommodation *43 bedrooms* **£B G2**
Check-in all day

Recent developments at this ancient high street hostelry have resulted in an additional 23 bedrooms for 1990. In similar style to existing rooms, they offer up-to-date extras like hairdryers and trouser presses as well as the present tea-makers, TVs, radios and direct-dial telephones. Most have carpeted private facilities, while those without share four public bathrooms. Fairly new, too, is the residents' lounge behind the comfortable and convivial single bar. Children welcome overnight. *No dogs.*

Credit Access, Amex, Diners, Visa

STOPHAM BRIDGE   NEW ENTRY   *White Hart*

Nr Pulborough RH20 1DS `FOOD`
Area Map 6 B3 *West Sussex*
Pulborough (079 82) 3321
Parking *ample*

Bar food *12.30–2.15 & 7–9.30, Sun 12.30–1.45 & 7–9*

Landlords *Bill & Elizabeth Bryce*
Brewery *Whitbread*
🍺 *Flowers Original; Wethered SPA; Strong Country Bitter; Guinness; Stella Artois; Heineken.* ⊖

The White Hart is a Sussex stone pub set picturesquely by Stopham Bridge on the river Arun, just off the A283 and a mile west of Pulborough. Inside, it is a delightful jumble of nooks and crannies, with beams, brasses and cottage-style furniture, painting an authentic picture of mellow Old England. The bar menu specialises in fish, from regular favourite whitebait to more exotic specials such as whole grouper. Soup, sandwiches and lasagne too.

Typical dishes Vegetable lasagne £2.50 Poached whiting £3.25

STOURBRIDGE   *Talbot Hotel*

High Street DY8 1DW `B&B`
Map 7 A2 *West Midlands*
Stourbridge (0384) 394350
Parking *limited*

Landlord *Mark Chatterton*
Brewery *Wolverhampton & Dudley*
🍺 *Banks's Bitter, Mild; Hanson's Black Country Bitter; Guinness; Kronenbourg 1664; Harp, Extra.* No real ale.

Accommodation *27 bedrooms* **£A G1**
Check-in all day

Stone-mullioned windows and oak panels dating back over 500 years lie behind the 18th-century facade. A splendid staircase leads to the attractively decorated bedrooms, including beamed executive rooms featuring antique furnishings (one has a four-poster). Standard, pine-furnished rooms are smaller but all categories offer good private facilities plus TVs, telephones and hairdryers. Leather Chesterfields grace the coffee lounge and there is a bright lively bar. Children welcome overnight.

Credit Access, Amex, Visa

STOW BARDOLPH   *Hare Arms*

King's Lynn PE34 3HT `FOOD`
Map 8 E1 *Norfolk*
Downham Market (0366) 382229
Parking *ample*

Bar food *12–2 & 7–10*

Landlords *David & Tricia McManus*
Brewery *Greene King*
🍺 *Greene King Abbot Ale; IPA, Mild; Guinness; Kronenbourg 1664; Harp.* 🍺 ☺

A pretty country pub in a delightful Norfolk village a few miles south of King's Lynn. David and Tricia McManus' conscientious and enthusiastic approach to pub-keeping is a model to others. The excellent bar food draws the crowds, so make sure you arrive early. Home-made pâtés and mousses vie with Stilton and bacon soup to get things going, but the real interest here is the super fresh fish from the Norfolk coast. Crabs and lobsters, oysters and sole are typical daily specials, and game is available in winter. Popular staples include steak and oyster pie, curries and well-filled sandwiches. Restaurant dishes are slightly more ambitious, and the lamb steak with a mint hollandaise sauce is delicious. There is a charming conservatory, and an intriguing coach house in the garden for children. Good wines.

Typical dishes Stilton & bacon soup £1.25 Steak & oyster pie £3.50 Crab salad £3.75 Pork steak on cream & green peppercorn sauce £3.75

We publish annually so make sure you use the current edition.

STRATFIELD TURGIS   *Wellington Arms*

Nr Basingstoke RG27 0AS `B&B`
Map 10 B3 *Hampshire*
Basingstoke (0256) 882214
Parking *ample*

Landlady *Marian Buchanan-Munro*
Owner *Badger Inns*
🍺 *Hall & Woodhouse Badger Best, Tanglefoot; Hofbräu Royal, Export.* 🍺

Accommodation *15 bedrooms* **£A G1**
Check-in all day

First a farmhouse and later a coaching inn, the Wellington Arms provides a commendably high standard of overnight accommodation. Behind a handsome Georgian facade a lot of care has gone into preserving character by way of flagstones and fine woodwork, open fires and inviting armchairs. Bedrooms (those in the main house are particularly attractive) feature well-chosen Continental or pine furnishings, direct-dial phones and remote-control TVs. Children welcome overnight.

Credit Access, Amex, Diners, Visa

STRATFORD-UPON-AVON   *Slug & Lettuce*

38 Guild Street CV37 6QY   `FOOD`
Map 10 A1 *Warwickshire*
Stratford-upon-Avon (0789) 299700
Parking *limited*

Bar food *12–10 pm, Sun 12–2.15 &
7–9.30*

Landlords *Mr & Mrs Harris*
Brewery *Ansells*
🍺 *Ind Coope Burton Ale; Tetley Bitter;
Slug Bitter; Ansells Bitter; Slug Light
Lager.* ⊖

Imaginative food prepared from market-
fresh local produce remains the winning
formula at this smart, popular pub-cum-
bistro. Daily-changing menus offer a tempting variety, from sausages dijonnaise and
prawns provençale to pork chop with
mushroom and Stilton sauce, roast guinea
fowl and plaice meunière. Sweets include
syllabubs and crumbles. Patio. Booking
advisable.
Typical dishes Pan-fried Brie & almonds
£3.50 Chicken breast & avocado £6

Credit Access, Visa

STUCKTON   *Three Lions*

Stuckton Road,   `FOOD`
Fordingbridge SP6 2HF
Area Map 7 F4 *Hampshire*
Fordingbridge (0425) 52489
Parking *ample*

Bar food *12.15–1.30 (Sun from 12) &
7.30–9 (Sat till 9.30)*
Closed *Sun eve & all Mon*

Landlords *Karl-Hermann & June
Wadsack*
Free house
🍺 *Wadworth 6X; Ind Coope Burton Ale;
Guinness; Castlemaine XXXX;
Löwenbräu.* 🍷 ⊖

German-born Karl-Hermann Wadsack's
superb cooking is the best available in any
bar in the country, although the smart red-
brick building is now strictly more of a
restaurant than a pub. Don't just drop in for
a drink! The blackboard menu changes
daily, offering delicious starters such as
flavourful, port-enriched game soup, salmon mousse with salmon roe, and Karl-
Hermann's own gravadlax. Game from the
nearby New Forest (including pheasant and
venison in season) features among main
courses, alongside Scotch salmon, veal
escalopes with mushrooms and a stunning
fricassee of seafood in a creamy, aromatic
curry sauce. Beautifully fresh accompanying vegetables are faultlessly prepared, and
sweets include rich, dark chocolate pot,
banana pancakes and hot apple strudel.
Carefully selected European cheeses are
served with celery or grapes, and there is
good strong coffee to follow. Booking
essential.

Typical dishes Spinach and cheese strudel £3.20 Sea bream with a lime and lemon
glaze £7.80 Medallions of venison £9.50
Chocolate marquise £3.25

Credit Access, Visa

SUMMERHOUSE   NEW ENTRY   *Raby Hunt Inn*

Nr Darlington DL2 3UD   `FOOD`
Map 4 D2 *Co. Durham*
Piercebridge (032 574) 604
Parking *ample*

Bar food *11.30–2*
No bar food *eves & all Sun*

Landlord *Mike Allison*
Free house ☙
🍺 *Theakston Best Bitter; Cameron
Strongarm; Bass (weekends only); guest
beers.*

Generous helpings of Barbara Allison's old-
fashioned home cooking bring lunchtime
appetites to a former farmhouse in a lovely
setting among rolling fields. Sandwiches,
salads, egg and ham flan, Cumberland
sausage and a daily roast show the range,
completed by a few simple sweets. The
lounge bar makes up in warmth what it
lacks in character, and visitors can always
rely on a friendly welcome from the whole
family.
Typical dishes Roast beef & vegetables
£2.90 Steak pie & vegetables £2.50

SURBITON   *Oak*

Maple Road KG6 4BX   FOOD
Map 10 D3 *Surrey*
01-399 1662
Parking *ample*

Bar food *12–2, Sun 12.30–2.30*
No bar food *eves*

Landlord *Mr V. Harrison*
Brewery *Charrington*
🍺 *Charrington IPA; Bass; Guinness;
Tennent's Extra; Carling Black Label.*

The Oak is spacious and pleasing, with wooden venetian blinds and rag-rolled dado panelling. You can eat anywhere (there is a separate dining room for families), but the food is appetisingly displayed along the mahogany counter of a separate bar. Home-cooked ham, beef, coronation turkey and pâté are always on offer, and there is a daily-changing choice of hot dishes. Garden.
Typical dishes Steak & kidney pie £3.50
Cauliflower cheese £3.50

SUTTON   *Anne Arms*

Suttonfield Road, Nr   FOOD
Doncaster DN6 9JX
Map 4 D3 *South Yorkshire*
Doncaster (0302) 700500
Parking *ample*

Bar food *12–2 & 7–9*
No bar food *Sun* 🌣

Landlords *Mr & Mrs J.R. Simms*
Brewery *John Smith*
🍺 *John Smith's Bitter; Guinness; John
Smith's Lager; Hofmeister.*
No real ale.

Locals are loyal to the Anne Arms, whose latest addition is a conservatory reached through an anteroom inhabited by caged birds. Besides a warren of ornament-filled rooms there is a garden packed with things for kids (but don't bring under-fives). Food is self-service, with an array of home-cooked dishes like braised lamb chops, lasagne and a roast, plus chips, fresh vegetables and salads. Apple pie and sherry trifle among the sweets.
Typical dishes Turkey escalopes £2.50
Deep-dish lasagne £2.50

SUTTON   *Sutton Hall*

Bullocks Lane, Nr   FOOD
Macclesfield SK11 0HE   B&B
Map 3 C4 *Cheshire*
Sutton (02605) 3211
Parking *ample*

Bar food *12–2.30 & 6.30–10*

Landlords *Robert & Phyllida Bradshaw*
Free house
🍺 *Bass, 4X Mild; Stones Bitter; Marston
Burton Bitter; Guinness; Tennent's
Extra.* ⊖

A splendid house dating from around 1500–1520 which was once a baronial residence, then a convent and is now an extremely atmospheric, attractive inn. Exposed beams, flagstone floors, fine old period furniture and roaring open fires make the bars mellow and traditional and you can enjoy some good bar food in these delightful surroundings. The food on offer ranges from standard fare such as pies and ploughman's to more imaginative dishes like duck and claret soup, seafood bake and moussaka with good garlic bread. More elaborate meals are served in the separate restaurant.

Typical dishes Chicken pancake £4.55
Steak & kidney pie with oysters £4.55

Accommodation *9 bedrooms* **£A G1**
Check-in all day

The homely, very characterful bedrooms, some panelled and some half timbered, are reached by a fine carved staircase; all have four-poster beds and solidly beautiful furniture. They are equipped with dressing gowns, trouser presses, tea-making facilities and compact, carpeted bathrooms – and one even boasts a priest's hole. Garden. Children are welcome overnight.

Credit Access, Amex, Visa

SUTTON HOWGRAVE
White Dog Inn

Nr Ripon DL8 2NS   `FOOD`
Area Map 4 D3 *North Yorks*
Melmerby (076 584) 404
Parking *ample*

Bar food *12–2*
No bar food *eves*
Closed *Sun eve & all Mon*

Landlord *B. H. Bagnall*
Free house
🍺 *Webster Pennine Bitter; Carlsberg Hof*. No real ale. 🍷

The pub's namesake, though fondly remembered in photos, has been replaced by a black dog, but little else has changed. The two bars are still as intimate as a villager's front room, with individual touches like hand-painted china ashtrays. Order at the bar and the landlady brings the meal, perhaps chicken and mushroom casserole with plenty of flavour, or inch-thick golden brown pastry-topped venison pie.
Typical dishes Fish pie £3.25 Chocolate roulade £1.75

SYMONDS YAT WEST
Old Court Hotel

Nr Ross-on-Wye HR9 6DA   `B&B`
Map 6 E3 *Hereford & Worcs*
Monmouth (0600) 890367
Parking *ample*

Landlords *John & Elizabeth Slade*
Free house ☕
🍺 *Flowers Original; Ruddles County; guest beer; Heineken; Stella Artois.*

Accommodation *20 bedrooms* **£B G2**
Check-in all day

Dating back over 400 years, this lovely manor house near the river Wye has a neat garden complete with swimming pool and children's play area. Inside, public areas like the oak-panelled bar and lofty Tudor dining room are full of period character, as are the spacious main-house bedrooms (three with four-posters). Remaining rooms in a modern wing are compact and well equipped, all offering private facilities. *No children under 12 overnight.*

Credit Access, Amex, Diners, Visa

TALKIN VILLAGE
Hare & Hounds Inn

Nr Brampton CA8 1LE   `FOOD`
Map 3 B1 *Cumbria*   `B&B`
Brampton (069 77) 3456
Parking *ample*

Bar food *12–1.30 & 7–9* ☕

Landlords *Joan & Les Stewart*
Free house
🍺 *Theakston Best Bitter, Old Peculier, XB; Hartley XB; Carlsberg.* ☕

Once used by monks as a resting place on the way from Armathwaite to Lanercost Priory, this homely 200-year-old village inn remains a pleasant place either to eat or to stay under the care of Joan and Les Stewart. Popular snacks are served in the traditional bars; these range from filled jacket potatoes (Talkin tatties) and generously layered sandwiches to pizzas, steaks, fried chicken and poached rainbow trout. Daily specials like pork in cider, beef in beer or spaghetti bolognese ring the changes, and there are plenty of ice cream-based sweets for afters, such as chocolate nut sundae or banana split. Children have their own menu of amusingly named dishes.

Typical dishes Rainbow trout £3.75 Barbecued bangers £2.25

Accommodation *4 bedrooms* **£D G2**
Check-in all day

One of the two handsomely furnished en suite bedrooms boasts a four-poster bed, while the remaining two rooms are more modern and functional in style. All four have washbasins, and TV is available in the simply furnished, upstairs residents' lounge. Garden. *No dogs.*

TANGLEY   NEW ENTRY   *Fox Inn*

Nr Andover SP11 0RU   `FOOD`
Map 10 B3 *Hampshire*
Chute Standen (0264 70) 276
Parking *ample*

Bar food *12–2 & 6.30–10*
No bar food *Sun eve*

Landlords *John & Gwen Troke*
Free house
● *Eldridge Pope Royal Oak; Bass; Courage
Best Bitter; Guinness; Kronenbourg
1664.* ▼

Well worth the diversion off the A343, the
Fox is a remote country pub with a
welcoming atmosphere in its tiny bars.
Here snacks like soup, ploughman's, filled
jacket potatoes and curries can be enjoyed,
while in the cosy restaurant more imaginative dishes (which can also be ordered in the
bar) such as Stilton-stuffed mushrooms,
chicken breast with fresh anchovies and
swordfish steak in garlic and lemon are
carefully prepared by Gwen Troke.
Typical dishes Chicken tarragon £2.50
Apple strudel £1.20

TARRANT MONKTON   *Langton Arms*

Nr Blandford Forum   `FOOD`
DT11 8RX   `B&B`
Area Map 7 D4 *Dorset*
Tarrant Hinton (025 889) 225
Parking *ample*

Bar food *11.30–2 & 6–10.30, Sun 12–
2.30 & 7–10* ☙

Landlords *Diane & Chris Goodinge*
Free house
● *Bass; Wadworth 6X; Toby Bitter;
Guinness; Carling Black Label; Tennent's
Lager.* ⊖

Thatched and creeper-clad, this mellow red-
brick pub in Hardy country is everybody's
idea of a traditional village inn. There is a
splendid 'local' atmosphere in the beamed
main bar, where a wide range of home-
cooked fare is available. Soup and pâté,
ploughman's, steak and kidney pudding
and fisherman's pie are all popular favourites from the regular menu, while the
blackboard offers more elaborate daily
specials: perhaps carrot and orange soup
followed by beef and aubergine curry or
braised lamb's hearts. Leave room for a
dessert such as gooey treacle tart or goose-
berry fool. Evenings bring speciality
themes for different nights of the week –
pizzas every Tuesday and Friday, for
example, and Chinese on Thursdays.

Typical dishes Braised oxtail and
dumplings £2.40 Lentil and onion soup £1

Accommodation *6 bedrooms* **£C G2**
Check-in by arrangement

Three single-storey blocks built around the
courtyard house six spacious bedrooms, all
furnished in pine and sporting pretty
duvets and curtains. TVs, tea-makers, telephones and large tiled bathrooms
throughout.

Credit Access, Amex, Diners, Visa

TEDDINGTON   *Clarence Hotel*

19 Park Road TW11 0AQ   `B&B`
Map 10 C3 *Middlesex*
01-977 8025
Parking *ample*

Landlords *Graham & Lorna Keeble*
Free house
● *Wadworth 6X; Ruddles County;
Guinness; Budweiser; Foster's.*

Accommodation *18 bedrooms* **£B G2**
Check-in by arrangement

New owners have refurbished accommodation at this sturdy town-centre pub. Light
and airy colour schemes, attractive fabrics
and modern furnishings (some with light
units, others dark) create a pleasant effect
and all rooms have duvets, remote-control
TVs and trouser presses. Downstairs, the
spacious bar with a small bistro area has a
lively, informal atmosphere and there is
also a separate nightclub (which can get
noisy). Terrace.

Credit Access, Visa

TERRINGTON   *Bay Horse Inn*

Nr York YO6 4PP   `B&B`
Area Map 3 B4 *North Yorks*
Coneysthorpe (065 384) 255
Parking *ample*

Closed *Mon lunch winter (ex. Bank Hols)*

Landlords *Mr & Mrs Stirk & Mr & Mrs Addy*
Free house
🍺 *John Smith's Bitter, Magnet Bitter; Carlsberg Hof. No real ale.*

Accommodation *4 bedrooms* **£D G3**
Check-in all day

Enthusiastic new owners have plans to refurbish the accommodation at their spotlessly kept village inn dating back over 400 years. At the time of our visit, the four rooms shared a single bathroom (soon to be increased to two) and had a neat, simple appeal. Downstairs, the atmosphere is relaxed and informal in the two cosy beamed bars with their crackling winter fires and open stone walls brightened by brass and copper pieces.

TESTCOMBE   *Mayfly*

Nr Stockbridge SO20 6AZ   `FOOD`
Map 7 B3 *Hampshire*
Chilbolton (026 474) 283
Parking *ample*

Bar food *12–2 (Sun till 2.30) & 7–9* 🍷

Landlord *Mr B. Lane*
Brewery *Whitbread*
🍺 *Flowers Original; Strong Country Bitter; Guinness; Heineken; Stella Artois.* 🍷

Visitors to the Mayfly can settle inside or outside depending on the weather: inside, in the quaintly traditional bar or bright conservatory, or out in the beer garden right beside the fast-flowing river Test. Bar food includes soup, salads from a help-yourself buffet, cold cuts, quiches and roasts, but for many the choice is a selection from an excellent array of mainly French cheeses.
Typical dishes Baked sugar ham £3 Selection of cheeses £2.50

Credit Access, Visa

THAMES DITTON   *Albany*

Queens Road KT7 0QY   `FOOD`
Map 10 C3 *Surrey*
01-398 7031
Parking *ample*

Bar food *12–2.30*
No bar food *eves*

Landlords *Dave & Wendy Weston*
Brewery *Charrington*
🍺 *Charrington IPA; Bass; Fullers ESB (winter only); Guinness; Tennent's Extra.* 🍷

Admire Hampton Court from the riverside terrace of this spacious Victorian pub offering a popular lunchtime buffet. Homecooked ham and beef, decent cheeses, quiche, pâté and salmon mousse can all be enjoyed with crisp salads, while the hot choice embraces soup, jacket potatoes, hearty cassoulet and steak and vegetable pie. Traditional roast Sunday lunch available. Book for waitress service, restaurant-style meals Monday to Thursday evenings.
Typical dishes Shooter's roll £2.95 Baked banana cream pie £1.25

THETFORD   *Historical Thomas Paine Hotel*

White Hart Street IP24 1AA   `B&B`
Map 8 E1 *Norfolk*
Thetford (0842) 755631
Parking *ample*

Landlord *Thomas Muir*
Free house
🍺 *Adnams Bitter; Stones Bitter; McEwan's Export; Carlsberg Hof.*

Accommodation *14 bedrooms* **£B G2**
Check-in all day

Reputedly the birthplace, in 1737, of the political pamphleteer Thomas Paine, this white-painted hotel offers good facilities. There is a spacious bar and, for residents, a split-level lounge with small circular tables for afternoon tea. Bedroom colour schemes range from autumnal to pink, and all have modern furniture, TV and beverage facilities. All but one have en suite bathrooms. Children welcome overnight. Accommodation closed three days Christmas, two days New Year.

Credit Access, Amex, Diners, Visa

THORNHAM   Lifeboat Inn

Ship Lane, Nr Hunstanton   FOOD
PE36 6LT   B&B
Map 8 E1 *Norfolk*
Thornham (048 526) 236
Parking *ample*

Bar food *12–2.30 & 7–10* ☙

Landlord *Nick Handley*
Free house
● *Greene King Abbot Ale, IPA; Adnams
Bitter; Carlsberg; Stella Artois.* ▮ ⊖

Sixteenth-century whitewashed stone farm
buildings in a charming rural setting make
the Lifeboat Inn a characterful pub. Low-
beamed ceilings, low doors and plenty of
rustic implements and copper jugs create a
mellowed atmosphere in the bars, and
families can relax in the knowledge that
there is a separate menu, room and outdoor
play area to keep the children happy.
Summer sees a buffet and barbecue under a
bright awning in the garden with interesting fare such as swordfish, frogs' legs and
red snapper on offer, as well as particularly
good composite salads and hearty hot
dishes like beef pepperpot. In the winter the
latter come to the fore and there is also a
deal of seafood, particularly local oysters
and mussels.

Typical dishes Fisherman's pie £4.75
Treacle tart & ice cream £1.35

Accommodation *2 bedrooms* **£D G2**
Check-in by arrangement

The two cottage bedrooms have a simple
appeal, with traditional furniture and TVs.
They share a neat bathroom. Accommodation closed two days Christmas. Garden,
patio, terrace.

Credit Access, Amex, Diners, Visa

TICHBORNE   Tichborne Arms

Nr Alresford SO24 0NA   FOOD
Map 7 C4 *Hampshire*
Alresford (096 273) 3760
Parking *ample*

Bar food *11.30–2 & 6.30–10, Sun 12–2
& 7–9.30*

Landlords *Chris & Peter Byron*
Free house
● *Wadworth 6X; Courage Best Bitter,
Directors; Tetley Bitter; Bass; Heineken.* ⊖

Real ales are served from the cask here in a
tiny red-brick, thatched pub in a picturesque rural hamlet in the Itchen valley. Home-
made soup, filled jacket potatoes, sandwiches and salads are supplemented by
daily specials such as flavoursome pork
and cider casserole, lasagne and poached
local trout. Leave room for an excellent
steamed syrup sponge and custard or bread
pudding.
Typical dishes Carrot and orange soup
£1.20 Pork and cider casserole £3.75

TIVETSHALL ST MARY   Old Ram

Ipswich Road, Norwich   FOOD
NR15 2DE
Map 8 F1 *Norfolk*
Pulham Market (037 976) 8228
Parking *ample*

Bar food *11.30 am–10 pm*

Landlord *Mr J. Trafford*
Free house
● *Webster Yorkshire Bitter, Greene King
Abbot Ale; Ruddles County; Budweiser.*

The charm of the beamed bar with its stone
floor and brick fireplace, coupled with the
attraction of home-made food, makes this a
highly popular venue, particularly with
families. There is always at least one
vegetarian dish on offer and fresh fish is
emphasised in the daily specials – you
might find cod, plaice, trout, salmon, turbot
and crab. Garden, terrace.
Typical dishes Steak & kidney pie £3.50
Lasagne £3.50

TORMARTON   *Compass Inn*

Nr Badminton GL9 1JB   `B&B`
Map 10 A3 *Avon*
Badminton (045 421) 242
Parking *ample*

Landlords *Monyard family*
Free house
🍺 *Wadworth 6X; Bass; Archers Village; Beck's Bier; Carlsberg Hof.*

Accommodation *19 bedrooms* **£A G1**
Check-in all day

Set amongst six acres of gardens, this creeper-clad coaching inn is conveniently placed for both the M4 and the M5, and makes a popular overnight stop with travellers and business people. Two extensions house the majority of good-sized bedrooms, which all now offer en suite bathrooms as well as TVs, tea-makers and direct-dial telephones. The characterful, Cotswold-stone bars and delightful enclosed orangery provide contrasting drinking venues. Garden. Children welcome overnight.

Credit Access, Amex, Diners, Visa

TOWERSEY   *Three Horseshoes*

Chinnor Road, Nr Thame   `FOOD`
OX9 3QY
Map 10 C2 *Oxfordshire*
Thame (084 421) 2322
Parking *ample*

Bar food *12–2 & 7–10*

Landlords *Mr & Mrs Worsdell*
Brewery *Aylesbury*
🍺 *ABC Bitter; Beechwood; Guinness; Carlsberg; Castlemaine XXXX.* 🍷 ☺

Parts of this red-brick pub date back as far as the 13th century, and it was once used as a milking parlour. Now the food is the high point. Starters include deep-fried mushrooms with garlic mayonnaise and minted fruit cup, followed by beef in beer, kidneys turbigo, vegetarian lasagne or split pea cutlets with apple rings. Steaks, fish, omelettes, salads and sandwiches complete the range.

Typical dishes Minted lamb & leek pie £3.45 Stuffed peppers £5.40

Credit Access, Visa

TREBARWITH   *Mill House Inn*

Nr Tintagel PL34 0HD   `B&B`
Map 9 B2 *Cornwall*
Camelford (0840) 770200
Parking *ample*

Landlords *Howard family Liddiard-Jenkin*
Free house ☙
🍺 *Flowers Original, IPA; Whitbread Best Bitter; Guinness; Heineken; Stella Artois.*

Accommodation *9 bedrooms* **£C G3**
Check-in by arrangement

Set in a dramatic wooded valley near the beach and cliffs of Trebarwith Strand, this converted corn mill retains much of its original character in the massively beamed and flagstoned bar. Residents have their own peaceful lounge, and there is a children's/games room. Homely bedrooms with pine furnishings and modern bathrooms (three not en suite) offer TVs, tea-makers, hairdryers and radio intercoms. Accommodation closed Christmas week. *No children under ten overnight.*

Credit Access, Visa

TRENT   NEW ENTRY   *Rose and Crown*

Nr Sherborne DT9 4SL   `FOOD`
Area Map 7 B3 *Dorset*
Marston Magna (0935) 850776
Parking *ample*

Bar food *12–2 & 7–9.30 (Sat till 10)*

Landlords *Chas & Nancy Marion-Crawford*
Free house
🍺 *Wadworth 6X; Fullers London Pride; Oakhill Farmers Best Bitter; Butcombe Bitter; Graf Arco Lager.* 🍷 ☺

Deep in rural Dorset is a gem of a pub – white painted, thatched and refreshingly unpretentious inside with its rug-strewn stone floor and log fires. Excellent bar food ranges from simple but delicious ham and eggs or cheese-topped steak sandwich to celeriac rémoulade, scampi in Pernod and venison with orange and juniper. Pleasant sweets and a good cheeseboard (including Dorset Blue Vinney). Garden.

Typical dishes Seafood pie £4.75 Boursin chicken £5.25

TROUTBECK   **Mortal Man**

LA23 1PL
Area Map 1 E3 *Cumbria*   **FOOD**
Ambleside (053 94) 33193   **B&B**
Parking *ample*

Closed *mid Nov–mid Feb*

Landlords *Annette & Christopher
Poulsom*
Free house
🍺 *Younger's Scotch; McEwan's Export;
Guinness; McEwan's Lager.*

A hotchpotch of antique seating, gleaming copper-topped tables, beams, horse brasses, pewter tankards, hunting horns and views of a gentle green valley through the windows give the bars at the Mortal Man plenty of rustic charm. One is kept mainly for residents, but it provides an overspill when the public bar is full. There is a plentiful supply of food on offer such as vegetable soup, lovely fresh summer salads with salmon mayonnaise, smoked trout, garlic sausage, rollmop herring and Cumberland sausage and, in the winter, a predominance of hot dishes like beef and vegetable pie.

Typical dishes Game pie £3.50 Spinach tortellini £4

Accommodation *12 bedrooms* **£A G1**
Check-in all day

The bedrooms are clean and comfortable, with attractive, homely decor in coordinated colours and well-cared-for furniture. All have smart, clean, en suite bathrooms, TVs and entrancing views. Housekeeping is excellent. Half board only. Garden. *No children under five overnight.*

Prices given are as at the time of our research and thus may change.

TUNBRIDGE WELLS   NEW ENTRY   **Sankey's**

39 Mount Ephraim TN4 8AA **FOOD**
Area Map 6 F2 *Kent*
Tunbridge Wells (0892) 511422
Parking *difficult*

Bar food *12–2.30 & 7–10*
No bar food *Sun*
Closed *Bank Hols*

Landlord *Guy Sankey*
Free house
🍺 *Harvey IPA; Murphy Stout; Beck's
Bier.* 🍷

Fresh fish dominates the menu at this friendly pub created by Guy Sankey from an old engineering works in a solid, late-Victorian house. The choice embraces fish soup, plump poached mussels and Dover sole as well as more elaborate offerings like stuffed baked grey mullet and the Australian fish barramundi. Fillet steak and a vegetarian daily special are also available, plus an outstanding spotted dick.
Typical dishes Aubergine parmigiana £3 Wing of skate £8

Credit Access, Amex, Diners, Visa

TURVILLE   **Bull & Butcher**

Nr Henley-on-Thames   **FOOD**
RG9 6QU
Map 10 C2 *Buckinghamshire*
Turville Heath (049 163) 283
Parking *ample*

Bar food *12–2 & 7.30–10*

Landlords *Peter David Wright, Sandie
Watson & Evie Harris*
Brewery *Brakspear*
🍺 *Brakspear Pale Ale, Special, Old;
Guinness; Stella Artois.* 🍷

A pretty black and white timbered pub with the inimitable atmosphere of the village local. Inside the black-beamed bar a large blackboard menu lists a range of fare such as soup, steak, gammon steak, beef and Guinness casserole, salads, Greek dips and Mediterranean prawns. Typical desserts are walnut pie and chocolate bombe. Monday nights in winter bring a fixed-price dinner (booking only), and in summer a barbecue in the garden.
Typical dishes Brakspear pie £4.50 Bo-peep Pie £4.50

TUTBURY   *Ye Olde Dog & Partridge*

High Street DE13 9LS
Map 7 B1 *Staffordshire*
Tutbury (0283) 813030
Parking *ample*

Bar food *12–2 & 6.30–10 (Sat 6.15–10.30), Sun 12–2.15 & 7.15–9.30*

Landlady *Mrs Y. Martindale*
Free house
🍺 *Marston Pedigree, John Marston; Bass; Marston Pilsner Lager; Stella Artois.* 🍷 ⊖

A splendid 15th-century half-timbered coaching inn offering a fine choice of food in its cosy, oak-beamed bars. The carvery is especially popular (it is essential to book there for Sunday lunch) and everything is very fresh and attractively presented, from imaginative salads, colourful starters like egg Mimosa decorated with prawns and excellent cold meats to such tempting hot dishes as crispy spit-roasted duckling served with black cherries in Kirsch. Look out for Staffordshire Tipsy Apple among desserts, or choose the well-kept Stilton and Cheshire cheeses.

Typical dishes Sirloin of beef £5.75 Apple charlotte £1.50

Accommodation *17 bedrooms* £A G1
Check-in all day

Three bedrooms in the main building have all the quaint character of beams and sloping floors, while best bedrooms (with four-posters) are in an adjacent Georgian town house. All offer en suite facilities, as well as TVs, tea-makers, direct-dial telephones and bedside radio-alarms. Garden and patio. *No children under ten overnight.*

Credit Access, Amex, Diners, Visa

We publish annually so make sure you use the current edition.

UMBERLEIGH   *Rising Sun*

EX37 9DU   B&B
Map 9 B1 *Devon*
High Bickington (0769) 60447
Parking *ample*

Landlords *Paul & Sandy Turner*
Free house
🍺 *Webster Yorkshire Bitter; Usher Triple Crown; Ruddles County; Guinness; Carlsberg; Foster's.*

Accommodation *6 bedrooms* £C G1
Check-in all day

Fishing rights on the neighbouring river Taw makes this 17th-century roadside inn a haven for salmon and trout anglers, and a rod room, racks and drying cabinets are provided. The cosy lounge bar has a very traditional appeal, and there is a flagstoned public bar and intimate residents' lounge. The bedrooms are charming, pretty little rooms with pine furniture, trouser presses, tea-makers, phones and TVs. Friendly, obliging staff are another plus. *No children under 14 overnight. No dogs.*

Credit Access, Amex, Diners, Visa

UPPER ODDINGTON   *Horse & Groom Inn*

Nr Stow-on-the-Wold   B&B
GL56 0XH
Area Map 4 D1 *Gloucs*
Cotswold (0451) 30584
Parking *ample*

Landlords *Mr & Mrs Howarth & Mr & Mrs Evans*
Free house
🍺 *Wadworth 6X; Hook Norton Best Bitter; Guinness; Löwenbräu; Castlemaine XXXX.*

Accommodation *8 bedrooms* £C G2
Check-in all day

Rustic character and charm abound in the cosy beamed and flagstoned bars of this 16th-century Cotswold inn surrounded by lovely countryside. Enjoy a pint by the fine inglenook fireplace or out in the garden, where a super play area, animals and an aviary keep the children happy. Eight appealing, comfortable bedrooms (including two in a separate cottage) with pretty fabrics and modern furnishings all have en suite facilities (mainly showers), TVs and tea-makers. Children welcome overnight. *No dogs.*

UPTON GREY — Hoddington Arms

Nr Basingstoke RG25 2RL FOOD
Map 7 C3 *Hampshire*
Basingstoke (0256) 862371
Parking *ample*

Bar food *12–2 & 7.30–9.30*
No bar food *Sun eve* ☙

Landlords *Ian & Irene Fisher*
Brewery *Courage*
🍺 *Courage Best Bitter; Directors; John Smith's Yorkshire Bitter; Beamish Stout; Foster's; Kronenbourg.* ⊖

Ian and Irene Fisher share the cooking at their welcoming 18th-century village pub. In the warm and inviting bars (or pleasant garden when it is fine), tuck into lunchtime offerings such as garlic mushrooms, seafood pie, country lentil crumble or a cheese platter served with crusty granary bread. Similar but more expensive evening selection of starters and main courses, including Ian's popular grilled steaks.
Typical dishes Seafood mornay £3 Moules marinière £2.95

Credit Visa

UTTOXETER — White Hart Hotel

Carter Street ST14 8EU B&B
Map 7 B1 *Staffordshire*
Uttoxeter (0889) 562437
Parking *ample*

Landlord *David D. Eccles*
Brewery *Allied Lyons*
🍺 *Ind Coope Burton Ale; Ansells Bitter, Mild; Guinness; Löwenbräu; Skol.*

Accommodation *26 bedrooms* **£B G1**
Check-in all day

Characterful accommodation is offered here at a black and white half-timbered hostelry. Spacious bedrooms (one with a four-poster and fine panelling) feature antique furnishings and bedsteads. All now have en suite facilities, including some splendid freestanding tubs, and TVs, telephones and teamakers are standard throughout. Downstairs, there is a convivial split-level bar and a small residents' lounge. Note the handsome 16th-century oak panelling in the function suite. Children welcome overnight.

Credit Access, Amex, Diners, Visa

WALKERN — White Lion

High Street SG2 7PA FOOD
Map 10 D1 *Hertfordshire*
Walkern (043 886) 251
Parking *ample*

Bar food *12–2 & 7–9.30*
No bar food *Sun & Mon eves*

Landlords *Mike & Jenny Windebank*
Brewery *Greene King*
🍺 *Greene King Abbot Ale; IPA; Guinness; Kronenbourg; Harp.* 🍷 ⊖

Freshly painted on the outside, warm and welcoming within, the Windebanks' 400-year-old pub makes a charming place to stop for a snack. Sound home cooking rules in the cosy beamed bar, where the choice ranges from soup and sandwiches to honeyroast duckling and mussels in wine with cream and herbs. Good cheeses and homely sweets like rhubarb crumble for afters. Garden.
Typical dishes Chilli con carne £3.50 Sausage and chips £1.50

WALL — Hadrian Hotel

Nr Hexham NE46 4EE B&B
Map 3 C1 *Northumberland*
Humshaugh (043 481) 232
Parking *ample*

Landlords *Kevin & Helen Kelly*
Brewery *Vaux*
🍺 *Vaux Samson; Lorimer's Best Scotch; Guinness; Stella Artois; Tuborg; Labatts.*

Accommodation *9 bedrooms* **£C G3**
Check-in all day

New landlords Kevin and Helen Kelly plan to redecorate the presently unassuming bedrooms, which would be a welcome move. Three are en suite, most of the others have shower units, and the two public bathrooms are clean and adequate. Teamakers and TVs are standard. Downstairs the bar and foyer/lounge are warm and inviting with deep luxurious armchairs and a coal fire in winter. An excellent base for visiting Hadrian's Wall and other Roman sites in the area.

Credit Access, Visa

WALTHAM ON THE WOLDS
Royal Horseshoes

Melton Road, Nr Melton Mowbray LE14 4AJ   `B&B`
Map 7 C1 *Leicestershire*
Waltham (066 478) 289
Parking *ample*

Landlords *Mr & Mrs Wigglesworth*
Brewery *John Smith*
🍺 *John Smith's Yorkshire Bitter; Courage Directors; Kronenbourg 1664; Foster's; Hofmeister.*

Accommodation *4 bedrooms* **£C G2**
Check-in by arrangement

A dazzling summer display of begonias outside the thatched old village pub and gleaming brass and oak within the single bar characterise the care and pride with which it is run by Mr and Mrs Wigglesworth. Compact modern bedrooms on the first floor of a skilfully converted stable block all have good lightwood furniture, duvets and tea-makers. Carpeted en suite bathrooms are spotlessly kept. Patio. Children welcome overnight. *No dogs.*

WARBLETON   NEW ENTRY
The War-Bill-in-Tun Inn

Nr Heathfield TN21 9BD   `FOOD`
Area Map 6 F3 *East Sussex*
Rushlake Green (0435) 830636
Parking *ample*

Bar food *12–2 & 7–9.30*

Landlords *Valerie & Bryan Whitton*
Free house
🍺 *Harveys Bitter; Flowers Original; John Smith's Bitter; Foster's; Stella Artois; Heineken.*

Food is a serious matter here: Bryan Whitton was for 30 years Crowborough's Master Butcher, and daily expeditions find the best in fish and vegetables. The menu runs from sandwiches, seafood and meat platters to curries, grills, steaks and sweets, with a roast for Sunday lunch. Staff at this 16th-century inn provide a particularly friendly welcome, paying personal attention to each customer.
Typical dishes Pheasant in grape sauce £6.95 Apricot and brandy gâteau £1.30

Credit Access, Visa

WARENFORD
Warenford Lodge

Nr Belford NE70 7HY   `FOOD`
Map 2 D5 *Northumberland*
Belford (066 83) 453
Parking *ample*

Bar food *12–1.30 & 7–9.30*
Closed *Mon lunch (except Bank Hols) & Mon eve & Tues lunch (Nov–April)*

Landlord *Ray Matthewman*
Free house
🍺 *McEwan's Best Scotch; Newcastle Exhibition; Drybrough Heavy; Carlsberg Pilsner.*

Look out for the village sign on the A1 or you could miss a meal to remember. The main pub building is full of character, solid stone with mullioned windows; inside all is cosy and friendly, the bar being a comfortably furnished L-shaped room on two levels. Ray Matthewman sees to the drinks, while his wife does a marvellous job in the kitchen; her menu changes twice yearly and her meals are the equal of anything in this part of the world. Dishes devoured with relish on a recent visit included plump grilled mussels with a light breadcrumb, parsley and garlic topping; Andalucian vegetable casserole – a generous serving of mixed vegetables, butter beans, bacon, ham and smoked sausage, perfectly seasoned and bursting with flavour; and an excellent Fen Country apple cake with molasses. Prawn fritters, salmon salad and lamb hotpot are other favourites, with ginger ice cream also among the sweets.

Typical dishes Grilled mussels £2.50 Cannelloni £3.50 Chicken curry £4.50 Choux swan £1.95

Credit Diners, Visa

WARMINSTER — Old Bell Hotel

Market Place BA12 9AN
Area Map 7 D1 *Wiltshire*
Warminster (0985) 216611
Parking *ample*

FOOD
B&B

Bar food *12–2*
No bar food *eves*

Landlord *Howard Astbury*
Brewery *Wadworth*
🍺 *Wadworth 6X; Hall & Houdhouse Tanglefoot; Guinness; Heineken; Stella Artois.* ⊖

Dominating Warminster's market place, this handsome old coaching inn boasts a fine colonnaded facade and an inner courtyard where al fresco lunches can be enjoyed. On cooler days the traditional beamed Chimes Bar makes a comfortable alternative setting for satisfying, straightforward dishes like home-made broth followed by, say, cottage pie, turkey curry or liver and bacon, with homely bread and butter pudding or apple crumble for afters. A cold buffet is always available, while Sundays bring a traditional roast lunch. Dinner can be taken in the cosy restaurant.

Typical dishes Beef curry £2.50 Steak and kidney pie £2.50

Accommodation *24 bedrooms* **£C G2**
Check-in all day

Neat and simply furnished bedrooms (recently increased by the addition of four en suite doubles in a new extension) offer functional overnight accommodation and front-facing rooms are protected from market noise by double glazing. Direct-dial telephones, TVs and tea-makers are standard throughout and over half offer private bath/shower facilities. The garden incorporates a children's play area. Children welcome overnight.

Credit Access, Amex, Diners, Visa

WARREN STREET — Harrow Inn

Nr Lenham ME17 2ED
Area Map 5 C2 *Kent*
Maidstone (0622) 858727
Parking *ample*

FOOD
B&B

Bar food *12–2.30 & 7–11, Sun 12–3 & 7–10.30*

Landlords *Sheila Burns & Alan Cole*
Free house
🍺 *Shepherd Neame Master Brew Bitter; Fremlins Bitter; Goacher Bitter; guest beer; Carlsberg Hof.* ⊖

Once the forge and rest house for travellers to Canterbury along the Pilgrim's Way, this carefully converted inn enjoys a peaceful downland setting yet is conveniently close to the A20 and the M2. Sturdy wooden furniture gleams with polish in the large, comfortable lounge bar warmed by a winter fire, and there is a pleasant garden for milder days. Light, creamy Camembert soup, hearty beef carbonnade and a decidedly stylish lobster salad typify the imaginative range of the bar menu, while puddings include spotted dick and whisky-enriched orange fool. Traditional roast Sunday lunch available.

Typical dishes Ham & lentil soup £1.10 Braised ox tongue with mustard sauce £5.25

Accommodation *7 bedrooms* **£C G2**
Check-in all day

Warm, well-kept bedrooms contrast dark-wood furniture with white walls and softly coloured carpets and curtains. Two share a neat public bathroom and the remainder have en suite facilities. Telephones are a recent addition, and a chintzy residents' lounge with TV is available. Accommodation closed four days Christmas. Children welcome overnight. *No dogs.*

Credit Access, Visa

WARRINGTON   Barley Mow

Golden Square WA1 1QB `A`
Map 3 B4 *Cheshire*
Warrington (0925) 51182
Parking *difficult*

Landlady *Susan Haskey*
Brewery *Tetley Walker*
🍺 *Ind Coope Burton Ale; Tetley Bitter,
Mild; Castlemaine XXXX; Skol;
Löwenbräu.* 🍷

A splendid genuine Tudor facade is
matched by an equally handsome interior
at this lively, atmospheric pub standing at
the end of a contrastingly modern shopping
precinct. Revamped throughout with a
sensitive touch, the rooms and bars retain
their historic charm with a wealth of oak
beams and panelling set off by old prints.
Note the particularly attractive book-lined
'library' room, ideal for a quiet browse
while enjoying a well-kept pint. Patio.

WARWICK-ON-EDEN   Queen's Arms Inn

Nr Carlisle CA4 8PA `B&B`
Map 3 B1 *Cumbria*
Wetheral (0228) 60699
Parking *ample*

Landlord *Tony Wood*
Free house
🍺 *Tetley Bitter; Theakston Best Bitter;
Marston Pedigree; Younger's Scotch;
Guinness; Castlemaine XXXX.*

Accommodation *7 bedrooms* **£D G2**
Check-in all day

Close to junction 43 of the M6, this pleasant
18th-century inn makes a convenient stopover. Neatly kept bedrooms (including
three in a separate cottage) feature attractive new floral fabrics and all offer TVs,
radio-alarms, tea-makers and compact
bathrooms (most with shower only). A sofa
bed and good-sized work area are useful
extras. Victorian prints and a display of
china add a homely note in the panelled bar
and there's a children's playground and
garden. Children welcome overnight.

Credit Access, Amex, Diners, Visa

WASDALE HEAD   Wasdale Head Inn

Nr Gosforth CA20 1EX `FOOD`
Area Map 1 C3 *Cumbria* `B&B`
Wasdale (094 06) 229
Parking *ample*

Bar food *11–2.50 & 6–10, Sun 12–2.50
& 7–10* 🍽
Closed *Mon–Fri (mid Jan–mid Mar &
mid Nov–28 Dec)*

Landlord *Mr E. Hammond*
Free house
🍺 *Jennings Bitter; Theakston Best Bitter;
Old Peculier; Yates Bitter; Slalom D;
Carlsberg.* 🍷 ☕

Accommodation *11 bedrooms* **£A G2**
Check-in all day

Standing in a secluded position at the head
of a particularly lovely and unspoilt Lakeland valley, this delightful inn is a haven for
walkers and climbers. In the homely, flagstone-floored Ritson Bar (named after a
former landlord, the 'World's Biggest Liar'),
good sound traditional fare is served.
Typical choices might include help-yourself French onion soup, beef bourguignon,
chicken casserole and meat pies, with
English farmhouse cheeses to finish. Residents have their own cosy little bar (note the
fine carved oak settles) and relaxing lounge
with an abundant stock of books and
magazines. A pool room and panelled
restaurant are also available for overnight
guests.

Typical dishes Cumberland tattie pot
£3.20 Shepherd's pie £2.25

Most of the comfortable, unfussy bedrooms
enjoy splendid views and all have modern
carpeted bathrooms, snug duvets and tea-
makers. Garden and patio. Accommodation
closed mid-January to mid-March and mid-
November to 28 December. *Half-board
terms only.*

Credit Access, Visa

WATERLEY BOTTOM — New Inn

North Nibley, Dursley `B&B`
GL11 6EF
Map 10 A2 *Gloucestershire*
Dursley (0453) 3659
Parking *ample*

Landlady *Ruby Sainty*
Free house
🍺 *Greene King Abbot Ale; Theakston Old Peculier; Smiles Best, Exhibition; Cotleigh Tawny, WB.*

Accommodation *2 bedrooms* **£D G3**
Check-in by arrangement

Narrow, winding country lanes lead to Ruby Sainty's extensively modernised old pub nestling in a beautiful secluded valley. The beamed lounge bar, which overlooks the delightful garden and its well-equipped play area, makes a characterful setting for a pint of excellent real ale. Pretty fabrics contrast with crisp white walls and furnishings in the neat, bright bedrooms. Both rooms have TVs and tea-makers and share a good modern bathroom. Children welcome overnight. *No dogs.*

WATH-IN-NIDDERDALE — Sportsman's Arms

Pateley Bridge, Nr `FOOD`
Harrogate H33 5PP `B&B`
Area Map 2 E4 *North Yorks*
Harrogate (0423) 711306
Parking *ample*

Bar food *12–2*
No bar food *eves*

Landlords *Ray & Jane Carter*
Free house
🍺 *Younger's Scotch; McEwan's Export; Guinness; Harp; Beck's Bier.* ⊖

Accommodation *6 bedrooms* **£C G2**
Check-in all day

An old sandstone coaching inn, set back from the road and reached by a windy drive crossing a hump-backed bridge, the Sportman's Arms is split into lounge, dining room and bar, where locals gather in the evenings to play dominoes. Both bar and restaurant (evenings and Sunday lunch only) always put on a fish special, often Nidderdale trout served in a variety of ways. Otherwise there is chicken liver pâté with good texture and flavour or roast best end of lamb with spinach and garlic pastry parcels in a herb and tomato sauce. Sweets are imaginative and tasty – passion cake, lemon torte. Traditional Sunday lunch can also be had in the bar.

Typical dishes Wath rarebit £3.80 Chicken sautéed with onions, mushrooms and garlic £4.25

Residents have the use of a lounge. Bedrooms are all good-sized, neat and well-kept with pretty fabrics, pine furniture and colour TVs. Two rooms are en suite while the remaining four share two bathrooms. Children welcome overnight.

Credit Access, Amex, Diners, Visa

WATTON-AT-STONE — George & Dragon

SG14 3TA `FOOD`
Map 10 D2 *Hertfordshire*
Ware (0920) 830285
Parking *ample*

Bar food *12–2 & 7.15–10*
No bar food *Sun*

Landlords *Christine & Kevin Dinnin*
Brewery *Greene King*
🍺 *Greene King IPA, Abbot Ale, XX Mild; Guinness; Harp; Kronenbourg 1664.*
No real ale. ⊖

A pink pebbledash pub where the bars are always busy at mealtimes, and the tables all have either candles or three-branch candelabras as a centrepiece. Millionaire's bun, which is fillet steak in a toasted roll with salad garnish, is popular, and weekly-changing specials might include seafood cooked in red wine and brandy, and calf's kidneys in a cream and Calvados sauce. Limited choice Saturday lunchtime.

Typical dishes Corsican fish soup £3 Pork fillet in chilli and lime £4

Credit Access, Amex, Diners, Visa

WELFORD-ON-AVON · Shakespeare Inn

Chapel Street CV37 8PX `FOOD`
Map 10 A1 *Warwickshire*
Stratford-upon-Avon (0789) 750443
Parking *ample*

Bar food *12–2 & 7–9.30*
No bar food *Sun eve*

Landlords *Mike & Jan Shaw*
Brewery *Whitbread*
🍺 *Flowers Original, IPA, Best; Guinness; Stella Artois.*

The menu looks ordinary, but everything is fresh and tasty at the Shakespeare, as a strong local following testifies. Ploughman's platters, pizzas, pot pies, jacket potatoes and omelettes are popular choices, along with daily specials like tagliatelle with a ham, cauliflower and tomato sauce. The pace is more leisurely in the evening, when trout, roast chicken, steaks and mixed grills join the repertoire.
Typical dishes Quiche £2.85 Treacle tart £1.05

Credit Access, Visa

WELL · Chequers

Nr Odiham RG25 1TL `A`
Map 7 C3 *Hampshire*
Basingstoke (0256) 862605
Parking *ample*

Closed *2 wks after Xmas*

Landlord *Robert Collins*
Free house
🍺 *Flowers Original; Marston Pedigree; Whitbread Best Bitter; Guinness; Stella Artois; Heineken.*

Deep in the heart of the Hampshire countryside, this 17th-century pub continues to provide a retreat from the modern world and an opportunity to enjoy the old-world charm. A flourishing vine covers the patio outside, and inside, the homely, quaint bar features low wooden ceilings, panelled walls and lots of old beams. Horse brasses, candlestick holders and other bric-a-brac add to the scene of country life – an ideal setting for a quiet drink.

Credit Access, Diners, Visa

Our inspectors never book in the name of Egon Ronay's Guides.

They disclose their identity only if they are considering an establishment for inclusion in the next edition of the Guide.

WENDRON · New Inn

Nr Helston TR13 0EA `B&B`
Map 9 A3 *Cornwall*
Helston (0326) 572683
Parking *ample*

Landlords *Bill & Gloria Standcumbe*
Brewery *Cornish Brewery Company*
🍺 *Cornish Wessex Royal; Newquay Steam Bitter; Guinness; Heineken; Stella Artois.*

Accommodation *2 bedrooms* £D G3
Check-in by arrangement

Landlords Bill and Gloria Standcumbe have been here for 16 years and have recently given their village pub a thoughtful face-lift. Outside, the new inn sign and harvest gold walls act as a colourful backdrop to hanging baskets, and within plush red carpets and varnished pine panelling combine well. The public bar retains a more traditional look. The two modest bedrooms have TVs and kettles, and share a bathroom. Accommodation closed two weeks at Christmas. *No children under 14 overnight. No dogs.*

WEOBLEY   *Red Lion Hotel*

Nr Hereford HR4 8SE   `FOOD`
Map 6 D3 *Hereford & Worcs*   `B&B`
Weobley (0544) 318220
Parking *ample*

Bar food *12–2 & 7–9.30*

Landlord *E.J. Townley-Berry*
Free house
🍺 *Flowers Original; Whitbread Best Bitter;*
Heineken. ⊖

In a picture-postcard village of black-and-white half-timbered houses stands a well-run little inn dating from the 14th century. A huge copper-canopied fireplace, exposed stone walls, old settles and comfortable sofas make the heavily beamed lounge bar a most inviting spot in which to enjoy simple lunchtime snacks: soup and sandwiches, pâté, ploughman's and egg mayonnaise. Hot and cold dishes are available at both sessions (except Sundays) in the pleasant carvery room, while the restaurant (12–2 & 7–9, Fri & Sat 7.30–9.30) offers more substantial meals such as hearty steak, mushroom and oyster pie accompanied by ample fresh vegetables. Tempting sweets include rich sherry trifle, profiteroles and butterscotch and walnut gâteau.

Typical dishes Steak sandwich £3.90 Chocolate fudge cake £1.75

Accommodation *7 bedrooms* £B G2
Check-in all day

Fresh curtains and some new furnishings have brightened the efficiently heated, individually decorated bedrooms, all of which are spotlessly kept and extremely smart and comfortable. Some boast brass beds and each has a private bath or shower room. Children welcome overnight.

Credit Access, Visa

WEST BEXINGTON   *Manor Hotel*

DT2 9DF   `B&B`
Map 7 A4 *Dorset*
Burton Bradstock (0308) 897785
Parking *ample*

Landlords *Richard & Jayne Childs*
Free house
🍺 *Wadworth 6X; Eldridge Pope Royal Oak;*
Palmer Bitter; Murphy Stout; Carlsberg.

Accommodation *10 bedrooms* £A G1
Check-in all day

Just a short walk from Chesil Bank is an old manor house offering ample space for relaxation in its stone-walled cellar bar and residents' lounge; and on sunny days the leafy conservatory is a delight. Books, magazines and dried flower arrangements add a homely, individual touch to the simply furnished bedrooms, all of which offer TVs, tea-makers, hairdryers and well-equipped private facilities. Accommodation closed two weeks Christmas. Children welcome overnight. *No dogs.*

Credit Access, Amex, Visa

WEST BROMWICH   *Manor House*

Hallgreen Road B71 2EA   `FOOD`
Map 7 B1 *West Midlands*
West Bromwich (021 588) 2035
Parking *ample*

Bar food *12–2 & 6–10 (Sat till 11,*
Sun 7–10)

Landlords *Lena & John D. Walker*
Brewery *Banks's*
🍺 *Banks's Bitter, Mild; Hanson's Black*
Country Bitter; Guinness; Kronenbourg
1664; Harp. ⊖

A derelict Victorian tenement used to hide this moated medieval manor house, now carefully restored and enjoying a new lease of life as a charming and atmospheric pub. The help-yourself servery offers a good daily variety of home-made dishes, including a flavoursome chicken curry packed with chunky meat, together with soup, ploughman's, cold meat salads and cheeses. Garden with play area. Children's menu.

Typical dishes Spaghetti bolognese £2.45 Beef and vegetable pie £2.45

Credit Access, Amex, Visa

WEST ILSLEY   *Harrow*

Nr Newbury RG16 0AR
Area Map 4 F5 *Berkshire*
East Ilsley (063 528) 260
Parking *ample*

`FOOD`
`B&B`

Bar food *12–2 & 7–9.30* ☙

Landlady *Heather Humphreys*
Brewery *Morland*
🍺 *Morland Mild, Bitter, Best Bitter;*
Guinness; Kaltenberg. ☙

Accommodation *2 bedrooms* **£D G3**
Check-in by arrangement

Christmas dinner is the only meal they do not serve in the Harrow, a friendly, down-to-earth inn overlooking the village pond and cricket green. Furnishings are simple and traditional, with one bar set mainly for eating, the other with log fire and darts. There is a decent choice of generously served, home-prepared fare, including soup, burgers, steaks, substantial main courses, cheese, ice creams and puddings. Sandwiches, too, and a couple of vegetarian dishes. Our latest visit showed standards staying starworthy with pleasures like fish pot in a creamy sauce, the heartiest of rabbit pies and a tangy fudge pie. Value for money is outstanding. Other features are a traditional Sunday lunch, children's room, menu and garden with play area.

Typical dishes Rabbit pie with lemon, bacon and herbs £3 Plaice with a spicy prawn stuffing £4.75 Home-baked ham with cider & raisin sauce £5.95 Carrot cake with cream cheese and honey £1.75

Two modest rooms with washbasins and tea-makers share a bathroom. The pub is well placed to receive weary walkers from the nearby Ridgeway Walk.

Credit Access, Visa

WEST LULWORTH   *Castle Inn*

BH20 5RN
Map 9 D2 *Dorset*
West Lulworth (092 941) 311
Parking *ample*

`B&B`

Landlords *Pat & Graham Halliday*
Brewery *Devenish*
🍺 *Devenish Wessex, Dry Hop, John Groves;*
Guinness; Steam Pils; Foster's.

Accommodation *14 bedrooms* **£C G2**
Check-in all day

Long and low under its heavy Dorset thatch is a quaint 17th-century roadside pub offering ample drinking space in its country-style bars (mind your head on the hanging pewter tankards) and large terraced rose garden to the rear. All but two of the homely bedrooms now have en suite facilities (sizes vary greatly), while thoughtful extras include biscuits, sweets, books and magazines as well as duvets, tea-makers and TVs. Children welcome overnight.

Credit Access, Amex, Diners, Visa

WEST PENNARD   *Red Lion*

Glastonbury BA6 8NN
Area Map 7 A2 *Somerset*
Glastonbury (0458) 32941
Parking *ample*

`B&B`

Landlords *Bryan & Caroline Channing*
Free house ☙
🍺 *Red Lion Best Bitter; Butcombe Bitter;*
Hall & Woodhouse Tanglefoot;
Worthington Best Bitter; Guinness;
Hofbräu.

Accommodation *7 bedrooms* **£B G1**
Check-in all day

A typical Somerset exterior with greystone walls, black timbers and shutters softened by pretty patches of garden and flowers. Inside, the low-ceilinged bars feature flagstone floors and exposed stonework. The bedrooms are situated in a converted barn away from the main building. Light, airy and comfortable, they are all equipped with TVs, dial-out phones, clock-radios and en suite bathrooms that are well fitted by pub standards. *No dogs.*

Credit Access, Visa

WEST WITTON   *Wensleydale Heifer*

Nr Leyburn DL8 4LS   `B&B`
Area Map 2 D2 *North Yorks*
Wensleydale (0969) 22322
Parking *ample*

Landlords *Major & Mrs Sharp*
Free house
🍺*John Smith's Bitter; Tetley Bitter;
McEwan's Export; Tuborg; Carlsberg
Hof.*🍺

Accommodation *19 bedrooms* £B G1
Check-in all day

Bedrooms have benefited from a recent
facelift at this 17th-century inn set amongst
lovely countryside on the A684 Leyburn-
Hawes road. New chintzy fabrics and
wallpapers have been used, and three
bedrooms in the main house (half are in
adjacent cottages) boast four-posters. TVs
and tea-makers are standard, and all have
neat private bath/shower rooms. Downstairs, drinks can be enjoyed in both the
beamed reception-lounge and cosy panelled
bar. Children welcome overnight.

Credit Access, Amex, Diners, Visa

WEST WYCOMBE   *George & Dragon*

High Street HP14 3AB   `FOOD`
Map 10 C2 *Buckinghamshire*   `B&B`
High Wycombe (0494)
464414
Parking *ample*

Bar food *12–2 (Sun till 1.45) & 6–10*
No bar food *Sun eve* ☙

Landlords *Mr & Mrs P. Todd*
Brewery *Courage*
🍺*Courage Directors, Best Bitter;
Guinness; Foster's; Kronenbourg
1664.*🍺 ⊖

Accommodation *10 bedrooms* £B G2
Check-in all day

A cobbled archway entrance is one of
several original features here at a Tudor
coaching inn, which reputedly extend to the
ghost of a 'White Lady'. Set in the National
Trust village beside the A40, period appeal
continues inside with large oak beams,
settles and Windsor chairs by roaring fires.
Friendly staff offer a promising menu
ranging from half a pint of prawns with dip
or Stilton and walnut pâté to an exemplary
stuffed pepper with tasty beef filling, a
blackboard special, and regular Cumberland sweet lamb pie. Follow with a rich,
gooey treacle tart or baked apple. Ploughman's, simple sandwiches and vegetarian
options are also available. Children's play
area in the garden.

Typical dishes Seafood pancakes £3.10
Lancashire hotpot £3.15

Creaking floors, ancient oak beams and
antique furniture, including a single four-
poster bed, compensate for the rooms' small
size. All are well equipped with TVs,
telephones and en suite bathrooms.
Unkempt stairways detract from good
housekeeping in rooms.

Credit Access, Amex

WESTON   *White Lion*

Nr Crewe CW2 5NA   `FOOD`
Map 6 E1 *Cheshire*   `B&B`
Crewe (0270) 500303
Parking *ample*

Bar food *12–2 (Sun till 1.45) & 7–9.30*

Landlords *Alison & Gordon Davies*
Brewery *Ind Coope*
🍺*Tetley Bitter; Ind Coope Burton Ale,
Bitter, Mild; Guinness; Löwenbräu.* ⊖

Alison and Gordon Davies offer a friendly
welcome and good eating at this black and
white village pub dating back to 1652.
Wooden settles, horse brasses and tack
characterise the atmospheric beamed bar,
and there is a bowling green in the garden if
you feel the need to work off lunch. Plates
come piled high here, whether your choice
is a toasted sandwich (perhaps featuring
chicken, bacon, lettuce and mayonnaise),
cold Dee salmon salad, a meat platter or the
daily-changing, weekday lunchtime roast.
A wide range of sandwiches and rolls is

also available, including filled granary batch cakes, while home-made sweets and fine cheeses round things off nicely.

Typical dishes Prawns in garlic butter £4.95 Tomato and tarragon soup 80p

Accommodation *17 bedrooms* **£B G1**
Check-in all day

A sympathetically designed extension with its own entrance and reception area houses the spacious bedrooms (including two suites). All have compact en suite bath or shower rooms. Accommodation closed one week Christmas. Children welcome overnight.

Credit Access, Amex, Diners, Visa

WHATCOTE   *Royal Oak*

Nr Shipston-on-Stour   `A`
CV36 5EF
Map 10 B1 *Warwickshire*
Tysoe (029 588) 319
Parking *ample*

Landlords *Matthews family*
Free house 🍷
🍺 *Marston Pedigree; Flowers Best Bitter; Guinness; Heineken; Stella Artois.*

Steeped in history, the Royal Oak has been an ale house for 800 years. Oliver Cromwell was quartered here during the Battle of Edge Hill, and in the huge inglenook fireplace are rungs leading to what could have been a hiding place. The beams in the bar are low enough to connect with unwary heads, and there are curios and knick-knacks all around. Outside are the remains of the tree that gave the inn its name. There is a garden for enjoying an al fresco pint.

WHITEWELL   *Inn at Whitewell*

Forest of Bowland, Nr   `FOOD`
Clitheroe BB7 3AT   `B&B`
Area Map 2 A5 *Lancashire*
Dunsop Bridge (020 08) 222
Parking *ample*

Bar food *12–2 & 7.30–9.30* 🍷

Landlord *Richard Bowman*
Free house
🍺 *Moorhouse Premier Bitter; Webster Yorkshire Bitter; Wilson Special Mild; Guinness; Carlsberg Hof.* 🍷 ☕

The handsome Inn has a splendid position above the River Hodder with views over unspoilt Lancashire countryside. A lounge/hall has oak tables and a fine fireplace; the tap room bar hums with local chatter. Food here is enjoyable and good. A robust home-made soup – no marks for subtlety but plenty for flavour – contains proper stock. Ham carved from the bone is accompanied by crisp salad and trifle or sticky toffee pudding (made by local ladies) are first-rate. English cheeses from Lancashire to Ribblesdale goat and ewe are complemented by high-quality AOC wines by the glass, although their L'Ecaillère vin de table is very drinkable.

Typical dishes Steak and kidney pie £3.50 Cumberland sausage with onion sauce £3.50

Accommodation *11 bedrooms* **£C G1**
Check-in all day

Characterful bedrooms of good size and proportions are attractive with warmly patterned wallpaper, period wardrobes and chests of drawers. Six of the eleven have adequate private facilities, the others sharing a clean, modern public bathroom. Garden.

Credit Access, Amex, Diners, Visa

John Selden
1854–1654

'Tis not the eating, nor 'tis not the drinking that is to
be blamed, but the excess.
Table Talk

Leon de Fos

For the man who would eat like a glutton,
A good stomach is worth more than mutton,
For what use is the best
If you cannot digest,
And your teeth are exceedingly rotten.
'Gastronomia'

William Shakespeare
1564–1616

Will the cold brook, candied with ice, caudle thy
morning taste, to cure thy o'-er-night's surfeit.
Timon of Athens

Mauduit

Intoxication . . . embraces five stages: jocose,
bellicose, lachrymose, comatose, and morotose.
The Vicomte in the Kitchen (1933)

Anonymous

The glances over cocktails
That seemed to be so sweet
Don't seem quite so amorous
Over the Shredded Wheat.
'Wine, Women and Wedding'

WHITNEY-ON-WYE *Rhydspence Inn*

HR3 6EU
Map 6 D3 *Hereford & Worcs*
Clifford (049 73) 262
Parking *ample*

Bar food *12–1.45 & 7–9.30*

Landlords *Peter & Pam Glover*
Free house
🍺 *Robinson Best Bitter; Wem Best Bitter;*
Mitchells & Butlers DPA; Guinness;
Carling Black Label. 🍷 ⊖

Flanked by two large terraces from which splendid views over the Wye Valley and Black Mountains can be enjoyed, this ancient half-timbered inn straddles the border between England and Wales. Inside, the heavily beamed bar is warmed by an open fire in winter. From simple but delicious snacks like grilled fresh sardines, crusty bread sandwiches and beef pasties served with chutney to more substantial offerings such as lemon sole mornay, vegetarian curry, succulent steaks and rack of lamb, all is imaginative and appetising. Seasonal specialities featuring game and seafood appear on the blackboard menu, while to finish there are home-made sweets and fine selection of English cheeses. Traditional roast lunch on Sundays.

Typical dishes Venison with ginger and walnut marinade £8.75 Devon farm sausages £3.25

Accommodation *5 bedrooms* **£C G1**
Check-in all day

Five attractively decorated bedrooms with beams and sloping floors all have private bathrooms as well as an armchair each, tea-makers and colour TVs. Children welcome overnight. *No dogs*.

Credit Access, Amex, Visa

WHITTLESFORD NEW ENTRY *Tickell Arms*

Village Green, North Road
CB2 4NZ
Map 10 D1 *Cambridgeshire*
Cambridge (0233) 833128
Parking *ample*

Bar food *10.30–2 (Sun from 12) & 7–10*

Landlords *S. Fisher & K. Tickell*
Free house
🍺 *Greene King IPA; Abbot Ale.* 🍷 ⊖

Eccentrically run by one Kim Tickell for over 25 years, the Tickell Arms is a favourite haunt of Cambridge undergraduates despite rude signs listing those the landlord won't serve (wearers of long hair, earrings, waistcoats without jackets, etc). Yet the pub itself, disguised as a mid-Victorian manor with ornate Gothic windows, is painted vivid navy blue and has taped opera played at disco decibels. Lovely walled garden and good food.
Typical dishes Dressed crab with salad £5.20 Lasagne £4.85

---

*Changes in data sometimes occur
in establishments
after the Guide goes to press.*

*Prices should be taken as indications
rather than firm quotes.*

WICKHAM   Five Bells

Nr Newbury RG16 8HH   `B&B`
Area Map 4·E5 *Berkshire*
Boxford (048 838) 242
Parking *ample*

Landlady *Mrs D. A. Channing-Williams*
Brewery *Usher*
🍺 *Usher Best Bitter; Webster Yorkshire Bitter; Ruddles County; Guinness; Carlsberg.* 🍷

Accommodation *4 bedrooms* **£C G2**
Check-in all day

On the Newbury-Lambourn road, the mellow thatched Five Bells boasts a large garden complete with children's swimming pool. Log fires warm the handsome beamed bar, where a good selection of ales and wines by the glass are served. An adjoining stable block houses four neat, bright bedrooms with simply painted walls and pretty curtains. They share a spacious bathroom and all have washbasins, TVs and tea-makers. Standards of housekeeping could be improved. Children welcome overnight.

Credit Access, Visa

WIDECOMBE-ON-THE MOOR   NEW ENTRY   Old Inn

Moretonhampstead   `FOOD`
TQ13 7TA
Map 9 C2 *Devon*
Widecombe (036 42) 207
Parking *ample*

Bar food *11.30–2 & 7–10 (summer 11.30–3 & 6.30–10), Sun 12–2.30 & 7–10*

Landlords *A. & S. Boult*
Free house 🛏
🍺 *Widecombe Wallop; Usher Best Bitter, Country Bitter; Guinness; Carlsberg; Skol.*

A 14th-century Dartmoor inn standing right next to St Pancras Church, known as the 'Cathedral of the Moors', with its 120-foot spire. The Old Inn has an extensive bar menu that ranges from soup and sandwiches via mackerel pâté to chicken curry, lamb in gin sauce and the popular country fish pie – a well-sauced mix of white fish, prawns and mushrooms under a mashed potato topping. There is a wider, and costlier, evening selection.
Typical dishes Stilton pâté £2 Vegetarian curry £3

WILLERBY   Grange Park Hotel, Cedars

Main Street, Nr Hull   `FOOD`
Map 4 E3 *Humberside*
Hull (0482) 656488
Parking *ample*

Bar food *12–2.30 (Sun till 2) & 6–10.30* 🛏

Landlord *Michael Bortano*
Free house
🍺 *Cameron Strongarm, Bitter; Guinness; Hansa.* ⊖

A combination of factors makes this an excellent family pub – parkland setting, all-day eating (snacks, sandwiches, pastas, morning coffee, carvery lunch, afternoon teas) plus children's play area, menu and portions. Service via uniformed waitresses in the restaurant is efficient and friendly. Daily specials might be minestrone served with a warm baguette or mildly curried chicken supreme.
Typical dishes Tagliatelli Bolzano £2.80 Sirloin steak (8oz) £4.95

Credit Access, Amex, Diners, Visa

WILMCOTE   NEW ENTRY   Mason's Arms

Nr Stratford-upon-Avon   `FOOD`
CV37 9XX
Map 10 A1 *Warwickshire*
Stratford (0789) 297416
Parking *ample*

Bar food *12–2 & 6–9.30*
No bar food *Sun eve (all Sun in winter)*

Landlord *Mr Snow*
Brewery *Whitbread*
🍺 *Whitbread Best Bitter; Flowers IPA, Original; Guinness; Stella Artois, Heineken.*

Wilmcote was the home of Shakespeare's mother, Mary Arden, and is just a short drive from Stratford along the A34. Right in the centre, the Mason's Arms is noteworthy for its interesting and well prepared bar food. Crispy squid rings or leek and potato soup might be followed by roast duck legs with black cherry sauce, poached salmon or pork kebabs with a spicy barbecue sauce. Sweets include rum banana mousse.
Typical dishes Lasagne £3.50 Lemon sole £6.50

Credit Access, Visa

WILMCOTE   **Swan House Hotel**

Nr Stratford-on-Avon
CV37 9XJ
FOOD
B&B
Map 10 A1 *Warwickshire*
Stratford (0789) 67030
Parking *ample*

Bar food *12–2 & 7–9.30 (Sun till 9)*

Landlords *Ian & Diana Sykes*
Free house
🍺 *Wadworth 6X; Hook Norton Best Bitter; Guinness; Carlsberg Hof, Pilsner.* 🍷 ☕

Accommodation *12 bedrooms* **£C G1**
Check-in all day

First-rate landlords Ian and Diana Sykes run their extremely friendly pub in exemplary fashion. It is a tall white-painted inn with a modern extension housing a well planned reception area. The bar is bright and cheerful, and serves freshly prepared bar snacks such as minestrone soup, mushroom omelette, jacket potatoes, steaks, pies and sandwiches. The restaurant (12–2 & 7.30–9.30) is spruce and immaculate, and the menu offers tender sautéed chicken livers with crisp croûtons, Dover sole, veal cordon bleu and grilled poussin. Sweets from the trolley include an enjoyable charlotte russe.

Typical dishes Steak & mushroom pie £3.25 Roast duck £4.25

Redecoration is progressively improving the bedrooms – most now have floral wallpapers and white furniture which give a cheerful look. All have en suite facilities, TVs, radio-alarms and tea-makers. One room sports a four-poster, while an executive suite includes a spa bath. Accommodation closed four days January, three days Christmas. *No dogs.*

Credit Access, Amex, Visa

Any person using our name to obtain free hospitality is a fraud.

Proprietors, please inform Egon Ronay's Guides and the police.

WINCHELSEA   **Winchelsea Lodge Motel**

Sandrock, Hastings Road
B&B
TN36 4AD
Area Map 5 B5 *East Sussex*
Rye (0797) 226211
Parking *ample*

Landlord *George Morgan*
Free house
🍺 *Webster Yorkshire Bitter; Ruddles Best Bitter; John Smith's Bitter; Kronenbourg 1664; Hofmeister; Carlsberg.*

Accommodation *24 bedrooms* **£C G2**
Check-in all day

A modern, impersonal establishment in sharp contrast to the quaint architecture of the ancient Cinque Port, Winchelsea Lodge offers quiet, private accommodation ideal for an overnight stay. The main bar is modern and large, with a peaked ceiling, and the bedrooms are situated at the rear of the building. All the rooms are identical, with brick walls, brown and beige furnishings and neat functional bathrooms. Two ground-floor rooms are suitable for the disabled. Children welcome overnight.

Credit Access, Amex, Diners, Visa

WINCHESTER   **Wykeham Arms**

75 Kingsgate Street
SO23 9PE
Map 5 C3 *Hampshire*
Winchester (0962) 53834
Parking *limited*

Bar food *12–2 & 6.45–8.45*
No bar food *Mon eve & all Sun*

Landlords *Graeme & Anne Jameson*
Brewery *Eldridge Pope*
🍺 *Eldridge Pope Royal Oak, Original IPA, Dorchester Bitter; Guinness; Faust Pilsner; Labatt's.* 🍷 ⊖

Accommodation *8 bedrooms* **£B G1**
Check-in all day

FOOD
B&B

An extremely well-run and characterful town pub hidden in the narrow cobbled streets near the school and cathedral. Jo Dockerty's skill and enthusiasm attract lovers of good food with such delights as Stilton and quince pâté, salmon fillet in filo pastry with ginger Hollandaise, or pan-fried pigeon breast with juniper and Madeira. Traditional pub fare also get a good look-in, with bangers and mash and cottage pie among the favourites; and soup, ploughman's, toasties and baked potatoes available for quicker snacks. Sweets are very good, too (prune and Armagnac tart, bread and butter pudding) and excellent wines accompany the fine food.

Typical dishes Lamb, watercress & mushroom bake £3.95 Salmon steamed in sake £8.95 Poached chicken breast with watercress mousseline £6.95 Crème brûlée £2.25

Bedrooms, individually and tastefully furnished by Anne Jameson, all have TVs, radio-alarms, dial-out phones and beverage trays. Five include en suite facilities, and residents have their own sauna. *No children under 14 overnight. No dogs.*

WINFORTON   **Sun Inn**

HR3 6EA
Map 6 D3 *Hereford & Worcs*
Eardisley (054 46) 677
Parking *ample*

Bar food *12–2 & 7–9.45 (Sun till 9)*
Closed *Tues in winter*

Landlords *Brian & Wendy Hibbard*
Free house
🍺 *Felinfoel Double Dragon; Robinson Best Bitter; Wadworth 6X; Flowers Best Bitter; Guinness; Stella Artois.* ⊖

FOOD

The Hibbards have run things here with genuine enthusiasm for five years now. A blackboard menu in the delightfully rustic, stone-walled bar of this roadside pub near the Welsh borders on the A438 offers everything from watercress soup and lunchtime sandwiches to cheesy seafood crumble, vegetable lasagne and venison pie. Finish with summer pudding, chocolate ginger crunch or cherries Jubilee. Children's menu and garden with play area.
Typical dishes Lamb casserole £4.25 Salmon in puff pastry £6.50

WINFRITH NEWBURGH   **Red Lion**

Nr Dorchester DT2 8LE
Map 7 A4 *Dorset*
Warmwell (0305) 852814
Parking *ample*

Landlords *Mike & Libby Smeaton*
Brewery *Hall & Woodhouse* ⊗
🍺 *Hall & Woodhouse Tanglefoot, Badger Best, Export Bitter; Guinness; Hofbrau Royal, Export.*

Accommodation *4 bedrooms* **£D G3**
Check-in all day

B&B

Cared for by the Smeaton family for over 40 years, this creeper-clad pub was rebuilt in 1965 after a fire destroyed the original 14th-century building. The main bar is pleasantly rustic with its beams and solid wooden furnishings, while the public bar retains its old flagstone floor. Upstairs, there is a multi-purpose lounge and four neat, homely bedrooms with floral wallpapers, candlewick bedspreads and simple white furniture. All have TVs and share an adequate bathroom. Garden and play area.

Credit Visa

WINKFIELD   Olde Hatchet

Hatchet Lane, Nr Ascot   FOOD
SL4 2EE
Map 10 C3 *Berkshire*
Bracknell (0344) 882303
Parking *ample*

Bar food *12–2.30 & 7–9.30*
No bar food *Sun eve*

Landlady *Christine Mace*
Brewery *Charrington*
🍺 *Charrington IPA; Bass; Guinness;*
Carling Black Label; Tennent's Extra,
Pilsner. ✆

Conifers and umbrella-topped tables at the
front and a garden to one side mark this
charming black and white country pub.
Straightforward, enjoyable snacks are
served in the low-beamed bar, with choices
like smoked chicken salad, ploughman's
with cheese, pâté or sausages, mushroom
soup and daily specials such as barbecued
spare ribs. Good service and presentation
(shame about the canned pop music).
Typical dishes Smoked salmon hoagie
£2.75 Whitebait and salad £2.50

Credit Access, Amex, Visa

WINKTON   Fisherman's Haunt Hotel

Salisbury Road,   B&B
Christchurch BH23 7AS
Area Map 7 F5 *Dorset*
Christchurch (0202) 484071
Parking *ample*

Landlord *James J. Bochan*
Free house ☎
🍺 *John Smith's Bitter; Worthington Best*
Bitter; Ringwood Best Bitter; Carling Black
Label; Carlsberg.

Accommodation *19 bedrooms* £C G2
Check-in all day

The river Avon runs alongside the grounds
here, at an immaculately kept, wisteria-clad
pub. Stuffed fish and an old well with
running spring water are unusual features
of the characterful beamed bars, and there
is an airy conservatory and cosy TV
lounge. Spotless bedrooms in the main
17th-century building, extended coach
house and nearby cottage blend pretty
fabrics with a mixture of modern and
traditional furnishings. Most offer en suite
facilities and all have TVs and telephones.

Credit Access, Amex, Diners, Visa

WINSFORD   Royal Oak Inn

Exmoor National Park   FOOD
TA24 7JE   B&B
Map 9 C1 *Somerset*
Winsford (064 385) 455
Parking *ample*

Bar food *12–2 (Sun till 1.30) & 7.30–9.30*

Landlord *Charles Steven*
Free house ☎
🍺 *Flowers Original, IPA; Guinness; Stella*
Artois; Heineken. 🍴 ✆

Winsford is a sleepy Exmoor village resist-
ant to street lighting and noise, the only
sound at night coming from the rustling
stream which bisects the village green.
The Royal Oak fulfils two functions –
firstly it is the local pub and secondly a
civilised and tranquil inn. Bar food has an
emphasis on good honest soup and excellent home-made savoury pies, such as
chicken and ham served with a crisp salad.
The restaurant (12–2 and 7.30–9.30) offers a
very English choice, deserving of praise for
both presentation and service. Menus
change daily, but favourites are venison,
lamb, duckling, veal and fish with good
soups among the starters.

Typical dishes Game pie £4.45 Steak &
kidney pudding £4.45

Accommodation *14 bedrooms* £A G1
Check-in all day

The bedrooms are either in the main house
or the modern annexe, recently refurbished.
Very well equipped, they are all en suite and
in tip-top order. Charles Steven is an
ebullient landlord who will ensure your
well-being, and breakfast is also a plus.
Children welcome overnight. *No dogs.*

Credit Access, Amex, Diners, Visa

WINSLOW   *Bell Hotel*

Market Square MK18 3AB   `B&B`
Map 10 C2 *Buckinghamshire*
Winslow (029 671) 2741
Parking *ample*

Landlords *Mr & Mrs William Alston*
Free house ☎
🍺 *Hook Norton Old Hookey; Adnams
Bitter; Marston Pedigree; Carlsberg Hof;
Foster's.* 🍷

Accommodation *15 bedrooms* **£B G1**
Check-in all day

Beer pumps that used to splatter the
floorboards in coaching inn days are all still
intact. Today the Georgian facade looks
superiorly over the market square. Heavy
beams, oak and leather furniture and an
inglenook fireplace complete the period
picture. Three bedrooms are in a separate
stable block. All are spacious with traditional furnishings. En suite facilities are
standard with one bedroom using a public
bathroom. TVs, telephones and tea-makers.
Pleasant first-floor residents' lounge.

Credit Access, Visa

WINTERTON-ON-SEA   *Fisherman's Return*

The Lane NR29 4BN   `B&B`
Map 8 F1 *Norfolk*
Winterton-on-Sea (049 376) 305
Parking *ample*

Landlords *John & Kate Findlay*
Brewery *Norwich* ☎
🍺 *Ruddles Best Bitter, County; Webster
Yorkshire Bitter; Carlsberg; Foster's;
Budweiser.* 🍷

Accommodation *4 bedrooms* **£D G2**
Check-in by arrangement

Its proximity to the village, the dunes and
the sea is just one of the attractions of the
Fisherman's Return, a brick and flint pub
dating back 300 years. Two snug, wood-
panelled bars are well populated with
locals, and upstairs there is a small residents' lounge with TV. The bedrooms are
neatly decorated, and their low doors,
sloping ceilings and small windows give
them plenty of character; one has a small
sitting room with Victorian furniture. Garden and patio.

WITHINGTON   *Mill Inn*

Nr Cheltenham GL54 4BE   `A`
Area Map 4 B2 *Gloucs*
Withington (024 289) 204
Parking *ample*

Landlady *Mrs Foley*
Brewery *Samuel Smith* ☎
🍺 *Samuel Smith's Old Brewery Bitter,
Museum Ale, Extra Stout; Ayingerbräu;
Prinz Lager.*

Splendid low-beamed ceilings, large open
fireplaces and stone walls combine with
simple rustic furnishings and country-style
artefacts to re-create the original atmosphere of this 500-year-old inn. Set in the
midst of a quaint Cotswold village, and
built to accommodate workers from the
nearby mill, inside it is delightfully traditional, but it also has a lovely garden by
the river Coln, complete with ducks, providing an idyllic setting for peaceful summer
drinking.

WITHYPOOL   *Royal Oak Inn*

Nr Minehead TA24 7QP   `B&B`
Map 9 C1 *Somerset*
Exford (064 383) 506
Parking *ample*

Landlords *Mr & Mrs Bradley & Mr &
Mrs Lucas*
Free house
🍺 *Usher Best Bitter; Ruddles County;
Webster Yorkshire Bitter; Guinness;
Carlsberg Hof.* 🍷

Accommodation *8 bedrooms* **£A G1**
Check-in all day

The convivial beamed bars of this 300-year-
old Exmoor inn are extremely popular with
the local farming population as well as
walkers, who should sleep soundly in the
eight characterful beamed bedrooms, all of
which enjoy lovely rural views. Pretty
fabrics, a light decor and fine period
furnishings are used to excellent effect and
most have smart modern bathrooms.
Direct-dial telephones, TVs and tea-makers
are standard throughout. *No children under
eight overnight.*

Credit Access, Amex, Diners, Visa

WOBURN   *Bell Inn*

21 Bedford Street MK17 9QD `B&B`
Map 10 C1 *Bedfordshire*
Woburn (0525) 290280
Parking *ample*

Landlords *Tim Chilton & Andrew Wadham*
Free house
🍺 *Greene King Abbot Ale, IPA; Guinness; Harp; Kronenbourg 1664.* 🍷

Accommodation *27 bedrooms* **£B G1**
Check-in all day

The main part of this scrupulously kept pub on the main street dates back to Tudor times, although its upmarket bar is a Victorian addition. The small main-house bedrooms all have darkwood furniture and varied fabrics. Opposite the inn a couple of Georgian houses contain the pretty, split-level residents' lounge and remaining bed-rooms, which are more characterful, with beams and old pine or antique furniture. Most have good bath or shower rooms. Children welcome overnight. *No dogs.*

Credit Access, Amex, Diners, Visa

WOLVERTON COMMON NEW ENTRY *Hare and Hounds*

Nr Basingstoke RG26 5RW `FOOD`
Map 10 B3 *Hampshire*
Kingsclere (0635) 298361
Parking *ample*

Bar food *11.30–2 & 6–10, Sun 12–2 & 7–10* 🍽

Landlords *Donald & Bernice Wilson*
Free house
🍺 *Wadworth 6X; Flowers Original; Guinness; Stella Artois; Heineken.* 😊

A busy 17th-century pub just off the A339 run in a friendly, efficient style by the Wilsons. Pot plants and pictures add a homely touch in the cosy beamed bar, where traditional snacks like ploughman's and sandwiches (lunchtimes only), she-pherd's pie and lasagne are supplemented by imaginative offerings such as aubergine and ricotta bake with herbs and yoghurt. Restaurant offering full à la carte menu.
Typical dishes Lamb cutlets with Parme-san £5.95 Cannelloni Sorrentina £4.80

Credit Access, Amex, Diners, Visa

WOOBURN COMMON   NEW ENTRY   *Chequers Inn*

Bourne End HP10 0JQ
Map 7 C2 *Buckinghamshire*
Bourne End (06285) 29575
Parking *ample*

Bar food *12–2.30*

Landlord *Peter Roehrig*
Free house
🍺 *Eldridge Pope Dorchester, IPA, Bitter, Royal Oak; Guinness; Eldridge Pope Faust.* 🍷 😊

The Chequers lies perched on the rolling Chiltern Hills, midway between the M4 and M40, and is a charming 17th-century inn which has been carefully and lovingly developed over the years by Peter Roehrig. Find him chatting to the locals in the convivial beamed bar, where quality wines by the glass are supplemented by simple but stylish lunchtime snacks. Choose from open sandwiches with rare roast beef or smoked salmon, chicken and cream cheese terrine, a tasty ploughman's or calf's liver sauced with avocado and pepper. Home-made sweets and good coffee to finish.

Typical dishes Carrot and orange soup £1.95 Tagliatelle with cream and mush-rooms £3.55

Accommodation *16 bedrooms* **£A G1**
Check-in all day

A sympathetically designed modern exten-sion houses 16 delightful bedrooms fur-nished in old stripped pine, with pretty patterned wallpapers and coordinating cur-tains at the leaded lattice windows. Double beds are standard throughout (including some four-posters), and all rooms have excellent bathrooms, and good facilities. Children welcome overnight.

Credit Access, Amex, Visa

WOODBRIDGE   **Bull Hotel**

Market Hill IP12 4LR   `B&B`
Map 8 F2 *Suffolk*
Woodbridge (039 43) 2089
Parking *limited*

Landlords *Neville & Anne Allen*
Free house
🍺 *Adnams Bitter; Younger's Tartan
Bitter; Guinness; Carlsberg; Heineken.*

Accommodation *29 bedrooms* **£B G2/3**
Check-in all day

Once a coaching inn, the Bull Hotel enjoys a position opposite the fine old Tudor shire hall. The two bars are simple and functional, and residents have a basic, homely, first-floor lounge. Bedrooms offer unassuming comfort, with painted walls, plain fabrics and a range of furniture from modern to period pieces. Most have en suite facilities, the remainder sharing three public bathrooms. Sadly, there is a somewhat shabby, untidy look about the place. Children welcome overnight.

WOOLER   **Tankerville Arms Hotel**

Cottage Road NE71 6AD   `B&B`
Map 2 D5 *Northumberland*
Wooler (0668) 81581
Parking *ample*

Landlords *Park family*
Free house 🐌
🍺 *McEwan's 80/-, Best Scotch; Newcastle Exhibition; Tetley Traditional; Warsteiner.*

Accommodation *15 bedrooms* **£C G2**
Check-in all day

A 17th century coaching inn on the A697 midway between Newcastle and Edinburgh. Creepers climb the sturdy stone exterior, and inside a certain amount of original charm survives in the bars. Most of the bedrooms are of a decent size, with neat, simple decor and a fairly traditional look. Each has a couple of armchairs, plus colour TV and tea-making equipment, and the best have their own modest bathrooms. Children's room and outdoor play area. Accommodation closed four days Christmas.

Credit Access, Visa

WOOLHOPE   **Butchers Arms**

Nr Hereford HR1 4RF   `FOOD`
Map 6 E3 *Hereford & Worcs*   `B&B`
Fownhope (043 277) 281
Parking *ample*

Bar food *11.30–2.15 (Sun 12–2) & 7–10
(Sat till 10.30)*

Landlord *Bill Griffiths*
Free house
🍺 *Hook Norton Best Bitter, Old Hookey;
Marston Pedigree; Carlsberg.*

Accommodation *3 bedrooms* **£D G3**
Check-in all day

Eight miles from Hereford, Ross-on-Wye and Ledbury, the Butchers Arms is a black-and-white half-timbered building with 14th-century origins. It is a delightful, down-to-earth place with few frills but all the important things: cheerful log fires, plenty of comfortable seats, a lovely garden, friendly staff, traditional beer, local cider and good, tasty food. Everything is home-made, from thick, warming apple and parsnip soup to vegetarian lasagne, chilli con carne and the very popular Woolhope pie packed with rabbit and bacon cooked in cider. Pâté, ploughman's platters and sandwiches are also available, and most customers cannot resist the amazing frozen ginger and coffee meringue cake.

Typical dishes Stilton & celery soup £1.25 Woolhope pie £3.95

The three homely bedrooms are spotlessly clean and of a decent size, with beams, white walls and furniture, duvets and electric blankets. They share a warm bathroom. A selection of books and games is kept on the landing. *No children under 14 overnight. No dogs.*

WOOLVERTON   Red Lion

Nr Bath BA3 6QS   `FOOD`
Map 7 A3 *Somerset*
Frome (0373) 830350
Parking *ample*

Bar food *12–3 (Sun till 2) & 7–10* 🍽

Landlords *Mr & Mrs B. Lander*
Brewery *Wadworth*
🍺 *Wadworth 6X, IPA; Bass; Guinness;*
Heineken.

Neat lawns front the Red Lion, a smart pub
set back off the A36, with flagstone floors,
open fires and exposed stonework. The bar
menu largely comprises hearty portions of
salads and jacket potatoes. The former
include seafood, Caribbean chicken and
savoyard (ham, cheese and walnuts with
garlic croûtons) while fillings for the
potatoes could be anything from bacon,
onions and cheese to corned beef, beans and
a fried egg.
Typical dishes Chicken korma salad
£5.75 Prawn avocado salad £3.85

WORCESTER   Slug & Lettuce

12 The Cornmarket   `FOOD`
WR1 2DF
Map 10 A1 *Hereford & Worcs*
Worcester (0905) 28362
Parking *difficult*

Bar food *12–2*
No bar food *eves & all Sun*

Landlord *Nigel Griffiths*
Brewery *Ansells*
🍺 *Ind Coope Burton Ale; Ansells Bitter;*
Tetley Bitter; Guinness; Löwenbräu;
Castlemaine XXXX.

A popular and atmospheric city-centre pub
with a clever open-plan design that still
retains some intimate corners. Now only
offering food at lunchtimes, the choice
remains as appetising and reasonably
priced as ever. Filled baps and salads are
supplemented by more substantial offerings such as chicken à la king, tagliatelle
carbonara and tasty vegetable quiche. Brie
served with fresh fruit makes a fine finale.
Typical dishes Beef stroganoff £2.95
Baked trout £2.95

Credit Access

WYE   New Flying Horse Inn

Upper Bridge Street   `B&B`
TN25 5AN
Area Map 5 D3 *Kent*
Wye (0233) 812297
Parking *ample*

Landlords *Barry & Anita Law*
Brewery *Shepherd Neame* 🍽
🍺 *Shepherd Neame Master Brew Bitter,*
Best Bitter; Beamish Stout; Hurlimann
Sternbrau; Steinbock Lager. 🍷

Accommodation *10 bedrooms* **£D G2/3**
Check-in all day

With a 400-year history, this white-painted
inn is characterised by low ceilings, black
beams, open brickwork and a large open
fireplace. The main bar has copper-topped
tables and simple chairs, and an adjoining
room provides easy chairs for more serious
relaxation. Rooms in the main building
vary in size and are modestly furnished, but
one has a four-poster and more traditional
pieces. In the old stable block the four
rooms are uniform and are all en suite.

Credit Access, Amex, Diners, Visa

WYKEHAM   Downe Arms

Pickering Road, Nr   `B&B`
Scarborough YO13 9OB
Area Map 3 D3 *North Yorks*
Scarborough (0723) 862471
Parking *ample*

Landlord *Viscount Downe*
Free house 🍽
🍺 *Younger's Scotch; Theakston Bitter;*
Guinness; McEwan's Lager.

Accommodation *10 bedrooms* **£C G2**
Check-in all day

Refurbishment has brightened the spacious
and popular public bar of a thoughtfully
extended roadside pub. A colourful aquarium provides a focal point of interest in the
contrastingly intimate little cocktail bar
and there are numerous conference suites.
Upstairs, good-sized bedrooms with simple
white furniture and attractive matching
fabrics all have TVs and tea-makers as well
as carpeted en suite bathrooms (some with
shower only). Children welcome overnight.

Credit Access, Amex, Diners, Visa

YARMOUTH   **Bugle Hotel**

The Square PO41 0NS   `B&B`
Map 7 B4 *Isle of Wight*
Isle of Wight (0983) 760272
Parking *ample*

Landlords *Chris Troup & Rinaldo Perpetuini*
Brewery *Whitbread*
🍺 *Whitbread Best Bitter; Flowers Original; Guinness; Heineken; Stella Artois.*

Accommodation *10 bedrooms* **£B G2**
Check-in all day

A lively seaside pub with weekend entertainment from a singing duo and summer barbecues in the back garden. 300 years have mellowed the day rooms, which include a nautically themed bar crammed with ship's planks, pennants and pictures. Bright bedrooms are decorated and furnished in an unfussy modern style, and all have TVs and dial-out phones. Four rooms have their own bathrooms en suite, the rest share two. Residents have assured parking. Children welcome overnight.

Credit Access, Visa

YATTENDON   **Royal Oak**

★   ★

The Square, Nr Newbury   `FOOD`
RG16 0UF   `B&B`
Area Map 4 F5 *Berkshire*
Hermitage (0635) 201325
Parking *ample*

Bar food *12.30–2 & 7.30–10* ☙

Landlords *Richard & Kate Smith*
Free house
🍺 *Wadworth 6X; Adnams Bitter, Hall & Woodhouse Tanglefoot; Guinness; Stella Artois.* 🍷 ☺

Accommodation *5 bedrooms* **£A G1**
Check-in all day

The rustic appeal of the 16th-century Royal Oak is considerable, but the hostelry's chief claim to fame is undoubtedly the culinary powers of owner Richard Smith. There is a fairly formal restaurant, but splendid food is also available in the snug bars. Salad of warm duck liver and chives, moules marinière, sirloin steak with rösti and raised pigeon and tongue pie with blackcurrant and orange sauce show the spread, and soufflé beignet makes an excellent finish.

Typical dishes Artichoke vinaigrette £3.75 Warm goat's cheese salad £5 Fricassée of Dover sole, monkfish & scallops with saffron sauce £8 Calf's liver & bacon £8.25

Bedrooms are appointed with considerable flair, and boast some fine fabrics and antiques. Beds are big, with good mattresses, and rooms are equipped with TVs, dial-out phones and thoughtful extras like magazines and mineral water. Bathrooms (all private, three en suite) are equally well provided. Good breakfasts. *No dogs.*

Credit Access, Amex, Visa

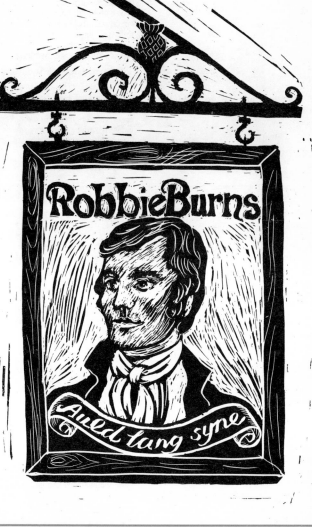

ABERDEEN   *Craighaar Hotel*

Waterton Road, Bucksburn `FOOD`
AB2 9HS `B&B`
Map 1 D3 *Grampian*
Aberdeen (0224) 712275
Parking *ample*

Bar food *12–2 & 6–10, Sun 12.30–2.30
& 6–9*

Landlord *Lewis Connon*
Free house
🍺 *Herriot 80/-; Guinness; Tennent's
Lager.*

A new chef is maintaining the high culinary standards already established at this unprepossessing modern hotel on a housing estate just five miles from the airport. The light and airy Concorde Bar and cosy, smaller Oyster Bar are attractive settings for an imaginative range of snacks with the emphasis on fresh seafood. Cider-steamed mussels, collops of monkfish in a julienne of leek, smoked salmon and pink peppercorn cream sauce and Dee salmon with a dill and saffron mayonnaise are typically imaginative offerings, while hearty meat dishes include char-grilled rib-eye steak, veal hongroise and pork chops with grilled tomato and spiced apple sauce. Finish with sticky toffee pudding or home-made white chocolate ice cream in a brandy basket. Traditional Sunday lunch available.

Typical dishes Sizzle steak £8.50 Cod in batter £4.95

Accommodation *41 bedrooms* **£B G1**
Check-in all day

Spotlessly kept little bedrooms with neat fitted furniture and duvets all offer trouser presses, tea-makers, mineral water and video recorders (film hire at reception). Compact en suite shower rooms. Children welcome overnight.

Credit Access, Amex, Diners, Visa

AIRDRIE   *Staging Post*

8/10 Anderson Street `B&B`
ML6 0AA
Map 2 C5 *Strathclyde*
Airdrie (0236) 67525
Parking *limited*

Landlord *David Barr*
Brewery *Welcome Inns*
🍺 *Younger's Tartan, 80/-; Guinness;
McEwan's Lager.* No real ale.

Accommodation *9 bedrooms* **£C G2**
Check-in all day

There are not many places to stay in Airdrie, so the Staging Post, in a quiet street near the centre, definitely serves a purpose. The accent is on convenience rather than luxury, bedrooms being on the small side; but there is room for an easy chair and a good-sized wardrobe, and all rooms offer TVs and telephones, plus little shower rooms in all but two. The lounge bar has more appeal than the rather down-at-heel Highwayman Bar. Children welcome overnight.

Credit Access, Amex, Diners, Visa

ANSTRUTHER   *Craw's Nest Hotel*

Bankwell Road KY10 3DS `B&B`
Map 2 C4 *Fife*
Anstruther (0333) 310691
Parking *ample*

Landlords *Clarke family*
Free house ☙
🍺 *McEwan's Export, Tartan Special;
Guinness; Carlsberg Pilsner, Hof.* No real
ale.

Accommodation *50 bedrooms* **£B G2**
Check-in all day

On the outskirts of Anstruther, the Clarke family's much-modernised Scottish manse offers functional overnight accommodation in uniformly decorated bedrooms divided between the main house and a recent wing. All have neat fitted furniture, TVs, tea-makers and compact bathrooms; five mini-suites are also available and there are two four-poster rooms. Public areas include a light and spacious lounge bar, cocktail bar and residents' TV lounge on the first floor. Garden. *No dogs.*

Credit Access, Amex, Diners, Visa

ARDENTINNY

Ardentinny Hotel

Loch Long, Argyll PA23 8TR
Map 2 B4 *Strathclyde*
Ardentinny (036 981) 209
Parking *ample*

`FOOD`
`B&B`

Bar food *12–3 & 6–9.30 (Sun till 9) & all day Sat & Sun in summer* ☙

Landlords *John & Thyrza Horn & Hazel Hall*
Free house
🍺 *McEwan's Export; Webster Yorkshire Bitter; Guinness; Foster's; Holsten Export.* ☺

Accommodation *11 bedrooms* £A G1
Check-in all day

Throughout the summer months sailing yachts and luxury cruisers on Loch Long float by the old white shoreside hotel, and all around the Argyll Forest Park beckons outdoor enthusiasts. The Ardentinny is now run by two sisters whose grandfather once owned it. Of several public rooms one commemorates Harry Lauder, another with a nautical theme is a popular place for hungry sailors. Chicken broth comes with excellent granary bread, and the beef olives are stuffed with savoury mincemeat and served with vegetables of the day. Vegetarians are offered their own salad and a main fish course is always available. Garden.

Typical dishes Stuffed mushrooms £2.75 Venison casserole £8.80

The accommodation is closed here between November and March, reflecting the importance of water sports holidays. Otherwise light, acceptably comfortable bedrooms of varying styles, from traditional to modern, are all en suite with TVs. 'Fyne' rooms overlook the loch. A small pleasant lounge is also available for residents.

Credit Access, Amex, Diners, Visa

We welcome bona fide recommendations or complaints on the tear-out pages at the back of the book for readers' comments.

They are followed up by our professional team, but do complain to the management on the spot.

BRAE

Busta House Hotel

ZE2 9QN
Map 1 D1 *Shetland*
Brae (080 622) 506
Parking *ample*

`FOOD`

Bar food *12–2 (Sun till 2.30) & 8–9.30* ☙

Landlords *Robin Black & Gordon Starks*
Free house
🍺 *Orkney Raven Ale, Lager; McEwan's Export; Tennent's Lager.* No real ale. 🍷 ☺

Rich in history, this substantial house with its own private harbour and tree-filled walled garden enjoys a lovely lochside setting. Home-made snacks are served in the beamed main bar and enchanting little garden bar. Choose from a menu offering cauliflower soup, meaty hamburgers or chicken curry among more standard bar snacks. Sweets include gâteaux, ice creams and fresh fruit salad.
Typical dishes Spiced Shetland herring £2.75 Sirloin steak £5.15

Credit Access, Amex, Diners, Visa

BUSBY   Busby Hotel

2 Field Road, Clarkston FOOD B&B
G76 8RX
Map 2 B5 *Strathclyde*
041-644 2661
Parking *ample*

Bar food *12–2 & 6–9, Sun 12.30–2 &
6.30–9* ☙

Landlord *John Hebditch*
Free house
🍺 *McEwan 80/-, Tartan Special;
Younger's No 3; Guinness; Beck's Bier.* 🍷 ⊖

Accommodation *14 bedrooms* **£C G2**
Check-in all day

Businessmen and travellers are frequent users of the Busby, which stands near the river Cart about eight miles from the centre of Glasgow. Snacks are served lunchtime and evening in the cocktail bar and traditionally styled lounge; though nothing out of the ordinary, they score on variety, and it is clear that some effort and care go into their making and presentation. The choice runs from soup and pâté to burgers, salads, deep-fried haddock, chicken and bacon kebabs and pork cordon bleu, with a trio of dishes catering for vegetarians.

Typical dishes Lasagne £2.55 Haddock mornay £2.65

Bedrooms, up on the third floor, are fairly simple in terms of decor but quite well equipped, all having a desk and easy chair, TV, radio, direct-dial phone and roomy, fully tiled bathrooms. Double glazing and central heating help keep things agreeably quiet and cosy. Staff are friendly enough, but a bit impersonal. Breakfast (at least on our latest visit) was unmemorable.

Credit Access, Amex, Diners, Visa

CANONBIE   Riverside Inn

DG14 0UX FOOD B&B
Map 2 C6 *Dumfries &
Galloway*
Canonbie (03873) 71295
Parking *ample*

Bar food *12–2 & 7–9*
No bar food *Sun lunch, Mon–Sat eves*
Closed *Sun lunch & 2 wks Feb*

Landlords *Robert & Susan Phillips*
Free house
🍺 *Ruddles Best Bitter; Yates Bitter; Hook
Norton Best Bitter; Guinness; Tennent's
Lager.* 🍷 ⊖

Accommodation *6 bedrooms* **£A G1**
Check-in all day

A white-painted old inn in a quiet village, the Riverside has a pleasantly rural air with tables made from old sewing machine bases, 'country' chairs and framed fishing flies on the walls. Robert and Susan Phillips share the cooking, producing straightforward, honest food that is never dull. You might choose a home-made soup as a starter, following it with tender lamb with celery, bacon and parsley pudding accompanied by flageolet beans with onions in a white sauce; finish with baked rhubarb cheesecake.

Typical dishes Wild salmon & salad
£5.55 Comfrey of duck £4.75

The spotless bedrooms have woodchip walls, matching bedcovers and curtains in pretty fabrics, comfortable armchairs, TVs, radios, and plenty of extras such as pot pourri, magazines and books. Two have bedhead drapes and there is one four-poster; all have modern bathrooms, two with shower only. There is also a chintzy residents' lounge with leather chesterfields in which to relax. Garden. Children welcome overnight. *No dogs.*

Credit Access, Visa

CASTLE DOUGLAS — King's Arms Hotel

St Andrew Street DG7 1EL   B&B
Map 2 C6 *Dumfries &*
Galloway
Castle Douglas (0556) 2626
Parking *ample*

Landlord *John Dickenson*
Free house
☞ *Younger's Tartan; McEwan's 60/-;*
Guinness; Carlsberg Hof; Tennent's Lager.
No real ale. ☟

Accommodation *18 bedrooms* £B G2
Check-in all day

A terrace of old town cottages with a central courtyard for enjoying a drink in the sun. Inside, several little rooms with armchairs and tartan carpets provide cosy spots for a convivial drink, and upstairs there is a quiet, homely residents' lounge. Bedrooms, most of which have private facilities en suite, are generally fairly modest in decor and furnishings, but all are comfortable enough and kept in decent order. The new owner is a Lancastrian manufacturer of agricultural equipment.

Credit Access, Amex, Diners, Visa

CLACHAN-SEIL — Tigh-an-Truish

Nr Oban PA34 4QZ   FOOD
Map 2 B4 *Strathclyde*   B&B
Balvicar (085 23) 242
Parking *ample*

Bar food *12–2.15 & 6–8.30* ☞

Landlords *Mr & Mrs Brunner*
Free house
☞ *McEwan's 80/-, Export; Younger's*
Tartan Bitter; Murphy Stout; Tennent's
Lager.

An unpretentious inn (also a filling station) by an old stone bridge on the rugged Atlantic edge of Scotland. It is mainly a haunt of locals, though a few tourists make their way there in summer and those who do so will find information about local events in the bar. The boarded ceiling is nicotine yellow, the bar counter of old pine, and a couple of dartboards pinpoint the entertainment. Soup and sandwiches are about all that is available in the winter, but in high season the choice gets wider with things like chicken liver pâté, burgers, crab or cold meat salads, jumbo prawns and a daily hot special. Traditional Sunday lunch.

Typical dishes Soup 90p Chicken casserole £3

Accommodation *2 bedrooms* £D G2
Check-in all day

The two good-sized bedrooms, one with private bath, the other with a shower, have their own kitchens stocked with breakfast provisions, as this is very much a self-catering place. The rooms are clean and tidy, with fine views. Garden. Accommodation closed in winter. *No dogs.*

Prices given are as at the time of our research and thus may change.

COMRIE — Royal Hotel

Melville Square PH6 2DN   B&B
Map 2 C4 *Tayside*
Comrie (0764) 70200
Parking *ample*

Landlady *Margaret Gordon*
Free house
☞ *McEwan's Tartan Special, 80/-, Pale*
Ale; Harp.

Accommodation *14 bedrooms* £C G2
Check-in all day

At the heart of this L-shaped inn on the village square is the convivial cocktail bar, decorated in the owner's tartan and stocked with over 50 malt whiskies. There is also a simpler public bar and a comfortable residents' lounge. Queen Victoria once stayed here and her visit is remembered by a four-poster sporting the royal coat of arms in one of the bedrooms. Other rooms have functional modern units, and all offer excellent private bathrooms. Children welcome overnight.

Credit Access, Amex, Diners, Visa

COYLTON   NEW ENTRY   *Finlayson Arms Hotel*

Nr Ayr KA6 6JT   `B&B`
Map 2 B5 *Strathclyde*
Joppa (0292) 570298
Parking *ample*

Landlords *Murdo & Rena Munro*
Free house
🍺 *Tennent's 80/-, 70/-, Light; Guinness; Tennent's Lager.*

Accommodation *4 bedrooms* **£D G2**
Check-in all day

Easy to spot with its brilliant white exterior, the Finlayson Arms stands on the A70 six miles from the birthplace of Robbie Burns and just four from Ayr racecourse. The bright, well-kept look continues both in the lively bar and in the neat little bedrooms, three of which have their own shower facilities (the fourth shares the family bathroom). Murdo Munro personally prepares a hearty breakfast guaranteed to start the day well.

Credit Access, Visa

DYSART   *Old Rectory Inn*

West Quality Street, Nr   `FOOD`
Kirkcaldy KY1 2TE
Map 2 C4 *Fife*
Kirkcaldy (0592) 51211
Parking *ample*

Bar food *12–2.30 & 7–10*
Closed *Mon eve & all Sun*

Landlords *Stuart & Kay Nelson*
Free house
🍺 *McEwan 80/-, Tartan Special; McEwan's Lager.* No real ale. 🍷

The splendid walled garden and cosy beamed bar of this Georgian inn perched above the harbour in a pretty village north of Kirkcaldy make agreeable areas for enjoying some imaginative snacks. At lunchtime the extensive cold buffet is supplemented by hot choices such as seafood au gratin and spaghetti neapolitan, while supper dishes include stir-fry chicken and prawn curry madras.
Typical dishes Mussel and onion stew £2.85 Tortellini al forno £3

Credit Access, Amex, Diners, Visa

EDINBURGH   *Cramond Inn*

Cramond Glebe Road   `FOOD`
EH4 6NU
Map 2 C5 *Lothian*
031-336 2035
Parking *ample*

Bar food *12–2.15 & 6–9.30, Sun 12.30–2 & 6–9*
Restaurant closed *Sat lunch, Sun eve & all Mon*

Landlord *Andrew Dobson*
Brewery *Samuel Smith*
🍺 *Caledonian 80/-; Marston Pedigree.* 🍷

A free house until last year the Cramond now trades under the aegis of Samuel Smith. The whitewashed 300-year-old inn continues to serve its commuter village with either standard pub food in the bar – ploughman's, quiches etc – or more serious meals in the separate restaurant (12–1.45 & 7–9.30) – from smoked mackerel pâté to braised chicken in red wine followed by lemon bavaroise cream.
Typical dishes Cream of asparagus soup £1.10 Steak and kidney pie £2.95

Credit Access, Visa

EDINBURGH   *Rutland Hotel*

3 Rutland Street EH1 2AE   `B&B`
Map 2 C5 *Lothian*
031-229 3402
Parking *difficult*

Landlords *Patrick & Anne O'Shea*
Brewery *Scottish Brewers* 🍷
🍺 *McEwan's 80/-, Export; Beck's Bier; Guinness; McEwan's Lager.*

Accommodation *18 bedrooms* **£B G2**
Check-in all day

Overlooking the Castle from its convenient position on Princes Street, the pub at No. 1 Rutland Place is a tremendously popular drinking venue, with two floors of heavily Victorian bars and a cellar wine bar offering serious wines. Double-glazed bedrooms, in contrast, are quiet and peaceful, with access at the back of the building by resident's key only. TVs, tea-makers and trouser presses are standard and most have modern bathrooms; the rest share four public ones. *No dogs.*

Credit Access, Amex, Diners, Visa

FOCHABERS   *Gordon Arms Hotel*

High Street IV32 7DH   `B&B`
Map 1 C2 *Grampian*
Fochabers (0343) 820508
Parking *ample*

Landlord *Raúl Suarez*
Free house
🍺*McEwan's Export, 80/-; Younger's Tartan Special, Pale Ale; Guinness; Harp.*

Accommodation *12 bedrooms* **£A G2**
Check-in all day

Antlers decorate the exterior of a former coaching inn standing alongside the A96, while the public bar sports a variety of fishing bric-a-brac – including stuffed prize catches. Simple overnight accommodation is provided by 12 well-equipped bedrooms (TVs, tea-makers, hairdryers and direct-dial telephones), which include both older rooms with large carpeted bathrooms and a number of smaller but quieter ones in the extension. Children welcome overnight.

Credit Access, Amex, Visa

GLASGOW   *Babbity Bowster*

16 Blackfriars Street   `FOOD`
G1 1PE   `B&B`
Map 2 B5 *Strathclyde*
041-552 5055
Parking *limited*

Bar food *8 am–9 pm*

Landlords *Fraser & Tom Laurie*
Free house
🍺*Maclay 70/-, 80/-, Porter; Murphy Stout; Tennent's Lager; Fürstenberg.* 🍷☻

A renovated Robert Adam town house in the city's business district is the setting for the splendidly informal and convivial Babbity Bowster – café, bar, restaurant and hotel. It is open seven days a week from 8 am, with breakfasts and snacks available until 11. The main café/bar menu, which comes on stream at noon and continues until 9 pm, includes Scotch broth, haggis and Loch Etive mussels as well as traditional Scotch pies, stovies and baked potatoes with various interesting fillings. Daily specials are well worth trying – our oxtail paprika was a very tasty dish. Besides the café/bar, which has an outdoor patio, there is also a restaurant – with a separate menu – on the first floor. Occasional musical evenings are a feature.

Typical dishes Chunky ham & leek pie £1.95 Loch Etive mussels £2.35

Accommodation *6 bedrooms* **£A G2**
Check-in all day

Bedrooms have neat fitted furniture, duvets and shower rooms. Phones, TVs and radios are not provided, but a parking space is reserved for each bedroom. Babbity Bowster is the name of an old Scottish dance. Children welcome overnight.

Credit Access, Amex, Diners, Visa

GLENDEVON   *Tormaukin Hotel*

Nr Dollar FK14 7JY   `B&B`
Map 2 C4 *Tayside*
Muckhart (025 981) 252
Parking *ample*

Closed *2 wks mid Jan*

Landlords *Mr & Mrs R. Worthy*
Free house
🍺*Ind Coope Burton Ale; Alloa 70/-, Export; Guinness; Skol.*

Accommodation *10 bedrooms* **£B G1**
Check-in all day

An old stable block has been converted to provide four additional bedrooms at a friendly black and white roadside pub pleasantly situated in hilly countryside. Spotlessly kept, all ten bedrooms have good pine furnishings and attractive coordinating fabrics. TVs, tea-makers, direct-dial telephones and hairdryers are standard throughout and compact modern bathrooms are well equipped. There is a peaceful little residents' lounge and a choice of beamed bars. Children welcome overnight.

Credit Access, Amex, Visa

Sir Thomas Elyot
1490?–1546

Abstinence is whereby a man refraineth from
anything which he may lawfully take.
The Governour (1531)

William Watson
1858–1935

And must I wholly banish hence
These red and golden juices,
And pay my vows to Abstinence,
That pallidest of Muses?
To a Fair Maiden who Bade Me Shun Wine

Walter de Map
fl. 1170–1200

Die I must, but let me die drinking in an Inn!
Hold the wine cup to my lips sparkling from the bin!
So when the angels flutter down to take
me from my sin,
'Ah, God have mercy on this sot',
the Cherubs will begin.
'The Jovial Priest's Confession' (c.1170)

Anonymous

God gave the grape
Good wine to make
To cheer both great and small.
But little fools they drink too much,
And big ones – none at all.
Cited by Walter James in Antipasto (1957)

Oscar Wilde
1854–1900

Work is the curse of the drinking classes.
Cited by H. Pearson in Life of Oscar Wilde

GLENFINNAN   Stage House Inn

PH37 4LT   `B&B`
Map 1 B3 *Highland*
Kinlocheil (039 783) 246
Parking *ample*

Closed *end Oct–1st April*

Landlords *Helen & Andrew Brooks*
Free house
🍺 *Youngers' Tartan Bitter; Guinness;*
Tennent's Lager.

Accommodation *9 bedrooms* **£B G2**
Check-in all day

Dating back to 1658, this welcoming inn occupies a picturesque setting alongside the A830 near Loch Shiel, where it owns extensive fishing rights. Six boats are also available for guests' use, making this a popular stopover with fishermen. Neat, clean bedrooms with smart modern furniture and pretty duvets all have private bath/shower rooms and electric blankets. Downstairs, there is a sunny little front lounge. Children welcome overnight. Accommodation closed end Oct–1 April.

Credit Access, Visa

INGLISTON   Norton Tavern

Edinburgh EH28 8XX   `FOOD`
Map 2 C5 *Lothian*
Edinburgh 031-333 1275
Parking *ample*

Bar food *12–9.45, Sun 12.30–2 &*
6.30–9.45

Landlord *Mr A. Forrest*
Free house
🍺 *Caledonian 80/-; McEwan's Export;*
Tennent's Special; Murphy Stout;
Tennent's Lager. 🍷 ☕

A popular tavern found down a driveway off the A8. Eating areas have simple wood furniture and the main bar features exposed stone walls and etched glass behind the bar. Enjoy American-style dishes such as Frisco Bay stew (fresh mussels casseroled with vegetables and herbs) or New York strip steak, plus various salads and puddings like Mississippi mud pie or apple pie.
Typical dishes Chicago pie £3.75 L.A. casserole £3.50

Credit Access, Amex, Diners, Visa

INVERMORISTON   Glenmoriston Arms

IV3 6YA   `FOOD`
Map 1 B3 *Highland*   `B&B`
Glenmoriston (0320) 51206
Parking *ample*

Bar food *12–2 & 5.30–8.30 (9.30 in*
summer) ☙

Landlords *Mr & Mrs Alan Draper & son*
Free house
🍺 *McEwan's 80/-; Guinness; Carlsberg*
Export. No real ale. ☕

Stuffed game birds, fishing flies and flint-lock rifles decorate the convivial bar at this solid, white-painted inn standing alongside the A82 by the shores of Loch Ness. The snack menu keeps things simple with a choice of home-made soup (including well seasoned vegetable broth), steak and kidney pie or gammon, filled jacket potatoes, sandwiches and various cold platters. More elaborate fare is available in the restaurant, where smoked venison with Cumberland sauce might be followed by veal stroganoff, local salmon with a prawn sauce or moist chicken breast richly sauced with whisky, cream and tomatoes.

Typical dishes Chicken and mushroom pie £3.20 Lasagne £3.20

Accommodation *8 bedrooms* **£C G2**
Check-in all day

Good-sized bedrooms are neat and well kept, with a light, pleasant decor and attractive coordinated fabrics. One room boasts some fine period furniture, while the others have modest modern pieces. Duvets, direct-dial telephones, TVs and small seating areas are standard throughout and all rooms now offer up-to-date carpeted bathrooms. Garden and patio.

Credit Access, Visa

INVERNESS   NEW ENTRY   *Coach House Inn*

Stoneyfield IV1 2PA   `B&B`
Map 1 B2 *Highland*
Inverness (0463) 230244
Parking *ample*

Landlady *Mrs Rena Kaspis*
Free house
🍺 *McEwan's Export, 80/-, Tartan Special;*
Guinness; Harp.

Accommodation *5 bedrooms* £C G3
Check-in all day

A solid, white-painted inn near the site of the Battle of Culloden, formerly the coach house of Georgian Stoneyfield House. The five neat, simply appointed bedrooms are centrally heated; each has a washbasin and there are two shared bathrooms. Rooms do not have TV or phones, but there is a TV in the little lounge. The bar opens onto a terrace that affords attractive views. The owners have plans to refurbish the inn and to increase considerably the number of bedrooms. *No children overnight.*

KILBERRY   *Kilberry Inn*

Nr Tarbert PA29 6YD   `FOOD`
Map 2 B5 *Strathclyde*
Ormsary (088 03) 223
Parking *ample*

Bar food *12–2, 5–6 & 7.30–9* 🍴
No bar food *Sun eve*
Closed *Jan–Easter & mid Oct–Xmas*
(except Fri & Sat eves & Xmas)

Landlords *John & Kathy Leadbeater*
Free house
🍺 *Younger's Tartan; McEwan's Lager.* ☺

Sixteen miles of single-track road run through lovely scenery to a converted croft with stone walls and exposed beams. John Leadbeater is a convivial host in the little carpeted bar, which has a peat fire at one end and a wood-burning stove at the other. The journey is well worth while, as Kathy Leadbeater's cooking will soon tell you. She bakes her own bread, makes her own jams and chutneys and produces some really splendid dishes to make up the daily blackboard menu. Typical lunchtime choices could include tomato and rice soup; a superb fish pie containing local salmon and prawns; marinated herring fillets; and a wonderful hot chocolate fudge cake. Similar evening menu, with perhaps steak and trout in addition. Between 5 and 6 there is a high tea menu, and Sunday lunchtime brings roast beef and Yorkshire pudding.

Typical dishes Country sausage pie £4.95 Beef cooked in Old Peculier £9.50 Salmon fish pie £5.50 Fresh strawberry fool with Cointreau £1.75

Our inspectors never book in the name of
Egon Ronay's Guides.

They disclose their identity only if they are
considering an establishment for inclusion
in the next edition of the Guide.

KILFINAN   Kilfinan Hotel

Nr Tighnabruaich
Map 2 B5 *Strathclyde*
Kilfinan (070 082) 201
Parking *ample*

Bar food *12–2 & 5–7.30*

Landlords *Tony & Gina Wignoll*
Free house
🍺 *McEwan's 80/-, No 3; Murphy Stout;*
McEwan's Lager. ✆

FOOD
B&B

A boast that the hotel has provided food and shelter for travellers between Strachur and Tighnabruaich for over 100 years doesn't exactly conjure a picture of bustling activity. Perhaps that's to this white-stoned coaching inn's advantage, for what it offers is rural tranquillity. To go with fine views of Loch Fyne and the coastal hills, good standards of modern comfort are blended with traditional character. There are two bars, one with intricate Kashmir curtains, but no lounge. The bar meals are relatively simple and modestly priced with a menu that includes home-made soup, ploughman's, deep fried haddock, steak and stout pie, jumbo sausage and salads.

Typical dishes Smoked mackerel pâté £2.60 Venison pasty £3.50

Accommodation *11 bedrooms* **£A G1**
Check-in all day

Half the bedrooms have pieces of antique furniture; the others are fitted with modern units. They have TVs, direct-dial telephones, radio-alarms and bowls of sweets. All bathrooms are carpeted and en suite and carry an imaginative assortment of toiletries. Children welcome overnight.

Credit Access, Amex, Diners, Visa

KILLIN   Clachaig Hotel

Falls of Dochart, Gray
Street FK21 8SL
Map 2 B4 *Central*
Killin (056 72) 270
Parking *ample*

Landlord *John Mallinson*
Free house
🍺 *Tennent's 80/-; Guinness; Tennent's Special, Lager.*

FOOD
B&B

Once a smithy, the Clachaig Hotel counts the Falls of Dochart which are practically on the inn's doorstep as a particularly spectacular distraction. The inn itself is rather basic, the remnants of character being usurped by a jukebox and pool table. Matters are somewhat rectified by tasty, filling food, albeit without frills. Pea soup, Loch Fyne kippers and haggis with potatoes and neeps are simple, well-cooked dishes. Healthy looking ploughman's comes with crisp apples. Palates requiring something less parochial are offered chilli con carne or quiche. Sweets run to cheesecake, lemon meringue pie and sherry trifle.

Typical dishes Steak and kidney pie £3.25 Lasagne £3.25

Accommodation *9 bedrooms* **£D G3**
Check-in all day

The bedrooms, like the food, offer no frills – unless you count the front rooms' views of the falls – and are simple, homely and clean. All have duvets, tea-makers and digital clocks. Interestingly, some rooms derive character from furnishings salvaged from the cabin of an ocean liner. Bathrooms again are functional but clean. Children welcome overnight.

Credit Visa

KIPPEN   *Cross Keys Inn*

By Stirling FK8 3DN
Map 2 C4 *Central*
Kippen (078 687) 293
Parking *ample*

FOOD
B&B

Landlords *Mr & Mrs Watt*
Free house ☙
🍺 *Younger's No 3; Broughton
Greenmantle Ale; Guinness; Murphy Stout;
McEwan's Lager.*

In the centre of an attractive village surrounded by rolling farmland, the 18th-
century Cross Keys is simple, honest and
welcoming. The lounge is beamed, has a
coal fire and stone walls above pitch pine
half-panelling. It is quieter than the more
popular public bar where a TV and fruit
machines hold sway. The food is carefully
cooked rather than imaginative. Soups are
home-made and the breaded haddock is
especially good, as are the accompanying
chips. Large portions make the meals here
excellent value. Children's menu, and
garden.

Typical dishes Home-made steak pie £3
Vegetarian flan £1.95

Accommodation *3 bedrooms* **£D G3**
Check-in all day

Three simple, homely bedrooms, one a
single, have newly installed washbasins,
and duvets on all beds. They are all
maintained in spotless condition and share
a plain and functional but equally clean
bathroom. The two most attractive rooms
are the one single and double under the
eaves, having sloping ceilings and fine
views. Children welcome overnight.

Credit Access

---

*Changes in data sometimes occur
in establishments
after the Guide goes to press.*

*Prices should be taken as indications
rather than firm quotes.*

KIRKWALL   *Kirkwall Hotel*

Harbour Street KW15 1LF
Map 1 D2 *Orkney*
Kirkwall (0856) 2232
Parking *limited*

B&B

Landlord *Leo Daly*
Free house
🍺 *Younger's Tartan Special; Tennent's
Extra.*

Accommodation *44 bedrooms* **£A G1**
Check-in all day

Airy, spacious front bedrooms enjoy fine
views over Kirkwall harbour at this handsome four-storey, stone-built inn. Simply
decorated throughout, all the rooms offer
direct-dial telephones and TVs and most
have private bath/shower rooms. Downstairs, cheery landlord Leo Daly extends a
warm welcome in the mellow saloon, where
a fine collection of malt whiskies is an
added attraction. Residents have the use of
the first-floor lounge. Children welcome
overnight.

Credit Access, Diners, Visa

LEWISTON
Lewiston Arms

Nr Drumnadrochit IV3 6UN **B&B**
Map 1 B3 *Highland*
Drumnadrochit (045 62) 225
Parking *ample*

Landlords *Mr & Mrs N. Quinn*
Free house ☜
🍺 *McEwan's Export; Murphy Stout; McEwan's Lager.* No real ale.

Accommodation *8 bedrooms* **£D G3**
Check-in all day

A pretty garden and specially prepared area in which to play boules are popular summer attractions at the Quinns' homely and welcoming pub. Inside, there is ample space for relaxation, with a choice of two lounges (one for residents only) and a pleasantly traditional lounge bar. Bright, neat bedrooms (half in an adjoining converted farmhouse) have a simple, cottage appeal and share two public bathrooms. Accommodation closed December to mid-January.

Credit Visa

LINLITHGOW
Champany Inn Chop & Ale House

Philipstoun EH4G 7LU **FOOD**
Map 2 C5 *Lothian*
Philipstoun (0506) 834532
Parking *ample*

Bar food *12.30–2.30 (Sun from 12.30) & 6.30–10 (Sat from 6)*

Landlords *Anne & Clive Davidson*
Free house
🍺 *McEwan's 80/-; Theakston Best Bitter; McEwan's Lager.* 🍷 ⊖

Subtitled the 'Chop and Ale House', the Champany is actually a sub-restaurant, sharing space with a starred restaurant in a prettily restored 16th-century building. Meat from the charcoal grill is the principal food, from best Aberdeen Angus beefburgers to T-bone steak. Buffet only at lunchtimes, but an exellent cold selection. Children's menu. Garden.
Typical dishes Herring and sour cream £2.15 Rib-eye steak £8

Credit Access, Amex, Diners, Visa

LOCH ECK
Coylet Inn

By Dunoon PA23 8SG
Map 2 B4 *Strathclyde*
Kilmun (036 984) 426
Parking *limited*

Bar food *11.30–2 & 5.30–10, Sun 12.30–2 & 6.30–10* ☜

Landlords *Richard & Helen Addis*
Free house
🍺 *McEwan's 80/-, Tartan Special; Younger's No. 3; Guinness; Harp.* ⊖

A lochside, roadside 17th-century inn, white-painted with a narrow terrace at the front and a small garden to one side. Open fires warm the entrance hall and bar as well as the throng who come here for the food. A standard bar food menu is supplemented by more imaginative blackboard specials – smoked trout or smoked salmon and spinach pancakes – and especially so in the evenings when peppered steak or chicken Kiev might appear. Mussel soup with a good flavour is liquidised, two or three mussels being left whole as a garnish. Pork and pepper casserole makes a tasty stew served with jacket potatoes, and the chocolate roulade is delicious.

Typical dishes Avocado mousse and prawns £1.95 Chicken and chips £2.85

Accommodation *2 bedrooms* **£D G3**
Check-in by arrangement

Just two bedrooms with pretty duvets and wallpaper make up the accommodation. They benefit from loch views but suffer once the curtains are drawn from being so tiny. The shared bathroom is also small.

We publish annually so make sure you use the current edition.

LYBSTER   *Bayview Hotel*

Russel Street KW3 6AG   B&B
Map 1 C1 *Highland*
Lybster (059 32) 346
Parking *ample*

Landlords *Bob & Lyn Ruddick*
Free house
🍺 *Tennent's Special, 70/-, Light; Murphy Stout; Tennent's Lager.* No real ale.

Accommodation *3 bedrooms* **£D G3**
Check-in all day

Conveniently placed for the A9, the Bayview, a little red and white painted inn, stands in the town centre just above the harbour. New owners have added a warm and cosy lounge bar, but it is in the plainer public bar that you will find the local fishermen and farmers. Modest overnight accommodation is provided by three efficiently heated bedrooms with simple modern furniture. All have washbasins and share a functional public bathroom. Children welcome overnight. *No dogs.*

Credit Access, Visa

MAIDENS   *Bruce Hotel*

Harbour Road, by   FOOD
Turnberry KA26 9NR   B&B
Map 2 B5 *Strathclyde*
Turnberry (0655) 31401
Parking *ample*

Bar food *12–2*

Landlords *Brian & Dorothy Sage*
Free house
🍺 *McEwan's 80/-, Tartan Bitter; Guinness; Carlsberg Hof.*
No real ale. 🍷

Not the most inviting of buildings from the outside, but the welcome within is warm and the accommodation is kept in apple pie order. Service throughout is above average, and the tartan-suited girls who serve the food are very smart and pleasant. Bar snacks are served at lunchtime, supplemented by some à la carte dishes from the evening restaurant menu (7–9). The latter gives quality and value for money: the salmon roulade has plenty of flavour, and duck breast with pink peppercorns comes with excellent fresh vegetables. Sorbets and ice cream in a brandy snap basket are a popular finale.

Typical dishes Chicken liver pâté with soft peppercorns £2.40 Avocado with scampi & cheese sauce £3.45

Accommodation *9 bedrooms* **£D G1**
Check-in all day

Bedrooms sport pretty floral duvets and matching curtains, whitewood furniture, tea-makers and TVs, but no phones. Bath/shower rooms are en suite, compact and carpeted. The place is bright and cheerful, and housekeeping generally is a strong point. Accommodation closed two weeks at Christmas.

Any person using our name to obtain free hospitality is a fraud.

Proprietors, please inform Egon Ronay's Guides and the police.

MELROSE   Burts Hotel

Market Square TD6 9PN
Map 2 C5 *Borders*
Melrose (089 682) 2285
Parking *ample*

FOOD
B&B

Bar food *12–2 (Sun from 12.30) &
6–9.30 (Sat till 10.30, Sun till 9.30)*

Landlords *Graham & Anne Henderson*
Free house
🍺*Belhaven 80/-, Heavy; Guinness;
Holsten; Foster's.* 🍷 ⊖

Long-standing owners Graham and Anne
Henderson continue to offer a warm
welcome and an appetising selection of
snacks at their distinctive old black and
white hotel on the 18th-century market
square. Popular lunchtime choices include
prawns, bacon and mushrooms in garlic
butter, spaghetti bolognese, pork chops
with Dutch apple sauce and grilled sirloin
steak, with perhaps rich lemon cheesecake
or peach and banana crumble for afters.
The bar supper menu is more elaborate
(chicken livers in red wine, marinated lamb
kebabs and calamari with lemon and prawn
sauce are typical). Traditional Sunday
lunch available.

Typical dishes Game casserole £3.25
Hazelnut, lentil and mushroom loaf £3

Accommodation *21 bedrooms* **£B G1**
Check-in all day

Smartly refurbished bedrooms, all new
with modern en suite bathrooms, have good
quality furnishings and co-ordinating
fabrics. Two larger rooms are especially
popular with families, and TVs, tea-makers
and direct-dial telephones are standard
throughout. Garden and play area. Children
welcome overnight. Accommodation closed
3 days Christmas and 3 days New Year.

Credit Access, Amex, Diners, Visa

MELROSE   George & Abbotsford Hotel

High Street TD6 9PD
Map 2 C5 *Borders*
Melrose (089 682) 2308
Parking *ample*

B&B

Landlady *Miss E.S. Crawford*
Free house
🍺*McEwan's Tartan Special, Pale Ale;
Broughton Greenmantle Ale; Guinness;
Carlsberg.*

Accommodation *31 bedrooms* **£A G2**
Check-in all day

A convenient spot to stop if you are visiting
the Border country, this town centre hotel
offers clean, simple overnight accommodation. Bedrooms range from those in the
main building which are traditionally furnished – some are large enough to be family
rooms – to more modern rooms in the recent
extension. All rooms have basic, clean
bathrooms, and all now have colour TVs.
There is a residents' lounge and, downstairs, a pleasant lounge bar. Children
welcome overnight.

Credit Access, Amex, Diners, Visa

MOFFAT   Black Bull

1 Church Gate DG10 9ES
Map 2 C5 *Dumfries &
Galloway*
Moffat (0683) 20206
Parking *limited*

B&B

Landlord *Jim Hughes*
Free house
🍺*Younger's No. 3; Tartan Special;
McEwan's 80/-; Guinness; Murphy Stout;
McEwan's Lager.*

Accommodation *3 bedrooms* **£D G2**
Check-in all day

Robbie Burns was reputedly a regular at
this 16th-century town-centre pub, whose
main bar has just been painted, papered
and upholstered in red. There is a certain
amount of red about the non-smoking bar,
too, but here some of the old stone wall is
painted white. A further bar, popular with
locals, features memorabilia of the old
Caledonian Railway. Three bedrooms
provide neat, clean accommodation with
TVs and tea-makers but few other frills.
They share a modern bathroom. *No dogs.*

Credit Visa

MUIR OF ORD   Ord Arms Hotel

Great North Road IV6 7XR   `B&B`
Map 1 B2 *Highland*
Inverness (0463) 870286
Parking *ample*

Landlord *William E. Grant*
Free house
🍺 *McEwan's Export, Pale Ale; Younger's Tartan Special; Harp.* No real ale.

Accommodation *11 bedrooms* **£C G2**
Check-in all day

Enthusiastic young owner William Grant is leading the extensive improvements being made at this mellow stone-built pub on the A862. Revamped public areas include a smart foyer, lively public bar and the quieter, plant-filled Garden Bar. There is also a tiny lounge and useful function suite. Tastefully redecorated bedrooms with matching wallpapers and fabrics all now offer en suite facilities, while TVs, tea-makers and telephones are standard throughout. Children welcome overnight.

Credit Access, Visa

NEW ABBEY   Criffel Inn

Nr Dumfries DG2 8BX   `FOOD`
Map 2 C6 *Dumfries &*   `B&B`
Galloway
New Abbey (038 785) 305
Parking *ample*

Bar food *12–2 & 4.30–7* 🍴

Landlords *Jenny & Herries McCulloch*
Free house
🍺 *Broughtons Special Bitter; Tennent's Heriot Brewery 80/-; McEwan 60/-; Guinness; Tennent's Lager.*

An unassuming inn on the village square, with a small garden for summer sipping. The McCullochs are the most welcoming of hosts, and Jenny keeps the customers well fed with a good variety of wholesome home cooking. Lunchtime brings soup – perhaps a warming vegetable broth – and a daily special like pork fillet with an onion and tomato sauce, supplementing toasted sand-wiches, quiches, salads, fish, gammon steaks and roast beef. It is worth leaving room for the day's special sweet, which could be a fruit pie or butterscotch flan. Children are welcome in the restaurant and have their own dishes. High tea (with cakes) and early evening menus are similar but shorter and on Sunday there is a roast lunch.

Typical dishes Fresh Solway salmon and salad £4.50 Sausage, bacon & tomato with French fries £3.60

Accommodation *5 bedrooms* **£D G2**
Check-in all day

Spotless bedrooms (TVs, but no phones) share an equally spruce tiled bathroom, and residents have their own lounge, a room decorated with more verve than taste. Garden.

Credit Visa

SPEAN BRIDGE   Letterfinlay Lodge Hotel

PH34 4DZ   `B&B`
Map 1 B3 *Highland*
Spean Bridge (039 781) 622
Parking *ample*

Pub closed *mid-Nov to mid-Mar*

Landlords *Forsyth family*
Free house
🍺 *Alloa Export Bitter; Löwenbräu.* No real ale.

Accommodation *13 bedrooms* **£D G2/3**
Check-in all day

A sturdy 19th-century hotel overlooking Loch Lochy and seven miles north of Spean Bridge, Letterfinlay Lodge has been run by the Forsyth family for over 25 years. A sun lounge takes advantage of the view and bar walls are stuck with old banknotes. Bed-rooms are modestly furnished, modern rooms are compact and fabrics are simple and traditional in style. Work is under way to make most spacious older bedrooms en suite. Public bathrooms retain Victorian fittings. Children welcome overnight.

TARBERT — *West Loch Hotel*

Loch Fyne PA29 6YF
Map 2 B5 *Strathclyde*
Tarbert (088 02) 283
Parking *ample*

Bar food *12–2 & 6.30–7.30*

Landlady *Mrs Sandy Ferguson*
Free house
🍺 *Tennent's 80/-, LA, Lager.*
No real ale.

Landlady Sandy Ferguson is into her second year here at the head of West Loch, and the influence of a new brush has not only swept clean but whitewashed the 200-year-old coaching inn's exterior. Both bar and lounge have peat fires, but their low tables are difficult to eat at, so the little dining room is preferable. A wide-ranging blackboard menu offers dishes like soup of the day, corn on the cob, seafood platter, sautéed peppered liver, corned beef hash, Eastern lamb casserole with cashew nuts and smoked trout with scrambled eggs, which all in all is perhaps a little over-adventurous as quality can be variable. Garden.

Typical dishes Haddock and chips £3.10 Orange beef and sweet potato pie £4

Accommodation *6 bedrooms* **£C G3**
Check-in all day

The six bedrooms are fresh, bright and modest, electric blankets serving as a reminder of the latitude here. They share two bathrooms. A neat little residents' lounge on the first floor houses the TV. Children welcome overnight.

Prices given are as at the time of our research, and thus may change.

TAYVALLICH — *Tayvallich Inn*

Nr Lochgilphead PA31 8PR
Map 2 B4 *Strathclyde*
Tayvallich (054 67) 282
Parking *ample*

Bar food *12–2 & 6–7.30 (Sun from 6.30)*
Closed *Mon in winter*

Landlords *Pat & John Grafton*
Free house
🍺 *Drybrough Heavy; Alloa Arrol's 70/-;
Guinness; Castlemaine XXXX.* No real ale. ⊖

Local seafood, including clams, prawns and oysters, is a popular attraction at the Graftons' neat little white pebbledash inn on the shores of Loch Sween. A wood-burning stove warms the small bar and next door is the dining room (with fine views across the water), where you can also tuck into creamy soup, meaty steakburgers or perhaps sweet and sour vegetables served on rice. Simple sweets.
Typical dishes Smoked salmon salad £5 Craignish mussels marinière £3

Credit Access, Visa

TURRIFF — *Towie Tavern*

Auchterless AB5 8EP
Map 1 D2 *Grampian*
Auchterless (088 84) 201
Parking *ample*

Bar food *12–2 & 6–9 (Sat till 9.30,
Sun 5–7.30)*
Closed *2 wks Jan*

Landlords *Douglas & Eileen Pearson*
Free house
🍺 *McEwan's Export, Lager.* ⊖

New owners are continuing to offer imaginative snacks with a healthy slant at this pebbledash pub on the A947. Ratatouille with pasta, cauliflower and aubergine moussaka and cheese and tomato-topped prawn and smoked haddock bake are typical offerings, while more traditional fare includes grilled steaks, hamburgers and salads. Banana and walnut toffee pudding to finish.
Typical dishes Lentil, mushroom and courgette pâté £2.50 Beef lasagne £3.95

Credit Access, Visa

ULLAPOOL   NEW ENTRY   Argyll Hotel

Argyll Street IV26 2UB   `B&B`
Map 1 B2 *Highland*
Ullapool (0854) 2422
Parking *ample*

Landlords *Brian & Janet Henderson*
Free house
🍺 *McEwan's 80/-, Export; Guinness; Harp; Carlsberg.*

Accommodation *8 bedrooms* £D G3
Check-in all day

A white-painted, family-run inn close to the shores of Loch Broom with plenty of local character in its modest, neatly kept bars. Equally spotless overnight accommodation is provided by eight cheerfully decorated bedrooms, furnished in up-to-date style and offering both quilts and electric blankets for added warmth. All rooms have their own washbasins and share three functional bathrooms. Residents have the use of a simple TV lounge. Children welcome overnight.

Credit Access, Visa

WEEM   Ailean Chraggan Hotel

Nr Aberfeldy PH15 2LD   `FOOD`
Map 2 C4 *Tayside*   `B&B`
Aberfeldy (0887) 20346
Parking *ample*

Bar food *12–2 & 6.30–9.30 (Sat & Sun till 10)*

Landlord *Mr A. Gillespie*
Free house
🍺 *Younger's Tartan Special; Carlsberg Export. No real ale.* 🍷

Accommodation *3 bedrooms* £C G2
Check-in all day

A delightful little inn in two acres of gardens with two terraces and views over the Tay valley. The bar is bright, sunny and well-kept with a central log-burning stove. A dining area by picture windows is served by friendly staff. The bar menu while not particularly exciting nevertheless offers simple, well-cooked food. Loch Etive mussels marinière come in huge, steaming portions with garlic bread. Fresh salmon salad has the fish carefully poached and moist, the salad crisp. Specials complement the printed menu and can feature game in season.

Typical dishes Loch Etive mussels marinière and garlic bread £4.75 Lasagne £2.65

Spacious, pleasantly bright bedrooms are comfortable and decorated with good pieces of antique furniture. All have duvets as well as cotton sheets, armchairs, coffee tables and TVs. Two incorporate small dressing areas and all three feature clean and simple bathrooms. The two front rooms have beautiful views, otherwise the back room is their equal. Children welcome overnight.

ABERGAVENNY   Llanwenarth Arms Hotel

Brecon Road NP8 1EP   FOOD
Map 6 D3 *Gwent*   B&B
Abergavenny (0873)
810550
Parking *ample*

Bar food *11–2 & 6–10, Sun 12–1.30
& 7–9.30*

Landlords *D'Arcy & Angela McGregor*
Free house
● *Wadworth 6X; Bass; Worthington Best
Bitter; Carlsberg; Tennent's Pilsner.*

Two stretches of salmon and trout fishing
on the river Usk are owned by this low,
whitewashed old inn perched on the banks,
and it also commands splendid views of the
Blorenge Mountain and Usk Valley. In the
two friendly bars and attractive conservatory, a wide choice of freshly prepared and
generously served food is available. As well
as stalwarts like home-made pâté, ploughman's, fish and steaks, there are weekly
changing specials such as cheese-topped
mushrooms with Madeira, prawns provençale and pork fillet sautéed with cream,
coconut liqueur and fresh pineapple.
Sweets might include rich truffle cake and
hot waffles. Barbecues are a popular summer feature.

Typical dishes French onion soup £2.25
Venison with red wine and mushroom
sauce £9.50

Accommodation *18 bedrooms* £B G1
Check-in all day

A three-storey annexe houses the compact
modern bedrooms, which all enjoy lovely
views. Floral fabrics contrast with darkwood furniture and all rooms offer tea-
makers, TVs and telephones. Private bathrooms are equally spotless. Children
welcome overnight. *No dogs.*

Credit Access, Amex, Diners, Visa

BABELL   Black Lion Inn

Nr Holywell CH8 8PZ   FOOD
Map 6 D1 *Clwyd*
Caerwys (0352) 720239
Parking *ample*

Bar food *12.15–2*
No bar food *eves, Sat & Sun lunches*
Closed *Mon eve (winter)*

Landlords *Mr & Mrs H.G.E. Foster*
Free house
● *Stones Best Bitter; Carling Black Label;
Carlsberg Hof. No real ale.* ☻

A peaceful country pub run since the mid-
1960s by friendly Mr and Mrs Foster. At
lunchtime food can be ordered from the à la
carte restaurant menu to eat in the mellow
bar: pâté, prawn cocktail or cheese salad for
something light, maybe veal in cream
sauce, grilled gammon or fillet of plaice
with lemon butter for a main dish. No bar
food in the evening, but a fixed-price
restaurant menu.
Typical dishes Poached haddock fillet
£4.55 Ham in mustard sauce £4.95

Credit Amex, Diners, Visa

BEAUMARIS   Liverpool Arms Hotel

Castle Street, Anglesey   B&B
LL58 8BA
Map 5 C1 *Gwynedd*
Beaumaris (0248) 810362
Parking *limited*

Landlords *Alex & Judith Borg*
Brewery *Scottish & Newcastle*
● *Younger's IPA, Scotch; Guinness;
McEwan's Lager; Beck's Bier.*

Accommodation *10 bedrooms* £B G1
Check-in all day

Although a hotel since 1700 the Liverpool
Arms is now completely modernised. All
that remains unsullied is a listed staircase.
Architectural heritage has given way to
theme, in this case maritime memorabilia.
There are some fine model sailing ships in
glass cases downstairs and the bedrooms
bear the names of famous admirals. These
simple, well-kept rooms have en suite bath
or shower rooms, colour TVs, direct-dial
telephones and tea-makers. Children
welcome overnight. *No dogs.*

Credit Access, Visa

BETWYS-YN RHOS   Ffarm Hotel

Nr Abergele LL22 8AR   FOOD
Map 5 C1 *Clwyd*
Dolwen (049 260) 287
Parking *ample*

Bar food *7–10*
Closed *lunches, all Sun & Mon (Oct–Easter)*

Landlords *Lomax family*
Free house
🍺 *Ind Coope Drum Mild; Tetley Bitter; Ansells Bitter; Wrexham Lager; Castlemaine XXXX.*

Eating is the favourite occupation in a pub that hides, signless, behind an impressive crenellated stone facade. Pleasant girls serve with a smile in the white-walled bars, where the printed menu and blackboard extras provide diners with a plentiful if mainly familiar choice. Liver and garlic pâté, prawns with a Marie Rose sauce or melon with fresh fruits could start the meal, with rack of lamb, seafood gratin or cannelloni to follow. Open evenings only.
Typical dishes Chicken creole £4.75 Vegetarian lasagne £4.25

BRECON   NEW ENTRY   Wellington Hotel

The Bulwark LD3 7AD   FOOD
Map 6 D3 *Powys*   B&B
Brecon (0874) 5225
Parking *ample*

Bar food *11 am–10.30 pm, Sun 12–10.30*

Landlords *Ian Blair & Anne Thomas*

Free house
🍺 *Hancocks HB Bitter; Bass; Allbright Bitter; Guinness; Tennent's Extra; Carling Black Label.*

The Wellington Hotel is a Georgian-fronted building in the centre of town. Besides providing excellent overnight accommodation it has an arcade with shops, a delightful coffee shop/bistro and a bustling pub called Duke's with whitewashed walls, wooden tables and a friendly, relaxed feel. A varied menu — the same for bar and coffee shop — makes good use of fresh ingredients for snacks such as croissants filled with cottage cheese and orange segments, spinach and cheese crunch, or variations on the ploughman's theme. Pancakes come with a temptation of fillings (ham and mushroom, ratatouille, chicken curry, stir-fried tuna with vegetables) and there are some lovely home-made sweets.

Typical dishes Stuffed pancakes £2.25 Beef bourguignon vol-au-vent £3.10

Accommodation *21 bedrooms* £B G1
Check-in all day

Good-sized bedrooms are very clean and attractively furnished, with bright bathrooms. Children are made particularly welcome, and family rooms and cots are available. Residents have a large, comfortable lounge. *No dogs*.

Credit Access, Amex, Diners, Visa

CARDIGAN   Black Lion Hotel

High Street SA43 1HJ   B&B
Map 5 B3 *Dyfed*
Cardigan (0239) 612532
Parking *difficult*

Landlord *Anthony Antoniazzi*
Free house
🍺 *Worthington Best Bitter, Dark Mild; Allbright Bitter; Guinness; Tennent's Extra; Carling Black Label.*

Accommodation *11 bedrooms* £C G2
Check-in all day

Hospitality has been a byword since 1105 at this much-enlarged town-centre inn, which later became an important coaching stop. Behind the present red-brick facade lies a characterful beamed interior, with some fine linenfold panelling featured in one of the bars. Pine-furnished bedrooms all offer en suite bath/shower rooms, colour TVs and tea-makers. Residents have the use of a comfortable upstairs TV lounge and quaint little writing room. Children welcome overnight. *No dogs*.

Credit Access, Visa

CENARTH — *White Hart*

Nr Newcastle Emlyn `FOOD`
SA38 9JP
Map 5 B3 *Dyfed*
Newcastle Emlyn (0239) 710305
Parking *ample*

Bar food *12–2.30 & 6.30–9.30
(Sun from 7)* ⛌

Landlords *Terry & Linda Parsons*
Free house
🍺 *Hancocks HB; Bass; Murphy Stout;
Carling Black Label.* ℮

Unpretentious, homely food is served at this characterful old pub in a tiny village. Low-beamed ceilings, a wood-burning stove and carved wooden pews set the scene for warming winter dishes like a hearty Welsh broth accompanied by crusty bread and cheese, chicken curry and steaks. In summer, the choice includes pizzas, filled jacket potatoes, salads and vegetarian specials. Children's menu. Garden.
Typical dishes Steak and kidney pie £2.75 Apple pie £1.50

CHEPSTOW — *Castle View Hotel*

16 Bridge Street NP6 5EZ
Map 6 E4 *Gwent*
Chepstow (029 12) 70349
Parking *ample*

Bar food *12–2 & 6.30–9.30*

Landlords *Martin & Vicky Cardale*
Free house
🍺 *Marston Burton Bitter, Pedigree;
Carlsberg Pilsner.*

Charming new owners Martin and Vicky Cardale make everyone welcome at this pretty, whitewashed inn just a stone's throw from Chepstow Castle. In the cosy bar with its highly polished tables and velvet-covered stools, tuck into simple snacks like leek and potato soup, sandwiches, ploughman's and home-made pâté, or opt for something more elaborate: perhaps salmon, prawn and cheese flan, pork with apple, bacon and cranberries in cider or vegetarian Gloucester cheese and chive lasagne. Sweets are interesting – hot apricots with yoghurt, or claret and blackcurrant jelly with orange.

Typical dishes Gloucester sausage and crusty bread £1.80 Prawns with stir-fry vegetables £4.50

Accommodation *11 bedrooms* £B G1
Check-in all day

Smart, well-kept bedrooms (including two in a modern annexe) are decorated in warm tones of brown, beige and copper and have an attractively cottage appeal. All offer en suite bathrooms, as well as mini-bars and hairdryers, TVs, tea-makers and telephones. The homely residents' lounge has glass doors opening onto a neat patio garden. Children welcome overnight.
Credit Access, Amex, Diners, Visa

CRICKHOWELL — *Bear Hotel*

NP8 1BW `B&B`
Map 6 D3 *Powys*
Crickhowell (0873) 810408
Parking *ample*

Landlords *Mr & Mrs Hindmarsh*
Free house ⛌
🍺 *Bass; Ruddles County; Webster
Yorkshire Bitter; Guinness; Holsten.*

Accommodation *27 bedrooms* £C G1
Check-in all day

On the A40 right in the town centre, this characterful old coaching inn has a splendid heavy-beamed main bar popular with locals and visitors alike. Overnight guests can also admire the many hunting trophies gathered in the homely panelled residents' lounge on the first floor. Solidly furnished bedrooms (some attractively grouped around a gallery) all have excellent bath-shower rooms as well as duvets, TVs and hairdryers. The honeymoon suite boasts a four-poster and whirlpool bathroom.
Credit Access, Visa

CRICKHOWELL   Nantyffin Cider Mill Inn

NP8 1SG   `FOOD`
Map 6 D3 *Powys*
Crickhowell (0873) 810775
Parking *ample*

Bar food *11.30–2.30 & 6–10,
Sun 12–2.30 & 7–9.30*

Landlord *John Flynn*
Free house
*Marston Pedigree; Worthington Best
Bitter; Whitbread Best Mild; Carlsberg
Hof.*

Pork and cider pie tops the popularity
stakes at this attractive former cider mill.
Other imaginative offerings to enjoy in the
cosy bar range from drunken chicken livers
and spicy beef with cashew nuts to daily
specials such as spinach-stuffed cannelloni
followed by lamb with fennel and Pernod.
Cold meat salads, grills and a fresh fish dish
are also available, with cider syllabub
among the desserts. Terrace and garden.
Typical prices Smoked haddock kedg-
eree £3.75 Sirloin steak £7

Credit Access, Visa

---

*We welcome bona fide recommendations
or complaints on the tear-out pages at the back
of the book for readers' comments.*

*They are followed up by our professional team,
but do complain to the management on the spot.*

EAST ABERTHAW   Blue Anchor

Nr Barry CF6 9DD   `A`
Map 6 D4 *South Glamorgan*
St Athaw (0446) 750329
Parking *ample*

Landlord *Jeremy Coleman*
Free house
*Theakston Old Peculier; Brains SA;
Wadworth 6X; Marston Pedigree; Murphy
Stout; Heineken.*

Jeremy Coleman has taken over the day-to-
day running of this ancient thatched pub
from his long-serving father, and it remains
an absolute delight to visit – despite the
deafening presence of Aberthaw power
station opposite. Dating back to medieval
times and dripping with ivy and creepers, it
is tiny inside, with thick old stone walls and
a maze of bars and drinking alcoves
reached by narrow passageways less than
two feet wide in places.

FELINDRE FARCHOG   Salutation Inn

Crymych SA41 3UY   `B&B`
Map 5 B3 *Dyfed*
Newport (0239) 820564
Parking *ample*

Landlords *Richard & Valerie Harden*
Free house
*Ansells Bitter, Mild; Ind Coope Burton
Ale; Tetley Bitter; Guinness; Castlemaine
XXXX.*

Accommodation *9 bedrooms* £C G2
Check-in by arrangement

The river Nevern runs through the grounds
of this cheerful pub beside the A487. Pale
wooden beams and pine pew seating characterise the two friendly bars, and there is a
bright, good-sized residents' lounge. Well-
kept bedrooms (including some family
rooms) in a modern wing contrast floral
quilts with plain white walls and all have
good desk space, radio-alarms, TVs and
fully fitted bathrooms with showers.
Garden.

Credit Access, Visa

FELINGWM UCHAF   NEW ENTRY   *Plough Inn*

Nantgaredig SA32 7PR
Map 5 C3 *Dyfed*
Carmarthen (0267) 88220
Parking *ample*

Bar food *12.15–2 & 7.15–9*
No bar food *Sun eve in winter*

Landlords *Leon Hickman & Eires Roberts*
Free house
🍺 *Bass; Worthington Best Bitter, Dark Mild; Tennent's Lager; Löwenbräu.* 🍷 ☺

FOOD
B&B

The Plough is jointly run with the adjoining Hickman's Restaurant. These linked 16th-century buildings are rooted on a steep incline that makes you wonder how coaches ever stopped here. The pub remains pleasantly rustic with its stone flagged floors, long bar, beamed ceilings and open fireplace. Bar food supplies most needs, with anything from sandwiches to moules marinière and pigeon breast in green peppercorn and Calvados sauce. Gourmets happy with bar surroundings may eat from the restaurant menu where chef-patrons Leon Hickman and Eires Roberts provide their respective specialities – duck en croûte and lobster thermidor.

Typical dishes Coq au vin £3.95 Open French apple tart £2

Accommodation *5 bedrooms* **£B G2**
Check-in all day

The bedrooms are across the road in a cottage. Beyond the panelled reception area, kitchen and breakfast room are five attractive bedrooms. Two have their own smart bathrooms; the other three share a large bathroom with a huge corner bath and bidet. Very clean, smart and new. Children welcome overnight. *No dogs.*

Credit Access, Amex, Diners, Visa

FFAIRFACH   *Torbay Inn*

Llandeilo SA19 6UL
Map 5 C3 *Dyfed*
Llandeilo (0558) 822029
Parking *ample*

Bar food *12–1.30 & 6–8*
No bar food *Sun lunch & Tues eve*
Closed *Sun eve*

Landlords *Callum & Vera Mackay*
Free house
🍺 *Buckley Best; Whitbread Mild; Welsh Bitter; Flowers IPA; Murphy Stout; Heineken.* ☺

FOOD

Homely, appetising bar snacks match the cosy, welcoming appeal of this tiny inn that is always packed at mealtimes. Squeeze in around a well-polished table in the beamed lounge bar for excellent fresh fish, including turbot, lobster salad and cod mornay, spicy vegetable curry, steak au poivre and cottage pie – all served in enormous portions. Stamina permitting, there is homemade fruit pie for afters. Children's menu. Garden.

Typical dishes Smoked trout pâté £2.75 Ham and vegetable pasta £3.25

GLYN CEIRIOG   *Golden Pheasant Hotel*

Nr Chirk LL20 7BB
Map 6 D2 *Clwyd*
Glyn Ceiriog (069 172) 281
Parking *ample*

Landlady *Jennifer Gibourg*
Free house
🍺 *Stones Bitter; Webster Yorkshire Bitter; Murphy Stout; Wrexham Lager; Carlsberg.* No real ale. 🍷

Accommodation *18 bedrooms* **£B G1**
Check-in all day

B&B

Old-world local and stylish country hotel come together in a delightfully peaceful valley setting that seems a million miles from urban bustle. Public rooms are crowned by a lovely bay-windowed lounge; there are two bars, one with Chinese Chippendale looks, the other with beams, slate and rustic trappings. Bedrooms are all prettily decorated, the best being quite grand in both decor and furnishings. Direct-dial phones and TVs in all rooms. Children welcome overnight. Garden and play area.

Credit Access, Amex, Diners, Visa

HAY-ON-WYE   **Kilvert Country Hotel**

Bull Ring HR3 5AG   `B&B`
Map 6 D3 *Powys*
Hay-on-Wye (0497) 821042
Parking *ample*

Landlord *L.K. Morelli*
Free house
🍺 *Bass; Flowers Best Bitter; guest beer; Guinness; Tennent's Extra; Carlsberg Pilsner.*

Accommodation *11 bedrooms* **£C G1**
Check-in all day

A pleasant town-centre inn dating from the late 17th century, and named after the diarist Reverend Francis Kilvert. The characterful single bar also doubles as reception, and behind a stained-glass partition is the intimate residents' lounge. Splendid brass bedsteads are a feature of the well-kept bedrooms, many of which are beamed. All have en suite shower rooms as well as hairdryers, trouser-presses, radios and tea-makers. Staff are young, bright and efficient. Children welcome overnight.

Credit Access, Amex, Visa

HAY-ON-WYE   **Old Black Lion**

Lion Street HR3 5AD   `B&B`
Map 6 D3 *Powys*
Hay-on-Wye (0497) 820841
Parking *ample*

Landlords *John & Joan Collins*
Free house
🍺 *Bass; Flowers Original, Best Bitter; Marston Pedigree; Whitbread Welsh Bitter; Guinness.*

Accommodation *10 bedrooms* **£C G2**
Check-in all day

The owners offer the warmest of welcomes in the cosy, comfortably appointed bar at their ancient coaching inn. Creaky, sloping floors and old beams characterise the warm, inviting main-house bedrooms, most striking of which is the Cromwell Room with its gallery. Annexe rooms are contrastingly modern and all but one of the ten bedrooms have neat private facilities. Wall-mounted TVs, direct-dial telephones, hairdryers and tea-makers are standard throughout. Children welcome overnight.

Credit Access, Amex, Visa

LLANARMON DYFFRYN CEIRIOG   **West Arms Hotel**

Nr Llangollen LL20 7LD   `B&B`
Map 6 D2 *Clwyd*
**Llanarmon Dyffryn Ceiriog
(069 176) 665**
Parking *ample*

Landlords *Tim & Carolyn Alexander*
Free house
🍺 *Worthington Best Bitter; Stones Bitter; Bass Mild; Tennent's Pilsner; Carling Black Label.* No real ale.

Accommodation *14 bedrooms* **£A G1**
Check-in all day

An attractive 400-year-old inn standing on the B4500 at the foot of the Berwyn Mountains. Individually decorated in pretty, cottagy style, the beamed bedrooms (including two suites) boast handsome antique furnishings and homely extras like potpourri and tissues. All have modern en suite bathrooms, and five rooms are reserved for non-smokers. Log fires warm the reception hall and delightfully traditional bars, and there is a peaceful residents' lounge with TV. Garden.

Credit Access, Amex, Diners, Visa

LLANDISSILIO   **Bush Inn**

Nr Clynderwen SA66 7TS   `FOOD`
Map 5 B3 *Dyfed*
Clynderwen (099 16) 626
Parking *ample*

Bar food *11–2.30 & 6.30–10.30,
Sun 12–1.30 & 7–10*

Landlords *Ken & Joyce Honeker*
Free house
🍺 *Crown Special Bitter, SBB; Guinness; Carlsberg.* ⊖

Paper money adorns the beams of the tiny bar within the small and characterful Bush. Polished tables, plants and dressers crammed with plates and ornaments provide a cosy background in the bright dining room, where help-yourself salads are displayed. Try them with turkey, ham or quiche, or choose something warming like steak and kidney pie. Good local cheeses and sweets such as treacle tart.
Typical dishes Turkey and vegetable soup £1 Chilli and salad £3.50

Credit Visa

LLANDOGO   *Sloop Inn*

Nr Monmouth NP5 4TW   `B&B`
Map 6 E4 *Gwent*
Dean (0594) 530291
Parking *ample*

Landlords *Grace Evans & George Morgan*
Free house
🍺 *Smiles Best Bitter; Wadworth 6X; Worthington Best Bitter; Murphy Stout; Hacker-Pschorr Lager.*

Accommodation *4 bedrooms* **£D G1**
Check-in all day

A friendly roadside inn, well patronised by the locals and named after the barges which once sailed here from Bristol. Plush red seating and warm red curtains make the bar a cosy spot, and there is a simpler public bar where darts and pool are played. Pretty pastel fabrics contrast attractively with darkwood furnishings in the excellent bedrooms, two of which enjoy lovely peaceful views. All have TVs, tea-makers and spotless en suite bathrooms. Children welcome overnight.

Credit Access, Amex, Diners, Visa

LLANDOVERY   *King's Head Inn*

Market Square SA20 0AB   `B&B`
Map 5 C3 *Dyfed*
Llandovery (0550) 20393
Parking *ample*

Landlords *Mr & Mrs D.P. Madeira-Cole*
Free house
🍺 *Worthington Dark Mild, Best Bitter; Hancock HB; Guinness; Carling Black Label.*

Accommodation *4 bedrooms* **£C G2**
Check-in all day

The Madeira-Coles have been welcoming visitors for over 18 years to their historic inn of medieval origins. Strikingly black painted with white woodwork, its projecting cornerstone (designed to protect the building from cartwheels) was used as a pulpit by the first Welsh Methodist. Inside, medieval stonework and massive low timbers (mind your head!) add to the charms of the neat bedrooms, all of which have tiled bathrooms en suite. Children welcome overnight.

LLANFRYNACH   *White Swan*

Nr Brecon LD3 7BZ   `FOOD`
Map 6 D3 *Powys*
Brecon (0874) 86276
Parking *ample*

Bar food *12–2.30 & 7–10.30, Sun 12–2 & 7–10*
No bar food *Mon*
Closed *Mon lunch & 3 wks Jan*

Landlords *David & Susan Bell*
Free house
🍺 *Brains Bitter; Flowers IPA; Whitbread Best Bitter; Guinness; Stella Artois.* ⊖

Flagstone floors, rough stone walls, beams and a vast inglenook create a simple rustic setting for the Bells' hearty, carefully prepared bar food at their pretty village pub. Welsh-style trout grilled with bacon, curries and tasty meat and fish pies are popular main dishes, while lighter bites range from potted shrimps to appetising bean and vegetable gratin. Pleasant sweets like chocolate cream mousse. Delightful flower-filled patio.
Typical dishes Chicken and mushroom pie £6.30 Baked crab £6.85

LLANGOLLEN   *Britannia Inn*

Horseshoe Pass LL20 8DW   `B&B`
Map 6 D2 *Clwyd*
Llangollen (0978) 860144
Parking *ample*

Landlords *Michael & Vicki Callaghan*
Free house
🍺 *Flowers IPA; Castle Eden; Whitbread Trophy; Chesters Best Mild; Stella Artois; Heineken.*

Accommodation *6 bedrooms* **£D G2**
Check-in all day

Rolling mountains and superb terraced gardens with a waterfall form the lovely setting for a white 15th-century hotel which originally sheltered monks. A burial area in the garden yields a good crop from their bones. Inside, ubiquitous 1950s furnishings are being removed, and the plain bar furniture offsets the magnificent views, also enjoyed from sloping ceilinged rooms. All have four-posters or half-testers, en suite bathrooms, TVs and trouser presses. Children welcome overnight.

Credit Access, Amex, Diners, Visa

LLANGORSE   *Red Lion*

Nr Brecon LD3 7TY   `B&B`
Map 6 D3 *Powys*
Llangorse (087 484) 238
Parking *ample*

Landlords *Ron Rosier & Geoff Hibbs*
Free house
🍺 *Flowers Original, IPA; Marston Pedigree; Whitbread Best Bitter; Stella Artois.* ❢

Accommodation *10 bedrooms* **£D G2**
Check-in all day

Nestling in a lovely valley between the Brecon Beacons and the Black Mountains is a pleasant village pub offering spotless accommodation in ten homely, comfortable bedrooms. Decor is either boldly chintzy or neatly neutral, and all rooms are equipped with tea-makers, TVs and radio-alarms. Half have simple but immaculately kept en suite bathrooms, the remainder showers and washbasins only. There is a tiny residents' lounge, and downstairs the two cosy, stone-walled bars positively gleam. Children welcome overnight. *No dogs.*

LLANGURIG   *Blue Bell Inn*

Nr Llanidloes SY18 6SG   `B&B`
Map 5 C3 *Powys*
Llangurig (055 15) 254
Parking *ample*

Landlords *Bill & Diana Mills*
Free house
🍺 *Samuel Powell Best Bitter; Welsh Bitter; Flowers Original; Whitbread Best Bitter; Stella Artois; Heineken.*

Accommodation *10 bedrooms* **£D G3**
Check-in by arrangement

A welcome in the hillside – courtesy of Diana and Bill Mills – awaits you in their charming fishing inn in Wales' highest village. An old black iron range stands on the slate floor of the simple, friendly bar. Enjoy a game of darts or dip into a book in the homely residents' lounge. Compact, rustic bedrooms have modern units and co-ordinated decor. One has en suite facilities; the others share two modern public bathrooms. Children welcome overnight. *No dogs.*

Credit Access, Visa

LLANNEFYDD   *Hawk & Buckle Inn*

Nr Denbigh LL16 5ED   `B&B`
Map 5 C1 *Clwyd*
Llannefydd (074 579) 249
Parking *ample*

Closed *Mon & Tues lunches in winter*

Landlords *Bob & Barbara Pearson*
Free house
🍺 *Bass, Mild; Carling Black Label; Tennent's Extra.*

Accommodation *10 bedrooms* **£C G2**
Check-in by arrangement

Standing opposite the Saxon church, the Hawk and Buckle dates from the 17th century. A splendid mural of the village adorns the residents' entrance, and a couple of original beams lend character to the main bar. Bedrooms, mainly in an extension at the back, have built-in wardrobes with curtains for doors, direct-dial phones, TVs and tea-makers, as well as decent modern bathrooms with showers over the tubs. *No accommodation for children under eight. No dogs.*

Credit Access, Visa

---

*Changes in data sometimes occur
in establishments
after the Guide goes to press.*

*Prices should be taken as indications
rather than firm quotes.*

LLYSWEN — *Griffin Inn*

Nr Brecon LD3 0UR
Map 6 D3 *Powys*
Llyswen (087 485) 241
Parking *limited*

FOOD
B&B

Bar food *12–2 & 7–9*
No bar food *Sun eve*

Landlords *Richard & Di Stockton*
Free house
🍺 *Flowers Original, IPA; Brains Bitter; Whitbread Best Bitter; Everards Bitter; Stella Artois.* ⊖

Accommodation *6 bedrooms* **£D G2**
Check-in all day

Whichever way you approach it, a beautiful scenic drive is the prelude to first-class eating in Richard and Di Stockton's charming old fishing inn. Fish features on an imaginative menu in the warm beamed bars, typified by cod and prawn au gratin, grilled mackerel and locally smoked salmon. Liver and bacon is a perennial favourite and soups are excellent. Desserts could include treacle tart, lemon crunch and a deliciously different hazelnut and coffee whirl made with yoghurt. Portions are enormous, so a good country walk is in order before and after a meal in this really delightful spot in the Upper Wye Valley.

Typical dishes Hunter's rabbit £4.25 Pigeon in cider £4.50 Lamb's liver & bacon £3.75 Smoked haddock & spaghetti cheese £3.25

Bedrooms are attractively decorated in cottage style, clean and very well maintained, with spotless bath or shower rooms and direct-dial phones. They do not have TVs, but there is a set in the landing lounge area.

Credit Access, Amex, Diners, Visa

MONMOUTH — *Queen's Head Inn*

St James' Street NP5 3DL
Map 6 E4 *Gwent*
Monmouth (0600) 2767
Parking *ample*

B&B

Landlords *Margaret & Alan Statham*
Free house
🍺 *Bass; Flowers IPA; Samuel Smith's Old Brewery Bitter; Stella Artois.* 🍷

Accommodation *3 bedrooms* **£D G2**
Check-in all day

Comfort combines with curios at this half-timbered inn whose history sweeps back to the Stuarts. Heavy beams span rough stone walls decorated with pewter mugs in the main bar. Pool is played in the public bar. Smallish bedrooms have colourful, co-ordinated, cottagy furnishings, good-sized beds with duvets and modern carpeted bathrooms fitted with hairdryers. Two rooms have shower only. Accommodation closed 25 and 26 December. Children welcome overnight.

Credit Access, Visa

MUMBLES — *Langland Court Hotel*

31 Langland Court Road,
Langland Bay SA3 4TD
Map 5 C4 *West Glamorgan*
Swansea (0792) 361545
Parking *ample*

B&B

Landlord *Mr C.R. Birt*
Free house
🍺 *Worthington Best Bitter, Dark Mild; Allbright Bitter; Carling Black Label; Tennent's Extra.* 🍷

Accommodation *21 bedrooms* **£B G1**
Check-in all day

A panelled entrance hall complete with grand oak staircase makes a striking first impression at this peaceful clifftop hotel. Leading off the hall is the pubby Polly's Bar, while the lounge has patio windows opening onto the garden. Best bedrooms overlook the garden and are furnished in luxurious style (some with four-posters), while remaining rooms in the converted coach house are more modest, but equally well equipped. Private facilities throughout. Children welcome overnight.

Credit Access, Amex, Diners, Visa

NOTTAGE   *Rose & Crown*

Heol-y-Capel, Nr Porthcawl   `B&B`
CF36 3ST
Map 5 C4 *Mid Glamorgan*
Porthcawl (065 671) 4850
Parking *ample*

Landlord *Mr J.W. Rout*
Owner *Westward Hosts*
🍺 *Webster Yorkshire Bitter; Ruddles Best Bitter, County; Truman Special Bitter; Carlsberg; Holsten.*

Accommodation *8 bedrooms* **£B G1**
Check-in all day

Very popular as an overnight stop, this old whitewashed pub offers excellent accommodation in eight pretty, pine-furnished bedrooms. All the rooms have neat, fully-tiled bathrooms with good showers over the tub, as well as trouser presses, TVs and direct-dial telephones. Downstairs, potted plants and well-polished brass counters add to the homely charms of the comfortable, beamed bars with their rustic stone walls and wooden settles. Children welcome overnight. *No dogs*.

Credit Access, Amex, Diners, Visa

PANT MAWR   *Glansevern Arms*

Nr Llangurig SY18 6SY   `B&B`
Map 5 C2 *Powys*
Llangurig (055 15) 240
Parking *ample*

Landlord *Mr W.T.O. Edwards*
Free house
🍺 *Bass; Worthington Dark Mild; Carlsberg Hof.*

Accommodation *8 bedrooms* **£C G2**
Check-in all day

Polished brass candlesticks and antimacassars give a pleasingly dated air to the charming little pub where Mr and Mrs Edwards have held sway for 38 years. The neat, cheerful bedrooms are just large enough for the TV and tea/coffee-making equipment; all have bathrooms, three with shower only. Ask for one of the front rooms, which have beautiful views down the upper reaches of the Wye valley. Children welcome overnight. Accommodation closed two weeks Christmas.

PEMBROKE   *Old King's Arms Hotel*

Main Street SA71 4JS   `B&B`
Map 5 A4 *Dyfed*
Pembroke (0646) 683611
Parking *ample*

Landlady *Ms G. A. Wheeler*
Free house
🍺 *Courage Directors; Worthington Best Bitter; Beamish Stout; Guinness; Carlsberg.*

Accommodation *20 bedrooms* **£C G1**
Check-in all day

Wall lamps cast lovely soft shadows in the cosy, stone-walled bars of this ancient coaching inn on the main street. Run by the same family for over 30 years, the welcome is genuinely warm and the service friendly and helpful. Homely bedrooms, including some with beamed ceilings in the main building, others in an extension, vary in size but all have good desk space and facilities, cheerful floral bedspreads and pristine bathrooms supplied with ample towels. Children welcome overnight.

Credit Access, Amex, Visa

PENLLYN   *The Fox at Penllyn*

Nr Cowbridge CF7 7RQ   `FOOD`
Map 6 D4 *South Glamorgan*
Cowbridge (044 63) 2352
Parking *ample*

Bar food *12–2.30 & 7–10*
No bar food *Sun eve*

Landlords *Sarah & Nigel Collett*
Free house
🍺 *Flowers Original; Whitbread Best Bitter; Fremlins Bitter; Stella Artois; Heineken.* ⊝

Sundays apart, lunch is an informal affair at gingham-covered tables in the bar of this pleasant, white-shuttered pub. Local fish dominates the blackboard list of daily specials, and you will also find soup, sandwiches, pasta and appetising meat dishes such as veal escalope stuffed with spinach and garlic cheese. Evening meals are served in the restaurant.
Typical dishes Salmon with chive and leek sauce £6.95 Deep-fried Brie with Cumberland sauce £3.85

Credit Access, Amex, Diners, Visa

PENMAENPOOL   *George III Hotel*

Nr Dolgellau LL40 1UD   `B&B`
Map 5 C2 *Gwynedd*
Dolgellau (0341) 422525
Parking *ample*

Landlady *Gail Hall*
Free house
🍺*John Marston Premium; Welsh Bitter;*
Guinness; Carlsberg Hof, Export.
No real ale.

Accommodation *12 bedrooms* £C G1
Check-in all day

Stay in the converted railway station house or at the inn proper at the head of the Mawddach estuary. An antique Welsh dresser has been cleverly divided to form the counter and bottle shelves, while fishing nets catch a nautical feel in the first-floor bar with terrace. The cellar bar has beams overhead and slate underfoot with tables at the roadside. Bedrooms have Stag furniture, carpeted bathrooms, TVs and telephones. Children welcome overnight. Accommodation closed two weeks Christmas.

Credit Access, Amex, Diners, Visa

PENYBONT   *Severn Arms Hotel*

Nr Llandrindod Wells   `B&B`
LD1 5UA
Map 6 D3 *Powys*
Penybont (059 787) 224
Parking *ample*

Landlords *Geoff & Tessa Lloyd*
Free house
🍺*Bass; Allbright Bitter; Worthington Best*
Bitter; Whitbread Welsh Bitter; Tennent's
Extra; Carling Black Label.

Accommodation *10 bedrooms* £D G2
Check-in all day

The A44 is the old coaching route from west Wales to the English Midlands, and this black-and-white pub was once a staging post. Two roomy bars cope well with the summer rush, and a large garden invites outside drinking. Ten bright, welcoming bedrooms include some that enjoy lovely views from a top-floor position. Private bathrooms, TVs, dial-out phones and clock-radios are standard. Children welcome overnight. Accommodation closed one week Christmas.

Credit Access, Visa

RAGLAN   *Beaufort Arms Hotel*

High Street NP5 2DY   `FOOD`
Map 6 D4 *Gwent*   `B&B`
Raglan (0291) 690412
Parking *ample*

Bar food *12–2.30 & 7–10*
(summer from 6.30) ☙

Landlords *Mr & Mrs Dorey*
Free house
🍺*Courage Best Bitter, Directors;*
Guinness; Foster's; Kronenbourg
1664.❦ ❸

Accommodation *10 bedrooms* £C G1
Check-in all day

Spotlessly maintained inside and out, this smart, whitewashed village inn dates from the early 15th century and features exposed stonework and original Tudor timbers in its popular little Castle Country bar, while an intricately carved counter provides an attractive focus in the relaxing lounge bar. Wholesome, home-made snacks such as creamy mushroom soup, sandwiches and ploughman's are supplemented by generously served daily specials like vegetable curry or chicken Portuguese (with wine, mushroom and tomato). Simple sweets like apple tart or sherry trifle to finish, and a traditional roast lunch on Sunday. Children's menu and outdoor play area in the garden.

Typical dishes Poached salmon £5.95 Deep-fried mushrooms with garlic cheese £1.95

Ten bright, comfortable bedrooms with pretty coordinating fabrics and practical modern furniture that includes a desk area; all have well-kept bathrooms as well as TVs, tea-makers and direct-dial telephones. There is a first-floor residents' lounge and patio for al fresco meals.

Credit Access, Amex, Diners, Visa

TRECASTLE   *Castle Hotel*

Nr Sennybridge LD3 8UH   `B&B`
Map 8 B3 *Powys*
Sennybridge (087 482) 354
Parking *ample*

Landlords *Clive Marshall & Tim Stanbury*
Free house
🍺 *Courage Directors; John Smith's Yorkshire Bitter; Guinness; Kronenbourg 1664; Foster's.*

Accommodation *9 bedrooms* **£D G2**
Check-in by arrangement

May 1989 saw the arrival of new owners Clive Marshall and Tim Stanbury here. Quite what renovations they plan at the Castle, an old coaching inn in the village centre, is uncertain. Of seven bedrooms, two had lace-trimmed four-poster beds, four were en suite (one with a bath, three with showers), and all had TVs and tea/coffee-making facilities. These would probably be a first priority. The bar's heavy oak beams and open fireplace will clearly stay. Children welcome overnight.

Credit Access, Diners, Visa

WHITEBROOK   *The Crown at Whitebrook*

Nr Monmouth NP5 4TX   `FOOD` `B&B`
Map 6 E4 *Gwent*
Monmouth (0600) 860254
Parking *ample*

Bar food *12–2 & 7–9.30*

Landlords *Roger & Sandra Bates*
Free house
🍺 *Whitbread Best Bitter; Warsteiner.* No real ale.

Feeling more like a little French-style auberge than a Welsh pub, the Crown is set in peaceful, secluded surroundings on a hillside. The atmosphere is informal under the new landlords Roger and Sandra Bates, he looking after the bar, she doing sterling work in the kitchen. Bar snacks run from soup and pâté to crab and prawn pancakes, home-made ices and apple tartlet glazed with apricots and Calvados. There are some first-class Welsh cheeses. Main courses on the fixed-price lunch and dinner restaurant menus include salmon, prawn and lobster mousse with a cherry brandy sauce, pork charcutière in puff pastry and sautéed chicken with a sauce of yoghurt, lime and tarragon. Vegetarian dishes and traditional Sunday lunch. Excellent wines.

Typical dishes Pâté, salad & toast £3.25 Allumettes au fromage et crevettes £3.95

Accommodation *12 bedrooms* **£B G1**
Check-in all day

Cheerful, spotless bedrooms offer crisp bed linen and good new towels, plus TVs, clock-radios, dial-out phones and tea-makers. A super breakfast starts the day. Children welcome overnight. Accommodation closed two weeks end January.

Credit Access, Amex, Diners, Visa

Our inspectors never book in the name of Egon Ronay's Guides.

They disclose their identity only if they are considering an establishment for inclusion in the next edition of the Guide.

WOLF'S CASTLE　　　　　　　*Wolfe Inn*

Nr Haverfordwest SA62 5LS
Map 5 A3 *Dyfed*
Treffgarne (043 787) 662
Parking *limited*

Bar food *12–2 & 7–10*
No bar food *Sun & Mon eve*
Closed *Mon in winter*

Landlords *Mr & Mrs Fritz Neumann*
Free house
🍺 *Felinfoel Best Bitter; Worthington Best Bitter; Guinness; Löwenbräu; Carlsberg.* ⊖

Accommodation *1 bedroom* **£D G3**
Check-in by arrangement

Standing on the A40, some seven miles from Haverfordwest, this welcoming little inn is conveniently placed for lunch before the afternoon ferry at Fishguard. Inside, the stone-walled public bar and plush lounge bar are cosy and inviting, and there is an attractive restaurant with polished tables and soft lighting. Appetising bar snacks make good use of local produce, with choices like spicy tomato soup and smoked trout pâté, tasty salads and daily specials such as steak pie or lasagne. The restaurant menu offers more elaborate fare, like trout with almonds and various ways with steak, while home-made sweets include orange soufflé and strawberry gâteau.

Typical dishes Beef and vegetable soup £1.25 Chicken and mushroom pie £3.25

The single twin-bedded room in a converted outhouse has its own smart bathroom and kitchen. Neat and bright, with pretty quilt covers, tea-making facilities, TV and a trouser press, a comfortable night's stay is assured. Breakfast is served in the room. Children welcome overnight. *No dogs.*

Credit Access, Visa

CHANNEL ISLANDS

ST ANNE — *Georgian House*

Victoria Street
Map 9 D2 *Alderney*
Alderney (048 182) 2471
Parking *ample*

Bar food *12–2.30*
No bar food *Sun lunch (except summer) & eves*

Landlords *Elizabeth & Stephen Hope*
Free house
🍺 *Guernsey Best Bitter; Guinness; Breda.*
No real ale. 🍷 ⊖

Accommodation *4 bedrooms* **£B G2**
Check-in all day

Elizabeth and Stephen Hope are the convivial hosts at this attractive whitewashed Georgian town house standing on a picturesque cobbled street in the heart of St Anne. The characterful bar makes a pleasant spot for enjoyable lunchtime snacks like chilled tomato soup, steak and mushroom pie and sandwiches, along with the best of the day's catch – including brill, sole and lobster. Finish with tangy lemon mousse or strawberry charlotte. A more elaborate menu is offered in the dining room, and throughout the summer there is a popular barbecue in the garden. Wednesday evenings and Sunday lunchtimes bring a carvery with a choice of roasts.

Typical dishes Sautéed kidneys with tarragon £4.50 Bread & butter pudding £1.25

Light and airy bedrooms with practical modern furnishings and pretty curtains all offer tea-makers, TVs, radio-alarms and well-kept private bathrooms. Residents have their own breakfast room and homely TV lounge. Children welcome overnight.

Credit Access, Amex, Diners, Visa

PLEINMONT — *Imperial Hotel*

Torteval
Map 9 C3 *Guernsey*
Guernsey (0481) 64044
Parking *ample*

Landlords *Mr & Mrs J.W. Hobbs*
Brewery *Randall*
🍺 *Randall Best Bitter; Worthington 'E'; Guinness; Breda.* No real ale.

Accommodation *16 bedrooms* **£C G2**
Check-in all day

A popular choice with families, this cheerful white-painted inn overlooking Rocquaine Bay and Portelet Harbour is run in friendly, informal fashion. Two comfortable residents' bars enjoy fine sea views and the convivial public bar is a favourite with the locals. Neat good-sized bedrooms with functional modern units and unfussy fabrics all offer TVs and tea-makers; most have tiled en suite bathrooms. Children welcome overnight.

Credit Access, Visa

ST AUBIN'S HARBOUR   Old Court House Inn

The Bulwarks
Map 9 D3 *Jersey*
Jersey (0534) 46433
Parking *difficult*

`FOOD`
`B&B`

Bar food *12.30–2.15 & 7.30–9*
No bar food *eves (in summer) & all Sun*

Landlord *Jonty Sharp*
Free house
🍺 *Mary Ann Special; John Smith's Yorkshire Bitter; Guinness; Stella Artois; Harp.* ⊖

Accommodation *9 bedrooms* **£A G1**
Check-in all day

A splendid position overlooking the characterful harbour is enjoyed by this tall, white-painted 15th-century inn. Simple but appetising lunchtime snacks are served in the lively, atmospheric cellar bars which boast exposed stone walls and low oak-beamed ceilings. Choose from ploughman's, salads or something more substantial – perhaps fresh local fish, lasagne, grilled king prawns or a daily special like devilled whole baby chicken. A second, quieter bar upstairs is shaped like a ship's cabin and panelled throughout in teak; there is a relaxing little lounge, too.

Typical dishes Moules marinière £3.75
Pint of prawns £3.75

The nine bedrooms tastefully blend pretty, co-ordinating wallpapers and fabrics with lovely old pine furnishings. All offer direct-dial telephones, tea and coffee making facilities and TVs, as well as excellent, stylishly tiled bathrooms. Many (including the penthouse suite) have the bonus of fine sea views. Children welcome overnight. *No dogs.*

Credit Access, Visa

ISLE
OF MAN

PEEL   Creek Inn

The Quayside
Map 3 A3 *Isle of Man*
Peel (062 484) 2216
Parking *ample*

`FOOD`

Bar food *11 am–11 pm, Sun 12–1.30 & 8–10*

Landlords *Robert & Jean McAleer*
Brewery *Okells*
🍺 *Okell Bitter, Mild; Guinness; Harp; Holsten Pils.* 🍷 ⊖

A bustling pub right by the quayside of Peel harbour, out of which working boats ply their trade. The industrious and friendly landlords Robert and Jean McAleer offer seafood specialities in their large, bright and unpretentious bar: kipper pâté and Manx scallops (known as Queenies) served on the shell in a mornay sauce are just two. Other dishes are meaty oxtail soup, lasagne, salads and pizzas. Apple pie or chocolate fudge gâteau to follow.

Typical dishes Steak & kidney pie £3.20
Queenies mornay £4.20

Index

This index has been split into the following sections: London, England, Scotland, Wales, Channel Islands and Isle of Man. Within the England, Scotland and Wales sections, the entries have been further grouped by county. The establishments have then been listed in alphabetical order by pub name, followed by town/village name, category (F = food; B&B = accommodation; A = atmosphere) and page number of the entry in the gazetteer.

An Offer for Answers

A Discount on the Next Guide (For UK residents only)

Readers' answers to questionnaires included in the guide prove invaluable to us in planning future editions, either through their reactions to the contents of the current Guide, or through the tastes and inclinations indicated. Please send this tear-out page to us *after you have used the Guide for some time*, addressing the envelope to:

Egon Ronay's Coca-Cola Pub Guide
City Wall House, Basing View, Basingstoke, Hampshire
RG21 2AP

As a token of thanks for your help, we will enable respondents resident in the UK to obtain the 1991 Guide post free from us at $33\frac{1}{3}$% discount off the retail price. We will send you an order form before publication, and answering the questionnaire imposes no obligation to purchase. All answers will be treated in confidence.

This offer closes 30 June 1990 and is limited to addresses within the United Kingdom

Please print *your name and address here if you would like us to send you a pre-publication order form for the next Guide.*

Name _____

Address _____

_____

_____ Postcode _____

Please tick

1. Are you?					
male?		*15–24?*		*45–54?*	
female?		*25–34?*		*55–64?*	
		35–44?		*over 65?*	

2. Your occupation

3. Do you have any children?   *Yes* ☐   *No* ☐

4. Do you have any previous editions of this Guide?
1987 ☐   *1988* ☐   *1989* ☐

5. Do you refer to this Guide

four times a week?		*once a week?*	
three times a week?		*once a fortnight?*	
twice a week?		*once a month?*	

6. How many people, apart from yourself, are likely to consult this Guide (including those in your home and place of work)?

7. Do you have our Hotel & Restaurant Guide?

1988 [____]   *1989* [____]   *1990* [____]

8. Do you have our Just a Bite Guide?

1988 [____]   *1989* [____]   *1990* [____]

9. How many times have you travelled overseas in the past year?

Business [____]   *Pleasure* [____]

10. How many nights have you spent in hotels during the past year?

11. Do you occupy more than one home?   *Yes* [____]   *No* [____]

Do you own the house you live in?   *Yes* [____]   *No* [____]

12. Your car

type   *year*

13. What is your daily newspaper?

14. What is the total annual income for your household?

under £5,000 p.a. [____]	*£20,000–£29,999 p.a.* [____]
£5,000–£9,999 p.a. [____]	*£30,000–£39,999 p.a.* [____]
£10,000–£14,999 p.a. [____]	*£40,000 p.a. or over* [____]
£15,000–£19,999 p.a. [____]	

15. Which of the following cards do you use?

Access [____]   *Diners* [____]

American Express [____]   *Visa* [____]

16. What fields would you like us to survey or what improvements do you suggest?

....

....

....

....

....

....

....

....

....

....

....

....

....

....

....

Readers' Comments

Please use this sheet to recommend bar snacks or inn accommodation of **really outstanding** quality – *not* full restaurant or hotel facilities. Your complaints about any of the Guide's entries will be treated seriously and passed on to our inspectorate, but we would like to remind you always to take up your complaint with the management at the time.

Please post to: ***Coca-Cola Pub Guide 1990***
Egon Ronay's Guides, City Wall House, Basing View,
Basingstoke, Hampshire RG21 2AP

Name and address of establishment
(Please state whether food or accommodation)

Your recommendation or complaint

NB We regret that owing to the enormous volume of readers' communications received each year, we will be unable to acknowledge these forms but they will certainly be seriously considered.

Name of Sender
(in block letters) _____

Address of Sender
(in block letters) _____

_____

Readers' Comments

Please use this sheet to recommend bar snacks or inn accommodation of **really outstanding** quality – *not* full restaurant or hotel facilities. Your complaints about any of the Guide's entries will be treated seriously and passed on to our inspectorate, but we would like to remind you always to take up your complaint with the management at the time.

Please post to: *Coca-Cola Pub Guide 1990*
Egon Ronay's Guides, City Wall House, Basing View,
Basingstoke, Hampshire RG21 2AP

Name and address of establishment
(Please state whether food or accommodation)

Your recommendation or complaint

NB We regret that owing to the enormous volume of readers' communications received each year, we will be unable to acknowledge these forms but they will certainly be seriously considered.

Name of Sender
(in block letters) _____
Address of Sender
(in block letters) _____

Readers' Comments

Please use this sheet to recommend bar snacks or inn accommodation of **really outstanding** quality – *not* full restaurant or hotel facilities. Your complaints about any of the Guide's entries will be treated seriously and passed on to our inspectorate, but we would like to remind you always to take up your complaint with the management at the time.

Please post to: *Coca-Cola Pub Guide 1990*
Egon Ronay's Guides, City Wall House, Basing View,
Basingstoke, Hampshire RG21 2AP

Name and address of establishment
(Please state whether food or accommodation)

Your recommendation or complaint

NB We regret that owing to the enormous volume of readers' communications received each year, we will be unable to acknowledge these forms but they will certainly be seriously considered.

Name of Sender
(in block letters) _____

Address of Sender
(in block letters) _____

Readers' Comments

Please use this sheet to recommend bar snacks or inn accommodation of **really outstanding** quality – *not* full restaurant or hotel facilities. Your complaints about any of the Guide's entries will be treated seriously and passed on to our inspectorate, but we would like to remind you always to take up your complaint with the management at the time.

Please post to: ***Coca-Cola Pub Guide 1990***
Egon Ronay's Guides, City Wall House, Basing View,
Basingstoke, Hampshire RG21 2AP

Name and address of establishment
(Please state whether food or accommodation)

Your recommendation or complaint

NB We regret that owing to the enormous volume of readers' communications received each year, we will be unable to acknowledge these forms but they will certainly be seriously considered.

Name of Sender
(in block letters) _____

Address of Sender
(in block letters) _____

Readers' Comments

Please use this sheet to recommend bar snacks or inn accommodation of **really outstanding** quality – *not* full restaurant or hotel facilities. Your complaints about any of the Guide's entries will be treated seriously and passed on to our inspectorate, but we would like to remind you always to take up your complaint with the management at the time.

Please post to: *Coca-Cola Pub Guide 1990*
Egon Ronay's Guides, City Wall House, Basing View,
Basingstoke, Hampshire RG21 2AP

Name and address of establishment
(Please state whether food or accommodation)

Your recommendation or complaint

NB We regret that owing to the enormous volume of readers' communications received each year, we will be unable to acknowledge these forms but they will certainly be seriously considered.

Name of Sender
(in block letters) _____

Address of Sender
(in block letters) _____

Readers' Comments

Please use this sheet to recommend bar snacks or inn accommodation of **really outstanding** quality – *not* full restaurant or hotel facilities. Your complaints about any of the Guide's entries will be treated seriously and passed on to our inspectorate, but we would like to remind you always to take up your complaint with the management at the time.

Please post to: *Coca-Cola Pub Guide 1990*
Egon Ronay's Guides, City Wall House, Basing View,
Basingstoke, Hampshire RG21 2AP

Name and address of establishment
(Please state whether food or accommodation)

Your recommendation or complaint

NB We regret that owing to the enormous volume of readers' communications received each year, we will be unable to acknowledge these forms but they will certainly be seriously considered.

Name of Sender
(in block letters) _____

Address of Sender
(in block letters) _____

'Dryblower' Murphy

I do not whine as others may
Of money I've misused;
Ah no, I only think today
Of pints that I've refused . . .
'Pints that I've Refused', Bulletin

Anonymous

The cheese-mites asked how the cheese got there,
And warmly debated the matter;
The orthodox said it came from the air,
And the Heretics said from the platter.
Notes and Queries

Anonymous

All animals are strictly dry,
They sinless live and swiftly die.
But sinful, Ginfull, Rum-soaked men
Survive by three-score years and ten,
And some of us – a Mighty Few –
Keep drinking 'till we're 92.
Rhyme printed on a tea towel

John Fletcher
1579–1625

Come landlord, fill a flowing bowl
Until it does run over,
Tonight we will all merry be –
Tomorrow we'll get sober.
The Bloody Brother

Ogden Nash
1902–71

Candy
Is dandy
But liquor
Is quicker.
'Reflections on Ice-Breaking', The Face is Familiar

Lake District

The glaciers of the Ice Age created a landscape in the north-west of England unique in its variety. The vast range of Cumbrian mountains, lakes and waterfalls include the austerity of Scafell Pike, the beauty of Buttermere and drama of Dungeon Ghyll. Secluded valleys, narrow mountain passes and remote footpaths offer choice walks and motoring tours. While tourism has been the only activity to wake the sleepy villages of Hawkshead, Coniston and Grasmere, industrial development has had a great effect along the Cumbrian coastline; harbours and seaside villages alternate with industrial towns including the busy coal and seaports of Whitehaven and Workington. Unspoilt regions of the Lake District, however, continue to inspire, as they did in the days of the well-known 19th-century poet, William Wordsworth. Visitors to the area can follow in the footsteps of artists and writers, such as Robert Southey, Beatrix Potter and the 20th-century walking enthusiast, A. Wainwright.

Places to Visit

1. Brockhole National Park Centre near Windermere, a house containing audio-visual exhibitions on all aspects of the Lake District; set in beautiful lakeside gardens with nature trails and summer launch trips. *D3*

2. Cartmel Priory Gatehouse (National Trust) Cavendish Street, Grange-over-Sands, the remainder of an Augustinian Priory, dating from about 1330. *D5*

3. Cockermouth *Wordsworth House* (National Trust) Georgian town house and birthplace of William Wordsworth. *B1*

4. Coniston *Brantwood* beautifully situated home of John Ruskin 1819–1900, containing a collection of Ruskin drawings and watercolours, exhibitions and the Lakeland Guild Craft Gallery. *D4*

5. Coniston Water *Steam Yacht Gondola* (National Trust) first launched in 1859, and renovated to provide a comfortable passenger service on the lake. *D4*

6. Grasmere *Dove Cottage* home of Wordsworth during his most creative years, and the Wordsworth museum houses a display of manuscripts and treasures associated with Wordsworth and British Romanticism. *D3*

7. Hawkshead *Beatrix Potter Gallery* (National Trust) The Square, including a selection of Beatrix Potter's original drawings and illustrations of her children's story books. *D4*

8. Kendal *Brewery Arts Centre* 150-year-old brewery, converted into an arts centre with a programme of exhibitions, theatre and music. *E4*

9. Lake Side & Haverthwaite Railway near Newby Bridge, steam locomotives haul trains on a steeply graded line through the lake and river scenery of the Leven Valley. *D5*

10. Levens Hall & Topiary Garden near Levens Bridge, an Elizabethan house with fine Jacobean furniture, panelling and plasterwork; the famous topiary garden was laid out in 1692. *E5*

11. Lingholm Gardens near Keswick, on the western shore of Derwent Water with formal and woodland gardens, rhododendrons and shrubs. *C1*

12. Mirehouse near Keswick, 17th-century manor house with original furniture; connected with Bacon, Wordsworth and Tennyson. *C1*

13. Near Sawrey *Hill Top* (National Trust) Ambleside, 17th-century house, home of Beatrix Potter, where she wrote many of her Peter Rabbit books. *D3*

14. Newby Bridge *Fell Foot Park* (National Trust) Ulverston, 18-acre country park with lakeside access and good views; rowing boats for hire. *D5*

15. Penrith Steam Museum including a collection of steam traction engines, steam models and vintage farm machinery and a working blacksmith's. *E1*

16. Ravenglass and Eskdale Railway 15-inch gauge railway providing a daily service in season, using steam or diesel engines. *B4*

17. Rydal Mount near Ambleside, Wordsworth's home from 1813 until his death in 1850, with a garden landscaped by the poet. *D3*

18. Sizergh Castle (National Trust) near Kendal, featuring the 14th-century pele tower and some fine Elizabethan overmantels, Strickland family portraits and furniture. *E5*

19. Temple Sowerby *Acorn Bank Garden* (National Trust) near Penrith, $2\frac{1}{2}$-acre garden with a vast display of daffodils beneath the oak trees. *E1*

20. Troutbeck *Townend* (National Trust) the fascinating home of the Brownes – a wealthy farmer's family – for over 300 years; built about 1626, it contains carved woodwork and family possessions. *D3*

21. Windermere Steamboat Museum a collection of steam, motor and sailing boats on the lakeside, many of them afloat and in working order. *D4*

Tourist Information Centres

Ambleside Old Courthouse, Church Street
Telephone (053 94) 32582

Cockermouth Riverside Car Park, Market Street
Telephone (0900) 822634

Kendal Town Hall, Highgate
Telephone (0539) 25758

Keswick Moot Hall, Market Square
Telephone (076 87) 72645

Penrith Robinson's School, Middlegate
Telephone (0768) 67466

Ravenglass Ravenglass & Eskdale Railway Car Park
Telephone (065 77) 278

Whitehaven St Nicholas Tower, Lowthern Street
Telephone (0946) 5678

Windermere The Gateway Centre, Victoria Street
Telephone (096 62) 6499

Area map 1

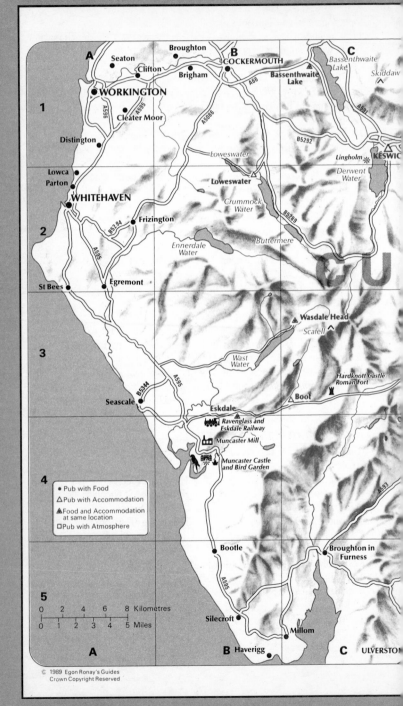

Broughton
Seaton
A
Clifton
B
COCKERMOUTH
Brigham
Bassenthwaite
Lake
Bassenthwaite
Lake
Skiddaw
C
WORKINGTON
A596
A595
A66
A5086
A591
1
Cleater Moor
B5292
Distington
Loweswater
Lingholm
KESWIC
Lowca
Parton
Loweswater
*Derwent
Water*
WHITEHAVEN
Crummock
Water
B5289
B5294
Frizington
*Ennerdale
Water*
Buttermere
2
A595
St Bees
Egremont
CU
Wasdale Head
Scafell
3
*Wast
Water*
B5344
A595
Hardknott Castle
Roman Fort
Seascale
Boot
Eskdale
*Ravenglass and
Eskdale Railway*
Muncaster Mill
A593
*Muncaster Castle
and Bird Garden*

• Pub with Food
△ Pub with Accommodation
▲ Food and Accommodation
at same location
□ Pub with Atmosphere

4
Bootle
**Broughton in
Furness**
A595

5
0   2   4   6   8 Kilometres
0   1   2   3   4   5 Miles
Silecroft
Millom
A
B Haverigg
C   **ULVERSTO**

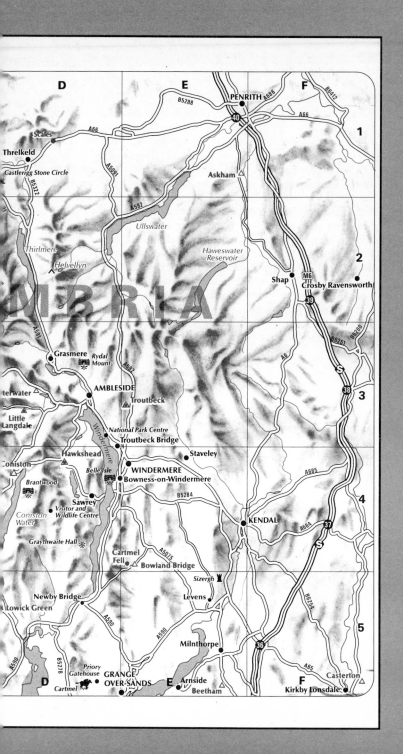

Yorkshire Dales

Popular walks in the Yorkshire Dales include The Three Peaks, a strenuous path over the summits of Pen-y-Ghent, Whernside and Ingleborough, and the Pennine Way which stretches up through the Dales across a landscape of secluded valleys, fields and becks. Green lanes, once used by monks, packhorses and villagers, offer pathways through such dales as Swaledale, the most remote of the Dales, and Wensleydale, generously wooded, broad and green. Natural features of the landscape are the limestone terraces, scars and crags, the potholes, rivers and waterfalls. Man-made features include the Norman castles of Richmond and Middleton, and the grand abbey ruins from the days of the great monastic landowners. Hamlets, barns and miles of limestone walls are common throughout the picturesque scenery; used mainly for farming and virtually free of modern industry, the countryside has remained unchanged for many years. An area of growth has been Harrogate, now popular both as a Victorian spa resort and as a cosmopolitan conference venue. The historic town of Richmond, market town of Hawes, and Skipton, the southern gateway to the Dales, are also busy with traders and admiring tourists.

Places to Visit

1. *Aysgarth Force* three waterfalls on the river Ure, also a carriage museum and nature trail. *D2*

2. *Bolton Abbey* remains of the 12th-century priory, set in beautiful surroundings with river walks to the Strid where water gushes between limestone ledges. *D5*

3. *Bolton Castle* impressive ruins beside the attractive village of Castle Bolton; built in 1379 for use as a fortified manor house by the first Lord Scrope, Chancellor of England. *D2*

4. *Brimham Rocks* (National Trust) blocks of millstone grit, eroded into strange shapes, creating an unusual landscape on the open moorland. *E4*

5. *Fountains Abbey & Studley Royal* (National Trust) Ripon, the dramatic ruins of the Abbey, founded in 1132, are the focal point of the 18th-century landscaped garden, with water garden, temples and follies. *F3*

6. *Grassington Museum* The Square, portrays life in upper Wharfedale, including items related to farming, local industries and trades. *D4*

7. Harrogate *Royal Baths Assembly Rooms* originally a hydrotherapy centre, now housing the Tourist Information Centre and Turkish baths. *F5*

8. Harrogate *Royal Hall* when opened in 1903, an entertainment venue for those taking the waters, now a theatre. *F5*

9. Harrogate *Royal Pump Room Museum* covers the strong sulphur well and contains local historical material. *F5*

10. *Jervaulx Abbey* founded as a Cistercian monastery in 1156, then owning large estates particularly in upper Wensleydale. The ruins are situated in attractive parkland. *E2*

11. Knaresborough *Mother Shipton's Cave* said to be the birthplace of the legendary 15th-century prophetess; also the site of the Petrifying Well. *F4*

12. Malham a focus of limestone country with nearby walks to Malham Cove and tarn. Gordale Scar can also be reached by a path alongside Gordale Beck and Janet's Foss, a tiny, pretty waterfall. *C4*

13. Middleham Castle now in ruins but known as 'the Windsor of North' when owned by the Neville family; Richard III acquired the castle in 1471. *D2*

14. Pateley Bridge *Nidderdale Museum* Old Council Offices, fascinating exhibition in a former Victorian workhouse, illustrating local life and history. *E4*

15. Reeth Swaledale Folk Museum Reeth Green, illustrates agricultural life, lead mining and past social conditions. *D1*

16. Richmond Castle a Norman castle with 11th century Scolland's Hall and fine views of the town from the 100-foot-high battlements on the keep. *E1*

17. Richmond *Georgian Theatre & Museum* Victoria Road, carefully restored theatre and collection of handbills and photographs; guided tours and regular programme of productions. *E1*

18. Ripon Cathedral a mixture of Gothic styles from 12th to 16th centuries but only the crypt remains of the original Anglo-Saxon church. *F3*

19. Skipton Castle once the 14th-century home of the Clifford family, rebuilt by Lady Anne Clifford and many of the remains today date from 1655–58. *C5*

20. Stump Cross Caverns between Hebden and Greenhow Hill, this magnificent cave system was discovered by lead-miners in 1858; splendid stalactite and stalagmite formations are floodlit in the main cave. *D4*

Tourist Information Centres

Harrogate Royal Baths Assembly Rooms, Crescent Road
Telephone (0423) 525666

Leyburn Commercial Square
Telephone (0969) 23069

Richmond Friary Gardens, Victoria Road
Telephone (0748) 3525

Ripon Wakemans House, Market Place
Telephone (0765) 4625

Settle Town Hall, Cheapside
Telephone (072 92) 3617

Skipton 8 Victoria Square
Telephone (0756) 2809

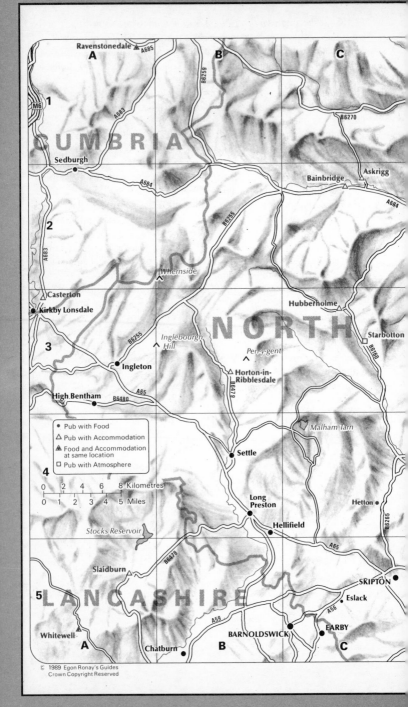

Pub with Food
△ Pub with Accommodation
▲ Food and Accommodation at same location
□ Pub with Atmosphere

0 2 4 6 8 Kilometres
0 1 2 3 4 5 Miles

© 1989 Egon Ronay's Guides
Crown Copyright Reserved

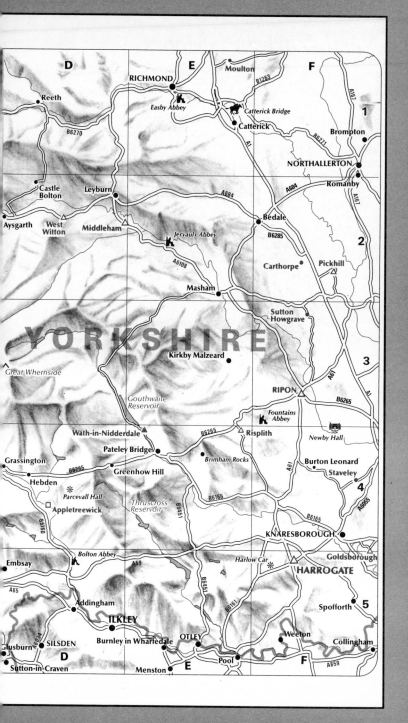

North Yorkshire Moors

The North Yorkshire Moors National Park is within easy reach of York, a city rich in history with architecture spanning centuries and remains dating back to the Vikings and Romans. Rising up from the flat Plain of York are the rolling Hambleton Hills and the escarpment of Sutton Bank, worth the steep ascent for its superb views. Central to the Park is the vast area of wild moorland, transformed in summer by a purple covering of heather. From the nearby Vale of Pickering the North Yorkshire Moors Railway passes through such attractive villages as Goathland, with its wide verges and greens, and Grosmont, the northern terminus where passengers can join the Esk Valley railway. The moors cross eastwards to the rugged coastline of cliffs, rocky shores and sandy beaches. The seaside resorts of Scarborough and Bridlington, the old harbour at Whitby and the fishing village of Robin Hood's Bay add further to the attractions of the coastline.

Places to Visit

1. Castle Howard built for Charles Howard, 3rd Earl of Carlisle, the work of architect Sir John Vanbrugh; in the 1,000-acre grounds there are two lakes, the Temple of the Four Winds and the Mausoleum. *C4*

2. Coxwold *Shandy Hall* home of clergyman and writer Laurence Sterne in the 18th century. *A3*

3. Helmsley Castle a few ruins of the 12th to 13th-century castle in this pleasant market town on the edge of the moors. *B3*

4. Hutton-le-Hole *Ryedale Folk Museum* an open-air museum incorporating a thatched Victorian cottage, reconstructed shops and farm buildings. *C2*

5. Kilburn *White Horse of Kilburn* a large turf-cut figure on the hillside, near the village where workshops and showrooms of 'The Mouseman', Robert Thompson, can be seen. *A3*

6. Kirby Misperton *Flamingo Land* near Malton, a fun park with rides, slides and shows, a cable car, monorail and animals. *C4*

7. Lastingham Church the Norman crypt dates back to about 1078 in the attractive church of this pleasant village. *C2*

8. Murton *Yorkshire Museum of Farming* near York, illustrates the history of farming, including demonstration crops, livestock and farm machinery. *B5*

9. Nunnington Hall (National Trust) York, mainly late 17th-century manor house on the banks of the River Rye, and houses the Carlisle Collection of Miniature Rooms. *B5*

10. Pickering *North Yorkshire Moors Railway* Pickering Station, passengers are taken, by steam locomotive, through the attractive countryside of the moors and dales as far as Grosmont. *C3*

11. Rievaulx Terrace & Temples (National Trust) Helmsley, a grassy terrace and woodlands offer views over the Cistercian Abbey and the Rye valley, across to Ryedale; temples include one in Ionic style with elaborate ceiling paintings. *B3*

12. Scarborough Castle above the bustle of the resort's seafront, the remains of this Norman castle have an imposing position on the headland. *E2*

13. Shipton-by-Beningbrough, *Beningbrough Hall* near York, an imposing 15th-century Georgian Hall built in 1716. *B5*

14. Whitby Abbey remains of a 13th-century abbey on the East Cliff of this picturesque fishing town. *D1*

15. York *Castle Museum* houses Dick Turpin's cell and collection of arms, armour and period costumes. A Victorian street has been recreated, complete with shops and stagecoach. *B5*

16. York *Jorvik Viking Centre* Coppergate, recreation of the Viking capital, also the original site where evidence of the settlement was discovered. *B5*

17. York *Merchant Adventurers' Hall* one of York's most fascinating medieval, timber-framed houses. *B5*

18. York Minster one of the greatest cathedral churches in the country; built between 1220 and 1470 its windows feature a large amount of medieval glass and the Undercroft houses an exhibition of Roman and Saxon remains. *B5*

19. York *National Railway Museum* contains the finest examples of the Nation's railway heritage, including a large collection of full-sized locomotives and carriages. *B5*

20. York *Treasurer's House* (National Trust) an elegant 17th to 18th-century town house with a fine collection of furniture and formal garden. *B5*

Tourist Information Centres

Bridlington 25 Prince Street
Telephone (0262) 673474
Pickering Pickering Station
Telephone (0751) 73791
Scarborough St Nicholas Cliff
Telephone (0723) 373333
Wetherby Council Offices, 24 Westgate
Telephone (0937) 62706

Whitby New Quay Road
Telephone (0947) 602674
York De Grey Rooms, Exhibition Square
Telephone (0904) 21756

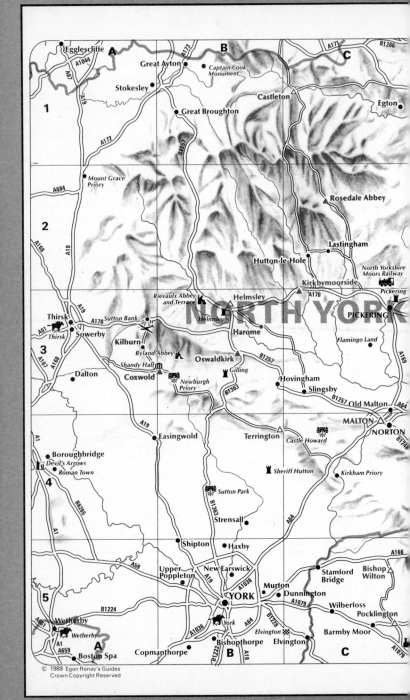

© 1989 Egon Ronay's Guides
Crown Copyright Reserved

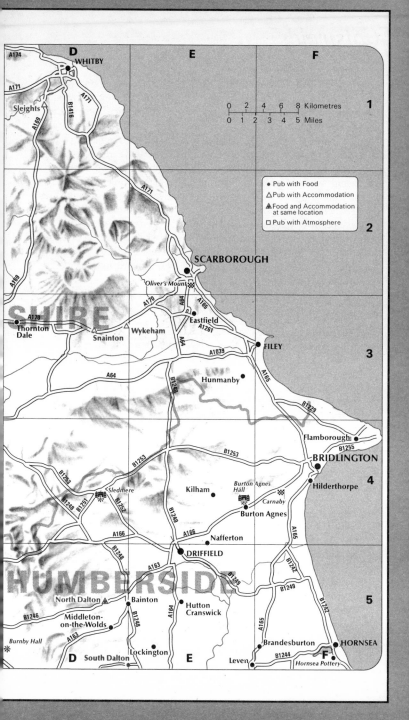

Cotswolds

Following a visit by George III in 1788, Cheltenham's reputation as a spa was established and its increased social status is reflected today in many fine Regency buildings. The town lies close to the scenic Cotswolds, an area of gently rising hills and picturesque villages where the use of local honey-coloured stone is characteristic. Also popular with sightseers is the university town of Oxford, a centre of learning for 800 years and a city of impressive architecture including the famous spires, ancient colleges and quadrangles. From Oxford, the surrounding Thames Valley area can be explored and from nearby Swindon the distinctive charm of such Wiltshire market towns as Malmesbury can be discovered, or Cirencester, the second most important city in Roman Britain. Swindon itself is a modern town, its present-day fortunes having been founded on the rich industrial heritage of the Great Western Railway. In contrast, on the ancient site of the Vale of the White Horse there are several relics left by prehistoric man, including the turf-cut figure of a horse.

Places to Visit

1. Bibury *Arlington Mill Cotswold Country Museum* A433, including a cornmill with working machinery and large museum. *C2*

2. Bourton-on-the-Water *The Model Village* Old New Inn, the actual village recreated in Cotswold stone to ⅑th scale. *C1*

3. Burford *Cotswold Wildlife Park* including tigers, leopards and zebra in parkland which surrounds a Gothic-style manor house, plus penguins, monkeys and tropical birds in the walled garden. *D2*

4. Cheltenham *Art Gallery and Museum* Clarence Street, with paintings, pottery and local history artefacts. *A1*

5. Cheltenham *Gustav Holst Birthplace* 4 Clarence Road, Pittville, a Regency house with 19th-century furnishings and working Victorian kitchen. *A1*

6. Cheltenham *Pump Room* Pittville Park, Albert Road, magnificent Regency buildings, where the spa waters can still be taken, also houses the Gallery of Fashion. *A1*

7. Cirencester *Park* 3,000 acres of parkland with woodland walks, Polo played every day through the summer. *B3*

8. *Cotswold Water Park* 5 miles south of Cirencester, off A419, 15,000 acres of lakes with facilities for angling, bird-watching, windsurfing and other water sports. *B3*

9. Faringdon *Buscot Park* (National Trust) 18th-century house with a collection of fine paintings and furniture, with park and water garden. *D3*

10. *Lydiard Mansion and Country Park* 5 miles west of Swindon, off A4, ancestral home of the Bolingbroke family, set in its own park and woodland. *C4*

11. Oxford *Ashmolean Museum* Beaumont Street, including art and

archaeology treasures, and the University of Oxford's collection of European paintings, bronzes and silverware. *F3*

12. Oxford *Botanic Garden* High Street, founded in 1621 it is one of the oldest in the country. *F3*

13. Oxford *Christ Church Cathedral* St Aldate's college chapel of Christ Church, dating from the 12th century. *F3*

14. Oxford *Divinity School* Broad Street, 15th-century with fine vaulted ceiling and exhibition of treasures from the Bodleian Library. *F3*

15. Oxford *Sheldonian Theatre* Broad Street, Wren's first work of architecture, used for conferment of degrees. *F3*

16. Oxford University Museum Parks Road, a Gothic building, designed with the help of John Ruskin, housing a natural history exhibition. *F3*

17. Swindon *Great Western Railway Museum* Faringdon Road, contains historic locomotives and other relics of the GWR, as well as a gallery devoted to I.K. Brunel. *C4*

18. Swindon *Oasis Leisure Centre* North Star Avenue, pools, water slides and other sports facilities, both indoor and outdoor. *C4*

19. Uffington Castle (National Trust) an Iron Age hill-fort dating from the 1st century BC, close to the figure of the white horse which is cut into the hillside. *D4*

20. Woodstock *Blenheim Palace* an 18th-century Baroque Palace by Vanbrugh, home of the 11th Duke of Marlborough and birthplace of Winston Churchill. *F2*

21. Yanworth *Chedworth Roman Villa* (National Trust) off A40/A429, remains of one of the best preserved Romano-British villas with well preserved pavements and bath house. *C2*

Tourist Information Centres

Abingdon 8 Market Place
Telephone (0235) 22711
Cheltenham Municipal Offices, Promenade
Telephone (0242) 522878
Cirencester Corn Hall, Market Place
Telephone (0285) 654180

Oxford St Aldate's
Telephone (0865) 726871
Swindon 32 The Arcade, Brunel Centre
Telephone (0793) 30328

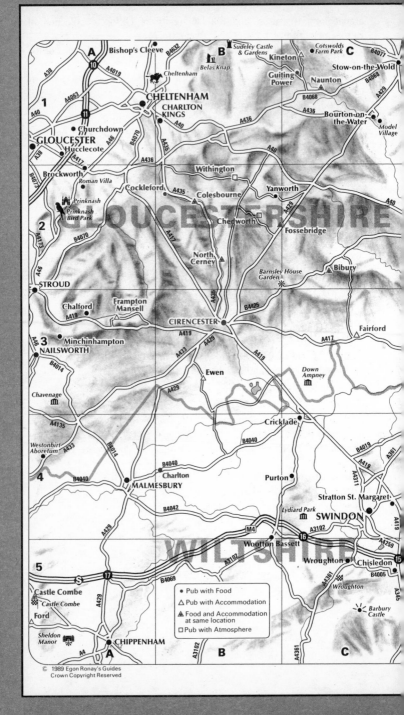

Pub with Food
△ Pub with Accommodation
▲ Food and Accommodation at same location
□ Pub with Atmosphere

© 1989 Egon Ronay's Guides
Crown Copyright Reserved

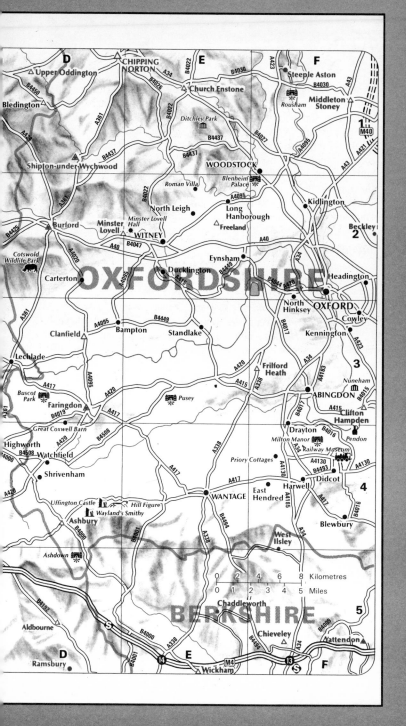

Kent

Kent has long been on the front line of England's defence as reflected in the many castle remains and fortifications, particularly in coastal areas. Rich in history, the county also boasts the oldest cathedrals in England (Canterbury and Rochester) and four of the five medieval Cinque Ports where old timbered houses and winding streets abound. Unspoilt coastal scenery ranges from the famous White Cliffs at Dover to the shingle spit and sandy beaches of Dungeness or Margate, and the marshlands between the estuaries of the Thames and Swale. Beautiful countryside includes the wooded slopes of the North Downs, the tranquil surrounds of the Medway, and the central fertile stretches of farmland, hop gardens and orchards.

Places to Visit

1. Bodiam Castle (National Trust) near Robertsbridge, built in 1385 but uninhabited since the 17th century, well preserved and remarkably intact. *B5*

2. Canterbury Cathedral site of Becket's martyrdom and shrine, also containing a Norman crypt, early-Gothic choir and 15th-century nave. *D2*

3. Canterbury Heritage Stour Street, a 'time-walk' museum with audio-visual displays telling the story of the city's history, set in the medieval Poor Priests' Hospital. *D2*

4. Canterbury *Pilgrims Way* St Margarets Street, re-creation of medieval England, depicting the journey taken by pilgrims to the shrine of Thomas Becket. *D2*

5. Chatham Historic Dockyard an area covering 80 acres, which includes a visitor centre, museum and ordnance collection. *A1*

6. Dover Castle (English Heritage) off Castle Hill Road, dominating the White Cliffs, a medieval fortress with 12th-century keep, rare Roman lighthouse and Saxon church. *F3*

7. Dover Museum & Gaol Ladywell, exhibition of Dover's local history, including model ships and displays of the town's defences and transport. *F3*

8. Folkestone a traditional seaside town which has managed to retain some of its charm, and the Leas promenade provides a cliff-top walk beside flower beds and lawns. *E4*

9. Herne Common *Brambles English Wildlife Park* Wealden Forest Park, unspoilt woodland area with a nature trail, children's farm, animals and a playground. *E1*

10. Lympne Castle near Hythe, a medieval castle overlooking Romney Marsh with Roman, Saxon and Norman history, rebuilt about 1360. *D4*

11. Maidstone *Allington Castle* off A20, 13th-century moated castle beside the river Medway and once the home of Thomas Wyatt, the Tudor poet. *A2*

12. Maidstone *Leeds Castle* 4 miles east of Maidstone, a fairytale medieval castle dating from the 9th century, built on two small islands in a lake and surrounded by parkland. *B2*

13. Margate Caves Lower Northdown Road, caverns hewn out of the chalk over 1,000 years ago, including two dungeons, and wall paintings. *F1*

14. Margate *The Shell Grotto* Grotto Hill, of Northdown Road, an ancient shell temple discovered over 140 years ago and including 2,000 sq ft of shell mosaic. *F1*

15. Otham *Stoneacre* small 15th-century, half-timbered manor house with a great hall and crownpost; restored in the 1920s. *B2*

16. Rochester Cathedral an imposing cathedral which is mainly Norman, dating from 1080; the crypt is particularly noteworthy. *A1*

17. Rochester *Charles Dickens Centre* Eastgate House, High Street, sound and light are used to animate characters from the novels of Dickens. *A1*

18. Rye *Lamb House* (National Trust) West Street, home of American writer Henry James from 1898 to 1916; including a display of James' personal possessions. *C5*

19. Sandwich in the Middle Ages one of the leading Cinque Ports, and today, with its many timbered buildings, the entire centre of the town is a conservation area. *F2*

20. Sissinghurst Castle Garden (National Trust) near Cranbrook, the famous garden created by Vita Sackville-West and her husband, also the study where she worked. *B4*

21. Tenterden *Smallhythe Place* (National Trust) a 16th-century half-timbered building and home of Ellen Terry for several years. *B4*

22. Wittersham *Stocks Mill* tallest Post Mill in Kent with a museum of old craft tools. *B5*

Tourist Information Centres

Canterbury 13 Longmarket
Telephone (0227) 766567
Dover Townwall Street
Telephone (0304) 205108
Folkestone Harbour Street
Telephone (0303) 58594
Maidstone The Gatehouse, Old Palace Gardens, Mill Street
Telephone (0622) 602169

Margate Marine Terrace
Telephone (0843) 220241
Rochester Eastgate Cottage, High Street
Telephone (0634) 43666
Rye 48 Cinque Ports Street
Telephone (0797) 222293

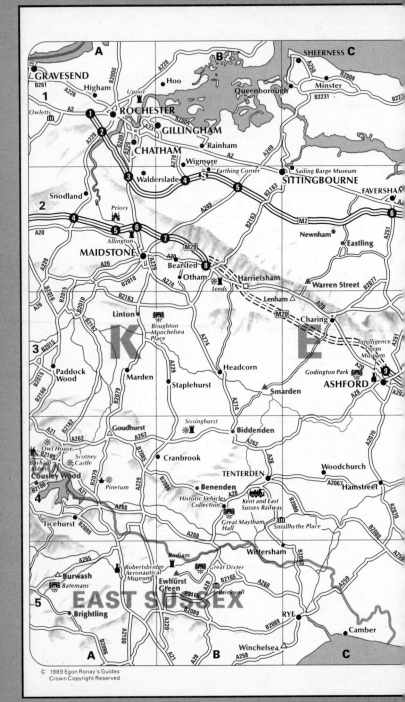

© 1989 Egon Ronay's Guides
Crown Copyright Reserved

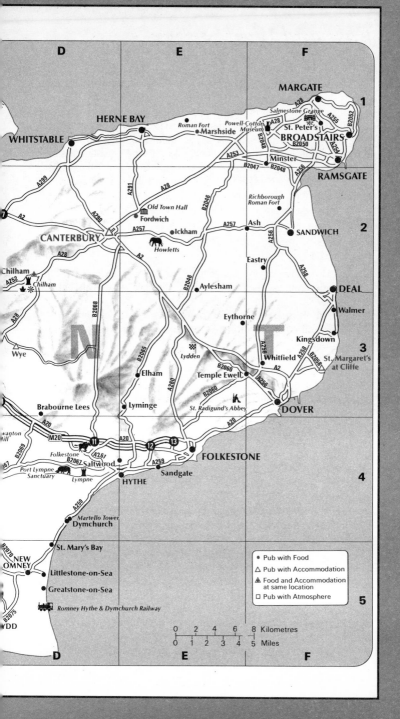

East and West Sussex

The elegant spa town of Royal Tunbridge Wells is found in the rolling countryside of the High Weald. Farnham, with its Tudor and Georgian buildings, and the cathedral town of Guildford have equally attractive surroundings including the heaths and wooded hills of Surrey and the beautiful North Downs. Southwards, the undulating range of the South Downs and Chichester, a county capital, lead to the coastline of sandy beaches and popular seaside resorts. Brighton, once a small fishing village, first became fashionable after George IV commissioned his unique palace, the Royal Pavilion. It has since become not only a holiday and retirement centre but also a university town and, more recently, a home for commuters.

Places to Visit

1. Alfriston Clergy House (National Trust) The Tye, Polegate, a 14th-century priests' house, half-timbered and thatched; medieval Hall and exhibition. *F5*

2. Ardingly *Wakehurst Place Garden* (National Trust) Haywards Heath, including a collection of exotic trees and shrubs; picturesque watercourse and rock walk. *D2*

3. Arundel Castle largely rebuilt in the 18th century; includes a 13th-century barbican, collection of armour and some fine paintings. *B4*

4. Arundel *Wildfowl Trust* Mill Road, beautiful grounds where ducks, geese and swans from all over the world can be seen. *B4*

5. Beachy Head magnificent views from a cliff top, 600 ft above sea level. *F5*

6. Bramber *St Mary's* an historic house c.1470 exhibiting a good example of late 15th-century timber framing. *C4*

7. Brighton *The Lanes* all that remains of the 17th-century fishing village lies within this district, where fascinating alleyways are filled with antique shops. *D4*

8. Brighton *The Royal Pavilion* a fascinating building with Indian Moghul-style minarets and white domes, and inside 18th-century 'chinoiserie' decor. *D4*

9. Chartwell (National Trust) Westerham, home of Sir Winston Churchill from 1924 and contains items associated with his career and interests. *E1*

10. Chichester Cathedral founded in the 11th century, rebuilt after a fire at the end of the 12th century. *A4*

11. Goodwood House near Chichester, an historic family home of the Dukes of Richmond with a fine collection of paintings, furniture and porcelain. *A4*

12. Handcross *Nymans Garden* (National Trust) near Haywards Heath, an impressive garden with plants, shrubs and trees from all over the world. *D3*

13. Newlands Corner near Guildford, on the crest of the Downs this is a famous beauty spot offering excellent views. *B1*

14. Petworth House (National Trust) superb stately home, with beautifully furnished rooms and a number of Turner's paintings amongst the collection of European masterpieces. *B3*

15. Pulborough *Parham House* Elizabethan house and gardens in the heart of a deer park. *B3*

16. Rodmell *Monk's House* (National Trust) Lewes, small home of Leonard and Virginia Woolf from 1919 until his death in 1969. *E4*

17. Sheffield Park Garden (National Trust) Uckfield, 100-acre garden and five lakes – originally landscaped by Capability Brown in the 18th century. *E3*

18. Shere a popular pretty village on the River Tillingbourne. *B1*

19. Singleton *Weald & Downland Open Air Museum* a collection of reconstructed local buildings, including medieval houses, farm buildings and a working watermill. *A4*

20. Standen (National Trust) East Grinstead, 1890s family house with carefully restored interior and period decorations; fine views across the Medway Valley. *E2*

Tourist Information Centres

Arundel 61 High Street
Telephone (0903) 882268
Brighton Marlborough House, 54 Old Steine
Telephone (0273) 23755
Chichester St Peter's Market, West Street
Telephone (0243) 775888

Guildford The Civic Hall, London Road
Telephone (0483) 575857
Seaford Station Approach
Telephone (0323) 897426
Worthing Town Hall, Chapel Road
Telephone (0903) 210022

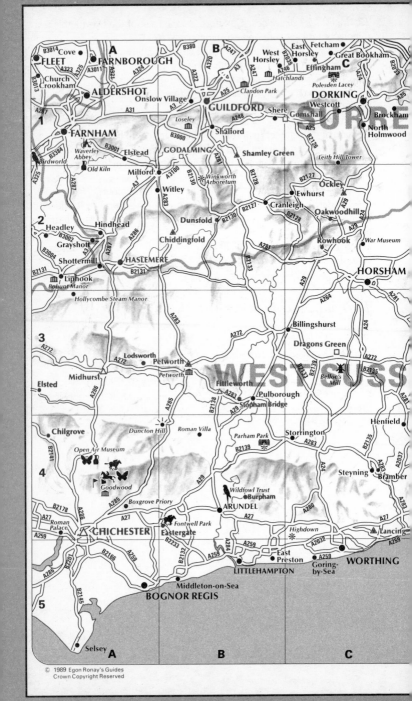

© 1989 Egon Ronay's Guides
Crown Copyright Reserved

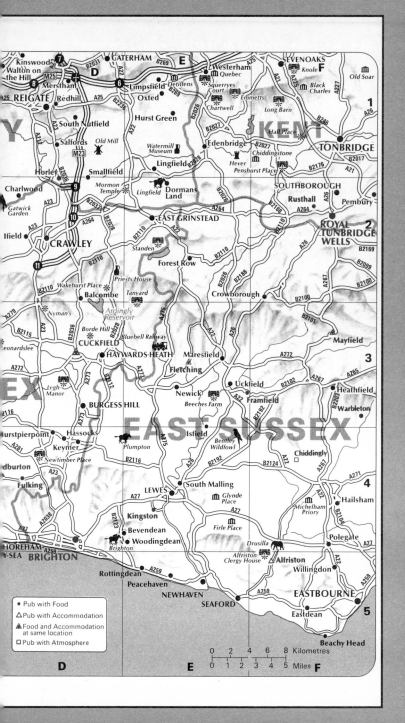

Legend

- Pub with Food
- △ Pub with Accommodation
- ▲ Food and Accommodation at same location
- □ Pub with Atmosphere

```
0   2   4   6   8  Kilometres
0  1  2  3  4  5  Miles
```

Dorset, Somerset and the Salisbury Plain

From between the busy resorts of Bournemouth and Christchurch, the wooded Avon valley leads to the peace of the Wiltshire Downs. Many sightseers will travel on to the ancient city of Salisbury and its magnificent 13th-century cathedral. Beyond lies the undulating landscape of the Salisbury Plain, and, westwards, Somerset and the Celtic myths of Glastonbury and its Tor. The abbey ruins of Glastonbury are also associated with St Patrick and the legendary figure of King Arthur. Wells, at the foot of the Mendip Hills, is connected with early-English Christianity, parts of its cathedral dating from the 13th century. In contrast, the Somerset town of Yeovil lost many of its old buildings in fires and the air raids of World War II, but throughout the county there are many unspoilt villages complete with delightful old churches of golden Ham stone. Thomas Hardy, born in 1840 near Dorchester, used the attractive landscapes of the south-east counties to full effect in portraying the natural world of his time; Shaftesbury is one of the many old towns in the area referred to in his well-known Wessex novels.

Places to Visit

1. Bournemouth *Russell-Cotes Art Gallery & Museum* including oil paintings from 17th to 20th century, watercolours, sculptures and Japanese and Burmese art. *E5*

2. Charlton Mackrell *Lytes Cary Manor* (National Trust) Somerton, a manor house with 14th-century chapel and 15th-century hall, and a hedged garden. *A3*

3. Dorchester Abbey was built by the Normans and enlarged in medieval times; here the famous Tree-of-Jesse window can be seen. *B5*

4. Dorchester *Dorset County Museum* High West Street, collections covering the geology of Dorset and illustrating its natural and local history. *B5*

5. Glastonbury the 'Cradle of Christianity' with its abbey, said to have been founded in AD700 on the site of a Chapel built by Joseph of Arimathaea. The Holy Grail is reputed to lie beneath the Chalice Spring. *A2*

6. Higher Bockhampton *Hardy's Cottage* (National Trust) near Dorchester, a thatched cottage where the poet and novelist, Thomas Hardy, was born in 1840. *C5*

7. Longleat House and Safari Park an Elizabethan mansion filled with old furniture, paintings and books; the grounds were landscaped by Capability Brown and the estate's safari park was the first of its kind in Europe. *C1*

8. Merley Park *Merley House* Wimborne, a Georgian building built in

1756, fully restored with period furniture; also a collection of model toys, including railway layouts. *E5*

9. Montacute House (National Trust) late 16th-century house with Renaissance features, formal garden and landscaped park. *A3*

10. New Forest 145 square miles of wood and heathland between the river Avon and Southampton Water. *F3/4*

11. Poole *Natural World* incorporating the Aquarium and Serpentarium where a range of living creatures can be seen from sharks to snakes and exotic fish to alligators. *E5*

12. Salisbury Cathedral set in an attractive walled Close, the cathedral is a fine example of early English architecture; the spire was added in the 13th century. *F2*

13. Salisbury *Mompesson House* the Close, an 18th-century house in the Cathedral Close with an elegant oak staircase and period furniture. *F2*

14. Sherborne Castle built by Sir Walter Raleigh in 1594, an historic house with fine furniture, paintings and porcelain. In the grounds are the 12th-century ruins of the old castle. *B3*

15. Stapehill *Knoll Gardens* water gardens and gardens with trees, shrubs, conifers and plants from all over the world. *E5*

16. Stonehenge (English Heritage) the famous stone construction, built between 2200BC and 1300BC, its original purpose is still a mystery. *F1*

17. Wells Cathedral has a magnificent west front and moving figures strike the hours on the cathedral's 14th-century clock. *A1*

18. Wilton House near Salisbury, with superb 17th-century state rooms by Inigo Jones and an excellent private art collection; large areas of lawn with giant cedars. *E2*

19. Wimborne Minster embraces several architectural styles from Norman to Gothic, and features a Saxon chest and one of the oldest astronomical clocks in the world. *E5*

20. Wimborne Minster *Kingston Lacy* (National Trust) 17th-century home designed for Sir Ralph Bankes by Sir Roger Pratt, with an outstanding collection of paintings and 250 acres of parkland. *E5*

Tourist Information Centres

Bournemouth Westover Road
Telephone (0202) 291715
Dorchester 7 Acland Road
Telephone (0305) 67992
Salisbury Fish Row
Telephone (0722) 334956

Shaftesbury Bell Street
Telephone (0747) 3514
Wells Town Hall, Market Place
Telephone (0749) 72552

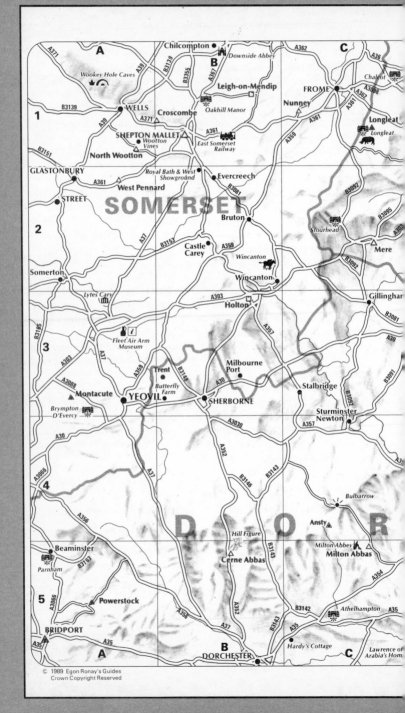

Chilcompton
Downside Abbey
A362
A36
Chalcot
A3088
FROME
Nunney
Longleat
Wookey Hole Caves
B3139
B3355
Leigh-on-Mendip
Oakhill Manor
WELLS
Croscombe
A371
Longleat
A39
B3139
A39
A361
A359
A361
SHEPTON MALLET
Wootton
Vines
East Somerset
Railway
North Wootton
B3151
GLASTONBURY
A361
Royal Bath & West
Showground
Evercreech
B3081
B3092
B3095
SOMERSET
West Pennard
STREET
Stourhead
A37
Bruton
Mere
B3092
Somerton
B3153
Castle
Carey
A359
Wincanton
B3185
Lytes Cary
A303
A303
Wincanton
Gillingham
A303
Holton
B3081
A37
A357
A30
Fleet Air Arm
Museum
A359
Trent
B3148
Milbourne
Port
A3088
Butterfly
Farm
A30
Stalbridge
B3091
Montacute
YEOVIL
SHERBORNE
B3092
Brympton
D'Evercy
Sturminster
Newton
A30
A3030
A357
A35
A37
A352
Bulbarrow
A3066
B3146
B3143
A358
Ansty
D   O   R
Hill Figure
Beaminster
Cerne Abbas
Milton Abbey
Milton Abbas
Parnham
B3163
B3143
A354
Powerstock
A3066
A358
B3142
Athelhampton
A35
BRIDPORT
A358
A352
B3143
A35
A35
A37
Hardy's Cottage
Lawrence of
Arabia's Home
DORCHESTER
B

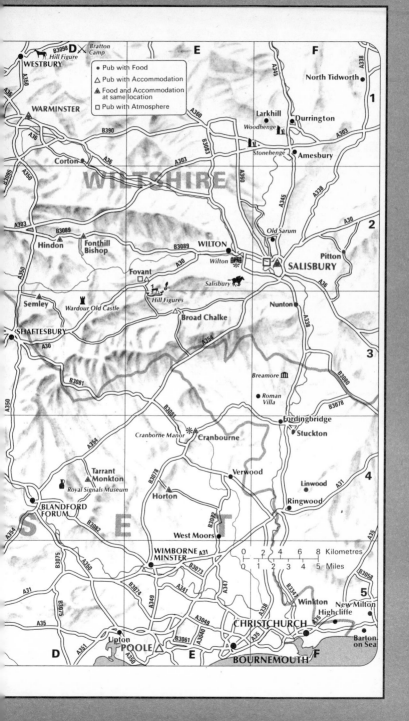

John Selden
1854–1654

'Tis not the eating, nor 'tis not the drinking that is to
be blamed, but the excess.
Table Talk

Leon de Fos

For the man who would eat like a glutton,
A good stomach is worth more than mutton,
For what use is the best
If you cannot digest,
And your teeth are exceedingly rotten.
'Gastronomia'

William Shakespeare
1564–1616

Will the cold brook, candied with ice, caudle thy
morning taste, to cure thy o'-er-night's surfeit.
Timon of Athens

Mauduit

Intoxication . . . embraces five stages: jocose,
bellicose, lachrymose, comatose, and morotose.
The Vicomte in the Kitchen (1933)

Anonymous

The glances over cocktails
That seemed to be so sweet
Don't seem quite so amorous
Over the Shredded Wheat.
'Wine, Women and Wedding'

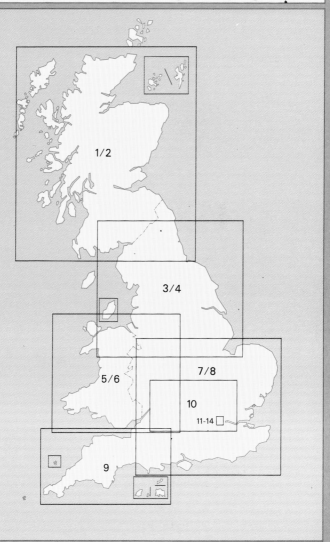

·MAP·SECTION·

Key to Maps

 M1   Motorways

A5   Primary Routes

A50   Selected 'A' Roads

————   County Boundaries

Guide Establishments

•   Pub with Food

△   Pub with Accommodation

⚠   Food and Accommodation at same location

□   Pub with Atmosphere

© Egon Ronay's Guides © Crown Copyright

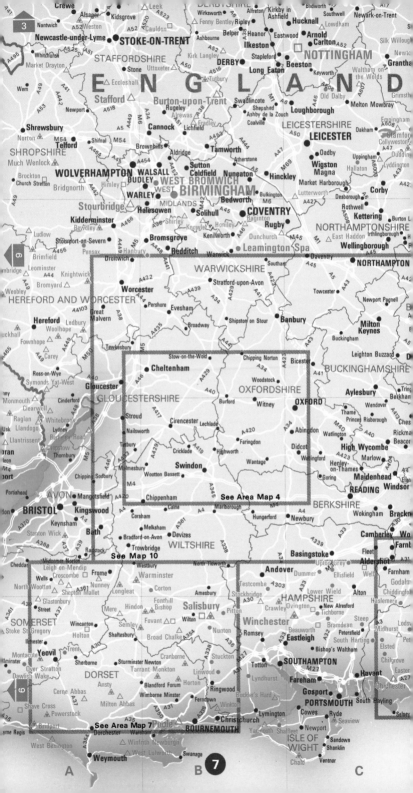

See Area Map 5

See Area Map 6

Pub with Food
Pub with Accommodation
Food and Accommodation
at same location
Pub with Atmosphere

0   10   20   30   40   50 Kilometres
0   10   20   30 Miles

© Egon Ronay's Guides © Crown Copyright

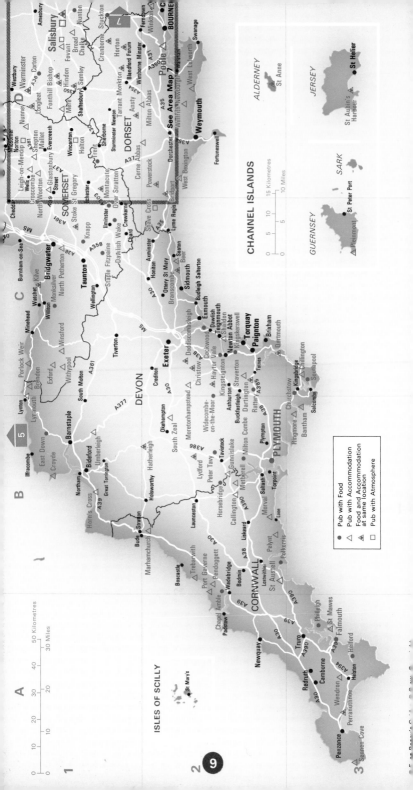

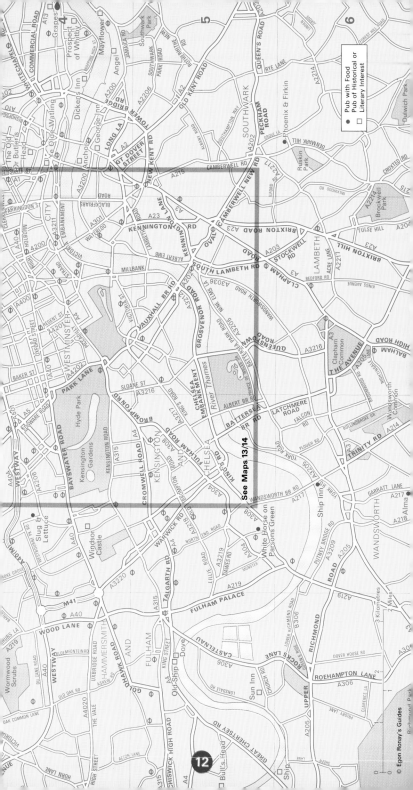

See Maps 13/14

Pub with Food
Pub of Historical or Literary Interest

12